Education and Society
in Hong Kong

Hong Kong Becoming China: The Transition to 1997

Ming K. Chan and Gerard A. Postiglione
Series General Editors

Because of Hong Kong's remarkable development under British rule for the past 150 years and its contemporary importance as a world economic and communications center on the Pacific Rim, and due to Hong Kong's future status as a Special Administrative Region of the People's Republic of China from 1997 well into the mid-twenty-first century, M.E. Sharpe has inaugurated this new multi-volume series. Published for an international readership, this series aims at providing both expert analysis and the documentary basis for a more informed understanding of Hong Kong's transition as a free society and capitalist economy toward socialist Chinese sovereignty under the "One Country, Two Systems" formula.

This series will explore various crucial dimensions of Hong Kong's current development in this transition process and their implications for the international community. Individual volumes in this series will focus on key areas and issues ranging from China's Basic Law for Hong Kong, education and social change, the existing common law legal system, the historical relationship between Britain, China, and Hong Kong, urban growth and infrastructural development, the control of the media, social movements and popular mobilization, the cultural identity of Hong Kong Chinese, to economic linkages with mainland China, the Beijing–Hong Kong–Taipei triangle, "brain drain" and migration overseas, as well as the internationalization of Hong Kong.

The Hong Kong Basic Law: Blueprint for "Stability and Prosperity" under Chinese Sovereignty? edited by Ming K. Chan and David Clark; *Education and Society in Hong Kong: Toward One Country and Two Systems*, edited by Gerard A. Postiglione; and *The Common Law System in Chinese Context: Hong Kong in Transition*, by Berry Hsu, are the first three books in this series.

Ming K. Chan is a member of the History Department, University of Hong Kong, and Coordinator of the Hong Kong Documentary Archives, Hoover Institution, Stanford University.

Gerard A. Postiglione is a member of the Education Department, University of Hong Kong.

Hong Kong Becoming China:
The Transition to 1997

Education and Society in Hong Kong
Toward One Country and Two Systems

Gerard A. Postiglione
Editor
with the assistance of
Julian Leung Yat Ming

An East Gate Book

LONDON AND NEW YORK

An East Gate Book

First published 1991 by M.E. Sharpe

Reissued 2018 by Routledge
2 Park Square, Milton Park, Abingdon, Oxon OX14 4RN
711 Third Avenue, New York, NY 10017, USA

Routledge is an imprint of the Taylor & Francis Group, an informa business

Copyright © 1991 by Taylor & Francis

No part of this book may be reprinted or reproduced or utilised in any form or by any electronic, mechanical, or other means, now known or hereafter invented, including photocopying and recording, or in any information storage or retrieval system, without permission in writing from the publishers.

Notices
No responsibility is assumed by the publisher for any injury and/or damage to persons or property as a matter of products liability, negligence or otherwise, or from any use of operation of any methods, products, instructions or ideas contained in the material herein.

Practitioners and researchers must always rely on their own experience and knowledge in evaluating and using any information, methods, compounds, or experiments described herein. In using such information or methods they should be mindful of their own safety and the safety of others, including parties for whom they have a professional responsibility.

Product or corporate names may be trademarks or registered trademarks, and are used only for identification and explanation without intent to infringe.

Publisher's Note
The publisher has gone to great lengths to ensure the quality of this reprint but points out that some imperfections in the original copies may be apparent.

Disclaimer
The publisher has made every effort to trace copyright holders and welcomes correspondence from those they have been unable to contact.

A Library of Congress record exists under LC control number: 90024658

ISBN 13: 978-1-138-89673-4 (hbk)
ISBN 13: 978-1-138-89674-1 (pbk)
ISBN 13: 978-1-315-48941-4 (ebk)

Contents

Contributors	vii
List of Tables	ix
Series General Editor's Foreword	xi
Introduction	xiii

Part I: Education and the Social Context

1. The Decolonization of Hong Kong Education
   Gerard A. Postiglione — 3

2. Hong Kong Education within Historical Processes
   Anthony E. Sweeting — 39

3. Hong Kong Education in an International Context:
   The Impact of External Forces
   Mark Bray — 83

Part II: Education and Politics

4. Educational Policymaking in Hong Kong: The Changing Legitimacy
   Cheng Kai Ming — 97

5. Preparing Pupils as Citizens of the Special Administrative
   Region of Hong Kong: An Analysis of Curriculum Change and
   Control during the Transition Period
   Paul Morris — 117

Part III: Education and Social Stratification

6. Egalitarianism and the Allocation of Secondary School Places
   in Hong Kong
   Ching-kwan Lee and Tak-sing Cheung — 149

7. The Schooling of Girls in Hong Kong: Progress and
Contradictions in the Transition
Grace C.L. Mak 167

Part IV: Educational Issues: Language and Labor

8. Cantonese, English, or Putonghua—Unresolved Communicative
Issue in Hong Kong's Future
Herbert Pierson 183

9. The Teaching of Putonghua in Hong Kong Schools: Language
Education in a Changing Economic and Political Context
Ora W.Y. Kwo 203

10. Educational Expansion and the Labor Force
Glenn Shive 215

Part V: Comparative Perspectives: One Country, Two Educational Systems

11. Pressure for Educational Excellence in China:
Implications for Education in Hong Kong
W.O. Lee 235

12. On the Characteristics, Strong Points, and Shortcomings
of Education in Hong Kong: A Mainland Chinese
Educator's View of Education in Hong Kong
Li Yixian 253

13. Education in Hong Kong and China: Toward Convergence?
Julian Y.M. Leung 265

Appendices 273

Appendix A: Education System of Hong Kong 274

Appendix B: The Policymaking and Administrative Bodies of
Education 275

Appendix C: Chronological Framework 276

Appendix D: Chronology of Important Documents Regarding
Hong Kong Education 282

Appendix E: A Comparison of the Educational Systems of the
PRC and Hong Kong 285

Selected References 287

Index 305

Series General Editor's Foreword

If there were any truth to the old British saying that the Battle of Waterloo was won on the playing fields of Eton, then the crucial importance of education in shaping the future development of postcolonial Hong Kong should not be underestimated. Although the process of decolonization began after the 1984 Sino-British Joint Declaration mandating its return to Chinese sovereignty in 1997, Hong Kong is still very much a colonial society, especially as exemplified in its educational system. Indeed, education in Hong Kong under British rule has been characterized by inequalities, privileges, patronage, discrimination as well as archaic hierarchies, inadequate planning and emphasis on quantity over quality.[1] It is with such a colonial heritage and institutional burden that the Hong Kong educational system is being influenced by and also helps to shape the transition to 1997.

Education and Society in Hong Kong: Toward One Country and Two Systems not only reviews these and other serious problems in the local educational system, but more importantly, it illustrates some of the transformative potentials of educational institutions in the following areas: the ongoing decolonization process; the training of indigenous political leaders for postcolonial administration as well as skilled manpower for continued economic development and to replace "brain drain" losses; the promotion of Hong Kong Chinese cultural identity; and the socialization of a new citizenry for the Hong Kong Special Administrative Region of the People's Republic of China.

The first essay by volume editor Gerard A. Postiglione and the other essays by education specialists in Hong Kong collectively have enhanced our appreciation of education as an instrument both for and against rational, positive sociopolitical evolution in an age of democracy. Their efforts help to bring into focus many of the factors underlining and undermining educational development in Hong Kong. They are rightfully critical of such twists and distortions perpetuated by the colonial regime as:

1. policymaking in the hands of an unrepresentative elite operating an undemocratic structure of territory-wide educational governance;

2. over-bureaucratized and illiberal administration of educational institutions, from primary schools to universities;

3. systematic official discrimination against mother-tongue teaching and learning;

4. curriculum design that not only prevented the promotion of nationalistic sentiments but also independent thought and critical-analytical ability. This ensured schools would not become a healthy force in democraticizing Hong Kong, but rather a hindrance to this long-overdue process; and

5. legal and administrative patronage favoring "British" (as against "non-British") degrees and qualifications in academic recognition, professional accredition, employment criteria, and scholarship awards regardless of merits.

Indeed, the Hong Kong government's highly political 1988 decision to eliminate non-British forms of tertiary education and the 1989 decision to double undergraduate enrollment by 1996, without consultation, only confirm the verdict delivered in the essays by Gerard Postiglione and his coauthors. That is, despite the inevitability of decolonization, localization and democratization in social institutions and public life during the transition era, there lurks the real danger of neo-colonial restoration by the sunset regime in ensuring that education will continue to be a key element of continued British influence in Hong Kong even after 1997 through the socialization of the local elites.[2] In this sense, the problems confronting Hong Kong education and society are much more than the future uncertainty under Chinese sovereignty, but also the competing claims of residual British influence and colonial mentality, traditional Chinese cultural bonds, and socialist authoritarianism. By offering honest description and expert analysis on these troubled aspects of education in transitional Hong Kong, this book is an especially fine addition to the *Hong Kong Becoming China: The Transition to 1997* series.

Ming K. Chan
Hong Kong
March 1991

Notes

1. Ming K. Chan and Michael Kirst, "Hong Kong: The Political Economy of Education," in *Education, Recession and the World Village: A Comparative Political Economy of Education*, ed. Frederick M. Wirst and Grant Harmon (London & Philadelphia: Falmer Press, 1986), pp. 49–66.

2. Ming K. Chan, *The British Sunset in Hong Kong: Historical Challenges in the Wilsonian Era of Transition* (Hong Kong: Hong Kong Economic Journal Press, 1989), chapter 7, "Full Restoration of British Style Education: The Education Commission's No. 3 Report and the Problems of Transition," pp. 42–52.

Introduction

Britain has entered the final phase of its colonial rule over Hong Kong. Its government in Hong Kong can no longer make major decisions without consulting Beijing, and even then, it is increasingly difficult to carry out these decisions without Beijing's full support. Although the planned new airport is the most cited example of this, it is likely that planning in other areas, including education, will soon experience a similar fate. Hong Kong education has yet to prepare itself for the challenges that will accompany the recovery of sovereignty by China. Nevertheless, education will be a key component of the major societal transition linking Hong Kong with the rest of China. In weathering the transitional period, education can act as a stabilizing force or a source of change. The collection of articles in this book constitutes a first attempt to address the implications of the 1997 transition for education in Hong Kong.

The first part of this volume comprises three chapters that introduce contextual aspects of Hong Kong education. The first chapter provides an overview of the basic dilemma of education in Hong Kong, that of resolving the contradictions of schooling for capitalism, socialism, and patriotism. The second chapter provides a rich historical background for viewing contemporary education. It accomplishes this by outlining several major historical processes, including colonization, industrialization, bureaucratization, and localization. Chapter three adds selected dimensions of the international context to the study of Hong Kong education.

Part two concerns itself with the political dimension of education. Chapter four looks at the policy-making process with a specific focus on the way that legitimacy is maintained. Chapter five focuses on political socialization, particularly the way in which Hong Kong prepares its citizens for the post-1997 period.

Part three considers education and social stratification in Hong Kong, an area increasingly thought of in terms of how it relates to the phenomenon of a capitalist society moving into the orbit of a socialist society. Chapter six analyzes the debate over egalitarianism and its bearing on the allocation of secondary school places. Chapter seven looks at the education of Hong Kong women within a stratified society.

Part four discusses two major issues facing Hong Kong education during the transitional period: the language medium and the emigration of talented individuals. Chapter eight cites the complexities of a society struggling over the choice of a language medium (English, Cantonese, or Mandarin) for education. Chapter nine focuses specifically on the economic and political context of Putonghua teaching. Chapter ten looks at the expansion of higher education and how it is being influenced by the large-scale emigration of talented individuals.

Part five compares and contrasts various aspects of the educational systems of Hong Kong and China. Chapter eleven considers the global trend toward excellence in education and what this means for education in China and Hong Kong. Chapter twelve encapsulates the view of a mainland Chinese educator on the role of Hong Kong education in the modernization of China. The final chapter identifies three dimensions around which Hong Kong's basic educational dilemma can be clustered.

This volume has tried to capture the plurality of thought on the subject of education in transitional Hong Kong, and it is written with the hope that a diversity of views will continue to exist in the future. I will not comment on the special qualities that each contributor has brought to his or her chapter, but rather leave this to the reader to discover. However, I thank the contributors for their cooperation throughout the time it took to prepare this volume. In addition, I would like to thank Mrs. Rico Kong for her assistance in typing parts of the manuscript and Y.M. Leung for his assistance in reviewing selected manuscripts during the early stages of this project. I also thank Doug Merwin, editor at M. E. Sharpe, for his encouragement and cooperation. Naturally, I take responsibility for any errors in this work.

Part I

Education and the Social Context

1

The Decolonization of Hong Kong Education

Gerard A. Postiglione

Introduction

Regarding the future of Hong Kong, Britain and China have created new contradictions for a new age. While the 1990s have become known as the decade of democracy in the world, Britain has willingly arranged for the recovery of sovereignty over Hong Kong by an authoritarian government, without the consent of the nearly six million people living in the territory. It may be too much to expect more from a colonial power, especially one that never practiced any form of genuine popular democracy in Hong Kong. Also, China has not been very successful in bolstering the confidence of the Hong Kong people, especially with its handling of student movements and its own turbulent domestic politics. Contrary to events in Eastern Europe, where socialist societies are taking on the trappings of capitalism, Hong Kong is impelled to accommodate to a socialist government. There is a similarity in that the former societies are working to situate themselves closer to the West without necessarily becoming capitalist, while Hong Kong is working to position itself closer to China without becoming socialist. In 1997, the British will retreat from their colony, after a period that saw the Hong Kong territory grow from a desolate outpost in the South China Sea to one of the world's largest financial and commercial centers. As Hong Kong confronts an uncertain future, its education system is attempting to position itself within the transitional process leading to the recovery of sovereignty by China. Education is expected to play a part in cementing the reunification. New educational reforms have the potential to act as vehicles for negotiating social transition processes, as well as instruments for resisting decolonization.

Since the signing of the *Sino-British Joint Declaration on the Future of Hong Kong* in 1984, there has been a steady stream of scholarship on various aspects of the imminent "one country, two systems" arrangement.[1] However, this scholarship has been concerned mainly with the significance of the restoration of Chinese sovereignty for Hong Kong's economy, politics, law, and government. An analysis of the implications of the transition for schools is virtually non-existent.[2] This is attributable to the secondary position of schools as a leading force of change in most social transformations. Schools in modern society have become organized to preserve the status quo.[3] Only in rare cases have they been catalysts for rapid social change, as they were during the cultural revolution in China.[4] The socialization processes within schools help to legitimize a society's dominant institutions. Education serves a conservative function by reproducing culture and social structure in a manner that ensures the survival of the social relations that underlie a particular form of economy and politics.[5]

Yet because education can also embody a society's vision and hope for the future, there is reason to expect the study of education in Hong Kong to take on a special importance during the transitional period leading to 1997. Although most people in Hong Kong are intent on preserving the status quo, as the status quo becomes more uncertain for the future, and as confidence in issues such as human rights and the future of representative government wanes, the potential of educational institutions to transform society is being reassessed and reasserted.[6] Thus education may come to play a transforming role after all, particularly when it is aligned with other institutions that promote social change.

A central question facing Hong Kong concerns how the new sovereignty will change the education system's potential to produce the kind of popular political leaders who will bolster the society's confidence enough to carry it through to postcolonial status. When colonial rule ended in the former British colonies, it led to a form of independence either through peaceful or violent means. In the case of Hong Kong, the end of the colonial period will lead directly to a restoration of China's sovereignty in 1997. The agreement between Britain and China promises that after 1997, the capitalist system and a high degree of self-government will be preserved in Hong Kong. Lau Siu-kai points out, "With only seven years remaining before 1997, Hong Kong is still in search of an organized group of political leaders who can be trusted by the people of Hong Kong and the two governments to make the arrangements stipulated in the Sino-British agreement and the Basic Law work."[7] The formula of "Hong Kong people running Hong Kong" cannot be successfully implemented without indigenous popular political leaders.

This chapter identifies some of the major implications that the transitional period leading to the restoration of Chinese sovereignty will have for educational and social transformations in Hong Kong. A discussion of education within transitional societies and a review of various aspects of the education system in Hong Kong, including the provisions of the Sino-British Declaration and the

Basic Law Drafting Committee for education, is followed by an examination of the way that contextual social processes favor a particular orientation for educational change and social transformation. We consider education's potential to harmonize capitalism, socialism, and patriotism within a "one country, two systems" arrangement, and to prepare popular political leaders who can gain the confidence of the Hong Kong people and guide them through the transitional period.

Toward 1997: Education and Its Intervention Points

Educational institutions and society's expectations of them are transformed dramatically only when a society's vision of its own future changes or when the conditions for the realization of that vision are perceived to change.[8] Societies approaching decolonization share a vision of their future as one in which they will gain autonomy from the colonial metropole.[9] This applies especially to the institution of education, which often spearheads the task of nation-building.[10]

With the formal signing of the Sino-British Declaration in 1984, Hong Kong's predominant vision of its future was one of continued stability and prosperity within a framework that would permit a great degree of autonomy under the sovereignty of the mother country. Until June of 1989, the conditions to carry out that vision existed, and were to be reflected in the Basic Law of the post-1997 Special Administrative Region (SAR) government. After June 4, 1989, the Basic Law Drafting Committee temporarily suspended work, revealing that the conditions for the fulfillment of the post-1997 vision had indeed changed.[11] Accordingly, the society's expectations of education also began to show signs of transformation, as the problem of reconciling capitalism, socialism, and patriotism became more pronounced. Hundreds of thousands of secondary and postsecondary students, teachers, and administrators joined demonstrations to express their sentiments toward political events in China.[12] Education Department officials ignored enforcement of the long-standing ban on politics in schools, and school principals and teachers wrestled with how to react to students' political poster displays in schools and their participation in territory-wide demonstrations.[13] Many months after the suppression of the democracy movement in Beijing, Hong Kong still found itself in a severe confidence crisis as cooperation between the British and Chinese governments became strained.

Such events added a new dimension to the already unusual nature of Hong Kong's decolonization process. Power had gradually shifted to the local elite and the new middle class, yet most power still resided with the British government. Hong Kong's people looked to the British government to press for a speedier pace of democratization even while Beijing denied its appropriateness. The local elite asserted that Hong Kong was not a colony in the classical sense, yet they expressed concern that in 1997 the mother country would gain the same influence wielded by the British in the territory's affairs, including education. Some referred to the transfer of sovereignty as the replacement of one hegemonic force with another because the future degree of autonomy gained by the territory would not be determined by the colonial metropole or even by the people of the territory itself, but rather by Beijing. Confidence in the Sino-British agreement on Hong Kong's future was won or lost within a plural society which favored decolonization and supported Chinese sovereignty, yet remained apprehensive in the face of interference by Beijing in Hong Kong's affairs. The degree to which decolonization, as opposed to the replacement of one force by another, was taking place became a complex question that could only await the outcome of struggles over representative government in Hong Kong, and the direction of future events in China. The precise nature and characteristics of Hong Kong as a transitional society became inseparable from the evolution of these factors during the crucial period before 1997.

Education plays a role in Hong Kong's transitional period insofar as it shapes the thinking of the generation that will lead Hong Kong after 1997. It influences the selection criteria for recruitment into important positions within the civil service of the transitional government; it works to maintain a highly skilled labor force in the face of the large-scale emigration of talented people from the territory; it determines, to some extent, the degree of interaction between the educational systems of Hong Kong and other parts of China; it influences school socialization processes that build a cultural identity essential for reuniting people in Hong Kong with the rest of China; and, finally, it bolsters or restrains the general process of democratization in the society.

From Colonial Development to National Development: The Role of Education

For most of Hong Kong's history, educational developments occurred within a colonial society built upon an *entrepôt* trade economy.[14] Beginning after 1949, skills and technology transferred from Shanghai, a steady immigration from the adjoining region of Guangdong, and increasing amounts of local investment combined with a laissez-faire economy and a British-style colonial government to promote Hong Kong's industrial foundation.[15] Successful textile manufacturing, followed by new international investments in other infant industries—through the 1960s and 1970s, including electronics—contributed to the socialization of a work force.[16] Government land sales, efficient infrastructural planning, and a growth rate averaging 10 percent each year further improved the investment climate, even as the British government entered into negotiations with the People's Republic of China on the question of sovereignty over Hong Kong. By 1990 Hong Kong had become a major international financial center with the second highest living standard in Asia, a key regional center for semiconductor manufacturing, and an important point for technology transfer to China.[17]

Hong Kong's burgeoning position as a textile trader within the European community in the 1970s led to pressure on the governor to ensure that child labor was not a factor in the territory's economic success. The implementation of free and compulsory schooling was used to indicate compliance. The rapidly expanding educational system, funded through both public and private efforts and managed through a combination of voluntary, government, and semi-government arrangements, was increasingly brought under the authority of the government's Education Department. The British tradition of elite education combined well with the Chinese tradition of examination-oriented selection for positions in government. By the early 1980s, Hong Kong had a highly bureaucratized, well-monitored, and tightly structured system of schools.

The future of Hong Kong society has always hinged on its contribution to national development. Hong Kong has long contributed to the economic dimension of nation-building in China. It continues to do so, and for this reason will be permitted to maintain its economic system for fifty years after the return of sovereignty in 1997. Hong Kong's political system, however, has made no such direct contribution to nation-building in China.[18] As a result, Hong Kong's future political system will be defined to a great degree by the Basic Law, promulgated by China's National People's Congress, thus strictly limiting its contribution to national political development to within the boundaries of the new SAR. A secluded bureaucratic polity has existed alongside an atomistic Chinese society to provide a high degree of nonintervention within the economic sphere, thus allowing capitalism to operate virtually unfettered by popular influence.[19] This, coupled with government control over land sale and the availability of low-wage labor (made possible through plentiful government-subsidized housing and inexpensive food and clothing from China), help to explain the tremendous success of the domestic economy.[20]

Education in Hong Kong has not yet deviated from its traditional colonial role. With the exception of minor revisions to the content of some school textbooks, schooling continues to socialize children into a sociopolitical system that has remained virtually unchanged for over 140 years.[21] Moreover, China has no plans to implement an explicit educational strategy of nation-building in Hong Kong after 1997. Nevertheless, as is noted above, education is increasingly seen as a key institution in the transitional period. Specific decisions about the expansion of higher education, which I have spoken about elsewhere, and the introduction of civics are just two examples.[22] Also, without a military acting to strengthen a particular brand of patriotic socialization, education may take on a more important ideological function.

Education for a Special Administrative Region: Autonomy under the Basic Law?

With the signing of the Sino-British Declaration in 1984, the territory was provided with a blueprint for its future. Although the agreement provides little detail aside from declaring the return of sovereignty over Hong Kong to China, it nevertheless permits Hong Kong to maintain its capitalist system, along with the general life-style of its people. According to the Sino-British Agreement and the Basic Law of the Hong Kong Special Administrative Region, education will maintain a great degree of autonomy.

> The Hong Kong Special Administrative Region Government shall on its own decide policies in the field of culture, education, science, and technology, including policies regarding the education system and its administration, the language of instruction, the allocation of funds, the examination system, the system of academic rewards and the recognition of educational and technological qualifications.[23]

> Community organizations and individuals may, in accordance with law, run educational undertakings of various kinds in the Hong Kong Special Administrative Region. Educational institutions of all kinds may retain their autonomy and enjoy academic freedom. They may continue to recruit staff and use teaching materials from outside the Hong Kong Special Administrative Region. Schools run by religious organizations may continue to provide religious education, including courses on religion. Students shall enjoy freedom to choose between educational institutions and pursue their education outside the Hong Kong Special Administrative Region.[24]

These statements place the control over education in the hands of the SAR government. An increasing number of groups in Hong Kong doubt that the SAR government will be autonomous and representative of the wishes of Hong Kong people, especially in the wake of the military crackdown on the democracy movement in China. Nevertheless, in 1997 the government of the People's Republic of China will inherit a government–education relationship that is, in one way, similar to its own. In both societies educational policy is the province of a small group of elites. The government of Hong Kong is not directly elected by the people of Hong Kong, yet it has taken on an increasingly large role in shaping the course of education over the last two decades.[25]

Transitional Dimensions in Comparative Perspective: The Hong Kong Factors

Although Hong Kong has little overall resemblance to most transitional societies, a number of similarities exist regarding education.[26] In colonial-to-postcolonial transitional settings, pre-independence education may remain largely unchanged throughout the transition, an exception being the specific role schools play in affirming national identity. Educational changes are found more in the content of education than in the form or structure of the system. For instance, social studies, history, and language curriculae may be revised. Colonial social structures may remain almost intact through the early postcolonial period, with the colonial power vacuum being filled by a national bourgeoisie. Hong Kong's economic system is to be retained through the transition, and the colonial elite have already begun to be replaced by the local bourgeoisie. Nevertheless, continued emigration of large numbers of local bourgeoisie prior to 1997 could result in a totally new set of circumstances. One scenario depicts the ever-increasing Beijing-sponsored capital within the territory coupled with new immigrants from China—born and educated under socialism—replacing the present bourgeoisie with a new "socialist bourgeoisie." This is bound to have a measurable influence on the cultural ethos of Hong Kong schools.[27] Another scenario depicts increasing internationalization of many spheres, including education, as a way to discourage Beijing's explicit interference after 1997.

The conditions of education in states where a socialist transition is underway are unique.[28] Here changes in the education system are complete and comprehensive, taking on the form, structure, and philosophical foundations of the system. But socialist transition theory may have limited relevance to Hong Kong's initial transition phase. It may take at least four decades as a Special Administrative Region before Hong Kong's transition to socialism could begin. It would be a transition for which, not unlike that of 1997, Hong Kong would need ten years to prepare. Such a situation is far too remote for most Hong Kong residents to consider now. However, even if one believes that socialist transition will not occur until 2047, then today's primary schoolchildren will be at the helm of the territory's socialist transition. For this reason, the education system might well begin to consider the question of how it should prepare students. Furthermore, there are indications that a socialist bourgeoisie may begin to gain greater influence in government departments such as the police—where the recruitment ban on graduates from the so-called leftist or patriotic secondary schools has been lifted—and in the government-run, post-secondary teacher training colleges, which have followed suit.[29] The patriotic secondary schools are also poised to join the government's proposed direct subsidy scheme for private schools, a plan considered elitist by many sectors of society.[30] The rejection by these schools of a formal curriculum in the 1960s and early 1970s, when the Cultural Revolution had spilled over into Hong Kong, led until recently to their exclusion from the colonial education system. The government has also established a Council for Academic Accreditation, which may consider the standing of educational qualifications from China (including Taiwan) as they relate to Hong Kong's occupational structure.[31] The increasing emigration of talented members of the Hong Kong work force and the territory's 1 percent unemployment rate have made the Council's work more vital. The American Chamber of Commerce and the Institute of International Education in Hong Kong have also addressed the problem of Chinese students not returning to China after completing their studies in the United States. These organizations have successfully lobbied both the Hong Kong and British governments to permit recruitment of these students to firms in Hong Kong as a temporary step before their eventual return to China. This move could supply much-needed professionally and technically skilled labor for Hong Kong. These are added factors affecting Hong Kong's transitional process and the role of educational institutions within that transitional period.[32]

Hong Kong begins to inform the study of education within transitional societies with such new factors as the expansion of externally sponsored national socialist capital, the increasing numbers of immigrants born and raised under socialism, and the further integration of patriotic elements into government organs and the occupational structure. At the same time, there has been an expansion of liberal groups in the territory, some going so far as to advocate the downfall of the Beijing government or of communism itself.[33] These developments become even more important when they are viewed in the context of Hong Kong's evolving cultural ethos and the dual identities it reflects, that of Chineseness and Hong-Kongeseness.[34] As a Chinese society with a long history of colonial rule, Hong Kong has structural features distinguishable from those of both traditional and modern China. This has fostered an ethos which represents "at once a departure from dominant Chinese values and a continuation of Chinese heritage."[35] Its dual nature is visibly a postwar phenomenon and has been particularly salient with the advent of the 1997 issue and the rise to prominence of the younger generation. Furthermore, the sharp value differences that are reflected in these two identities become more distinct in the education system, which differs on such important cultural, social, and political features as the medium of instruction (English or Chinese), the political leaning of the school (in support of Beijing or Taipei), the connection of the school with various clansmen and provincial associations in China, and the school's social class composition.[36] The plurality of Hong Kong schools has existed and flourished alongside a highly centralized educational policymaking bureaucracy. This bureaucratic polity has enjoyed a high degree of insulation as part of a government not directly representative of the people. Nevertheless, through a variety of formal and informal consultative channels, the educational policy process maintained a threshold level of legitimacy within the Chinese community, even though schools with stronger ties to the colonial elite enjoyed greater influence.

Trajectories for Educational Change: Limited Options

We can identify three broad options or orientations relating to school politics and educational change in Hong Kong's transitional period. Each deals in a different way with reconciling emerging problems. The first option, most likely in the short run, sees a maintenance of the status quo. The second hinges on increased democratization of the society, which would bring the pluralism of Hong Kong schools more into the forefront of the reform process, resulting in a less consensus-bound, more conflict-prone reform process. The third option envisions the replacement of the influence of one central government by another, and sees the shoring up of traditional consultative mechanisms for ensuring support for educational changes, with greater influence exerted by those individual schools and groups of schools having or building closer ties with mainland institutions.

The potential role of education in Hong Kong in solving the complex problems that will emerge during the recovery of sovereignty by China will be determined by the specific characteristics of the transitional society. Whether education will work toward reconciling or heightening the contradictions between capitalism, socialism, and patriotism, and whether schools will assume a new role in political socialization and the preparation of popular political leaders will also depend in part on the dual identities reflected in the cultural ethos of Hong Kong, as well as on how selected contextual features are brought to bear on education. Before examining these contextual features, we will review the basic characteristics of Hong Kong education, including the organization of selection, governance, policy, and reform.

Hong Kong Education: The Organization of Selection

Throughout Hong Kong's history, a combination of government, government subsidized, and private forms of education flourished.[37] For most of its history, education in Hong Kong generally followed a colonial pattern, although Chinese education was always an accepted part of the system.[38] However, after the Second World War, a gradual move away from traditional colonialism took place as educational influence shifted slightly away from total dependence on developments in the United Kingdom. Hong Kong's population is 98 percent Chinese, and aside from the few schools established specifically for the children of expatriates, the school system is designed to serve the needs of the local populace.

In 1978, Hong Kong achieved a nine-year universal, free, and compulsory education system.[39] By 1980, most (87 percent) of the student population chose to continue beyond nine years, with 40 percent studying in government or government-aided schools and the rest in self-financing private schools. The number of private schools declined continually until 1988, when a Direct Subsidy Scheme (to be discussed later) was proposed as a measure by which more private schools could survive.

The government places students according to a Primary One Admission Scheme after kindergarten, a Secondary School Allocation Scheme after primary school, and a Junior Secondary Education Assessment (JSEA) after junior secondary school.[40] The JSEA (which will be gradually phased out as the number of subsidized places in senior secondary schools increase) is aimed at insuring fairness and equal opportunity; yet, while its standardized testing insures a more objective means of placement, social class and gender-related factors have already worked themselves into the system in a systematic way by the time the JSEA is administered.[41] This point is discussed in more detail in chapter seven.

Students who remain in secondary school until form five will sit for a Certificate of Education Examination. About a third of these students go on to the two-year sixth form education. They may sit for the higher level examinations after the first year to gain entrance to the four-year program of the Chinese University of Hong Kong, or the advanced level examinations after the second year to gain entrance to the University of Hong Kong. Reforms in 1988 called for changes that lead to a unified admission system for a standard three-year university education.[42]

The vocational-technical sector of the school system has grown since 1981, when only 3 percent of the form three graduates continued their studies in technical institutes. By the end of the 1980s this figure more than doubled, as the number of these institutes grew to eight. Aside from offering post–form three craft courses lasting two years, the technical institutes also offer post–form five technical courses. The latter took in an increasingly large segment of the population as opportunities to enter universities expanded less rapidly than the secondary-school levels below.[43]

University entrance increased from 2 percent of the relevant age group in 1980 to 8 percent in 1990. Other postsecondary institutions, such as the two polytechnics, teacher and nurse training institutes, and the other colleges including the Hong Kong Baptist College and Lingnan College, have provided places for about another 8 percent of the age group. Many of these are upgrading their diploma and certificate courses to degree-level offerings. In 1978, Hong Kong entered into an ongoing debate concerning the expansion of tertiary education. A government report on diversification of the economy gave a larger role to education in Hong Kong's economic development.[44] This was interpreted by some as a signal to expand higher education. However, other factors acted to prevent any significant expansion. Among these were the rise of credential inflation in other parts of the world; concern over the establishment of an indigenous intellectual elite that might constitute a threat to political stability; and the high cost of financing tertiary education.[45] The government, through the Universities and Polytechnics Grants Committee, decides on the establishment and rate of expansion of university-level education.[46] Until 1990, the government kept the growth of university places to a snail's pace. Before then, it chose to release the pressure for the creation of more university places by a rapid expansion of vocational and technical education.

Hong Kong Education: Governance, Policy, and Reform

Under the Education Ordinance, the director of education controls all government schools and supervises all other kindergarten, primary, secondary and postsecondary institutions in the territory—with the exception of the universities and polytechnics.[47] The ordinance provides the director with broad-ranging powers over the life and practice of schooling, its staff and pupils, and in particular anything that seems like politics in schools. Most of the schools in the territory are publicly funded but privately operated. Each school has an unpaid management committee and supervisor appointed by the sponsoring body. In most cases, members of the committee are people who are not involved in policymaking or the day-to-day affairs of the school. The supervisor has considerable legal responsibility and usually works closely with the school principal in policy and personnel decisions. School principals, who have absolute power over the staff and pupils, are appointed to government schools by the education department and to other schools by the sponsoring agencies. According to the government's Code of Aid, all aided schools are funded according to the same formula, regardless of location, sponsorship, or prestige. Schools in the small private sector are financed mainly by tuition fees.

Educational policy in Hong Kong has been characterized as lying somewhere between a centralized and a decentralized system. It would be more accurate to say that decision making and policy are part of the centralized system, yet there is a broad and complex consultative process that has evolved since the late 1970s. Although the educational system is modeled closely on that of the United Kingdom in its structure, organization, admission and examination regulations, and curriculum, it is far from a duplicate of that or any other system. Traditionally, educational policy has been the province of an influential elite of the colony who are not representative of the people as much as reflective of the powers that be. As the system expanded in the 1960s and 1970s, the policy process became more complex, with a variety of education associations, unions, and pressure groups all entering into the consultative process.

In general, the highest decision maker is the governor-in-council. Four committees advise the governor on educational matters (Appendix B). The Board of Education concerns itself with education from kindergarten to sixth form, the Universities and Polytechnics Grants Committee is responsible for funding and development of university education, and the Vocational Training Council is responsible for technical education. A lack of coordination led to the founding of a fourth committee, the Education Commission, composed of appointed members of the community and representatives from the other three committees. It provides consolidated advice to the governor on the overall development of the education system.[48]

A key feature of educational policy in Hong Kong as it bears on transitional processes concerns the maintenance of legitimacy, as noted in chapter four. Colonial societies carry with them an inherent suspicion of government and an opposition to its policies. The Hong Kong government has skillfully minimized this problem of maintaining support for its educational policies by building an extensive consultative network. Having the chance to be heard by government increases the satisfaction of groups, which thereby yields a threshold level of legitimacy to the government's policies. This occurs within a system that has a marked degree of pluralism under a centralized, non-representative structure of territory-wide educational governance.

The most controversial issue involving the membership of the Education

Commission concerned Szeto Wah, president of the Hong Kong Professional Teachers' Union and one of the few elected (rather than appointed) members of the Hong Kong Legislative Council.[49] As a long-time critic of the government Education Department and a liberal member of the council, he opposes many of the policies of the Beijing government toward Hong Kong. Szeto Wah was not appointed to the Education Commission even though he enjoyed broad support among the rank-and-file of the teaching profession and large sectors of the community as a leader of the liberal movement during the political transition. Although Szeto Wah was eventually appointed to the Education Commission, this case illustrated a challenge to the government's ability to gather the support of the public for changes in education. As we shall see in the following sections, other characteristics of the transitional period further threaten the government's legitimacy. Furthermore, these characteristics work to determine whether education will lean toward the colonial status-quo consultative or nonconsultative, the emergent conflict-prone democratic, or new, restructured consultative patterns of formulating changes in education.

Educational Transformations:
The Shifting Social Context

Educational changes in Hong Kong's history have occurred within the context of a minimally integrated sociopolitical system. A British-controlled autonomous bureaucratic polity has existed alongside an atomistic Chinese society.[50] Until the latter part of the 1980s, the government was able to remain largely secluded from Chinese society. However, more activism from society, particularly in the struggles for more representative government, has brought a new sociopolitical context to bear on educational issues. It is to this context that we now turn.

Decolonization and the Transformation of the Length of University Education

A local British economist once described Hong Kong as "a part of China that happens, for the time being, to be administered by someone else."[51] This statement does little to alter the fact that Hong Kong is still a colonial society, even though decolonization has already begun. The first section of Hong Kong was obtained by the British as a result of the First Opium War (1840–1842). Through the Sino-British treaties of 1842, 1860, and 1898, the area of what is today known as Hong Kong was ceded or leased to the British.[52] These treaties are not recognized as valid by the People's Republic of China. Nevertheless, negotiations have been completed for recovery of the territory. Initial indications are that the colonial elite will be replaced by an elected and appointed group of local residents of Chinese descent. It is not yet clear how and to what degree the new leadership will represent Beijing's interests. At present the Xinhua News

Agency, Beijing's official representative organization in Hong Kong, already exerts considerable influence.

Educational issues during decolonization have long been a serious problem in former British colonies such as India, Kenya and Malaysia, where history shows that events leading to drastic changes in tertiary education have been repeated again and again. Political observers and educational reformers have suggested that in the past, education was used as a powerful tool for Britain to keep control over its colonies following decolonization. The elite education system allowed the British government to continue its influence on those who received tertiary education and would become community leaders. This would ensure a favorable link with the territory after British withdrawal.[53]

The Hong Kong Education Commission appears to be working toward a continuation of British-style higher education. Its most controversial educational reform proposal had a direct bearing on the issue of decolonization.[54] This reform was directed at sixth form education, but had major implications for Hong Kong's two universities. The reform's stated intention was to standardize sixth form education, reduce examination pressure, and unify the admission scheme to universities. Its effect was to bring the issue of length of university education to the forefront.

Prior to the Education Commission's recommendations, the University of Hong Kong had recognized the problem of sixth form education as it affected the quality of the pool of candidates from which it drew its students. The university decided to develop a foundation year, which would be attached to the beginning of the already existing three-year program.[55] The foundation year was designed to provide new students with a broad curriculum and language improvement opportunities. This change would have brought the University of Hong Kong into line with the Chinese University of Hong Kong, thus eliminating the need for sixth form students to surmount the dreaded Advanced Level examinations before entering the University of Hong Kong.

The Education Commission's report cited the narrowness of sixth form education and how it fostered students "who lack maturity, initiative, and innovation."[56] However, the commission favored broadening the sixth form rather than making modifications at the university level. A major reason cited was the high financial cost of extending university education and the concern with finding competent lecturers to staff it.

This reform was unique in the way that it broke the past pattern of consensus-bound educational reform and delivered the policymaking process into a conflict-prone mode of educational reform. At one time, 4,000 university students marched on the government in protest against the plan. Many educational groups in Hong Kong entered the fray, revealing a deep split in preference for and against the reform.[57] Although the heads of the major postsecondary institutions were opposed to the reform, the Legislative Council voted, by a narrow margin, in favor of it.

The government's strong ties to British higher education were enough to stifle any movement toward a four-year university system. With encouragement from the government, the influential subsidized secondary schools council came out in favor of the proposal, tipping the balance in favor of maintaining upper sixth form schooling. The proposal had important resource implications, thus acting to unite secondary school principals who received government subsidies for the upper year of their secondary schools. The funding for this year stood to be eliminated if a four-year university structure came into being.

The issue of truncating the Chinese University program from four to three years was not new.[58] Although it had been debated before, the context of the deliberations surrounding the latest debate was different in that the Sino-British Declaration added strength to the case for bringing Hong Kong university education into line with that in China. At one time, opposition groups even appealed, although unsuccessfully, to China's quasi-ambassador in Hong Kong, asking him to become involved and support the four-year structure of higher education since it coincided with that in the rest of China. Thus, some have come to view this case as signifying neither an abandonment of the Chinese character of the Chinese University of Hong Kong, nor the embracing of colonial values, but rather an acknowledgment that groups in Hong Kong are prepared to exercise their right, as spelled out in the Joint Declaration, to resist following the model of education in China.

The way in which government handled this reform highlighted a break with the past tradition of activating the elaborate consultation network and soliciting outside expertise in order to create the legitimacy needed to carry out its reforms more smoothly.[59] Moreover, since that time the government has seemed less concerned about its legitimacy in educational matters. This was evident more than a year later when it acted without consultation and proposed to double the number of places in tertiary education by 1996.[60] In contrast to the earlier reform, the government neither seemed concerned about the cost of financing the dramatic expansion, nor the difficulty of finding competent lecturers to staff the expanded system. While some have seen this as a way of rewarding tertiary institutions for their compliance with the earlier reform, others saw it as a genuine effort to develop human resources that were lost to the increased exodus of talented people that followed the June 4 tragedy in China.

Transforming Political Socialization and Preparing Political Leaders

"Power, both administrative and executive, is in the hands of civil servants who are in law primarily responsible, through the governor, to the United Kingdom."[61] Until 1985, the people of Hong Kong could neither appoint these public servants to office nor remove them. Nevertheless, government officials and others often proclaim that Hong Kong is essentially democratic. Until 1980, the only major body even partly elected was the Urban Council. Its main functions are municipal (e.g., street cleaning, control of peddlers, public libraries). As late as the mid-1970s, only 10 percent of the adult population was entitled by education to vote in Hong Kong's elections, and in 1969, for example, only 0.05 percent bothered to do so. In 1983, a district administration scheme was set up in order to permit some forms of public consultation and participation. A portion of the membership of these district boards is elected in the same way as a portion of the members of the Urban Council. At the end of 1983, there were 904,916 registered voters representing only 32 percent of the total potential electorate. Moreover, voter turnout was sparse. In the urban regions, for instance, only 250,000 of the potential electorate of 708,119 were registered to vote, and of this group only 35 percent actually cast ballots. The first concrete effort to permit election to a governing body that wields any real power and influence took place in 1985. This astonishing reform opened indirect elections of a small section of the recently enlarged Legislative Council. The election involved only 1 percent of the population and of that number only 50,000 bothered to vote. Elections for the district board in 1988 showed a disappointing 17 percent turnout.[62] A government green paper on representative government, published in 1987, contained several graduated options ranging from a continuation of the status quo to a "one person, one vote" system of electing a majority of the legislature before 1997.[63] The Beijing government viewed this document as potentially interfering with the smooth transfer of sovereignty, since the Basic Law Drafting Committee, established by the 1984 Sino-British Agreement, was also to take up the issue of representative government and had not yet reported to the National People's Congress. At that time, a large sector of the general public considered it wise that Hong Kong avoid confrontation with Beijing over this issue. However, the 1989 suppression of the democratic movement in China fueled calls to escalate the pace of political reform in Hong Kong, resulting in a tremendous surge of support for direct elections of all legislative councillors before 1997. Nevertheless, final deliberations over the Basic Law concluded that only 33 percent (twenty of the sixty seats) of the Legislative Council would be directly elected in 1997. Before 1990 the total number of people that had the right to vote in the Legislative Council elections was very small, approximately 1 percent of the total population of Hong Kong and less than 3 percent of the adult population. In 1990 the Legislative Council consisted of fifty-six members, with elected members being in the minority.[64] The first direct elections of a small number of legislative councilors were to take place in September 1991.

The schools have never been a force in democratizing Hong Kong, and, if anything, have hindered the process. The school curriculum has, until the late 1980s, virtually ignored raising political consciousness. The planned return of sovereignty changed that to some degree by leading to minor modifications of the school curriculum. However, political democracy remained a topic to be avoided. Nevertheless, the government is concerned with doing what it can to ensure that popular political disruptions do not mar the return of sovereignty.[65]

Changes in the school curriculum, as noted by Morris in chapter five, provide much-needed legitimacy to a colonial government that has often been accused of dragging its feet for many years before introducing opportunities for representative government. In this sense, people view the curriculum as an instrument to bolster their attempts at expanded representative government.

After the signing of the Joint Declaration in 1984, the number and range of school curriculum topics dealing with political awareness increased. Although this may be associated in any society with a general trend toward more affluence and a growing middle class, it derived at least equally from the expected return of sovereignty in 1997. The greatest stress is placed on the responsibilities of good citizenship, while activities that encourage political involvement are minimized. Two quotations from the government guidelines for civic education reflect this: "In light of Hong Kong's recent political development, evolution should be the watch-word and the emphasis in this guide will be on civic education as a politically socializing force for promoting stability and responsibility," and, "Democracy means different things to different people . . . so education for democracy per se would be difficult to interpret."[66]

Education officials have also lifted the taboo on teaching about post-1949 China. However, many school principals want to teach children about modern China but are encountering difficulties. In particular, it is difficult to get teachers to analyze the present regime. Most teachers are reluctant to discuss Beijing's generally feared and often despised regime, with the result that Hong Kong is fostering a generation of young people who have only the slightest understanding of their future as Chinese citizens. While some academics support the new courses, others criticize them as reflecting a new defensiveness in the Education Department to appease Beijing.

Following the recommendation of the *Education Commission Report No. 3*, a working group named the Working Group on Sixth Form Education was set up in June 1988 to consider the curriculum reform.[67] In July 1989, the working group submitted its report to the Secretary for Education and Manpower, who endorsed the recommendations. One recommendation was the introduction of a new course entitled "Liberal Studies," which would be offered beginning in September 1992 as a way of broadening the curriculum and making it more relevant to Hong Kong's future. The main modules included in the course were entitled Hong Kong Studies, Environmental Studies, The Modern World, Science Technology and Society, China Today, and Human Relationships.[68] Despite the benefits of such a long-overdue reform, the curriculum's restriction to the sixth form and its status as an optional course act to relegate this reform to the backwaters. Its successful implementation has been further threatened by the universities which have refused to make it an admission requirement.

These curriculum changes are occurring against a backdrop of important changes in the political culture of Hong Kong during the late 1980s. The sociopolitical landscape has been gradually transformed from its traditionally apolitical orientation. Rapid economic growth, expanded educational opportunity, and a younger population have led to a decline of traditional institutions and social customs. Social and economic issues have been pushed into the political arena, leading to demands for more government action. After a long period in which a secluded bureaucracy existed apart from the Chinese society, there have been new efforts to formalize government–people relationships. An increasing number of people believe that the government is responsible for solving their personal and family problems. The people of Hong Kong are fast adopting an active, even interventionist concept of government, and they would like to see the government measure up to their expectations. Moreover, as the growth of political pressure groups continues, it is apparent that the people of Hong Kong are becoming more favorably disposed toward many kinds of political activism. A prominent Hong Kong political scientist notes that "tactics which involve a quantum of confrontation or violence are increasingly rated as effective means to compel the government to give in."[69] This is no small change. However, there is still a lack of adequate local structures for social and political participation, including areas of educational decision making. Nevertheless, the curriculum changes discussed, coupled with the general move toward more political activity within schools and the increasingly activist role played by teachers in grass-roots politics, point to a move away from a status quo orientation that prevents schools from taking a more visible role in territorywide education reforms.

Political leaders are slowly beginning to emerge from the school system. In fact, teaching professionals are expected to dominate the first direct elections to the Legislative Council in September of 1991.[70] Political analysts believe that teaching professionals could have an edge because they can make use of holiday periods to organize campaigns and canvass for support. Moreover, the nature of the profession, and the knowledge among the public that teacher salaries are not nearly as high as for other occupations that command an equal level of educational qualifications, contribute to the image of the teacher as a dedicated politician.

However, in order for schools to become more effective in producing popular political leaders, they will have to integrate themselves into their surrounding communities. They are now isolated units. A 1982 report by a visiting panel stated:

> At the school level, there is little sense of community despite the fact that many schools can be found clustered together geographically. Even when the citing of new facilities has been premeditated, these can not be regarded as community schools in the usual sense of the phrase. The extensive devolution of authority and responsibility of voluntary agencies in the education portfolio and the fact that these agencies are not federated on a neighborhood basis makes it impractical to contemplate "local control" beyond that currently being contemplated in the school net schemes.[71]

The schools' isolation from the surrounding community is intensified by the lack of parental involvement in their operations. Parental involvement within schools is usually limited to formal parent–teacher association meetings (where they exist) and to rare school visits when a child's problems prompt the teacher to call for a parent. There is a strict and still widely accepted separation of roles between parents and teachers, and between home and school, deriving partly from the alienation many parents feel due to their own lack of schooling. Education authorities introduced a school management initiative in March 1991 that could be used to increase parental involvement in school affairs.

Despite the densely populated nature of the Hong Kong community, and the geographic position of schools within residential areas, the schools are not integrated into the communities. The social distance of the school from the surrounding community derives not only from the lack of contact between teachers and parents, but also from the lack of contact between school leaders and the community. School management boards do not see themselves as directly accountable to the surrounding community. The only perceived accountability is to the Education Department, which makes financial allocations and inspects the schools. Although they are essentially powerless, District Board officials are elected by members of the community and could provide a way for residents to channel their opinions about school problems to the government. However, District Board officials are seldom approached on educational matters.[72]

During the territorywide demonstrations of May and June 1989, some popular leaders did emerge from the schools because they embodied the sentiments of many Hong Kong people. Moreover, these demonstrations were also an opportunity for some young political leaders to emerge from the ranks of the large number of secondary and tertiary school students.

Decolonizing the Selection System: Language as Cultural Capital

Localization, a process in which local people are increasingly given priority in appointments to high-level posts in government and industry, was never taken as a serious objective until the signing of the Joint Declaration on Hong Kong's future in 1984. Before then, expatriates were clearly favored for recruitment to upper-level government posts. Just prior to the Sino-British Joint Declaration, the political scientist Myron Mushkat expressed the following view:

> A more subtle explanation for the extent of expatriate recruitment is that it dovetails with the higher objectives of "colonial control." Hong Kong, after all, is a British dependent territory and in order to fulfill its role with a measure of effectiveness the United Kingdom must have at its disposal reliable mechanisms for providing societal direction. The presence of a fairly large number of Britons in key policy-making posts may thus be construed as a factor which facilitates "colonial management." One could argue, however, that this legitimate objective no longer requires the balancing of each local appointment with an expatriate one and that a ratio more favorable to the local component need not detract from the U.K.'s grip over Hong Kong.[73]

The Hong Kong government officially adopted localization of the civil service as official policy as early as 1947, but by the mid-1980s a significant number of high-level positions continued to be held by expatriates.[74] Expatriates comprised almost half of all directorate officers and almost one-third of those at the top of the Master Pay Scale.[75] According to the Sino-British Declaration on Hong Kong, after 1997, "The government and legislature of the Hong Kong Special Administrative Region shall be composed of local inhabitants."[76] Furthermore, while foreign nationals may be employed by the future Hong Kong civil service, they may not hold posts as heads of major government departments, including the police department, or as deputy heads of some of those departments.[77] In his study of government planning with respect to government localization policy, John Burns concluded that

> it indicates a failure of the government's policy of localization over the years. Coherent plans to localize problem grades and departments are urgently needed. Hong Kong must develop a confident, forward-looking civil service for the years up to and beyond 1997. Much needs to be done.[78]

Since then, however, the government appointed the first non-expatriate as director of education.[79] Local Hong Kong Chinese are increasingly appointed to top posts in other government departments as well. Nevertheless, because of the great exodus following the Sino-British agreement, the pace of localization has slowed, particularly in the middle-level civil service. In an effort to stall the exodus of key individuals, the British government is proposing to make available 50,000 "insurance" passports, carrying the right to live in the United Kingdom, and is encouraging other nations with large interests in Hong Kong to do the same.[80] This may confound the educational policy process by creating strong loyalty to the United Kingdom, even after 1997. China has already asserted that it will not recognize the overseas passports of local residents of Chinese descent, and will undoubtedly develop countermeasures throughout the transitional period for what it sees as an illegitimate means to limit its sovereignty.

By gearing up to teach English-language courses that encourage success on linguistically based civil service examinations, educational changes have been increasingly fashioned to dovetail with the recruitment of native Hong-Kongese to the civil service. This has been accomplished through a policy process that reflects the colonial support for elite schools and the preservation of the University of Hong Kong as a wholly English-medium institution. English-language facility and cultural consonance are essential for the recruitment and promotion of graduates from the University of Hong Kong in the civil service.

This emphasis also led to the creation of a large Anglo-Chinese system of secondary schools. By the early 1980s this sector of the educational system peaked, surpassing the number of Chinese instruction schools by nine to one.[81] However, although the official medium of instruction in the Anglo-Chinese schools was English, the limited number of competent English-speaking teachers led to many variations in the quality of language instruction. Even when competent English-speaking teachers were available, a great many students were not able to learn in English. Parents resisted pleas by educators to reconsider educating their children in Anglo-Chinese schools instead of Chinese instruction schools. The Education Department eventually took steps to increase the number of schools in the Chinese sector by providing incentives to those questionable Anglo-Chinese schools to convert to Chinese instruction. This, it was hoped, would result in an increase in the number of Chinese-medium secondary schools, and a corresponding influence on the ethos of many Hong Kong secondary schools.

The medium of instruction in most secondary schools in Hong Kong is still officially English, which places a tremendous burden on students since most have little contact with native English speakers. The effects of this practice on culture and identity is of more interest to researchers than parents, most of whom continue to opt for as much English-medium education for their children as possible.[82] Children who attend elite English-medium schools are at an advantage, because they will be recruited to government civil service posts. Public policies do not seek to redress this, as noted again by a visiting panel.

> There also seems to be an element of safeguarding privilege by an elite whose children are more or less bilingual. Everyone should try by the best legitimate means to secure the best start for his own child, but we feel the public policies should look particularly to the needs of those whose starting positions are not so favorable.[83]

This pattern may be reinforced further by a new set of language-policy proposals the government is considering. These would make entrance into English-language secondary education dependent on an examination administered after primary six.[84] The proposals' stated aim is to improve competency in at least one language and eliminate the use of "Chinglish," a mixture of English and Chinese words in the teaching–learning process. The outcome of the proposals, as I have explained elsewhere, will be to further extend elitist elements in the educational system and further restrict access for those in the English streams to the University of Hong Kong and to government civil service positions.[85]

However, all past government-initiated language proposals have fallen short of implementation. The medium-of-instruction controversy dates back to the end of World War II, the government forever being in the bind of eliminating either parental choice or sound educational practice. Some accuse the government of being halfhearted. In the case of Putonghua (Mandarin) teaching, the government recommended the language as an option but failed to make it a requirement. As noted in chapter nine, the Education Commission recommended that the schools teach Putonghua either before or after hours or as an extracurricular activity, but only two schools have adopted it as the main medium of instruction.[86] Researchers such as Bauer and Pierson (chapter eight) are confident that Putonghua will replace English and Cantonese as the language of power and the official language of government, and that everyone will be required to learn it.[87]

Growing business opportunities in the China trade and investment area, along with an expansion of interactions between China and Hong Kong, have added to a new ground swell favoring schooling in the Chinese mother tongue over English-language schooling. In fact, the battle to preserve Hong Kong's status as an English-speaking territory is far from won. At the same time, many educators in China have criticized Hong Kong's return to Chinese mother tongue education because Hong Kong Chinese consider Cantonese, rather than Putonghua, to be their lingua franca.[88] The majority of Hong Kong educators strongly resist the use of Mandarin as a learning medium in their schools. This represents yet another example of how the dual identity of Hong Kong's cultural ethos manifests itself within educational issues, even as it impinges on localization and recruitment into the government civil service. Thus, school language policy, and the extent to which individuals can function competently in Putonghua, Cantonese, and English, can easily come to influence the legitimacy of emerging political leaders and the orientation that educational reform will take.

Social Stratification and the Transformation of Elite Education

There is a staggering degree of income inequality in Hong Kong. While the average citizen enjoys the third-highest living standard in Asia, many still live without running water or legal electricity.[89] In most societies, such levels of inequality generate class conflict and industrial hostilities. However, when industry, trade, and commerce are prosperous and the labor market is active, the wages of workers in Hong Kong are still much better than those of their counterparts on the mainland. The Gini coefficient, which measures income inequality in a population, fell from 0.49 in 1961 to 0.43 in 1971 and remained about the same in 1981, with little change to the present. This was still considerably higher than what was observed in the United States (0.25), Taiwan and Korea (0.3), and Singapore (0.4).[90] Forty percent of the population is engaged in manufacturing, 22 percent in government and science occupations, 16 percent in commerce, and 5 percent in agriculture. In 1976, the working class (all manual employees) comprised 51.6 percent of the population, the new middle class (non-manual employees) 36.5 percent, and the capitalist class (all employers and self-employed persons) 11.9 percent.[91] In 1981, the poorest 10 percent of all households received 1.4 percent of the population's total household income, whereas the richest 10 percent received 35.2 percent of that income. The working class has had no political power in the legislature despite the fact that its political orientation and ideological identifications run the gamut from extreme right (in support of Taiwan) to extreme left (in support of Beijing).[92] Except for the street riots of 1952, 1967, and 1984, since the end of World War II the territory has been stable, with little overt social unrest and conflict. There are signs indicating the emergence of a politically conscious middle class that is beginning to play a more active role in organizing itself in community political affairs. This emerging class is gaining more control over the educational system, which helps ensure that their children inherit their middle-class status. A future concern with regard to China's regaining sovereignty over Hong Kong is less its willingness to tolerate capitalism than its tolerance of the great gaps that exist among social classes in Hong Kong.

Access to opportunity has increasingly been placed within the domain of formal education. Chinese tradition holds education in high esteem, and the idea of having a scholarly examination system as a key determinant for access to high positions, especially in government, is not new to the Chinese.[93] However, the character of the school selection process in Hong Kong is brutal. Even though education is compulsory (and free) until age fifteen, less than 8 percent survive to enter postsecondary, university-level education in Hong Kong. The extent of equity within this system is questionable although, as is often the case in other industrial societies, the meritocratic ideology (at least the notion that anyone who is capable and works hard in school, regardless of social class factors, can achieve success) has remained quite durable.

Research on educational success in Hong Kong has consistently confirmed what has been all too evident in the Western developed nations—that family background, however measured, is the best predictor of school achievement.[94] However, school characteristics also play a large role. In this regard, there is a great disparity among schools, as confirmed in the visiting panel's report:

> There are striking variations indeed. Hong Kong has some of the best schools in the world in terms of student attainment ... most of the schools however, leave something to be desired. Facilities, teacher qualifications, examination results and other indicators of quality rank low. Students are allocated to these schools for various reasons, including their test performance and lack of opportunity owing to the educational and economic status of their parents.[95]

Little has been done to relieve this problem. If the economy goes through a period of crisis, as is expected in the mid-1990s, this could highlight the gap between the social classes and increase the likelihood that the schools will become an arena of social class conflict. Whether or not social class conflict can work itself into the cultural fabric of the Chinese society in Hong Kong in such a way as to avoid becoming dangerously divisive remains an important question. If it cannot, then it may pose yet another threat to the realization of extended democratic educational changes.

A reform known as the Direct Subsidy Scheme is directed at privatization of education and has major implications for social stratification in Hong Kong.[96] When a large-scale international move toward privatization of education occurred in the 1980s, Hong Kong was heading in the opposite direction.[97] Private schools flourished in Hong Kong during the 1950s and 1960s when the school system was experiencing its initial expansion. Private primary schools virtually disappeared as the government's inspection standards under its Code of Aid became the measure of the viability of keeping a school open. By the 1980s, the Code of Aid was used to bring all primary and most secondary schools under the umbrella of the Education Department. When three years of junior secondary education became universal, free, and compulsory, there were not enough places for students in the government-subsidized schools, so the government began to buy places from the private secondary schools. Private school places were generally inferior to those in the government sector. The government increased the number of schools under its control, and the number of private schools declined. However, beginning in the late 1980s a number of factors such as organized opposition by the private schools led to a new reform proposal to save them. The major change came in 1988 with a new proposal by the Hong Kong Education Commission.

The Education Commission recommended that the Bought Places Scheme be phased out. This scheme permitted the government to buy places from private secondary schools as a way to supplement the supply of free secondary school places. While one of the new proposal's major selling points is to throw a lifeline to the private schools by allowing them to apply for government subsidies, it has other implications as well. It was argued that the high-quality secondary schools will opt to come under this Direct Subsidy Scheme (DSS) rather than the existing Code of Aid. Under the DSS, schools that receive a financial subsidy from the government could charge school fees. Moreover, they would not have to accept students through the government's centralized scheme. The other selling point of this scheme is that it expands parental choice. Parents could send their children to DSS schools by applying directly to them.

Critics of the scheme note that the new system would allow parents to pay a weighty school fee to send their children to the exclusive secondary schools, which would still be supported by public funds. For the first time, these publicly subsidized schools could have the power to accept or refuse students as they see fit. Thus, the financial scheme, which evolved over several decades to ensure more equality of educational opportunity, would be severely compromised. Social distinctions could become further institutionalized (see chapter six).

The DSS proposal has nevertheless been welcomed by a number of educators who point to international trends and contend that the system would more closely match Hong Kong's free market ideology. Naturally, the proposal was welcomed by the heads of the most prestigious schools. But it also received support from the pro-Beijing or patriotic schools, which have long been excluded from financing through the government's Code of Aid.

Interdependence and Academic Exchange

There has been a growing interdependence, both economically and politically, between Hong Kong and the People's Republic of China. China is well-justified in its assertion that it is responsible for the economic success of Hong Kong. Through immigration, it provides the indispensable manpower needed to fuel Hong Kong's industrialization. China also subsidizes a large percentage of Hong Kong's foodstuffs and provides relatively inexpensive clothing. Moreover, the mainland provides the colony with 35 percent of its water supply. Hong Kong remains a useful contact point with the West for China. The most common explanation for China's position with respect to Hong Kong has been, and remains, mutual advantage. This is not to suggest that it would be unwilling to sacrifice some level of mutual economic advantage for sovereignty. China has the military power to overrun Hong Kong in a few hours. Alternatively, it can use its supporters in Hong Kong to destabilize it.

The points of interdependence between China and Hong Kong are unique to ideologically opposed economic systems. Hong Kong is the largest market for China's exports, while China has become the second-largest export market for Hong Kong.[98] In short, Hong Kong is a major source of China's investment capital and will continue to play a major role in financing China's modernization. By 1980 China's net foreign exchange earnings from Hong Kong had already reached $6.9 billion, representing 36.5 percent of China's total foreign exchange for that period.[99]

By far, the major form of interdependence derives from migration from the mainland to Hong Kong. When the British were ceded Hong Kong in 1842, the population of Hong Kong Island was estimated to be only about 23,000. With the New Territories and Kowloon, the estimate was about 100,000.[100] The Japanese invasion of China in the 1930s caused a mass exodus in which 750,000 people migrated to Hong Kong between 1937 and 1939, bringing the total population to 1.6 million.[101] By 1945, as a result of the Japanese occupation of Hong Kong, movement back to China and abroad left the entire territory with only 600,000 people. The population increased again in the 1950s to 2.5 million as a result of the Communist victory in China. A steady increase since then has left it at about 5.5 million.[102] In 1971, approximately 56 percent of the population was born in China, and by 1985, due to a leveling out of migration, only 40 percent of the population originated in China. Thirty-nine percent of the population is under twenty years old. Only 2 percent of the population is non-ethnic Chinese. While immigration has been a major factor in Hong Kong's development, new policies have restricted the previously free flow of immigrants from China. Nevertheless, a heavy flow of legal immigrants, about 27,000 per year, and illegal immigrants, of whom more than forty are arrested each day, continues to enter the territory.[103]

The large majority of Hong Kong's population is from Southern China, particularly Guangdong Province. However, there are significant numbers as well from Northern and Central China. The Shanghainese, for instance, who number only 3 percent of the total population, have a larger influence than their numbers would suggest; their special contribution to the industrialization of Hong Kong occurred soon after 1949, when they transferred much capital and skills to the territory. Census figures do not highlight the range of regional Chinese groups that occupy Hong Kong. For example, the Fujianese and Shanghainese are grouped together in census figures, but the differences between them and their salience as ethnic groups in Hong Kong cannot be denied. Census figures do show that the composition of recent immigrants is shifting. A larger percentage are migrating from regions that lie to the north of the adjoining province of Guangdong. It is also worth noting that the data on migrant characteristics suggests that if educational characteristics can be taken as surrogates for social position, the recent migrants "did not come from either the poorest areas or the poorest sections of society."[104]

The cultural system of the Hong Kong Chinese is heterogeneous. Among the 98 percent ethnic Chinese majority, according to Lau, there are "variations in dialect, customs, and styles of living as well as lingering hostilities among locality groupings which would be readily available cleavage lines to divide society into antagonistic frameworks."[105] Hong Kong's Chinese society is the product of a continual adjustment process in a society of Chinese people who are divided by ethnic, territorial, dialectical, and ideological identifications. The urbanization of Chinese regional groups within the Hong Kong context seems to have converted these regional groups into ethnic groups. This process has been noted in detail with three Chinese regional groups in Hong Kong—the Shanghainese, Fujianese, and Chao Zhouese.[106] As long as we do not consider ethnicity to be a rigid set of beliefs, behaviors, or customs, but rather one dimension of beliefs, behaviors, and customs that articulate closely with other dimensions of life and culture, then we can more easily see how Chinese regional groups take on the characteristics of ethnic groups when they migrate to an urban area like Hong Kong. Instead of viewing ethnicity as isolated, we see it as part of a process and a situational construct. As such, it exists only as a specific adaption and orientation to a given set of circumstances during a given period of time. Chinese regional groups who migrate to Hong Kong, such as the Shanghainese, Fujianese, or Chao Zhouese, engage in such a process of adaption and develop situational orientations, allowing them both to become a part of and remain apart from the Hong Kong Cantonese culture.

The diversity of regional groups in Hong Kong is not outwardly reflected in a varied regionally based school system. With the exception of the handful of Chinese secondary schools that draw students from particular regions, most are heterogeneous. Therefore, the schools cannot be viewed as institutions that preserve regional ethnic cultures. Except for two or three secondary schools that use Putonghua (Mandarin) as the medium of instruction, Cantonese mixed with varying amounts of English is the norm. Schools expose students of non-Cantonese origin to local Cantonese culture. This does not eliminate regional subcultures and the identities that derive from them, but it provides students from other regions with sufficient access to the local cultural milieu.

Economic interdependence with China has not been accompanied by educational or academic interdependence. There is virtually no structural interdependence between the two educational systems. Few formal institutional agreements have been signed between universities in Hong Kong and those in other parts of China. The number and diversity of Chinese universities would make it difficult to choose only a few with which to set up formal arrangements, since agreements with many institutions could easily become overwhelming given the size of Hong Kong's two universities. Informal exchanges allow links to be maintained with a large number of higher educational institutions in China. Thus, most formal academic exchanges and research projects are conducted through faculty or academic department agreements, although each university sets aside funds that members of departments and faculties can use in academic exchange.

Since the early 1980s there has been an increasing amount of academic exchange between Hong Kong and the rest of China. I have noted the imbalance of these exchanges in favor of science and engineering until the late 1980s.[107] The early phase brought university staff together but resulted in little substantive cooperative work. The later phase initiated joint cooperative projects between departments or faculties of different institutions, including those facilitated by the World Bank and other international agencies. There are also organizations within Hong Kong, such as the Beijing–Hong Kong Academic Exchange Center and the Peihua Foundation, which encourage and sponsor academic exchange between universities in Hong Kong and other parts of China.[108] Student exchanges in both directions have also increased. Special scholarships have led the way for an increasing number of Hong Kong students to study at China's leading universities, although the number dropped after June 4, 1989. By June 1990, postgraduate enrollment had decreased by 75 percent. China's State Education Commission coordinated the selection of Hong Kong students for admission to graduate study and scholarships were provided to cover expenses at more than forty tertiary institutions in China, including key-point universities such as Beijing University and Qinghua University.[109] This adds to the already large number of Hong Kong students attending universities in South China, in close proximity to Hong Kong. More students from China are enrolled in graduate than undergraduate programs in Hong Kong's two universities, and their numbers have steadily increased.

Hong Kong's interdependence goes beyond linking itself with China. As an international trading center, it has developed economic interdependence with many other nations, and this has made itself felt in the educational arena. Many of the university staff in Hong Kong earned their credentials outside of the territory and in the rest of China. Furthermore, there are at least 30,000 Hong Kong students earning postsecondary degrees outside of Hong Kong, a figure more than double the number studying at the territory's two universities.[110]

Given that it is strengthening ties with universities in other parts of China where academic freedom is often limited, there has been surprisingly little concern expressed within Hong Kong's universities over academic freedom—even with the crackdown on universities in China following the Tiananmen tragedy. The tenure system in Hong Kong's universities protects the critical scholar. However, a large number of non-tenure, three-year renewable contracts offered to new recruits have shown their potential to make critical academics more vulnerable. Unlike Hong Kong's journalists, who have steadfastly battled the forces that threaten their future openness, the universities have yet to bring this issue to the forefront. This may be partly due to the fact that the universities have seldom been viewed as openly critical of government policy, whether it be Hong Kong's or China's. On the only occasion when both universities challenged the government's Educational Commission on the issue of the length of university education, the commission prevailed.

Interdependence with the rest of China has a tremendous potential to influence the educational reform process in Hong Kong and in China as well (see chapter eleven). The extent of Beijing's influence will be determined by whether it is mediated through an educational reform process that is essentially democratic, or exerted through a restructured consultative system designed to align educational developments with mainland interests. Even if Beijing makes an unlikely effort to leave Hong Kong educational politics in their present form, the status quo orientation noted earlier could hardly continue. Local leaders would be hard-pressed to pick up where the colonials left off without establishing a new source for government-initiated educational changes.

Cultural Tradition, Educational Transformation, and the Hong Kong Identity

Traditional Chinese society was perpetuated by a state-dominated social order, which has existed for one hundred and fifty years in colonial Hong Kong. However, a different conception of the state–society relationship has appeared. Only in the last two decades has this conception undergone changes, while the basic nature of the political order has remained intact. Thus, the state-dominated society of Hong Kong is different in many ways from that of traditional Chinese society and of mainland China.

Governance in Hong Kong is characterized by such elements as authoritarianism, benign and enlightened rule, separate but blurred public and private spheres, and the rule of law. As Lau Siu-kai and Kuan Hsin-chi state:

> The establishment of colonial rule in Hong Kong was based until several decades ago on military force. In the long span of colonial rule, subtle versions of the doctrine of the economic prowess and cultural superiority of the white people, and the civilizing mission of the colonizer, had occasionally emerged to justify colonial dominance. Still, there has not been an elaborate, systematic theory, explicitly articulated, to buttress the legitimacy of authority in Hong Kong.[111]

Confucianism, for instance, disappeared from the content of Hong Kong civil service examinations. This deprived the residual Confucian presence of instrumental value and relegated it to cultural backwaters. The Confucian influence lingers, but is contingent more on the natural influence of social customs and family socialization than on any institutional underpinning, such as schooling.

Hong Kong Chinese society differs from traditional and modern Chinese society in a number of ways: its high degree of modernization, industrialization, and urbanization; its dominance by market forces; the erosion of tradition; the adapted changes in the family and other primary and quasi-primary structures; the lack of a moralizing elite; and the dominance of an economic elite. Furthermore, the values embodied in the Hong Kong Chinese elites differ from their counterparts in China. Their moral status is shaky and they lack a sense of cultural or moral mission.

Hong Kong's history has left the school system with the task of resolving the tensions that have resulted from a long colonial period. Dora Choi Po-king recognizes in the identity crisis of Hong Kong students the strains between cultural tradition and modern education. She goes part way toward explaining the source of this tension in the 1970s:

> The post-war generation was, therefore, bombarded with Western cultural influence both in and outside the school. Yet they were constantly reminded of their Chinese cultural heritage, and they did acquire a national cultural identity which was, however, never substantiated by any concrete ties, nor even candid discussion of relevant political developments. Caught in this ambiguous situation, the Hong Kong–born post-war generation met with a severe crisis of cultural identity.[112]

Lau and Kuan also note the distinctive ethos of the Hong Kong people as a post-war phenomenon that has become more salient with the onset of the transition to 1997, and the rise of the younger, more educated generation. They suggest the existence of two identities in Hong Kong, Chinese and Hong-Kongese:

> Sudden and dramatic confrontation with one's fellow "compatriots" who differed from oneself in many significant ways willy-nilly forced one to ask the soul-searching question of "Who I am?" ... Hong Kong Chinese are made more conscious of their distinct identity when placed in juxtaposition with the mainland Chinese people.[113]

These local scholars continue to raise questions about the implications of the reincorporation of Hong Kong in 1997, especially as it relates to the apparent tension in the cultural identity of Hong Kong students. They identify the educational challenge of 1997 as socialization into a "one country, two system" society. Hong Kong education will be beset with a major dilemma, that of building an educational system that can reconcile the ideological contradictions between capitalism, socialism, and patriotism, and preparing local political leaders who can guide Hong Kong through the postcolonial transition.

Conclusion: Education and Social Transformations

As decolonization proceeds and Hong Kong becomes closer to China, the potential for social transformation will become more closely tied to the ability of educational institutions to prepare popular political leaders. This will require a fundamental change in the manner of political socialization in secondary schools and tertiary institutions. The government's guidelines on civic education, the modification of the ban on political activity in schools, and the liberal studies curriculum go part way to this end. Moreover, an increasing number of teachers and school principals are becoming active in local elections aimed at guaranteeing more representative government. However, much more will have to be done to have any effect upon the factors, noted by Lau, that have impeded such leadership. These include the nature of colonial governance; the character of the Chinese community; the institutional features of the local sociopolitical system; time constraints; the inconsistent and incoherent leadership policy of the British and Chinese governments; and elusive and erratic mass support for leaders.[114] The educational changes discussed above have only begun to approach this important challenge. However, future educational reforms can be expected to pay increasing attention to this issue.

Each of the three broad orientations identified earlier in this chapter has the potential to reconcile or heighten contradictions. The likelihood of any single one prevailing will depend on the way in which the other macroscopic social transformations affect education during the period before and after 1997. At a minimum, the contextual processes outlined above reveal a tension developing between each of these orientations. The apparent increased vulnerability of the policy process places the long-term future of the first orientation in serious doubt. Hong Kong's ability to secure its preferred model of representative government from Beijing before 1997 is certain to shape events in favor of the second policy option. However, the degree to which the people of Hong Kong can acquire, accept, and work within the conflict-prone policy process of a more representative government will determine whether or not a centralizing force will be asserted after 1997. Such a centralizing influence would rebuild the traditional consultative mechanism for maintaining the legitimacy of the educational policy process. Given the uncertainty of future events, each option remains a possibility.

The degree to which each of the three broad orientations reconciles or heightens the contradictions between capitalism, socialism, and patriotism will also be determined in large measure by the way in which the macroscopic social transformations affect education. As is apparent from the experience of Eastern European societies, the contradictions between capitalism and socialism can only be reconciled by allowing the citizenry to become actively engaged in social transformation. This leaves only the second policy option as holding out any real hope for reconciliation. In this respect, the others will only delay real progress. The challenge will be to show that patriotism must be harmonized in such a way as to allow opposition groups to thrive within a democratic framework. The response of the people of Hong Kong to the events of 1989 in China and other parts of the world makes clear their determination to tie the development of democratic institutions to patriotism.

How Hong Kong's educational system handles this situation in years to come will be of interest to scholars of social change. Unfortunately, the colonial history of Hong Kong shows some cause for disappointment. It supports the idea that the Hong Kong educational system of the 1990s will resist the changes necessary to reconcile such contradictions, specifically in the area of more popular democratic participation in the educational reform process. As Eastern European societies have learned, sacrifices are necessary if reforms are to take place. Hong Kong will have a strong tendency to shy away from significant reforms because of its long-standing economic success under the colonial government. This is understandable to an extent. However, carrying on as usual will only lead Hong Kong education into a greater dilemma. The territory will have to show greater flexibility—channels for active participation by all sectors of the society in educational matters must be widened, and resulting conflicts must be viewed in a constructive manner as part of a mature reforming society, not just as threats to stability and prosperity.

Education will play an important role in the transition because of its position within a series of complex, shifting factors. Education can cushion the changes and contradictions of the transition, and at the same time be used to resist selected features. It may provide a cultural transmission process that helps legitimize continued British influence through the transition years by regulating the production and distribution of its status culture. In this sense, through the socialization of its elites in Hong Kong, education is still an important element of continued British influence. However, it is doubtful that China will be content to limit itself to merely economic influence over Hong Kong. Moreover, as a result of unrest in China, local Hong Kong students have become more politicized, and it is only a matter of time before they become a formidable challenge both to London's and to Beijing's influence. The 1997 situation has plunged Hong Kong into a quagmire of uncertainty, which has given the territory a sharpened sense of its identity but at the same time has revealed a lack of consensus about the direction of education. This lack of consensus places the government's legitimacy at risk at a time when it is attempting to shore up its influence in order to exert control after 1997 on institutions of cultural transmission.

Notes

I would like to thank Lee Wing On for his useful comments.

1. See John Burns and Ian Scott, *The Hong Kong Civil Service and Its Future* (Hong Kong: Oxford University Press, 1988); Joseph Y.S. Cheng, ed., *Hong Kong in Transition* (Hong Kong: Oxford University Press, 1986); Christopher Howe, "Growth, Public Policy, and Hong Kong's Relationship with the People's Republic of China," *China Quarterly*, no. 95, pp. 512–33 (September 1983); Y.C. Jao, Leung Chi-keung, Peter Wesley-Smith, and Wong Siu-lun, *Hong Kong and 1997: Strategies for the Future* (Hong Kong: Center of Asian Studies, University of Hong Kong, 1985); Lau Siu-kai and Kuan Hsin-chi, "The Changing Political Culture of the Hong Kong Chinese," in Joseph Y.S. Cheng, ed., *Hong Kong in Transition* (Hong Kong: Oxford University Press, 1986), pp. 26–51; Gerard Postiglione, "The Structuring of Ethnicity in Hong Kong," *International Journal of Intercultural Relations* 12, pp. 247–67 (1988); Lucian W. Pye, "The International Position of Hong Kong," *China Quarterly*, no. 95 (September 1983); A.J. Youngson, ed., *China and Hong Kong: The Economic Nexus* (Hong Kong: Oxford University Press, 1983); Ian Scott, *Political Change and the Crisis of Legitimacy in Hong Kong* (Hong Kong: Oxford University Press, 1989); Albert H. Yee, *A People Misruled: Hong Kong and the Chinese Stepping Stone Syndrome* (Hong Kong: API Press, 1989); Katherine Cheek-Milby and Myron Mushkat, eds., *Hong Kong: The Challenge of Transformation* (Hong Kong: Center of Asian Studies, University of Hong Kong, 1989).

2. Paul Morris, "The Effect on the School Curriculum of Hong Kong's Return to Chinese Sovereignty in 1997," *The Journal of Curriculum Studies* 20, 6 (November–December 1988), pp. 509–28 and Gerard A. Postiglione, "Hong Kong Education within Transition," *Comparative Education Review* 35, 5 (November 1991).

3. See Joseph Scimecca, *Education and Society* (New York: Holt, Rinehart, and Winston, 1980) and *Society and Freedom* (New York: St. Martin's Press, 1981); also, John Boli, Francisco O. Ramirez, and John W. Meyer, eds. "Explaining the Origins and Expansion of Mass Education," in P. Altbach and G. Kelly, eds., *New Approaches to Comparative Education* (Chicago: University of Chicago Press, 1986).

4. See Stanley Rosen, *Red Guard Factionalism and the Cultural Revolution in Guangzhou* (Boulder: Westview Press, 1982); Julia Kwong, *Cultural Revolution in China's Schools* (Stanford: Hoover Institution Press, 1988).

5. See Henry A. Giroux, "Theories of Reproduction and Resistance in the New Sociology of Education," *Harvard Educational Review* 53, pp. 257–93 (1983); Jerome Karabel and A.H. Halsey, eds., *Power and Ideology in Education* (New York: Oxford University Press, 1977).

6. University of Hong Kong Faculty of Law, *Hong Kong's Bill of Rights: Problems and Prospects* (Hong Kong: University of Hong Kong Faculty of Law, 1990); Tsim Tak-lung, "The Implementation of the Sino-British Declaration," in Richard Y.S. Wong and Joseph Y.C. Cheng, eds., *The Other Hong Kong Report: 1990* (Hong Kong: The Chinese University of Hong Kong Press, 1990).

7. Lau Siu-kai, "Decolonization without Independence and the Poverty of Political Leaders in Hong Kong" (Hong Kong: The Chinese University of Hong Kong, Hong Kong Institute of Asian Pacific Studies, Occasional Paper No. 1, November 1990).

8. See Robert Church, *Education in the United States: An Interpretive History* (New York: Free Press, 1976).

9. See Philip G. Altbach and Gail P. Kelly, eds., *Education and Colonialism* (New York: Longman, 1978).

10. See Ingemar Fagerlind and Lawrence J. Saha, *Education and National Development: A Comparative Perspective* (Oxford: Pergamon Press, 1983).

11. Among the first to resign from the Basic Law Drafting Committee were the outspoken liberal legislative councilors Lee Chu Ming and Szeto Wah. The editor of the *Ming Bao* daily newspaper, Louis Cha, who formerly had supported the Beijing government, also resigned after June 4, 1989.

12. See *Hong Kong Standard* and *Wen Hui Bao*, June 5, 1989.

13. See "Call to End Politics Ban in Schools," in *South China Morning Post*, June 7, 1989. On June 16, 1989, the University of Hong Kong Faculty of Education conducted a territorywide meeting of school teachers and principals in which accounts of student activism within and outside of schools were discussed. Most students were involved in territorywide demonstrations; however, many had organized activities at school such as speeches, political poster displays, letter writing, and student assemblies.

14. See Anthony E. Sweeting, *Education in Hong Kong, pre-1841 to 1941: Fact and Opinion* (Hong Kong: University of Hong Kong Press, 1990).

15. See Wong Siu-lun, *Emigrant Entrepreneurs: Shanghai Industrialists in Hong Kong* (Hong Kong: Oxford University Press, 1988).

16. See Edward K.Y. Chen, *Multinational Corporations, Technology, and Employment* (London: Macmillan, 1983).

17. See Jeffrey Henderson, "Hong Kong: High Technology Production and the Makings of a Regional Core," in Jeffrey Henderson, ed., *Global Option: Society, Space, and the Internationalization of High Technology Production* (London: Croom Helm, 1987).

18. In its early history, however, Hong Kong at times became the base for the launching of radical activities that contributed to nation-building in China. An example is the case of Sun Yatsen's anti-Manchu uprisings.

19. See Lau Siu-kai, *Society and Politics in Hong Kong* (Hong Kong: The Chinese University of Hong Kong Press, 1982).

20. See Manuel Castells, *The Shek Kip Mei Syndrome: Public Housing and Economic Development in Hong Kong* (Hong Kong: Center of Urban Studies and Urban Planning, January 1986).

21. See Lau, *Society and Politics in Hong Kong*.

22. "Academic Hits Out at Crisis Intervention," in *South China Morning Post*, November 5, 1989; and, "Tertiary Doors Will Open to More Students," in *South China Morning Post: Year in Review*, January 14, 1990.

23. *A Draft Agreement between the Government of Great Britain and Northern Ireland and the Government of the People's Republic of China on the Future of Hong Kong* (Hong Kong: Government Printer, 1984).

24. The Secretariat of the Consultative Committee for the Basic Law, *Draft Basic Law of the Hong Kong Special Administrative Region of the People's Republic of China* (Hong Kong: The Secretariat of the Consultative Committee for the Basic Law, 1988). See also those Chinese sources on the subject of the "one country, two system" policy: Zhao Qiuyi, *Yiguo liangzhi gailun* (Jilin University Press, 1988); Zhao Xiaowang, Deng Yun, and Zhou Bingyin, *Yige guojia liang zhong zhidu* (Liberation Army Press, 1989); *Xianggong wenti wenjian: xuanji* (Beijing: Renmin chubanshe, 1985); *Xianggong jiaoyu mianguan* (Guangdong renmin chubanshe, 1988); and Lei Qiang, Wu Fuguang, Zhong Guang, and Zheng Tainxiang, *Xianggong gaodeng jiaoyu* (Guangdong gaodeng jiaoyu chubanshe, 1988).

25. See *The Hong Kong Education System* (Hong Kong: Education Department, 1981). For an earlier historical account, see Sweeting, *Education in Hong Kong, pre-1841 to 1941: Fact and Opinion*, and Bernard Luk Hung-Kay, "Chinese Culture in the Hong Kong Curriculum," paper presented at the Annual Conference of the Comparative and International Education Society, Harvard University, March 31, 1989.

26. See Philip G. Altbach and Gail P. Kelly, eds., *Education and Colonialism*, pp. 1–52.

27. See Lau Siu-kai and Kuan Hsin-chi, *The Ethos of the Hong Kong Chinese* (Hong Kong: The Chinese University of Hong Kong Press, 1988).

28. See Martin Carnoy, *The State and Political Theory* (Princeton: Princeton University Press, 1985).

29. "Leftist School Leavers Gain Acceptance," *South China Morning Post*, October 2, 1989. What distinguishes these so-called patriotic, leftist, or pro-China schools is that they have traditionally supported the Beijing government's policies. During the Cultural Revolution, for instance, they rejected the formal curriculum of the Hong Kong education department. These schools have the strongest links with schools in mainland China.

30. See "Pro-China Schools in Subsidy Bid," *South China Morning Post*, October 8, 1989.

31. See section entitled "Provisional Hong Kong Council for Academic Accreditation," in chapter entitled "Education," in Aladin Ismail, ed., *Hong Kong 1989* (Hong Kong: Government Printer, 1989).

32. See *Returning to Hong Kong: 1990*, Glen Shive, ed. (Hong Kong: American Chamber of Commerce with the Institute of International Education, 1991).

33. See *South China Morning Post*, January 1, 1990.

34. See Lau and Kuan, *The Ethos of the Hong Kong Chinese*.

35. Ibid., p. 187.

36. See *Xianggong jiaoyu shouce* (Xianggong: Shangwu shuguan, 1988); Huo Guoqiang, *Xianggong zhongxue gailan* (Xianggong: Xianggong zhonghua jidujiao qingnianhui, 1988).

37. See Anthony E. Sweeting, "The Reconstruction of Education in Post-War Hong Kong) 1945–54: Variations in the Process of Policy Making," Ph.D. dissertation, University of Hong Kong, 1989.

38. See Ng Lun Ngai-ha, *Interaction of East and West: The Development of Public Education in Early Hong Kong* (Hong Kong: The Chinese University of Hong Kong Press).

39. Hong Kong Government, *Hong Kong: 1984* (Hong Kong: Government Printer, 1985).

40. See Education Department, *Report of the Allocation of Senior Secondary School Places—1981–83 Cycle* (Hong Kong: Government Printer, 1983); Education Department, *Report of the Working Group Set Up to Review the Secondary School Place Allocation System* (Hong Kong: Government Printer), January 5, 1985.

41. See Education Department, *Report of the 1983 Junior Secondary School Assessment*, prepared by the Junior Secondary School Assessment Section of the Education Department (Hong Kong: Government Printer, 1983); Education Department, *Report of the 1989 Junior Secondary Assessment*, prepared by educational records and the Junior Secondary Education Section of the Education Department (Hong Kong: Government Printer, 1989); Education Department, *Report of the Working Party on the Review of the JSEA System*, prepared by the Junior Secondary School Assessment Section of the Education Department (Hong Kong: Government Printer, February 1986).

42. Education Commission, *Education Commission Report No. 3* (Hong Kong: Government Printer, 1988).

43. Hong Kong Government, *Vocational Training Council: Annual Reports* (Hong Kong: Government Printer, 1985–90).

44. See Hong Kong Government, *Report of the Advisory Committee on Diversification* (Hong Kong: Government Printer, 1979).

45. See Gerard Postiglione, "International Higher Education and the Labor Market in Hong Kong: Functions of Overseas and Local Higher Education," in *International Education* 17, 1 (Fall 1987); Gerard Postiglione, "Higher Education and the Labor Market in

Urban Hong Kong," in L.Y. Choi, K.W. Fong, and Y.W. Kwok, eds., *Planning and Development in Open Coastal Cities* (Hong Kong: Center of Urban Studies and Urban Planning of the University of Hong Kong, 1986).

46. See Hong Kong Government, *Universities and Polytechnics Grants Committee of Hong Kong: Interim Report for 1985–88* (Hong Kong: Government Printer, 1985).

47. See Bernard Luk Hung-Kay, "Education," in Tsim Tak-lung and Bernard Luk Hung-kay, eds., *The Other Hong Kong Report* (Hong Kong: The Chinese University of Hong Kong Press, 1989).

48. See Hong Kong Government, *A Perspective on Education in Hong Kong: Report by a Visiting Panel* (Hong Kong: Government Printer, 1982).

49. See Luk, "Education," p. 178.

50. See Lau, *Society and Politics in Hong Kong*.

51. Youngson, *China and Hong Kong: The Economic Nexus*, p. 1.

52. Gregor Benton, *The Hong Kong Crisis* (London: Pluto Press, 1983), p. 4.

53. See Frank Choi, "Education Report Criticized for Promoting Elitist System," *Hong Kong Standard*, October 25, 1988.

54. See Education Commission, *Education Commission Report No. 3* (Hong Kong: Education Department, 1988).

55. See documents of the University of Hong Kong's planning committee for the foundation year 1987–88.

56. *Education Commission Report No. 3*, p. 230.

57. See "Split over Educational Reforms," *South China Morning Post*, October 27, 1988.

58. A.E. Sweeting, "The Cat among the Pigeons: Education Commission Report Number 3," in A. E. Sweeting, ed., *Differences and Identities: Educational Argument in Late Twentieth Century Hong Kong* (Hong Kong: Faculty of Education).

59. Kai Ming, Cheng, "Educational Policy-Making in Hong Kong" (Working paper, University of Hong Kong, Department of Education, 1988).

60. See the speech of Sir David Wilson, governor of Hong Kong, regarding the expansion of higher education, in November of 1989; see also "Academic Hits Out at Crisis Intervention," *South China Morning Post*, November 5, 1989; and, "Tertiary Doors Will Open to More Students," *South China Morning Post: Year in Review*, January 14, 1990.

61. John Rear, "One Brand of Politics," in Keith Hopkins, ed., *Hong Kong: The Industrial Economy* (Hong Kong: Oxford University Press, 1971), p. 55.

62. Norman Miners, *The Governance and Politics of Hong Kong*, 4th ed. (Hong Kong: Oxford University Press, 1986).

63. See Hong Kong Government, *Green Paper: The 1987 Review of Developments in Representative Government* (Hong Kong: Government Printer, 1989).

64. See Norman Miners, "Constitution and Administration," in *The Other Hong Kong Report: 1990*.

65. Morris, "Effects on the School Curriculum," p. 514.

66. See Education Department, *Guidelines on Civic Education in Schools* (Hong Kong: Government Printer, 1985).

67. Education Department, *Report of the Working Group on Sixth Form Education* (Hong Kong: Government Printer, July 1989).

68. See Curriculum Development Council, *Liberal Studies* (Hong Kong: Curriculum Development Council of the Hong Kong Government Education Department, 1991).

69. See Cheng " The Changing Political Culture of the Hong Kong Chinese," pp. 37–38.

70. See Andy Ho and Daphne Cheng, "Educators Set to Dominate Legco Polls," in *South China Morning Post*, August 10, 1980.

71. Llewelyn Commission, *A Perspective on Education in Hong Kong* (Hong Kong: Government Printer, 1982), p. 17.

72. See Spencer Liu Wing-kei, "The Role of Teachers as a Political Force in the Period of Transition: A Case Study of the Professional Teachers Union," Master's thesis, University of Hong Kong, Faculty of Education, 1990.

73. M. Mushkat, *The Making of the Hong Kong Administrative Class* (Hong Kong: Center of Asian Studies, University of Hong Kong, 1982) p. 60.

74. See Civil Service Branch, "Civil Service Personnel Statistics," mimeo (Hong Kong, Civil Service Branch, Government Secretariat, 1986), pp. 11–12.

75. Ibid.

76. Hong Kong Government, *A Draft Agreement between the Government of the United Kingdom of Great Britain and Northern Island and the Government of the People's Republic of China on the Future of Hong Kong* (Hong Kong: Government Printer, September 26, 1984), p. 17.

77. Ibid.

78. John Burns, "Succession Planning and Localization," in J. Burns and I. Scott, eds., *The Hong Kong Civil Service and Its Future* (Hong Kong: Oxford University Press, 1984).

79. Mr. Michael Leung became the director of education.

80. See *South China Morning Post*, January 31, 1990.

81. See Education Department, *Report of the Working Group Set Up to Review Language Improvement Measures* (Hong Kong: Government Printer, 1989).

82. See John Gibbons, "The Issue of the Language of Instruction in the Lower Forms of Hong Kong Secondary Schools," *Journal of Multilingual and Multicultural Development*, no. 3, pp. 117–128.

83. Llewelyn Commission, *A Perspective on Education in Hong Kong*, p. 36.

84. See *Report of the Working Group Set Up to Review Language Improvement Measures*.

85. "Jiaoyu shiqu tigong jihui xiaoyong fenliu jiaoxue tuzeng fenhua maodun," *Jingji Ribao*, Hong Kong, November 24, 1989; "Zhongchan jieji zinu jiaoyu yaoqiu zengzhuan shangxuewei mianliu xianggong rencai," *Xin Bao*, Hong Kong, November 27, 1989.

86. See Ora Kwo, "Language Education in a Changing Economic and Political Context: The Teaching of Putonghua in Hong Kong Schools," paper presented at the First Hong Kong Conference on Language and Society, Hong Kong, April 1989.

87. Herbert Pierson, "Language Attitudes and Use in Hong Kong: A Case For Putonghua," paper presented at the First Hong Kong Conference on Language and Society, Hong Kong, April 1989; Robert Bauer, *The Hong Kong Cantonese Speech Community*, manuscript, Center of Asian Studies, University of Hong Kong.

88. S.W. Wai, "Secondary Schools Favor Teaching through Chinese," *South China Morning Post*, November 12, 1986, p. 3.

89. See Benton, *The Hong Kong Crisis*, p. 19.

90. M.K. Lee, "Emerging Patterns of Social Conflict in Hong Kong Society," in Joseph Y.S. Cheng, ed., *Hong Kong in the 1980s* (Hong Kong: Summerson Eastern Publishers, 1982), p. 25.

91. Census and Statistics Department, *Hong Kong Census, 1976* (Hong Kong: Government Printer, 1976).

92. Lau, *Society and Politics in Hong Kong*, p. 4.

93. See Max Weber, *The Religion of China* (New York: The Free Press, 1951); J.M. Menzel, *The Chinese Civil Service* (Boston: D.C. Heath, 1963); and E.A. Kracke, "Religion, Family and Individual in the Chinese Examination System," in John K. Fairbank, ed., *Chinese Thoughts and Social Institutions* (Chicago: University of Chicago Press, 1957).

94. See Alan Brimer and Patrick Griffin, *A Study of Mathematics Achievement in Hong Kong* (Hong Kong: Center of Asian Studies, University of Hong Kong, 1985); R.E. Mitchell, *Pupil, Parent and School: A Hong Kong Study* (Taipei: The Orient Culture Service, 1972); Pedro Ng, *Access to Educational Opportunity: The Case of Kwun Tong* (Hong Kong: The Chinese University of Hong Kong Social Research Center, 1975); David Post and Pong Suet-ling, "Socio-economic Indicators and Higher Education Access in Hong Kong," paper presented at the Comparative and International Education Association Annual Meeting, Harvard University, March 31, 1989.

95. *A Perspective on Education in Hong Kong*, p. 58.

96. Llewelyn Commission, *Education Commission Report No. 3*.

97. See Condy Wan Ho-yee, "Issues of Efficiency and Equity in the District Subsidy Scheme From the Perspective of Parents," Master's thesis, University of Hong Kong Faculty of Education, 1990.

98. See Lau Pui-king, "Economic Relations between Hong Kong and China," in Joseph Y.S. Cheng, ed., *Hong Kong in Transition* (Hong Kong: Oxford University Press, 1986), pp. 235–267.

99. See Y.C. Jao, "Hong Kong's Role in Financing China's Modernization," in A. J. Youngson, ed., *China and Hong Kong: The Economic Nexus*.

100. See D. Podmore, "The Population of Hong Kong," in K. Hopkins, ed., *Hong Kong: The Industrial Colony* (Hong Kong: Oxford University Press, 1971).

101. See F.S. Sit, "Postwar Population and Its Spatial Dynamics," in F.S. Sit, ed., *Urban Hong Kong* (Hong Kong: Summerson Eastern Publishers, 1981).

102. See Youngson, *China and Hong Kong: The Economic Nexus*.

103. See Hong Kong Government, *Hong Kong 1990: A Review of 1989*. (Hong Kong: Government Printer, 1990).

104. Ronald Skeldon, "Hong Kong and Its Hinterland: A Case of International Rural-to-Urban Migration?" paper presented at the International Geographical Union Symposium No. 6, Commission on Population Geography, Migration, and Cities, 1984, pp. 23–26.

105. Lau, *Society and Politics in Hong Kong*, p. 4.

106. See Siu-lun Wong, *Emigrant Entrepreneurs: Shanghai Industrialists in Hong Kong* (Hong Kong: Oxford University Press, 1988); Gregory Guldin, "Overseas at Home: The Fujianese of Hong Kong," Ph.D. dissertation, University of Wisconsin at Madison, 1977; D.W. Sparks, "The Teochiu of Hong Kong," Ph.D. dissertation, University of Texas at Austin, 1978.

107. See Bai Jierui, *Jinggong xueshu jiaoliu xiankuang yu qiandan* (Xianggong: Jinggong Xueshu Jiaoliu Zhongxin, 1985).

108. See various issues of the monthly journal *Mainland–Hong Kong Academic Exchange*, published by the Beijing–Hong Kong Academic Exchange Center in Hong Kong.

109. See "Neidi jinliushijian gaodengyuanxiao shuoshi boshi kecheng shou gangao sheng," in *Da Gong Bao*, Hong Kong, January 4, 1991.

110. See Mary Louise Taylor, ed., Institute of International Education, *Annual Report, 1986* (New York: Institute of International Education, 1987).

111. Lau and Kuan, *The Ethos of the Hong Kong Chinese*, p. 19.

112. Choi Po King, "Cultural Identity and Colonial Rule: The Hong Kong–China Connection," paper presented at the Chinese University of Hong Kong, Conference on Chinese Cultural Tradition and Contemporary Modern Education, November 7, 1988, p. 31.

113. Lau and Kuan, *The Ethos of the Hong Kong Chinese*, p. 1.

114. Lau, "Decolonization without Independence."

2

Hong Kong Education within Historical Processes

Anthony E. Sweeting

Introduction

The main purpose of this chapter is to identify and to characterize historical processes which serve as a context for educational development in Hong Kong. The chapter may, therefore, help provide at least a glimpse of *gestalt* and hence of connections between the other studies discussed in the book.

Three salient processes which seem to have interacted with educational quantity and quality in many societies are colonization, industrialization (as often prefaced and accompanied by commercialization), and bureaucratization. A consideration of how these three processes operated historically to affect Hong Kong society and especially its educational enterprises might evoke interesting variations on the general themes. There are in addition three other processes which, in their operation, may be less obvious but more particular to Hong Kong. One is "transitization" (or the process-effects of migration which, for a long time, transformed Hong Kong into a transit area). Then there is localization, attended by "vernacularization," a relatively recent process which might appear in some ways to be an obverse of colonization. Finally, one may now also consider the process, however belated and incomplete, of democratization. Together, these six historical processes illuminate political, economic, social, and cultural dimensions of education in Hong Kong. They may also throw light on the educational connotations of the major transition that now confronts the territory. The change due to take place in 1997 is much more than a switch in sovereignty. It is already beginning to have recognizable effects on the formal curriculum of Hong Kong schools.[1] Further attempts at understanding the wide range of social and educational implications can only benefit from an examination of their historical roots.

Six Historical Processes

1. Colonization

Colonization as the social science concept of a historical process is protean in its applications. It commonly assumes the settlement of foreign territories by some metropolitan country and the separation of incoming and indigenous peoples by legal means, thus fostering the growth of racialism. For this reason, colonization has appeared to sharpen "the pluralist dilemma in education."[2] The concept also includes the organization of economic relations within a colonized territory to be of direct benefit to the metropolitan society and it encompasses the deliberate use of the colonized territory as a strategic base. It might also involve the conversion of souls and the enlightenment of minds, within a spirit of paternalistic obligation epitomized by the "white man's burden." Quite clearly, it has educational implications. In its crudest form, it assumes a type of cultural imperialism through which the language, literature, and other customary manifestations of the metropolitan country overwhelm the culture of the colonized.[3] As a convenient control mechanism, schooling might be used selectively by the colonists, with the masses deliberately deprived of educational opportunities, in order to encourage the creation of an amenable elite among the colonized.[4]

In practice, colonization has had even more forms and aspects than those sketched above. To make sense of its educational repercussions, some commentators distinguish between the different "styles" of such colonizing nations as Britain, France, and Germany.[5] Others recognize the limited powers of colonial governments and emphasize the part played by the culture of the colonized in shaping the political, social, and educational experiences of different colonies.[6] Both lines of thinking have application to educational developments in colonial Hong Kong.

Within Hong Kong, the manifestations of colonization have been special and several. For the sake of historical accuracy, one should note that the first and, in every sense, the fullest case of colonization occurred about a thousand years ago. This was the colonization, by conquest, of the region and its original inhabitants (probably of Malay-Oceanic stock) by the Chinese.[7] The process was, however, so complete and is so distant in time that it is difficult, if not impossible, to attribute to it now any clear implications for future educational developments other than the significance of the fact that now over 98 percent of Hong Kong's population is ethnic Chinese. One turns, therefore, to the more commonly recognized case of colonization: the much more recent assertion of control over various parts of the territory by the British.

From the very outset of Hong Kong's existence as a British colony, both governors and governed have recognized that the settlement of a large and permanent population from the metropole neither served as a major motivating force nor emerged as a significant consequence. Instead, Hong Kong became a *pied-à-terre*, a bolt-hole,* or a transit camp for disproportionate numbers of people from the uncolonized parts of the adjoining empire and its successor republics. In demographic and metaphorical terms, Hong Kong experienced further waves of colonization by the Chinese. Since the mid-nineteenth century, Hong Kong's *raison d'être* has been largely as a work place, a mart, and, additionally from the British point of view, as a strategic outpost. For this reason, commercial, diplomatic, and military considerations loomed large in all discussions of the future of the colony. Furthermore, the agenda of these discussions never included as a realistic option the possibility that Hong Kong would itself become an independent nation. Thus, Hong Kong's experience of colonization differed markedly from almost all other territories that underwent a colonial period. Each of these variations of classic colonization was directly related to developments in China.

The migration of people into Hong Kong from uncolonized China began in the early 1840s and has continued throughout the later nineteenth century and for much of the twentieth century, despite discouragement by successive Chinese governments. In general, what it has meant is that, for a very large proportion of the population, cultural loyalties belonged to China. For them, colonization by the British was close to being irrelevant. All important aspects of their lives, including the education of their children, reflected Chinese traditions and practices. Schools existed in the Hong Kong region (including the island of Hong Kong, the Kowloon peninsula, and the part of the Xinan district that became known as the New Territories) long before the British arrived there.[8] Other schools, based on Chinese models, continued to be established after, and largely unconnected with, the British arrival. Thus, for at least some of the present population of Hong Kong the type of "convergence" required during the transition to Chinese sovereignty is not between colonialist education and Chinese education but between different variations of Chinese education. These are not trivial distinctions. They affect the type of spoken and written Chinese used in educational discourse. Especially since 1945, they have engendered sharp divergence over the more politically oriented components of the curriculum, such as history, Chinese history, civic education, economics, and government and public affairs.

Educational repercussions of the primacy accorded to trade include the early concern of finding sufficient translators and interpreters to be go-betweens in diplomatic and commercial intercourse with China. In Hong Kong's case, trade did not so much follow the flag; it vindicated it. As Hong Kong developed into

---

* an escape route

an *entrepôt*, some of its upwardly mobile population responded positively to the attractions of the middleman role. The most successful became fully fledged "compradores."[9] Not only could they profit personally by acting as middlemen between the new foreign companies and their Chinese suppliers, buyers, and workers, they could often also invest their commissions and trade on their own behalf. Several used these opportunities in ventures that contributed to the modernization of China. To become qualified for such opportunities, they required at least a smattering of the English language, which they normally obtained at school. It is not surprising, therefore, to find that most members of the emerging elite in the later nineteenth century and early twentieth century had been educated either at schools founded by religious bodies or in the principal government school.[10] In light of the more simplistic versions of the colonization-as-cultural-imperialism thesis, it is perhaps ironic to note that, for much of Hong Kong's colonial history, it has been the parents of Chinese schoolchildren who have pressed for priority to be given to English education. Their attitudes were, however, rarely those of an exploited "lumpen-colonized." Indeed, if labels are to be attached on the basis of motives and practice, Chinese parents might be considered to be the exploiters, since, for their family's advancement, they were deliberately taking advantage of the situation created by the dependence of foreign firms on go-betweens. Most parents felt sufficiently confident in the strength and, indeed, what they felt to be the superiority of their traditional culture to assume responsibility for ensuring, via private tuition or through a parallel system of schools, that their children would not lose their Chinese identity. Some of the individuals emerging from this deliberately limited and pragmatic form of acculturation demonstrated their motives and their enterprise, as well as their Chinese identity, by becoming what might be described as "educational compradores." Far from relying supinely on curriculum materials imported from the United Kingdom, they took the initiative to produce courses and books that catered to new cohorts of Hong Kong Chinese who aspired to improve their English and thus their lot.[11] The role of both commercial and educational middlemen is either disregarded or dismissed as Uncle Tom-like by the more macro-oriented interpretations of the effects of colonization. Hong Kong's experience suggests, however, that their contributions were catalytic. During the transition to Chinese sovereignty, new commercial and educational compradores are emerging. Their contributions, too, are likely to be very significant.

Evidence certainly exists to support the identification of more familiar effects of the British colonization of Hong Kong on the development of education within the territory—or at least, effects that will seem more compatible with general analyses of "classic" colonization. Much of this relates to attitudes. Legally sanctioned presumptions of racial superiority appear, for example, in the first set of "Rules" issued in the 1850s by the Education Committee appointed by the British governor of Hong Kong to shape behavior in government-assisted schools.[12] Even earlier evidence suggests that the commonly observed connection between Christian missionary presuppositions and openly colonialistic pretensions applied to the first Western-model school ever opened in Hong Kong and that this connection may well have engendered types of cultural alienation and *anomie*.[13] At various times during Hong Kong's colonial history, non-Chinese teachers at government schools and at schools run by religious bodies have revealed (or, at least, have been perceived to display) arrogant or patronizing and racially biased attitudes. Similarly, in the early period and subsequently, influential individuals, both religious and lay, expressed a pronounced opinion in favor of separate formal schooling for the different races. Toward the end of the nineteenth century, there were even attempts to ensure that such instances of informal education as the City Hall Museum were subject to separate opening hours for the two principal races.

At the very beginning of the twentieth century, an official report recommended that priority be accorded to the education of a Chinese elite.[14] Distinct traces of the effects of colonialist attitudes on policy decisions about the quantitative provision of education also appeared in the "Introductory" section of the Annual Report for 1924 by the Hong Kong government's Education Department. It reads, in part:

> The number and circumstances of British children in this distant Colony make it at once feasible and desirable to provide them all with an education in Government schools as nearly as possible equal and similar to what they could find *at home*. . . .
> Other communities for which separate provision for education is needed are the Portuguese and the Indian. . . .
> The problem of Chinese children is different. Their numbers are so large that it is impossible for the Government to take charge of the education of all. The principle adopted is to endeavour to set a good standard of work in Government Schools while giving assistance by grants or subsidies to all private schools which meet the required modest standard of efficiency.[15]

It was not until the 1935 Burney Report and, more effectively, until after the Japanese occupation of Hong Kong, that the government acknowledged the importance of giving priority to the provision of vernacular primary education—in other words, to the education which would benefit the majority of the population.[16]

The relatively small proportion of the relevant age group for whom any type of tertiary education was provided in Hong Kong is sometimes considered the result of a colonialist conspiracy. It is at least consistent with the commonly cited predilection of colonial regimes for using education to facilitate the entrenchment of a collaborationist native elite.

British colonization may be seen to have affected the curriculum of Hong Kong schools, initially by encouraging an Anglo-centric approach to such subjects as history, geography, and literature. Moreover, it is not unusual to find colonialism blamed for the markedly apolitical tenor of the curriculum. One explanation for Anglo-centricity (or, at least, Euro-centricity) in the curriculum of government and grant schools during the earlier period rests with the composition of the teaching profession and the nature of teacher education. For approximately a century after the British occupation of Hong Kong island, the teaching profession in colonial-type schools reflected colonialistic-style relations. The headmasters, senior teachers, and other important knowledge-brokers were non-Chinese, usually of British, other European, or American stock. These were the people who planned, developed, and implemented the curriculum. For the day-to-day running of an "upper grade" school, they were able to make use of the services of "Chinese assistants," who received far inferior employment terms. They were frequently former pupils and often continued to be supervised by the non-Chinese staff.[17] Professional preparation for these Chinese assistants and for Chinese teachers at lower grade schools was, for much of the earlier part of the period, via the pupil–teacher scheme, a variation of the monitorial system, which did not encourage creativity. Moreover, at least until the middle of the twentieth century, the rare alternatives to the pupil–teacher scheme were equally dominated by non-Chinese senior staff.[18]

Widespread and long-standing dissatisfaction with "the system" bequeaths further problems to today's educational planners. Teachers have tended to shun liability for curriculum reform and to blame poor teaching practices on the demands of public examinations, rigid syllabuses, and syllabus-echoing textbooks. Until very recently, many have been content to wait for and follow initiatives from "the authorities."

It is not fair to conclude, however, that the process of colonization yielded in an invariable and uniform manner ethnically harmful or culturally imperialistic results. Whether one refers to society in general or focuses on specific educational developments, cases can be quoted of racial cooperation, relatively harmonious side-by-side coexistence, or at least the emergence of a symbiotic relationship between the Chinese and the British in Hong Kong.[19] Pressure for a type of educational apartheid existed over time in counterpoint to pleas for integration.[20] On the linguistic and cultural front, arguments in favor of ensuring that Chinese pupils in Hong Kong's government and grant schools should have a solid foundation of Chinese studies came from such colonial officials as Frederick Stewart, and served to offset the more openly "pragmatic" aspirations in favor of concentration on English acquisition shared by most Chinese parents.[21] Stewart, the first headmaster of the Government Central School and inspector of schools, also pressed, as early as 1866, for the introduction of a special education tax, which would have affected mainly the non-Chinese, and for compulsory school attendance by the Chinese.[22] Moreover, although a later inspector of schools, E.A. Irving, campaigned for separate education for the different races and supported the idea of devoting a disproportionate portion of scarce resources to the education of a Chinese elite through the medium of the English language, the British

Colonial Office made it clear that this was unacceptable policy "in a large native community such as exists in Hong Kong."[23] Furthermore, highly selective admission to tertiary education was not necessarily the result of colonial attitudes or policies. To establish such a connection one would need to show that the situation was and is different in noncolonized societies such as the United Kingdom or even China. With regard to the curriculum, despite some moves to make Hong Kong education Anglo-centric and to depoliticize it, local Chinese students have certainly retained their Chinese identity and, especially in the twentieth century, have been directly involved in political issues, a fact that demonstrates either the ineffectiveness of colonial rule or its irrelevance.

In the case of Hong Kong, such qualifications to conventional interpretations of the colonization's effects on education suggest that one might need to consider it as a chronologically as well as a geographically variable process. Clearer understanding might therefore be gained if an attempt were made to periodize the British colonization of Hong Kong, based on an overview of its history:

1843–1913: The Heyday of Applied Colonization
1914–1945: Colonialism under Challenge
1945–1965: Applied Decolonialization
1966–1997: Colonialism as a Shibboleth

The first sixty years of Hong Kong's existence as a British colony have been labeled "the heyday of applied colonization" partly because it was in this period that the colony was set up, its social, economic, and political infrastructure developed, and, therefore, because it was then that Hong Kong's colonial status seemed to have most impact on society, on interracial attitudes, and on educational developments. The term "applied" is used to emphasize the particularity of Hong Kong's brand in contrast to concepts of "pure" colonization. The 1913 Education Ordinance, which empowered the Hong Kong government to inspect even privately owned schools, represents in some ways the high-water mark of colonial power and authority over education.

Even before 1913, however, there were signs of colonization being overtaken by other forces, especially Chinese nationalism. This was the force that increasingly challenged colonialist attitudes in Hong Kong in the period that lasted roughly from the beginning of World War I to the end of World War II. Its impact on education in Hong Kong can be seen clearly in the growing numbers of vernacular schools founded in this period and, most dramatically, in the part played by secondary school students in the 1925–26 general strike and boycott of British goods. One curricular innovation in the early 1930s that derived from the tensions between Chinese nationalism and colonial rule within Hong Kong during the interwar period was the introduction of civics to offset what was considered disruptive propaganda from the "New Life Movement" of the Guomindang.[24] The Japanese made deliberate use of anticolonialist feelings in their propaganda and their attempts to legitimize their occupation of Hong Kong (1941–45), which itself differed little in practical repercussion from crude colonization.

The two decades succeeding World War II witnessed decolonization in various parts of Asia and Africa. They also saw the emergence of the People's Republic in China, which happened to coincide with the increasingly obvious decline of Britain as a world power and with the equally widespread atmosphere of the Cold War. These developments led to a situation in which, although it was not deemed appropriate to de-colonize Hong Kong in the "pure" and formal sense, British unreadiness to help Hong Kong deal with the accelerating influx of refugees from China ensured that colonialist attitudes became even less acceptable. The same factors also encouraged growing economic independence from Britain. One side effect was that Hong Kong learned to deal with its educational problems by itself and not to rely on the metropole. Thus, although Hong Kong continued to receive visits from British advisers (e.g., Fisher, 1951; Jennings and Logan, 1953; Fulton, 1959; Marsh and Sampson, 1963), the important decisions tended increasingly to be made in Hong Kong (e.g., the Keswick Report, 1952; the Seven Year Plan, 1954; the White Paper on Educational Policy, 1965). Allowing room for some fluctuations, it appears justified, therefore, to treat the years 1945–65 as a period of applied decolonialization. Without ceasing to be a colony in the constitutional sense, Hong Kong became conspicuously less colonial in all important operational senses.

From about 1966 onward, colonialism has been used as a pejorative slogan or ubiquitous scapegoat at a time when there has been little trace of colonization as a policy determinant. Recourse to anticolonialistic rhetoric was made by protesters and rioters in 1966 and 1967. It also colored the vocabulary of leaders of the Students' Movement in the 1970s and, in the later 1980s, sharpened emotions in attempts to conserve the right of American-influenced tertiary educational institutions in Hong Kong to admit students one year earlier than the other such institutions. By the 1970s and 1980s it had become more significant as a catchall shibboleth than as a directive and was at least partly an extraneous force. In the early 1970s, much was made of the claim that the prominence of English in the Hong Kong curriculum was a direct result of colonization.[25] However, since then the Burney Report of 1935 has been criticized as colonialist because it proposed that Hong Kong students should learn only "such and so much English as they were likely to need for their subsequent careers, and no more," on the grounds that this recommendation treated Hong Kong Chinese as inferiors by depriving them of full rights to English culture.[26] Thus, there appears to be a Hong Kong version of the "damned if you do, damned if you don't" syndrome which Remi Clignet identified as characteristic of colonizer–colonized relations.[27]

The above attempt at periodization, however tentative, incorporates the view that colonization, in one form or another, has had its impact on education in Hong Kong. The result has been less than a full-blooded pluralist dilemma because the knowledge-managers in Hong Kong have always had to cope with an overwhelmingly Chinese population and its self-confident culture. It would be less than impartial to assert that, at the present time, as the territory approaches its next important transition, most of Hong Kong's educational problems can be attributed to its "colonial scars."[28] On the other hand, there can be little doubt that questions related to the legitimation of educational policy have been exacerbated by the cultural distance between rulers and ruled.[29] Colonization, with its offshoot, colonialization, is certainly one of the strands that history has woven into the contextual tapestry of the transition. Hong Kong's constitutional status as a colony contributed to the generation of a range of patronizing or, at least, paternalistic attitudes which may be categorized as "colonialist." These attitudes influenced both the intentions and the outcomes of educational policy at the general system level and at the chalk-face.* At the same time, however, even though it has become increasingly unfashionable to recognize the point, Hong Kong's colonial status brought some advantages for the territory's educational policies and practices. It made Hong Kong less parochial. Government officers might bring to their work the benefits of having helped to administer other parts of the colonial empire. Comparisons and the recognition of general trends were facilitated. Especially in the twentieth century, visits by experts from "home" often stimulated educational debate and sometimes led to improvements in educational practice. Thus, the colonization strand in Hong Kong's historical tapestry appears, on deeper analysis, multihued, not uniformly black in color.

2. Industrialization

Another quite conspicuous strand is industrialization. From the very beginning of its existence as a British colony, Hong Kong's rationale has been based largely on economic advancement. In the early period, the main avenue for such advancement was through activities connected with the *entrepôt* trade. Even then, however, industries began to develop. As early as 1846, Sir John Davis, second governor of Hong Kong, noted:

> A large number of Chinese are employed in their respective shops in the exercise of industrial trades and manufactures, and there are scarcely any wants of the inhabitants which do not meet with a ready supply within the town.[30]

These economic activities were genuine industries in the sense that they involved division of labor and applied inanimate sources of power to mechanize, in however rudimentary a way, the manufacture of goods or the production of services. The early industries included rattan ware, ginger preserving, and flash-

---

* in the classroom itself

light production[31] as well as the more directly *entrepôt*-related enterprises such as shipbuilding and ship repairing, which increased in number during World War I when overseas supplies were interrupted.[32] Further encouragement for the fledgling Hong Kong industries came with the Ottawa agreements of 1932 which sanctioned forms of colonial preference within the British Commonwealth. Thus there was some interaction between the processes of colonization and industrialization (or at least their products) in the case of Hong Kong. In this respect, Hong Kong's colonial status brought with it some advantages even above and beyond the security of contract and property which came as accompaniment to the introduction of the British legal system.

Japanese occupation of Hong Kong in the early 1940s not only suspended British colonization of the territory, it also effectively halted local industry. When the British returned to reoccupy Hong Kong in the latter part of 1945, initially it was the *entrepôt* trade that helped the society find its economic feet. Within two years, however, a resumed and accelerating influx of labor and capital into Hong Kong encouraged the expansion of the textiles industry and enabled the establishment of the plastics industry.[33] The Korean War (1950–53) and, especially, the American-inspired United Nations' embargo on trade in strategic materials with China (1951), by restricting opportunities for *entrepôt* services, acted as further incentives to industrialization.

Thus, extraneous contingencies combined with both immigrant and native enterprise and hard work to fuel Hong Kong's Industrial Revolution. No single event, not even the trade embargo, acted as a sufficient condition for the exponential increase in industrialization after World War II. Instead, a special blend of what may appear now to be either necessary conditions or at least components of a conducive milieu produced the "economic miracle." The ingredients in that potion included the entrepreneurial know-how of such immigrants as the "Shanghai Industrialists," some of whom brought their whole businesses, manufacturing equipment, and venture capital with them to Hong Kong when they fled China in the late forties.[34] The special ingredients also included the readiness of countless "smaller" immigrants to hazard their life savings in ventures that might offer them and their children a step up in the desperate effort to climb out of refugee squalor and insecurity.[35] The new factors were added to a preexisting industrial base, however elementary, a social ethos which encouraged and rewarded business initiative,[36] an enabling rule of law, and "a loose system of support for industrial development in Hong Kong" from the colonial government.[37]

Partly as a result of the growing sophistication of the local economy as well as competition from more recently industrialized nations in southeast and eastern Asia (including China itself), Hong Kong has witnessed a switch of emphasis, at least in quantitative terms, from manufacturing to tertiary, service-oriented industries such as banking, insurance, transport, communications, and the hospitality sectors.[38] Accompanied by the rapid growth of high technology industries, this development resembles "postindustrialization" in Europe, North America, and Japan.

Periodization of the industrialization process is, then, a relatively simple matter. One may think in terms of three phases: (1) the early "prerevolutionary" phase up until the late 1940s, a period during which industries, especially small-scale and often *entrepôt*-related ones, gradually grew; (2) the fully fledged industrial revolution starting shortly after the end of World War II, with its massive emphasis on manufacturing; and (3) the expansion of tertiary, infrastructure-related industries from the mid-1970s, the current phase of which combines manufacturing-style industry with *entrepôt* activities. Much of the remainder of this section attempts to analyze, and seek evidence of, the effects of industrialization on education in Hong Kong.

One possible effect relates to the connection between industrialization and pressure to secure compulsory school attendance of children under a particular age. Factory legislation has encouraged this move in several industrializing societies.[39] There were few calls for compulsory education in Hong Kong during its first "proto-industrialization" period. One of the earliest was in 1921 when the Commission on Child Labour considered the possibility of introducing compulsory education in order to protect young children from exploitation. This was largely at the behest of the Reverend H. R. Wells, a commission member.[40] Another member, E. A. Irving, then director of education in Hong Kong, was instrumental, however, in securing the failure of this move when he baldly declaimed that "the first point to be considered is the money." Subsequently, despite Britain's example and exhortations from UNESCO about ultimate objectives for all communities, compulsory education even up to the end of primary schooling was not achieved until 1971, late in the second period of full-blooded industrialization. Hong Kong's Industrial Revolution coincided with a massive population influx, especially of young people. This exacerbated social and particularly educational problems. It also heightened awareness of them. Operating in the same direction, therefore, as the influence of Britain and the advocacy of United Nations agencies, local pressure for social welfare reforms persuaded officials to plan for educational expansion and, eventually, to achieve universal and compulsory schooling. By the middle of the 1970s, the very success of Hong Kong's manufacturing revolution had led to the specter of protectionist trade policies being implemented by such important economic units as the United States and the EEC. There can be no doubt that, when, in 1978, free and compulsory education in Hong Kong was extended up to the age of fifteen, this was not done in response to calls from educational radicals. Instead, it was seen to be a way of disarming criticism from within the EEC that Hong Kong's industry, particularly its textile industry, exploited child labor. Although there has been no further extension of compulsory education during the third phase of industrialization, the tendency for young people to stay in school longer and/or to seek alternative, "open" educational opportunities after they have left school suggests that the positive correlation between industrialization and educational quantity still holds firm.

Industrialization also served as a model for the organization and daily processes of schooling in Hong Kong. As in other industrializing societies, the success of the factory system was an example that encouraged the move away from all-age, single-class, single-teacher schools with a loosely defined curriculum to the age-differentiated, multiclass schools with specialist-teachers and a more explicitly defined curriculum. This was partly also an effect of the colonization of Hong Kong by the British who had already gained experience of the newer, less tutorial-like schools. The end result was the classification of a chronological/scholastic hierarchy and a division of labor within schools. It took some time, however, before the distinction between elementary (or, a little later in history, primary) and secondary schools was recognized and implemented.[41]

Factory-style procedures were introduced into the early schools. Strict timetables, the reliance on monitors from among the pupils to behave like foremen and help maintain discipline, the related use made of the pupil–teacher (apprentice-style) system,[42] and the general management/worker–type relations between teachers and pupils may all be connected with industrialization, at least metaphorically. More directly, industrial apprenticeship schemes began to be introduced in Hong Kong in the nineteenth and early twentieth centuries. They coexisted, however, with older forms of apprenticeship whose almost characteristic inclination toward nepotism owed more to Chinese traditions than it did to the requirements of industrialization or to some deliberate conspiracy by the colonizers. It was only in the second and third phases of Hong Kong's industrialization that the government made serious efforts to regulate apprenticeships and to coordinate their educational input with provisions for part-time day-release and opportunities for study at technical institutes.

As the form of industrialization itself changes, one might expect alterations in its metaphorical and direct effects on education. The size or even existence of "classes" in schools, the application of sophisticated educational technology, and the switch to more resource-based learning and less expository teaching appear compatible with the processes of tertiary industry and, therefore, likely to become increasingly acceptable to the educational institutions of Hong Kong's future.

In Hong Kong's past, the most commonly recognized link between industry and education was in the impetus it provided for an improvement of facilities in technical education. This link was reinforced by an awareness of both the problems and opportunities associated with industrialization. Even the "prerevolutionary" phase of industrialization in Hong Kong brought with it the type of social problems that had characterized developments elsewhere: inadequate housing for the working class, child labor, difficult working conditions, insufficient attention to public health, the disruption of the extended family and the weakening of even nuclear family loyalties among some of the displaced proletariat. Such problems were exacerbated in later, more intense periods of industrialization. On the other hand, industrialization also offered opportunities for learning new skills, and these were not circumscribed by centuries of tradition or medieval guild-type restrictions. The opportunities, too, expanded along with the increased scale of industrialization.

Hong Kong's earliest experiment in technical education was linked to these two factors—both the social problems and the opportunities. This was the West Point Industrial Reformatory, which was established in 1863. From the outset, it was supported by government officials and other persons of standing as a way of dealing with delinquent, orphaned, or abandoned youths. What better hope for reform was there than through useful industry? Social misfits received training in carpentry, tailoring, shoemaking, printing or bookbinding and thus became equipped for gainful employment. The West Point Reformatory appealed to the religious-minded because, like the Ragged School Movement in England, it represented "good works." It also appealed to pragmatic businessmen because the reformatory could be seen to be a useful and realistic institution, keeping potential criminals off the streets. Moreover, it attracted official government aid because it was cheap. Industrialization was beginning to have an impact on opinions about the responsibilities of government. It stimulated a paternalistic attitude on the part of both the reformers and their principal supporters, which, through the association of industrial training with the rehabilitation of juvenile offenders, tended to attach a stigma to technical education.[43]

The actual extent of financial commitment to technical education, official and voluntary, remained very limited throughout the early period, partly because of this stigma, partly because education as a whole did not attract large sums of public or private money. This sometimes led to friction between what was advocated in Britain and what was implemented in Hong Kong.[44] Developments in technical education during the early twentieth century were characterized by the enthusiastic backing of some local businessmen, but lacked wholehearted support from officials. The usual reason advanced for the latter feature was financial—the Hong Kong government should not be expected to bear the costs of institutions that would benefit all southern China. The result was that the next major developments in the history of Hong Kong's technical education did not take place until the 1930s when they were connected with the onset of the Great Depression.[45]

Changes in the effects of industrialization on education during the full-blooded industrial revolution phase were rarely as rapid as those taking place in industry itself. This was at least partly because recovery from the Japanese occupation was necessarily slowest in the field of technical education. Equipment looted earlier could not be quickly replaced in a period of postwar shortages. People with technical and technological qualifications were under such demand by industry itself in many parts of the world, including Hong Kong, China, and Britain, that there were few on hand to take up the challenges of technical teaching or technical teacher education. Some vestigial stigma associated with technical education might also help explain the relative slowness of developments, especially in a period when the priority of general education appeared overriding.[46]

The cause of technical education in the colonies received official blessing from London and at least some gradually increasing practical help in the decade following the end of World War II.[47] In the specific case of Hong Kong, however, the main input from Britain with regard both to industrialization itself and to the improvement of technical education was confined mainly to exhortatory circulars and visits by Colonial Office advisers.[48]

Meanwhile modest developments were taking place in Hong Kong itself. During the Japanese occupation, two Salesian-run industrial schools had continued to operate[49] and were, therefore, able to resume their tasks shortly after the British returned to Hong Kong. The Government Trade School, under its new name, the Hong Kong Technical College, reopened in stages between 1948 and 1950, with the Junior Technical School initially occupying some of its premises in 1948. The demand for places in all these institutions was from the outset very high.

By the early 1950s, the official annual reports of the Education Department were beginning to recognize "the increasing importance of Hong Kong as a manufacturing and industrial centre," together with the implications of this for education.[50] More confidential sources make it clear that time and effort were now being devoted to the development of technical education.[51] Other signs of changing attitudes included the support that technical education received in the local Chinese press and the fact that Sir Robert Ho Tung, a well-known philanthropist, chose to donate a large sum so that a Technical School for Girls could be built and then handed over for the government to run.[52]

The appointment of a Technical Education and Vocational Training Investigating Committee in October 1951 to collect information about the facilities available in Hong Kong and to obtain evidence about future requirements publicly signaled that the government meant business. Both the interim and the final report of this committee (usually named the Burt Report, after the committee's chairman, Mr. S. J. G. Burt) stimulated action. The former, produced in October 1952, led directly to extensions of the Hong Kong Technical College. The latter, dated October 1953, became the blueprint for further expansion and, via its endorsement by the Board of Education, led to the establishment of the Standing Committee on Technical Education and Vocational Training (July 1954).

Details of expansion have been outlined clearly elsewhere.[53] They include the opening of the Kowloon Tang King Po School in 1953, another Salesian initiative in technical education; the Hong Kong Technical College's move to handsome new premises in Kowloon (1957) and its later (1971) transformation into the Hong Kong Polytechnic, as well as the establishment of the first Technical Institute at Morrison Hill in 1970 to provide sub-polytechnic training; and the appointment of the nonstatutory Hong Kong Training Council in 1973 to advise on measures necessary to ensure a comprehensive system of manpower training geared to Hong Kong's changing needs. The technical education system in Hong Kong appeared increasingly autochthonous and less dependent on the pronouncements of visiting experts. By the mid-1950s, the government had decided to rely upon home-grown inputs such as those of the Investigating Committee, the later Standing Committee, and on the financial contributions of such bodies as the Chinese Manufacturers' Association. It was the latter's contribution of $1 million, made on condition that the government would spend an equal amount of money and provide the land, that led to the new and improved version of the Hong Kong Technical College in Kowloon in the mid-1950s and ultimately to its upgrading into the Hong Kong Polytechnic in 1971. By the early 1960s, there was a widely recognized link between industry and technical education.[54] And by the mid-1970s, educational discourse and documents professed the need to increase the proportion of the curriculum devoted to "practical education" in general secondary schools.[55]

The latest phase of industrialization has brought a further expansion of technical education. The increasing number of technical institutes (especially after 1975), the establishment of a second polytechnic, named the City Polytechnic of Hong Kong, in 1984, and the official incorporation of a third university, named the Hong Kong University of Science and Technology, in 1988, are the most obvious instances of this trend. The link between such developments and the newer infrastructure and high-technology related forms of industrialization was clearly outlined in the Report of the Advisory Committee on Diversification of the Economy in 1979. In the spirit of this report, the replacement of the Hong Kong Training Council by the Vocational Training Council, a statutory body, in 1982, and the establishment of a new Department of Technical Education and Industrial Training as its executive arm, improved the coordination of vocational training schemes and opened up opportunities for more sophisticated manpower planning exercises. A further indication of the importance that the Hong Kong government now attaches to the connection between education and manpower planning occurred in February 1983 when the Education Branch of the Government Secretariat was renamed the Education and Manpower Branch.

Industrialization has had a limited but gradually increasing impact on the curriculum of schools. As early as 1866, electricity and chemistry were introduced into the curriculum of the Government Central School, but this was mainly thanks to the enthusiasm of Sir Richard MacDonnell, then governor of Hong Kong, rather than a recognition of the importance of industrial progress. The concern expressed by Lau Chu Pak in 1916 about the English standards of Chinese pupils was more directly connected with the interests of commerce and industry. He was able to use his position as a legislative councilor to secure a review of the curriculum, but few changes actually ensued. Efforts to introduce "handwork" into secondary schools in the late 1930s were partially successful, but in 1953 the Burt Committee commented that secondary courses were "almost entirely academic." The phase of rapid industrialization in Hong Kong led to more widespread acceptance of the relevance of "practical education" even within the "grammar school" tradition, but the lingering stigma contributed to the failure of the experiment with Secondary Modern schools in the early 1960s and vacillating attitudes toward the newer prevocational schools. The latest phase of industrialization has witnessed an increasing recognition of the importance of technical and, more especially, technological subjects. Perhaps the clearest manifestation of this trend has been the introduction of computer studies into the secondary school curriculum as a pilot scheme in 1982 and this subject's rapid take-up. Recent apprehension about English language standards also derived at least partly from the renewed concentration on infrastructure-related industry and, in this sense, may be compared with Lau Chu Pak's earlier anxieties. A different but equally interesting effect of industrialization upon both formal and informal education may be seen in the concern shown for the environment. Ecology has taken a large part in school subjects such as biology and geography, especially since the mid-1970s. In approximately the same period, generated both by worldwide developments and by responses to some of industrialization's negative effects in Hong Kong, several organized groups have started to mobilize opinion against pollution and other forms of environmental waste in the territory.[56]

Industrialization has also helped fashion the conditions that led to educational developments at the two extreme ends of schooling: early childhood education and adult education. The first genuine kindergarten for Chinese children in Hong Kong was established by the Basel Mission in 1892. Apart from the "good works" and proselytizing aspect of its missionary-oriented foundation, it clearly catered to children of the Chinese working class. Dr. E.J. Eitel, the German-born inspector of schools who was an enthusiastic supporter of the kindergarten movement, attempted to convert other government officials in Hong Kong and in Britain to the cause by pointing out that the Basel Mission's kindergarten gave "gratuitous teaching to young Chinese children in Saiying-pun,[57] not merely combining play with work but giving rudimentary instruction in the rudiments of industry by systematic training of hand and eye."[58] The dramatic increase in kindergartens for Chinese in Hong Kong during the interwar period derived both from the need for mothers to work in factories and from the strengthening of the feminist movement during the May Fourth Movement in China. An even more direct effect of industrialization on the development of early childhood education can be seen in the opening of a number of factory schools and crèches for the very young.[59] The exponential expansion of kindergartens and child care centers after World War II was directly related to the needs of working mothers and to the breakdown of the extended family, both of which were exacerbated by the continued and accelerating influx of a young refugee population. That influx has moderated and changed in nature during the third phase of industrialization. The expectations of growing numbers of working mothers have ensured, however, that institutionally based early childhood education has become the norm and that more attention is paid to the quality of that education.

The first Hong Kong venture into the field of formal adult education began in 1907 and was named the Technical Institute. It provided "extension classes" in the evenings at the leading government secondary school in a range of technical subjects intended to qualify young adults for employment in industry. However, as might be expected, it was during the period of rapid industrialization that adult education really took off. Details of these developments are clearly outlined elsewhere.[60] Part of the motivation for adult education classes in the late 1940s and adult education centers in the 1950s stemmed from official anxieties about the spreading of political propaganda if no government-supported opportunities were provided. Once started, however, they served as a means of delayed initial education (and thus a means of reducing illiteracy), as a source of elementary technical education, and as a form of recreational and cultural relief from the drudgery of factory employment. Recently, adult education has become much more ambitious and much more sophisticated—especially by utilizing modern forms of information technology[61]—and has, in this way, reflected the changing nature of Hong Kong's industrialization.

The "high tech" aspects of Hong Kong's latest phase of industrialization, and above all its newer role as regional distribution center (i.e., *entrepôt*) and local market for sophisticated electronic equipment, have served to enhance facilities for communications, especially among the upwardly mobile middle classes. The use of personal computers, radio telephones, and, more recently, facsimile machines has increased very noticeably. One effect of this is to diminish still further parochial attitudes among people and to ensure that they are closely acquainted with developments in other parts of the world. This has important educational connotations and quite clearly will affect problems of absorption into a China which periodically seems to revert to forms of isolationism.

In all periods of Hong Kong's colonial history, the effects of industrialization on education have included various stimuli to change, particularly in relation to the curriculum and to the structure of schooling. They have also generated new problems. The same may be said for the effects of education on industrialization. In general, increasing educational provision and improving educational quality have led to an extension of expectations. These expectations apply to working conditions, living conditions, and changes in attitudes about the scope of the responsibilities of the individual vis-à-vis the government. Perhaps the clearest indications of such changes have occurred in preschool education, where parental attitudes are very different now from what they were in, say, 1945. Education has helped promote a concern for the environment and may, perhaps, affect the actions of some industrialists. To the extent that education has become increasingly concerned with certification, a type of "diploma inflation" has affected Hong Kong, as it has affected other parts of the world. In fact, much of the reason for this derives from other parts of the world in that the large number of "returned students" from overseas institutions arrived with more paper qualifications than Hong Kong employment possibilities actually required. The situation was, therefore, not immediately open to control by the Hong Kong government. Nevertheless, the 1977 Green Paper on Senior Secondary and Tertiary Education and the White Paper of 1978 both emphasized the dangers of producing overqualified or inappropriately qualified young people and recommended more rigorous manpower forecasting geared to the precise needs of the Hong Kong economy. It is true that, during Hong Kong's Industrial Revolution, very few successful entrepreneurs had any form of relevant qualification (in technical or technological education) for their ventures. Instead, most were products of the academically oriented Chinese middle schools.[62] In one sense, however, education still had an effect. Middle school leavers had difficulties finding opportunities for higher education. Some of them, therefore, devoted their energies to making their fortunes through industry! In the newer, infrastructure-related industries especially, however, qualifications required for entry have become ever more demanding. The result has been that opportunities for refresher training or, indeed, re-training are increasing in industry, partly thanks to concepts of in-service education.

Education has interacted with the economy during all phases of Hong Kong's history. In some form or another, industrialization is likely to persist as a historical process. It will continue to affect and to be affected by education. The record of past interaction is clear enough to indicate the insufficiency of doctrinaire interpretations which almost instinctively equate industrialization, as well as education, with exploitation and fail to see how both processes are capable of offering opportunities. Although there have been plenty of problems caused by industrialization—not least the spread of materialism and instrumentalism, the increased sense of displacement and *anomie*, and the classic social inequities—it has also been accompanied by a general improvement in the standard of living, the benefits of specialization and diversification, and a substantial augmentation of Hong Kong's value to China and to the rest of the world. Each of these general outcomes, whether they be problem or benefit, has tended to influence education in Hong Kong. In turn, education is certain to continue influencing industrialization.

3. *Bureaucratization*

Bureaucratization is another social science buzzword which, in its post-Weberian usage, has become a catchword, like colonialism, that critics use to belabor the government. The term connotes something to be deplored, as was industrialization by many Romantics. It is not surprising, therefore, to discover links between the concepts and the historical processes of bureaucratization, colonization, and industrialization, at least in the Hong Kong experience.

Whatever the precise manifestation of colonialist attitudes and their effects on the educational system, there can be no doubt that for much of Hong Kong's colonial history the cultural distance between rulers and ruled suggested the need for some control mechanisms. This control implied an increase in the responsibilities of the government via an expanded body of government officers. For several commentators, the mere quantitative increase in the civil service represented bureaucratization. Other commentators concentrated on the manner of administration by officials. Effective interference in customary Chinese practices, which might to a Westerner appear nepotistic or in some other way corrupt, entailed additional officials armed with additional regulations. It was, thus, differences (in the sociological rather than the aesthetic sense of "culture") between the colonial government and the majority of the people in Hong Kong that encouraged the former to oversee and control the latter. In the case of the first Education Ordinance of 1913, the quest for legislative control and practical supervision was, in itself, a defensive strategy against burgeoning Chinese nationalism. Largely because of the overt political motivation, it was perceived by some opponents to constitute "autocratic and inquisitorial legislation,"[63] a frequently identified aspect of bureaucratization.

A second reason for seeking to increase control and, thereby, to encourage bureaucratization derived from the expansion of the educational system itself and, more particularly, of educational expenditure from public funds. In other words, financial or, more generally, economic considerations may be added to cultural and political ones as stimuli for bureaucratization. As early as 1848, a formal committee was appointed to superintend government-sponsored schools, precisely because of the money involved. Although this was only $10 per school per month, there can be no doubt that the perceived need to show "value for money" was one of the prime motives behind the appointment of the first Education Committee. Later, as educational expenditure expanded along with enrollment figures, so did the control mechanisms. This was particularly true once the idea of scholarships and fee remissions gained currency. Industrialization was one of the major reasons for the increase in enrollment figures, as well as the introduction of scholarships and fee remissions.

Industrialization also affected bureaucratization by providing a model of the advantages of specialization. Despite a hankering after the virtues attributed to generalism by people modeling themselves on the typical English gentleman or the typical mandarin, the case for division of labor within the administration of education gradually came to be accepted. Again, this process was aided by the expansion of the system. It eventually became too big for an inspired and amateur generalist to handle.

Each of these trends, identified in relation to the whole educational system and, specifically, to the role of government officers or government-appointed committees within it, also applies at the individual school level. There, too, the days of charismatic individual leadership gave way to a strengthening of the responsibilities of the school office and of various staff members who attained functional and hierarchical positions, such as dean of discipline. Both at system level and at individual school level, bureaucratization tended to become self-justifying, self-perpetuating, and self-expanding.

One of the problems in dealing with bureaucratization as a historical process is that the term "bureaucracy" has been used in various ways. Historically, it simply meant administration by government officials. Later, it developed meanings within sociology relating to a form of administration found in various organizations following a range of goals. Max Weber associated it with the most rational, rule-directed, and, therefore, efficient way of pursuing organizational goals. It implied a high degree of specialization, with responsibilities clearly defined and delimited, an explicable hierarchical structure based on size of responsibility and of talent, and impersonal relationships both between members of the organization and with clients. Its keystone was rationality and its major characteristic was predictability. Later sociologists,[64] concentrating largely on the microsociology of business, have shown how bureaucracies can become very rigid, countercreative, and, thereby, basically inefficient. It is with the latter overtones that the word "bureaucratic" is normally used today in Hong Kong, as elsewhere. The school in Hong Kong has itself become a bureaucracy with the Weberian advantages and the post-Weberian frailties combined within an unstable environment and a "loosely coupled system," as modern sociological overviews suggest schools in other countries have developed.[65]

Historically, however, bureaucratization in Hong Kong education includes the whole range of meanings—literal, Weberian, and post-Weberian. For this reason, it is impossible to periodize the process. The first committees and Board of Education were roundly criticized for being amateurish and, in one sense, therefore, of being not sufficiently bureaucratic.[66] As late as 1935, Edmund Burney criticized education policymaking in Hong Kong partly on the grounds that the government still relied upon laterally promoting various generalists, inexperienced and unqualified in educational administration, to the post of director of education.

The quantitative expansion of the administrative infrastructure for education in Hong Kong was relatively slow to begin. In 1865, the amateurish Board of Education was dissolved and replaced by a one-man department of education, Frederick Stewart. It was not until 1909 that the department gained a director of education (rather than inspector of schools) and, at that time, the total administrative staff of the department comprised three persons (the director himself, the sub-director of girls' schools, and the sub-director of vernacular schools), plus two junior staff and two "minor staff." Even immediately after World War II, the total administrative staff of the education department could comfortably sit around one Chinese dining table.[67] Not long after this, the crucial quantitative expansion and organizational diversification of the educational administration took place.[68] Further expansion of the bureaucracy at the system level in the

1960s, 1970s, and 1980s has tended to be more closely related to the size of the system and to its tendency toward more precise functional demarcations (e.g., within the field of technical education). In this way, Hong Kong has experienced similar trends to those elsewhere. At the school level, bureaucracies expanded in the postwar period largely for the same reasons and also to deal with the additional work created by increased government regulation.

The effects of bureaucratization upon education in Hong Kong have included an increase in efficiency and a decrease in opportunities for overt corruption. Specialization, clear lines of authority, and impartiality brought obvious benefits. Planning has led to the achievement of such predefined goals as the provision of universal, compulsory, and free primary education in 1971. Bureaucratization has also provided employment opportunities for the locally educated within the local educational administration, especially as the policy of localization became more rigorously pursued and as the system became ever larger.

There can be little doubt, however, that the characteristics identified by post-Weberian sociologists have also at times seemed conspicuous in the educational administration in Hong Kong. These include the temptation toward centralization, unthinking standardization, and impersonalization or dehumanization, rather than impartiality. Bureaucratic defense mechanisms and bureaucratic "empire-building" have served to frustrate the individuals who sought to influence policy (e.g., Bishop Hall, Szeto Wah), or, sometimes, to incorporate and reward them honorifically. Bureaucratic inertia or conservatism, allied with political anxieties, has often appeared to stifle curriculum initiatives. The Textbook Committee, out of which developed the Syllabus and Textbook Committee, out of which eventually developed the Curriculum Development Council, was appointed to ensure that propaganda unfriendly to Hong Kong's interests was not purveyed in schoolbooks. In recent years, curriculum development in Hong Kong seemed wedded to the center–periphery model.[69] In the 1970s, controversies led to allegations that the administrative structure had outgrown its ability to communicate appropriately to the circumstances. In particular, the "Certificated Masters Dispute" of 1973 and the "Precious Blood Jubilee School Dispute" of 1978 provoked adverse comments about the responsiveness of the Education Department, and these comments were at least partly endorsed by the T.K. Ann Report (1975) in the case of the former dispute and the Rayson Huang Report (1979) in the case of the latter, as well as by the Llewellyn Report of 1982. Since then, however, reforms within the administration (including the regionalization of some of the Education Department's work, together with the establishment of the Education and Manpower Branch of the Government Secretariat, the Vocational Training Council and the Education Commission) apparently have succeeded in making the bureaucracy more responsive as well as more efficient.

If the effects of bureaucratization on education in Hong Kong have been mixed, then so have the effects of education on bureaucratization. On the one hand, the expansion and improvement of education have produced a supply of local candidates for the bureaucracy and have probably contributed to the liberalization and humanizing of that bureaucracy. On the other hand, diploma inflation has affected educational administration, too, the result being that promotions may depend more upon paper qualifications in areas such as business administration than on the ability to deal sensitively with educational "clients" (the pupils, teachers, and parents) or the ability to appraise sympathetically (and not merely according to current fashion) policy options open to Hong Kong schools in their peculiar circumstances.

That bureaucratization has brought problems for education (especially the tendency toward centralization and standardization together with a lack of innovation from bodies such as government-run colleges of education and committees dominated by officials concerned with day-to-day administration) hardly needs emphasis. It should be recognized, however, that the same process has benefited education through the removal of at least gross inequities and opportunities for corruption.

4. Localization/Vernacularization

Localization means the deliberate policy of employing local people in positions of responsibility within the government's administrative structure and within commerce and industry. It is related to vernacularization within the educational system since there the officially sponsored, or, at least, tolerated, use of the vernacular of the majority of the local people is likely to enhance their eligibility for employment.

Only very rarely can one substantiate the view that localization and vernacularization historically proved to be the obverse of colonization, despite the simplistic conceptual attractions of so doing. Both processes have far longer histories than those with which they are often credited. From the very beginning of Hong Kong's colonial existence, efforts were made to promote opportunities for some "local" people to contribute to the welfare and efficiency of the new colony.[70] The need for interpreters was generally acknowledged. In 1847, the Reverend S.G. Brown, former headmaster of the Morrison Education Society School, went to the extent of taking back with him to the United States three former pupils so that they could continue their education and, eventually, return to Hong Kong or China more equipped to play a constructive role. Other Chinese from the colony including Ng Choy (Wu Ting Fang) and Ho Kai (later Sir Kai Ho Kai) were educated in Britain and returned to play prominent parts in the development of Hong Kong.[71] Within the colony itself, from 1848 opportunities (and subsidies) were provided for local teachers by the Hong Kong government, and from 1853 there was a small teacher education scheme in the form of pupil–teacher classes at St. Paul's College. Frederick Stewart launched a rather more ambitious pupil–teacher scheme at the Central School in the 1860s, but discovered, to his intense frustration, that most trainees left the program for more lucrative posts as soon as they felt they had learned enough English for the purpose. Even so, many of these young, upwardly mobile Chinese remained in Hong Kong and contributed, as translators, interpreters, members of professions (especially lawyers and doctors), or compradores, to the continued development of the local society and economy. The importance of the vernacular in Hong Kong education was also recognized from the earliest days. Disparaging remarks were sometimes made about the nature of the Chinese language, and colonialistic comments were uttered about the civilizing effects of learning English. Even so, most of the early educators took pains to become fluent in Chinese (e.g., S.R. Brown, Charles Gutzlaff, James Summers, James Legge, Frederick Stewart, Ernest Eitel). Furthermore, throughout the period, a Chinese "stream" of education, based on traditional *sishu* and more advanced tutorial establishments, continued to exist in Hong Kong and in neighboring parts of China. These schools continued to attract pupils, some of whom would begin their "Anglo-Chinese" education in government or mission schools only after they had completed their "Chinese education."

The provision of employment opportunities for locals and the use of the Chinese language within education happened even during what was earlier described as "the heyday of applied colonization" and it was not totally incompatible with colonialistic attitudes. The real boost to vernacularization and eventually to more comprehensive localization came from two basic sources: the emergence of Chinese nationalism as a major political force and changes in official British attitudes toward the colonies. Both processes certainly had important effects long before the Sino-British Agreement of 1984.

The establishment of the Board of Chinese Vernacular Primary Education in 1911 is sometimes interpreted as evidence of the Hong Kong government's active collusion with the less aggressive forms of Chinese nationalism. Actually, it was a tentative attempt to supervise the small new private vernacular schools which had sprung up from about the turn of the century, while mollifying the Hong Kong Chinese of the new elite, who were represented on the board. A lack of enthusiasm is reflected in the facts that the board was given no legal sanction to control schools, that altogether it managed to open only two schools and to recommend subsidies for ten others, that it lasted only two years and, on its demise in 1913, this type of vernacularization-from-above was pronounced a failure by the new governor.[72] Other evidence shows that vernacularization-from-below, especially in the years following the May Fourth Movement of 1919, was much more successful.[73] For a time, the Hong Kong government was content to leave the establishment of new vernacular schools to "the Chinese community and their worthy representatives."[74] It was not long, however, before industrial and political strife in the form of the Seamen's Strike of 1922 and the General Strike and Boycott of 1925–1926 encouraged the government to take a more direct role over vernacular education. The first fruits of this change of attitude may be seen in the establishment of the Government Taipo Normal School to provide teacher education for the New Territories in 1925 and the Government Vernacular Middle School (later renamed Clementi College), which also absorbed the Government Normal School for Men, in 1926.

The increasing number of schools in Hong Kong in which the medium of instruction was Chinese obviously provided more employment opportunities for Hong Kong Chinese within the educational system and, thus, contributed to localization. The system retained, however, some colonialist attitudes, which showed themselves most clearly in salary discrimination. Although several Chinese and Eurasian teachers reached positions of responsibility within Hong Kong's educational system from quite an early period,[75] they were not employed on equal terms with expatriates of Caucasian origin. Such obvious discrimination provided fuel for anti-British propaganda by the Japanese immediately before and during their occupation of Hong Kong. The occupation itself, however, provided plenty of evidence to the surviving Hong Kong population that the slogan "Asia for the Asians" did not mean, in practice, "Hong Kong for the Hong Kong people."

The second main source of support for the movement toward localization and vernacularization came from Britain. It was manifested in a new sense of commitment to the development and welfare of the colonies. There can be little doubt that it was at least partly stimulated by a perceived need to counter anti-British and specifically anticolonialist propaganda. It should be noted, however, that signs of the onset of the change could be detected before Japanese propaganda began in earnest. The establishment of the Advisory Committee on Education in the Colonies (ACEC) in 1929 had more to do with Britain's response to criticisms about colonial rule in Africa (included in the Phelps-Stokes Commission Report of the earlier 1920s) than it did with Asian colonies. Even so, eventually the ACEC, which advised the secretary of state for the colonies, had important influence on educational policy in Hong Kong. General statements about the importance of localization appeared in the White Paper of 1940. The subsequent Colonial Development and Welfare Acts gave practical encouragement to locally run industries, agriculture, and welfare services within the colonies. In addition, two other, more specific documents, issued soon after the war, made it clear that localization within colonial civil services was ensconced as official policy and that the British government recognized the consequential need for an improvement of training facilities.[76] These policy statements had an effect on Hong Kong. For example, Duncan Sloss, vice-chancellor of the Hong Kong University, was able to make use of the Command Paper on the Organization of the Colonial Service to support his arguments to reestablish and strengthen teacher education programs in his university. The statements of intention did not, of course, transform the situation overnight; attitudes were too deeply entrenched for that. But they did herald changes. By 1983 (a year before the signing of the joint declaration about the future of Hong Kong by the governments of China and Britain), over 98 percent of available posts in the civil service were staffed by locals. Although there have been significant variations within this process of localization, even at the highest levels of the civil service considerable progress has been made.[77] The chief localization-related problem facing Hong Kong in the 1980s and 1990s appears to be how to attract, train, and retain competent locals in the civil service. This problem is due to the extent to which non-government employment opportunities (in particular, within the professions, business, and industry) have been taken up by local Hong Kong people, as well as to anxieties about the future and the resulting brain drain.

In the first few decades after World War II, a period that witnessed both a continuation and acceleration of the refugee influx and the beginnings of decolonialization, vernacularization also proceeded apace. By this time, primary education was already almost entirely conducted in Cantonese. An attempt by the Hong Kong government in 1946 to extend the use of Cantonese as the medium of instruction to what would now be termed the first two years of secondary education was resisted successfully by the mainly missionary-sponsored grant schools on which the government depended so heavily for secondary education in the first postwar years. However, vernacularization at the higher levels of education received further sanction from the Hong Kong government through several important measures, including the establishment of the government's Evening School for Higher Chinese Studies in 1951. Even more important, the Keswick Report on Higher Education recommended in 1952 that the University of Hong Kong should conduct parallel courses in arts and science through the medium of Chinese. There were two significant results of the university's inability to meet this challenge. First, a type of bridging-course was started, which enabled pupils from Chinese middle schools to attend a "Special Sixth Form" at Clementi College to gain sufficient English and other basic matriculation requirements to be eligible to enter the University of Hong Kong. Second, the Hong Kong government decided to offer financial support to some of the more substantial of the mushrooming Chinese postsecondary colleges in Hong Kong. This led eventually (in 1963) to the establishment of the Chinese University of Hong Kong.[78]

The Chinese Language Movement,[79] which, by 1974, had succeeded in elevating Chinese to equal status with English as an official language of Hong Kong, especially when accompanied by the rhetoric of the Students' Movement from 1971, further strengthened the image of vernacularization within Hong Kong's educational system as well as outside it. The reality, however, was different. This was a period when predominantly economic considerations persuaded parents to seek educational opportunities for their children in Anglo-Chinese schools rather than middle schools. The result was that, whereas the Keswick Committee could write in 1952 that "for every three students from the Anglo-Chinese secondary schools, there are four from the Chinese secondary schools,"[80] by 1987, less than 10 percent of secondary school pupils were attending secondary schools in which the official medium of instruction was Chinese.[81]

On the other hand, the relatively rapid changeover from a selective form of secondary education to mass secondary education, which occurred in Hong Kong from the late 1970s onward, brought with it doubts about the quality of education, especially about language standards. Linguistic insecurities of pupils and teachers led to distinctions between what a school officially claimed as its language policy and what actually happened in the classroom—often an admixture of English and Cantonese, with a gradual predominance of Cantonese.[82] This, in turn, contributed to the further lowering of standards in both languages. Thus, when the Hong Kong government, influenced by the Llewellyn Report's (1982) arguments for mother-tongue education and, perhaps more directly, by the Education Commission's Report No. 1 (October 1984), decided to implement a policy of "positive discrimination" in favor of the use of the local vernacular in secondary education, many principals and teachers were happy to seize the opportunity, even though parents still valued English for pragmatic purposes. The Joint Declaration of the Chinese and British governments about the future of Hong Kong served to reinforce the importance of the "Chinese language" in Hong Kong education as one way of seeking convergence with China. It certainly gave an impetus to the growth of Putonghua as a curriculum area in Hong Kong. Somewhat paradoxically, it also seemed to strengthen the case for Cantonese as medium of instruction.

The effects of localization and vernacularization on education in Hong Kong are numerous. They are also disputed. In the final analysis, however, there is no reason to deny that certain effects apply in the case of some people and schools, but not in the case of others. Thus, localization and vernacularization are often assumed to increase warmth and closeness, the sense of belonging to Hong Kong, among teachers and pupils. Proponents of localization argue this on the grounds that the teachers and pupils come from similar linguistic and cultural backgrounds, and there is no doubt that this is often the case. In some cases, however, personality problems or socioeconomic differences may outweigh the sense of togetherness. It is also possible that local teachers will exhibit a greater sense of commitment to and knowledge about the Hong Kong curriculum than expatriates. On the other hand, especially during periods of high "transitization," such as the brain drain of the 1980s, expatriates working in Hong Kong for a lengthy period of time who have the good fortune to possess secure passports may actually prove to be more stable than local teachers concerned to establish their credentials elsewhere. Vernacularization is certainly likely to improve the learning opportunities of the majority of Hong Kong students. A recent intervention study has shown that the language of instruction makes no significant difference in the case of the top 30 percent of the ability range, who might benefit in other than academic ways from learning through the medium of English, but proposals to sanction a two-tier system have been criticized as socially divisive.[83] Other evidence of the thin-skinned sensitivities involved in the language issue included the open signs of resentment among local pupils and teachers of the government-backed scheme to import native English language users into Hong Kong in an effort to improve secondary pupils' use of English.[84] There is little doubt that morale has risen within the teaching profession as senior positions in both the public and private sectors became open to and, eventually, dominated by local educators. The crisis of the 1980s and 1990s, however, concerns their successors, since many of the most talented younger teachers are either leaving Hong Kong to establish rights of abode elsewhere or are leaving teaching for more lucrative employment opportunities, which have themselves been created by the brain drain. The result is that the average age of teaching professionals is declining, the proportion of professionally qualified to unqualified teachers is improving, but problems certainly exist in the filling of posts of responsibility with suitable local staff.

Education has also affected localization and vernacularization. Since the very earliest days, as the careers of Yung Hung, Ng Choy, and Ho Kai testify, educational qualifications have served as "entry tickets" to senior posts. The basic difference between the later twentieth century and the later nineteenth century is quantitative. Now there is an expectation that success in the certification aspects of education will lead to socioeconomic advancement, as well as the expectation that it will serve as a "passport" and contribute to a local citizen's emigration credit points. Education has also affected vernacularization in the sense that it has modified the more traditional Chinese approaches. Simplified characters, modern literature, and Putonghua are consequently now much more accepted as part of a vernacular package deal than they were in the past.

The advantages outlined above that have come from localization and vernacularization are widely acknowledged. It is possible, however, that the processes have been accompanied by disadvantages. It could be that parochialism increases as the number of expatriates with experience in several other countries decreases. There is even a danger of corruption, especially nepotism, spreading as competition from abroad declines. The argument might also be made that reliance on locals in government, for instance, actually tends to increase the salary bill since attempts have to be made to induce people from well-paid occupations in the private sector. Despite these possibilities, it remains clear that one of the chief hopes for the future of Hong Kong is that it is, and will continue to be, run by Hong Kong people. For this reason, the promise held out by the Chinese government that, after 1997, there will be "one country, two systems" and that Hong Kong will be governed by Hong Kong people is psychologically and educationally of utmost importance.

5. *Transitization*

With only very rare exceptions, Hong Kong has never been a melting pot. Instead, it has resembled a Chinese *wok* in which various separate ingredients are rapidly and briefly stir-fried in a very heated and high-pressured atmosphere.

Therefore, their tastes rarely mix. Metaphorically, this agrees with Lau's comments about the atomistic or minimally integrated nature of Hong Kong society.[85] This primarily results from the way in which migration has affected Hong Kong. As pointed out earlier, one of Hong Kong's most important roles (in a sense, its main function) has been to serve as a temporary work place or mart and, on many occasions of social, economic, or political distress in China, as a bolt-hole for people from the mainland—predominantly, but not exclusively, from parts close to Hong Kong. The artisans who came to Hong Kong during the 1840s to find work usually intended to return to their homes in China, and often did return periodically and then to retire. They were followed in the 1850s by Chinese people, sometimes of more substantial means, who were escaping the ravages of the Taiping uprising. Other political movements engendered reasons for people to leave China and to treat Hong Kong either as a stepping-stone on their way to some other place or as a place of temporary refuge.[86] To these must be added the various natural disasters (droughts, floods, storms, epidemics) that have periodically blighted the nation,[87] as well as a persistence of the basic urge to make a better living, which the earliest newcomers to Hong Kong manifested. The transitization of Hong Kong has been reciprocal. Thus, in times of trouble within Hong Kong (e.g., the plague of the 1890s and early 1900s, the 1925–26 strike and boycott, the Japanese occupation from 1941 to 1945, the 1966 and 1967 disturbances, the crisis of confidence in the late 1980s), many residents left the territory—in some cases for mainland China.

Hong Kong also served as a work place, mart, career stepping-stone, and, sometimes, refuge for its non-Chinese inhabitants. These have included European and American administrators, businessmen, missionaries, and professionals. They have also included people originally from the Indian subcontinent, Thais, Japanese, Koreans, and, more significantly in recent times, Filipinos and Vietnamese. The result of this transitization process has been that Hong Kong did not develop as a typical town in China, but rather as a "Chinatown," with contiguous and small enclaves of other various groups.

Possibly the only period in which transience was not a major characteristic of Hong Kong society was the 1960s and 1970s. In these decades, something approaching a sense of Hong Kong identity developed. Lau and Kuan found the "Chinese identity" of ethnic Chinese in Hong Kong to have undergone "slow and subtle changes" and noted with astonishment the proportion of respondents to their 1985 questionnaire who identified themselves as "Hong Kongese."[88] At least part of the reason for this change relates to Hong Kong's achievements in the economic and social spheres since World War II. It is also due to the obvious distinctions between the Hong Kong Chinese and the Chinese in China with regard to life-styles, rights, and liberties. It is more than possible that education in Hong Kong in all its informal as well as formal aspects has also contributed to this change.

This was, however, not the only development in the later postwar period. At the same time, illegal immigrants from China resumed importance as a problem and were associated in the public mind with an upsurge in crime. The increase in numbers of Filipinos, mainly employed on contract terms in domestic service, also ensured that the transient nature of Hong Kong society persisted. But by far the most important development that has reinvigorated the transitization process in Hong Kong has been the "brain drain" associated with anxieties about Hong Kong's future. One side effect of this has been the phenomenon of Hong Kong Chinese returning to Hong Kong for finite periods of time, having secured their residence rights elsewhere (the "green card" for the United States, a Canadian or Australian passport)—in local parlance, the "astronauts."

The most commonly recognized effect of transitization is the alleged lack of Hong Kong identity. One manifestation of this is the way both Chinese and non-Chinese expatriates think of "home." Perhaps in the 1970s, Hong Kong began to be regarded as home by some members of both groups. Some may retain this concept in the 1980s and into the 1990s. Most do so, however, with a certain amount of trepidation which has increased since June 4, 1989. And, as already emphasized, many Chinese and non-Chinese are taking active steps to set up a family home outside Hong Kong.

Transitization's effects on education have been largely negative. The transient nature of the Hong Kong population has often been used as an excuse to avoid long-term planning and, especially, as a reason to refuse to improve both quantitative and qualitative aspects of education. Thus, E.A. Irving, the first director of education, wrote, "What becomes of the hopes of those who aspire to raise the standard of education in Hong Kong to a uniformly high level? As well hope to raise the standard of education in Charing Cross Hotel!"[89] Over forty years later, a successor, T.R. Rowell, hardly changed the metaphor from this British Railways theme in his attempt to justify only selective education for the Chinese: "For the considerable semi-permanent population little can be done educationally. It would be rather like 'setting up a school on Victoria Station for those who pass through.' "[90] Both directors (and other like-minded persons) failed to mention, however, the government assistance which, since 1903, had been given to the educational welfare of children of the semi-permanent European population. It was only from the early 1950s that official policy, as outlined by Rowell's successor, D.J.S. Crozier, accepted that priority should be given to providing education for the Chinese population and that other means should be found for mollifying the non-Chinese. These other means included private schools. Eventually (by 1967), the establishment of the English Schools Foundation, which received government assistance on the same basis as it was offered to schools for the Chinese majority of the population, provided a subsidized alternative to the non-Chinese.

A related argument, made on several occasions during Hong Kong's history, to justify government inaction and economy with regard to education in Hong

Kong, was that if the government effected improvements in Hong Kong's educational facilities, this would simply encourage further immigration of transients from China. This was one of the reasons for niggardly support for technical education in the 1920s. It was also initially used to justify not providing educational services for the floods of immigrants arriving in Hong Kong in the late 1940s and early 1950s. It is not coincidental that the first signs of long-term planning for Hong Kong's educational services occurred during the 1960s and 1970s (e.g., the White Paper of 1965 and the various Green and White papers of the 1970s), the very period in which, as noted above, something approaching an "identification" process was beginning to affect the residents of Hong Kong.

Transitization has also increased the importance of the certification aspects of education. As mentioned above in the sections on industrialization and bureaucratization, this has meant that educational qualifications have been valued as types of passports or, at least, emigration credit points. Unfortunately, such an effect has led to a rapid turnover of the teaching force, which lowers the morale of the profession. It has tended also to reinforce an already existing inclination among Hong Kong Chinese to prize education only for what it is instrumental in achieving. Currently, there is a clear emphasis in education as well as in industry and the property market on short-term returns. Students are beginning to avoid courses—including teacher education—that require an investment of time.

Transitization has also had a negative influence on the development of local culture and, specifically, of an interest in local history. Because, until very recently, Hong Kong Chinese people considered themselves primarily as Chinese rather than as Hong Kongese, they have tended to disparage local culture and local history. This tendency was reinforced by the fact that so much of the local recorded history refers to the colonial period. The marked increase in interest in local history during the past ten or so years, as manifested in publications and in a willingness to incorporate local history into the curriculum of secondary and tertiary educational institutions, is clearly related to the beginnings of a sense of Hong Kong identity in the 1960s and 1970s and to a desire to be distinct from the (less advanced?) Chinese of the People's Republic in the years immediately before the constitutional absorption of Hong Kong by China. The earlier refugee/transient mentality similarly contributed toward the inclination of many people in Hong Kong not to be involved in local politics. A newcomer's first priority was to make a living and set up opportunities for leaving Hong Kong. More recently, the sense that Hong Kong distinctiveness could be threatened by the resumption of Chinese sovereignty has made many Hong Kong citizens much more interested in political matters.

Education's effects on transitization have been largely enabling. In other words, the diplomas issued by educational institutions have helped many people leave Hong Kong. However, in the present circumstances especially, the requirements of the new host country might, in turn, have effects on Hong Kong's education. Thus, it is currently argued that the fact that Canada does not give immigrant "credit" for professional teacher qualifications has adversely affected enrollments into Hong Kong's teacher education establishments. A second possible effect of education on transitization has been gradually to moderate it. Informal and formal education may have contributed toward the emergence of a Hong Kong identity among its disparate people.

Transitization has created problems for Hong Kong—generally, related to a lack of community and loyalty. If there have been any benefits to Hong Kong from transitization, they must be associated either with the material advantages accompanying transient entrepreneurs and transient labor or, more generally, with the cosmopolitanism brought by coming and going. Because many of them have recently come from elsewhere and many are about to go elsewhere, people in Hong Kong tend to be both informed about and responsive to international trends. This can be regarded as a strength in a society that is beginning to depend increasingly on its tertiary industry.

6. Democratization

If one defines democratization as the assumption of participatory responsibilities by people who are not civil servants, based on some form of popular sanction, then it has a longer history in Hong Kong than is often supposed. For many decades, the *kaifongs*, or neighborhood associations, various voluntary associations (such as the Man Mo Temple Committee, the District Watch Committee, and the Board of Directors of the Tung Wah Group of Hospitals), and lineage or district groups in the New Territories have provided channels for the emergence of leaders or "representatives" by some form of consensus. Among the much smaller non-Chinese communities, overt espousal of political reform which involved a call for elected representatives on the Legislative Council and/or a municipal council can be traced back to the earliest days of Hong Kong's colonial existence. At the same time, the study groups of the late nineteenth and early twentieth centuries, in which coteries of Hong Kong Chinese debated reform or revolution for China, were usually imbued with the spirit of democracy, if not always with the mechanics. The same may be said of local organizations which sprang up to support and, later, to mourn the pro-democracy movement in China during the summer of 1989. Throughout Hong Kong's colonial history, non-Chinese pressure groups, such as the China Association, the various chambers of commerce, and municipal reform or even educational reform movements, usually respected democratic procedures.

Numerous superficial observers point to the "political apathy" of the Chinese people. They use this alleged ethnic trait to explain political stability in Hong Kong and the prolonged existence of unrepresentative colonial rule. It is possible, however, that the reason for overt political inactivity on the part of many Hong Kong Chinese has, in the past, concerned more their status as refugees and transients than it has their inherent Chineseness. Secondly, the expression "political apathy" has been used undiscriminatingly.[91] It has concealed such questions as whether the people have felt knowledgeable and comfortable about the channels open to them for political participation. Furthermore, especially when it is applied in a derogatory or patronizing manner to Hong Kong students, as it so often has been, it reveals considerable ignorance about the history of Hong Kong.[92]

Progress toward formal representation of the people in Hong Kong has been slow, but it has not been nonexistent. Early moves in this direction tended to concern either the non-Chinese population (e.g., the election of a member of the chamber of commerce to the Legislative Council in the nineteenth century) or to constitute forms of tokenism (e.g., the appointment of the first Chinese members of the Legislative Council). Plans for municipal reform were emasculated by the relative unimportance of the responsibilities that a municipal or urban council exercised. The first genuine attempt to change this, shortly after the end of World War II, was popularly known as the "Young Plan," after its principal author, Sir Mark Young, governor of Hong Kong immediately before the war and, briefly again, following the British Military Administration of 1945–46. The Young Plan, which would have reformed both the Legislative and the Urban councils on democratic lines, originated in discussions in London and had more to do with the British government's concern about the future status of Hong Kong, especially in a period of decolonization, than it did with a grass-roots pro-democracy movement in Hong Kong. Basically, it was overshadowed by the circumstances of the Chinese civil war, the continued and increased influx of economic and political refugees, the establishment of the People's Republic in China, and the heightening of the Cold War in various parts of the world. In these circumstances, and particularly with a new governor in Hong Kong, a quite widely shared "don't rock the boat" attitude, especially among Hong Kong government officials and the local Chinese, Eurasian, and European "establishment," ensured that the Young Plan was shelved.[93] Further tinkering with the system (e.g., minor changes in the composition of the Legislative, Executive, and Urban councils) became the substitute for fundamental democratization. Various reasons (especially the impact of the 1967 riots) persuaded the Hong Kong government to try to improve its public relations and its general responsiveness to public opinion in the late 1960s and 1970s through such means as the Government Information Services and the District Office scheme. By the 1980s, these had extended to elected district boards, a regional council for the New Territories, and a system of indirect election by "functional constituencies" for a minority of Legislative Council seats. Green and White papers on constitutional development have differed significantly in their prognoses of the progress that can realistically be made along the road to democratic representation of the people before 1997. There is no doubt, however, that, first the Sino-British Joint Declaration over the future of Hong Kong in 1984 and, most recently, the trauma associated with the events of June 4, 1989, in Peking have spurred on efforts to democratize Hong Kong, albeit belatedly.

Even in its earlier, very incomplete form, democratization has had effects on education in Hong Kong. There have been occasions, for example, when one might talk of an upsurge of "Student (or Pupil) Power." To the general political examples already given (1925–26, 1967, the Students' Movement of the late 1960s and 1970s, and the aftermath of June 4, 1989), one might add the Precious Blood Jubilee School Dispute of 1978, in which educational and financial issues combined to arouse the idealism and activism of pupils and teachers. As might be expected, such open political activity on the part of pupils and students has tended to affect also the normal interaction (or lack of interaction) patterns of Hong Kong classrooms, as well as to encourage more democratic, or at least more responsive, forms of school governance. Not all teachers and administrators have welcomed these changes, and there are some who would attribute an alleged increase in disciplinary disorders to democratization and, especially, to student activists. Teachers may feel pressed to be less expository and more interactive with the students. Some welcome the change, others resent it. Students' input into course evaluation is becoming more common in Hong Kong, with a similarly mixed reaction from teachers. Moreover, a general increase in concern for elective government, the quality of life in Hong Kong, a protected environment, and the equality of the sexes have led to curriculum initiatives, both from the Hong Kong government and by special interest groups, particularly in the 1980s. This may explain the current support for political education, civic education, environmental education, and moral education.

The effects of education on democratization are also significant. As the level of education of Hong Kong people has improved, the case for democratization has become stronger. It is not a case, as the Forster Act in Britain is often said to be, of education following political gains in order to make them work. Instead, in Hong Kong, it is more a matter of education heralding and justifying political gains. The direct link between education and the franchise is obvious when one of the qualifying criteria for the right to vote in Urban Council elections remains a pass in the General Certificate of Education. Finally, there is every possibility that, as educational provision continues to improve, old-style, demagogic political leaders will lose credence even within democratic forms. As the populace becomes more educated and sophisticated, so should their representatives.

Conclusions

One important conclusion that an analysis of historical processes offers is clear confirmation of their close interconnections. Colonization, industrialization, bureaucratization, localization, transitization, and democratization have interacted with, and fed off each other over a relatively long period of time in Hong Kong's history. This interaction has had significant impact on education in the colony. It has affected the nature of the educational system, especially in a structural sense.

It has contributed toward policy concerning both quantitative provision and qualitative concerns. It has engendered curriculum change—or, sometimes, conservatism. It has helped shape the attitudes of all those involved in educational encounters—the pupils, the teachers, the parents, the administrators, and the general public. All these effects have happened over a longer time span than is often recognized.

Laissez-faire is probably the most commonly used term to describe the general attitude of the Hong Kong government. Perhaps equally strong claims could be made for "benign indifference" or "enlightened inertia." Except when faced with threats to its own survival (and sometimes threats to its "face"), the Hong Kong government has usually taken a noninterventionist stance until some form of crisis management has indicated the desirability of action. This has been particularly important in a society that has resembled a confederation of communities characterized by energy, disparateness, cultural self-confidence, and transience.

It is important to recognize, too, that Hong Kong has *always* been a place of transition, not merely a place of transit for many of its inhabitants. Change has been an important fact of Hong Kong life, whether one concentrates on the physical environment or on political and socioeconomic relationships. The Hong Kong curriculum has been influenced by political factors, and especially developments in China, for more than a century before the Sino-British accord over its future. Education in all its aspects has *always* been influenced by both endogenous and exogenous factors.

This suggests that although the imminent transition occupies the thoughts and feelings of millions of present-day inhabitants of Hong Kong, there is nothing unique about the situation. The trends and factors that have affected Hong Kong in the past are likely to continue to affect society during and after the transition.

Unfortunately, some commentators "raid" history in a very selective way for the booty they can seize in attempts to justify their predetermined generalizations. Intense suspicion should be directed at conspiracy theories, which pay more credit to the foresight and intelligence of colonial administrators than their achievements warrant; at the cruder forms of Marxist dogmatism; at hindsight-dependent concepts, which fail to understand the historical context; and at all ex post facto prescriptions that predict with confidence. Usually, they derive from the shoddiest, most superficial, and least primary-source-oriented views of Hong Kong's past. They are also often the product of individuals who, whatever their ethnic origin, bring with them conceptual baggage that weighs them down so much that they are unable to appreciate the particularities of the situation, as Mackerras has recently noted about Western images of China. Indeed, in the final analysis and especially because of the interconnections which hard evidence indicates, one might query the very existence of "historical processes," since a process presupposes a product and the basic product of history is the present.

Notes

1. See, for example, P. Morris, "The Effects on the School Curriculum of Hong Kong's Return to Chinese Sovereignty in 1997," *Journal of Curriculum Studies* 20, 6, pp. 509–20, 1988.
2. See B. Bullivant, *The Pluralist Dilemma in Education: Six Case Studies* (Sydney: Allen and Unwin, 1981).
3. See M. Carnoy, *Education as Cultural Imperialism* (New York: Longman, 1974).
4. Examples of this tendency are cited in P. Altbach and G. Kelly, eds., *Education and the Colonial Experience* (New Brunswick: Transaction Books, 1984) and S.J. Ball, "Imperialism, Social Control and the Colonial Curriculum in Africa,' in *Defining the Curriculum: Histories and Ethnographies*, ed. F. Goodson and S.J. Ball (London: Falmer Press, 1984).
5. See, for example, R. First, *The Barrel of a Gun: Political Power in Africa and the Coup d'etat* (London: Allen Lane, 1970); P. Gifford and T. Weiskel, "Education in a Colonial Context," in *France and Britain in Africa*, ed. P. Gifford and W.L. Louis (New Haven: Yale University Press, 1971).
6. See C. Whitehead, "Education in British Colonial Dependencies, 1919–39: Reappraisal," *Comparative Education* 17, 1, 1981, and "Education in Far Away Places: Evidence from the Periphery of Empire of the Problems of Developing Schooling in British Colonies," *Education Research and Perspectives* 16, 1, pp. 51–69, 1989; G. Kelly, "Colonialism, Indigenous Society, and School Practices: French West Africa and Indo-China," in *Education and the Colonial Experience*, ed. P. Altbach and P. Kelly (New Brunswick, NJ: Transaction Books, 1984).
7. See K.M.A. Barnett, "Hong Kong before the Chinese: The Frame, the Puzzle, and the Missing Pieces," *Journal of the Hong Kong Branch of the Royal Asiatic Society* 4, pp. 42–67, 1964; J. Hayes, *The Hong Kong Region, 1850–1911: Institutions and Leadership in Town and Countryside* (Hamden, CT: Archon Books, 1977); S. Bard, *In Search of the Past: A Guide to the Antiquities of Hong Kong* (Hong Kong: Urban Council, 1988).
8. See H.L. Lo, *Hong Kong and Its External Communications before 1842: The History of Hong Kong prior to the British Arrival* (Hong Kong: Institute of Chinese Culture, 1963); A.E. Sweeting, *Education in Hong Kong, pre-1841 to 1941: Fact and Opinion* (Hong Kong: Hong Kong University Press, 1990).
9. "Compradore" is derived from the Portuguese term *comprador*, meaning "provider" or "provisioner." On the China coast in the later nineteenth century, it came to mean a Chinese or Eurasian middleman in commercial and labor relations between foreign companies and Chinese clients, customers, and workers. Most large foreign companies appointed a chief compradore who, in turn, set up a staff of assistant compradores, usually from among his relatives and friends.
10. C.T. Smith, *Chinese Christians: Elites, Middlemen, and the Church in Hong Kong* (Hong Kong: Oxford University Press, 1985).
11. A.E. Sweeting, "Snapshots from the Social History of Education in Hong Kong: An Alternative to Macro-Mania," *Education Research and Perspectives* 16, 1, pp. 3–12, 1989.
12. For example, "7. When any European gentleman, especially a Government Officer, or any of those gentlemen who superintend the Schools, enter the school-room, the teacher should instruct the boys to stand up and be silent and respectful . . ." (The Reverand Wilheim Lopscheid, "A Few Notes on the Extent of Chinese Education and the Government Schools of Hong Kong, with Remarks on the Religious Notions of the Inhabitants of the Island," *Hong Kong China Mail*, pp. 2–3, 1859). Another example from a half-century later is offered by the Education Department's official definition of grades

of schools. This made a form of racial discrimination very clear: "An Upper Grade School means one in which at least part of the Staff is European. Lower Grade Schools are those under purely native management" (*Hong Kong Government Gazette*, June 30, 1905, p. 1023). That such attitudes were shared by Colonial Office personnel in London can be detected in the dismissive minute written by an official about a qualified Chinese teacher's application to be treated as equal to expatriate staff: "I don't think that the fact that Mr. Hee has found an Englishwoman foolish enough to marry a Chinaman is an argument for increasing his salary [as Headmaster of Wanchai District School]" (Colonial Office Files [hereafter, CO] Series 129, "Hong Kong: Original Correspondence," File 341, p. 342).

13. See, for example, the specimens of essays about the history of Hong Kong written by pupils of the school of the Morrison Education Society, *Chinese Repository* 12, pp. 362–68, July 1843; also quoted in A.E. Sweeting, "Reconstruction of Education in Post-War Hong Kong, 1945–54: Variations in the Process of Policy Making" (Ph.D. diss., Hong Kong University, 1989). Another document published in the *Chinese Repository* (12, pp. 620–30, the "Report of the Morrison Education Society," December 1843, signed by S.R. Brown) suggests that missionaries were not averse to forms of cultural alienation. Thus, Brown wrote (p. 628): "I have heard them, when some instance of falsehood or low cunning has occurred among the natives around them, say with a look of disgust, 'that is Chinese.'"

14. The actual terms used by the 1902 Education Committee were: "The Committee hold that what education is given should be thorough, and that better results will be obtained by assisting to enlighten the ignorance of the upper classes of Chinese than by attempting to force new ideas on the mass of the people. Civilized ideas among the leaders of thought are the best and perhaps the only means at present available for permeating the general ignorance; for this reason much more attention has been paid to the Anglo-Chinese [English-medium] schools than to the Vernacular" (*Hong Kong Government Gazette*, April 11, 1902, p. 518).

An obvious comparison suggests itself with other cases of colonialistic elitism, but, as further examination reveals, the Hong Kong view was not supported by the Colonial Office in London (see below).

15. "Annual Report of the Director of Education for the Year 1924" (Hong Kong: Education Department, 1925), p. 2. Italics added.

16. See, for example, Edmund Burney, *Report on Education in Hong Kong* (London: Crown Agents, 1935), pp. 24–26; it was only in 1954 that a director of education could refuse to give preferential treatment to children of expatriate civil servants on the grounds that the more urgent and important problems that he had to tackle related to the overwhelming majority of the population, the Chinese.

17. In 1883, for example, the Hong Kong government's surveyor-general reported on "classrooms arranged as requested by Mr Wright [Headmaster of the Government Central School] in such manner that each large class-room opens into two smaller class-rooms with glass doors to enable one European teacher to supervise two Chinese assistant teachers" (CO129/210, p. 253).

18. These included the short-lived Normal School (1881–83), evening extension classes in pedagogy at the Technical Institute (from 1907), the University of Hong Kong's department of education (from 1916), and the first of the government's Teacher Training Colleges (Northcote Training College, from 1939).

19. H.J. Lethbridge, *Hong Kong: Stability and Change* (Hong Kong: Oxford University Press, 1979), p. 209; A.E. Sweeting, "Hong Kong," in *Schooling in East Asia: Forces of Change*, ed. R.M. Thomas and T.N. Postlethwaite (Oxford: Pergamon, 1983), p. 274.

20. For example, the London Missionary Society made it clear to Sir Henry Pottinger, first governor of Hong Kong, that the school they wished him to support, Ying Wa College, was intended for the education of both Chinese and European children (their letter of August 18, 1843, appears in CO129/2, pp. 258–63). More than a half century later, Dr. George Bateson Wright protested vigorously against the proposed restriction of admission into his school, Queen's College, to Chinese on the grounds that the aim of Queen's College was not merely to produce efficient copying clerks, but to offer an all-round, general education (CO129/311, pp. 62ff.).

21. See Sweeting, *Education in Hong Kong, pre-1841 to 1941*.

22. Annual Report on Education, 1865 (in *The Hong Kong Blue Book*, 1865, pp. 277ff.).

23. The secretary of state for the colonies to the governor of Hong Kong, September 12, 1902; in CO129/311, pp. 48f. It might also be noted that, over thirty years earlier, Frederick Stewart had explicitly argued, concerning the education received by the boys in the Government Central School, that it was important "not to neglect the *many* for the benefit of the *few*" (Annual Education Report, 1866).

24. For concern about Guomindang propaganda, see A.E. Sweeting, *Education in Hong Kong, pre-1841 to 1941*, p. 332. Civics acquired renewed importance in the later 1940s and 1950s when, in the atmosphere of the Cold War, it became one of the instruments of a "Counter-Communism" strategy (Sweeting, "Reconstruction of Education in Post-War Hong Kong," pp. 740–42).

25. See, for example, N.L. Cheng et al., "At What Cost? Instruction through the English Medium in Hong Kong Schools," privately published pamphlet, 1973.

26. M.W. Bentley, "Language, Culture, and Education in Hong Kong before 1941," seminar paper at the Centre of Asian Studies, University of Hong Kong, November 10, 1988.

27. R. Clignet, "Damned If You Do, Damned If You Don't: The Dilemmas of Colonizer-Colonized Relations," in *Education and the Colonial Experience*, ed. P.G. Altbach and G.P. Kelly (New Brunswick, NJ: Transaction Books, 1984), pp. 77–96.

28. D.M. Kwok, "Language Attitudes and Tri-Lingual Oral Learning during Hong Kong's Countdown toward being a Post-Colonialistic Region of China," paper presented at the First Hong Kong Conference on Language and Society, April 1988.

29. K.M. Cheng, "The Concept of Legitimacy in Educational Policy-Making: Alternative Explanations of Two Policy Episodes in Hong Kong" (Ph.D. diss., University of London, 1987).

30. Cited in Matthew Turner, *Made in Hong Kong: A History of Export Design in Hong Kong* (Hong Kong: Urban Council, 1988), pp. 8–9. Turner goes on to point out that by 1846 (i.e., only five years after the first official British landing in Hong Kong), a third of all Chinese properties were registered as factories and that the further expansion and diversification of local industry in the later 19th century included "feather-dressing, match factories, soap, coal, briquette and rattan works, sugar refineries, cement works, and spinning mills."

31. M. Topley, "The Role of Savings and Wealth among the Hong Kong Chinese," in *Hong Kong: A Society in Transition*, ed. I.C. Jarvie (London: Routledge and Kegan Paul, 1969).

32. Phelps Brown E.A., "The Hong Kong Economy: Achievements and Prospects," in *Hong Kong: The Industrial Colony*, ed. K. Hopkins (Hong Kong: Oxford University Press, 1971).

33. A.J. Youngson, *Hong Kong Economic Growth and Policy* (Hong Kong: Oxford University Press, 1982).

34. S.L. Wong, *Emigrant Entrepreneurs: Shanghai Industrialists in Hong Kong* (Hong Kong: Oxford University Press, 1988).

35. V. Sit and S.L. Wong, *Hong Kong Manufacturing* (Tokyo: Institute of Developing Economies, 1988).

36. S.K. Lau and H.C. Kwan, *The Ethos of the Hong Kong Chinese* (Hong Kong: Chinese University of Hong Kong Press, 1988).

37. V. Sit, S.L. Wong, and T.S. Kiang, *Small Industry in a Laissez-faire Economy* (Hong Kong: Centre of Asian Studies, 1979), pp. 398–99.

38. K.S. Yeung, "Manpower Training in New Technologies," speech to open the Hong Kong University/UNESCO Conference on the Popularization of Science and Technology, September 4, 1989, p. 9.

39. See, for example, Papers for the 8th Session, International Standing Conference for the History of Education, 1986.

40. Frederick Stewart, Inspector of Schools, had floated the idea of compulsory education, along with the possibility of a special Education Tax, as early as 1866, but was clearly aware that it was unlikely to attract much support ("The Annual Report on the State of the Government Schools for the Year 1865," signed by Frederick Stewart and dated February 12, 1866, *The Hong Kong Blue Book, 1865*, p. 278). In 1893, the Marquis of Ripon, secretary of state for the colonies, reminded Hong Kong officials that compulsory education had been "introduced into more than one of the Protected Malay States, and with more than satisfactory results, as far as can be judged" (CO129/256, pp. 961ff.). On the other hand, the 1902 Report of the Education Committee and various subsequent annual reports had dismissed as unfeasible and unjustifiable the argument for compulsory education. Wells's case appeared in the *Report of the Commission on the Industrial Employment of Children*, 1921, Appendix 2.

41. A clear distinction between primary and secondary education was not achieved in Hong Kong until the early 1950s, well into the second phase of Hong Kong's industrialization. It occurred at least partly as a result of the visit by Mr. Norman Fisher, the director of a local education authority in Britain and his subsequent Report on Educational Expenditure. See Sweeting, "Reconstruction of Education in Post-War Hong Kong," pp. 386, 596–97.

42. The pupil-teacher scheme, which St. Paul's College adopted in 1853 and the Central School from the mid-1860s onward, was, like the monitorial system in England, a clear example of how education borrowed factory-style methods from industry. Another was the type of specialization and even the use of simulation practiced in the short-lived (1881–1883) Wanchai Normal School. "Extension-courses" for teachers-in-training at the Technical Institute (established in 1907) were, in a sense, a halfway house between apprenticeships to "Masters of Method" and more modern concepts of teacher education.

43. This attitude was common both among office-bound bureaucrats and among people imbued with the literary inclinations of Chinese cultural tradition.

44. In 1902, for example, as well as disapproving of the Education Committee's recommendations that education should follow the lines of race, Joseph Chamberlain, the secretary of state for the colonies, made it clear that he was not satisfied with the fate of a second Industrial Reformatory which had been established less than five years before in a surge of enthusiasm. This Industrial Reformatory had attracted generous financial backing from Mr. E.R. Belilios, a well-known businessman and philanthropist, after whom it was named. It was opened in 1898. Despite early claims about the indispensability of the institution and in the face of Belilios' own arguments for the establishment of a full technical school, by 1902 plans were being made to use the premises of the Belilios Reformatory simply as a prison. The governor, Sir Henry Blake, rated the establishment of a separate school to cater exclusively for Europeans as a higher priority, arguing that the establishment of a technical school "was not considered practicable." And so it transpired. The separate school for Europeans was established. The Belilios Reformatory lapsed. And, although in 1907 a "Technical Institute" was established, this was more

significant as an early development in adult education. It utilized the principal government school's premises in the evenings to provide "extension-classes" in a range of subjects including technical and teacher training.

45. Thus, it took a group of influential Chinese and Eurasian businessmen nearly fifteen years of pressure and frustration before they succeeded in gaining government support for the establishment of a trade school for poor children (eventually opened in Aberdeen in 1935), and, in this case, the onset of the Great Depression probably had more impact on persuading officials about the urgency of the need for technical education than the eloquence of the original group of supporters. Two years earlier, largely as a result of the depression-influenced report by a committee appointed in 1930 to look into the possibility of increasing facilities for practical education and on the feasibility of establishing a government trade school, the Junior Technical School (later renamed Victoria Technical School) was opened, providing a program for the pre-apprenticeship training of artisans. The need for such an institution was clearly demonstrated when, from the outset of its existence, there were eleven applicants for every single place in the school. In 1937, partly thanks to a critical "Report on Education in Hong Kong" written by the British visitor, Edmund Burney, the Government Trade School was finally established.

46. The new "workers' children's schools," which were opened shortly after the war by an alliance of leftist trade unionists with Anglicans led by the "Red Bishop" (Bishop R.O. Hall), strongly espoused practical education. The initial government support for these schools was replaced, however, by efforts to control or even close them as suspicions about their political purposes grew. See Sweeting, "Reconstruction of Education in Post-War Hong Kong," pp. 682–724.

47. The prospect of officially sponsored expansion in the field had been signaled before the war by the British Colonial Office's surveys of vocational and technical education facilities within the colonial empire and, more specifically, by the fact that in the survey of 1940, Hong Kong had for the first time been included. The famous White Paper on Colonial Welfare and Development marked a decisive policy change, most pertinently in its new sense of commitment about Britain's role in the welfare and development of the colonies. This was reinforced by the second Colonial Development and Welfare Act in 1946, with its even greater emphasis on profitable economic development.

48. Such visits included that of Sir Patrick Abercrombie, financed by C.D. & W. funds, to advise on town planning, as well as the more explicitly technical education orientated visits of F.H. Harlow (1951 and 1954) and F.H. Reid (1952). A direct, though short-lived, effort to aid Hong Kong industry by switching the whole of China's allocation of engineering scholarships to Hong Kong, under a scheme organized by the Federation of British Industries, soon experienced difficulties, even though it received some support from the Foreign Office. The offer was made in 1949, but circumscribed by conditions that made it clear that the original objective—to enhance British trade prospects with China—was still paramount. The Hong Kong government withdrew from the scheme in 1950.

49. The Catholic Order of the Salesians of Don Bosco had taken over the running of the West Point Reformatory, which had earlier been renamed the St. Louis Reformatory, in 1927. The Salesians had also been represented during the protracted negotiations over the founding of a trade school in Aberdeen and became responsible for the management of the school as soon as it opened in 1935. The Japanese authorities allowed the Salesians to reopen their schools in May 1942 partly because the priests running the schools were nationals of countries with which Japan had no quarrel, partly because of the espousal of such schools both by the priests themselves and such supporters as Aw Boon Haw, a prominent member of local councils under the Japanese, and partly because the Japanese themselves recognized the value of technical education.

50. See, for example, the Annual Report, 1950–51, p. 64.

51. See. for example, Minutes of the Board of Education, October 1950 onwards.

52. See, for example, *Wah Kiu Yat Pao*, January 10, 1949; (editorial) December 6, 1950; November 16, 1951; December 13, 1951; May 9, 1952; January 26, 1954; *Sing Tao Yat Pao*, April 23, 1951; March 15, 1954; April 1, 1954. The persistence of the plea for further attention to technical education suggests, however, less than complete satisfaction with the ongoing situation. See also the *South China Morning Post*, Tuesday, June 17, 1947, p. 1, for news of Ho Tung's donation. It is more than likely that Sir Robert consulted with senior members of the government about this gift, as he did in connection of his donation of $1 million toward the cost of a hall of residence for women at the University of Hong Kong. The Ho Tung Technical School for Girls did not open until March 1953.

53. See, for example, S.F. Bailey, *The Hong Kong Polytechnic: The First Ten Years* (Hong Kong: Hong Kong Polytechnic, 1983); D.D. Waters, "The Planning of Craft and Technician Education in Hong Kong, 1957–1982" (Ph.D. diss., Loughborough University of Technology, 1985).

54. Thus an official in the Education Department wrote, "The increase in the facilities for technical education in Hong Kong has been encouraged by, and has in turn stimulated, the expansion of local industry which has replaced the *entrepôt* trade as the mainstay of the Colony's economy" (Triennial Survey, 1958–61, Education Department, p. 36).

55. For example, in the Green Paper on the Expansion of Junior Secondary Education of 1973 and the White Paper of 1974.

56. While it cannot be claimed that a "Green" movement has assumed an overt political form in Hong Kong, the activities of the Conservancy Association (established in Hong Kong in 1968, in abeyance 1980–1986, and revived in the latter year), the World Wide Fund for Nature (Hong Kong branch founded in 1981), the Friends of the Earth (Hong Kong branch founded in 1983), and the shorter-lived but active Heritage Society (1977–1983), together with official government support in the form of such bodies as the Antiquities and Monuments Office (established in 1976), the Environmental Protection Advisory Committee (appointed in 1984, as a successor to the Advisory Committee on Environmental Pollution, first appointed in 1974), and the Environmental Protection Department (formed in 1986 out of an earlier "unit") have helped focus attention on some of the negative ecological effects of industrialization in Hong Kong. These included the various forms of pollution, together with the sacrifice of buildings of historic or aesthetic value in the interests of commercial developments aimed at fostering economic growth. Each of the organizations named, whether an interest group or a government agency, has also become a part of Hong Kong's informal educational system. As the transition to Chinese sovereignty approaches, however, it is possible that the activities of some of these groups in Hong Kong may create tension, especially when juxtaposed against certain developments within the People's Republic of China. The reason for this is not an absence of official bodies within China charged with environmental protection. Despite their existence and sincerity, however, "modernization" and development programs are not always quite so scrupulous about environmental matters as enthusiasts in Hong Kong would wish. Protests over the nuclear power station at Daya Bay, for example, might herald further dissension between Hong Kong people and Chinese authorities.

57. Saiying-pun was, and is, a largely working class area in the western part of Hong Kong island.

58. Annual Report on Education, 1896; in *Supplement to the Hong Kong Gazette*, no. 31, July 3, 1897, p. v.

59. Evidence for this is provided by the Report of the Commission on the Industrial Employment of Children, Hong Kong Government Sessional Papers, 1921, p. 123.

60. See, for example, K.C.D. Law, "A History of Adult Education in Hong Kong: An Analysis of Role, Scope and Change from 1955–1975" (Ph.D. diss., Florida State University, 1979); S. Wong, "Development of Adult Education in Hong Kong since World War II" (Ph.D. diss., Edinburgh University, 1975).

61. Probably the clearest indication of this trend was the establishment of the Open Learning Institute in 1989.

62. See Sit, Wong, and Kiang, *Small Industry*.

63. The quotation is taken from a letter by a prominent barrister, F.B.L. Bowley, which appeared in the correspondence columns of the *South China Morning Post* on July 16, 1913. An extract from the letter also appears in Sweeting, *Education in Hong Kong, pre-1841 to 1941*, p. 283.

64. See, for example, R.K. Merton, *Social Theory and Social Structure* (Glencoe, IL.: Free Press, 1957), and M. Crozier, *The Bureaucratic Phenomenon* (London: Tavistock, 1964).

65. See, for example, L.A. Bell, "School as an Organization: A Reappraisal," and W.B. Tyler, "Organizational Structure of the School," *Culture and Power in Educational Organizations*, ed. A. Westoby (Milton Keynes, England: Open University Press, 1988), pp. 3–14, 14–40.

66. For example, in comments about the improvements made by the appointment of the first inspector of schools, in the *Hong Kong Government Gazette*, 1862, pp. 106–7, and specifically critical of members of the Board of Education, in the China Mail, March 30, 1865, p. 50.

67. As a photograph in Sweeting, "Reconstruction of Education in Post-War Hong Kong," p. 160, illustrates.

68. Juxtaposed charts for the administrative structure in the years 1946–49, 1949–51, 1951–52, 1952–53, 1953–54, and 1954–55, by showing the number and the nature of changes made, clearly prove that the critical time for the bureaucratization of education in Hong Kong was at the very end of the 1940s and in the early 1950s and that the motive force was at this time political anxieties about the activities of various leftist schools. See Sweeting, "Reconstruction of Education in Post-War Hong Kong," pp. 162–67.

69. See, for example, Sweeting, "Hong Kong," pp. 289–90. It is even doubtful whether an ostensible conversion of officials to the virtues of school-based curriculum development will make much difference in practice. See P. Morris, "Bureaucracy, Professionalization, and School Centred Innovation Strategies," *International Review of Education*, 1990 (forthcoming).

70. As discussion of colonization and of transitization makes clear, "local," especially in the early years of the colony's existence, did not necessarily mean "native to the island of Hong Kong."

71. Thus, Ng Choy, a barrister trained at the Inns of Court in London, was the first Chinese member of the Legislative Assembly and also a member of the 1880–1882 Education Commission. Ho Kai, his brother-in-law, who gained qualifications in both law and medicine while in Britain, was a later member of the Legislative Council, founded the Alice Memorial Hospital, and helped to base on this the Hong Kong College of Medicine. He was also a member of the 1901–1902 Education Committee.

72. L.N.L. Ng, *Interactions of East and West: Development of Public Education in Early Hong Kong* (Hong Kong: Chinese University Press, 1984), p. 111.

73. See, for example, T.C. Cheng, "Changes in Local Vernacular Schools," *Hong Kong University Journal of Education*, January 1939, pp. 46–52; M.Y. Fong, *The First Hundred Years of Hong Kong Education* (Hong Kong: China Learning Institute, in Chinese, 1974); C.L. Wong, *A History of the Development of Chinese Education in Hong Kong* (Hong Kong: Po Wen Book Co., in Chinese, 1982).

74. "The Government has assisted in the building of the present school [the Chung

Wah Shu Yuen] by means of a grant-in-aid and will always be ready to cooperate with the Chinese community in education work, but I am confident that the best result will be obtained if the matter is left as largely as possible in the hands of the Chinese community and their worthy representatives" (Sir Reginald Stubbs, governor of Hong Kong, quoted in the *South China Morning Post*, December 2, 1920, p. 3). "Representatives," here, cannot be treated literally, in its democratic sense, since no formal mechanism for representation existed at the time. Presence on the committees of certain voluntary associations (e.g., the District Watch Committee and the executive committees of the Tung Wah Hospital Group, the Po Leung Kuk, and the Confucian Society) tended, however, to be taken as evidence of leadership caliber. Such presence was usually the result of self- (or, at best, a type of consensual) election.

75. For example, Mr. Young Hee was headmaster of the government Wanchai District School in the early 1900s; Mr. Sung Hok-P'ang was appointed headmaster of Belilios Public School in 1905 and later, in 1913, became inspector of schools for the New Territories; Dr. Catherine F.C. Woo became principal of the St. Paul's Girls' (later Coeducational) College in 1916, stayed in charge until after the end of World War II, and was succeeded in 1952 by Dr. Bobbie Kotewall.

76. Colonial Command Papers 197 (The Organization of the Colonial Service) and 198 (Post-War Training for the Colonial Service), H.M.S.O., 1946.

77. See I. Scott and J.P. Burns, *The Hong Kong Civil Service: Personnel Policies and Practices* (Hong Kong: Oxford University Press, 1984), pp. 29–32.

78. The Chinese University, like the Evening School for Chinese Studies and the Keswick proposal of degree courses through Chinese at Hong Kong University, was initially designed to cater to school-leavers from local Chinese middle schools. Many of these found that the traditional practice of seeking higher education opportunities in China no longer seemed so attractive. The change in attitude was affected by the Communist victory in the Chinese civil war, the establishment of the People's Republic of China, and the beginning of its "Soviet phase" of development, the Korean War, and the continuation of the Cold War. In these circumstances, the Hong Kong government was particularly concerned to offer alternatives to these students.

79. For further details of the Chinese Language Movement, see, for example, N. J. Miners, *The Government and Politics of Hong Kong* (Hong Kong: Oxford University Press, 1975). As Miners points out, the Chinese Language Movement was an example of the type of pressure group that disbands as soon as it recognizes that it has achieved its objective (in this case, in 1974).

80. *The Report on Higher Education* (Hong Kong: Government Printer, 1952), p. 6.

81. Education Department Annual Report, 1986–7, pp. 46–47.

82. R.K. Johnson, "Bi-lingual Switching Strategies: A Study of the Modes of Teacher-Talk in Bilingual Secondary School Classrooms in Hong Kong," *Language Learning and Communication* 2, 3, pp. 267–85, 1983.

83. Results of the original intervention study appear in M.A. Brimer, ed., "The Effects of the Medium of Instruction on the Achievement of Form 2 Students in Hong Kong Secondary Schools," mimeo, 1985. An oblique reference is made to this research and a recommendation formulated which calls for secondary schooling through the medium of English to be confined to a minority in the Report of the [Education Department's] Working Group Set Up to Review Language Improvement Measures (Hong Kong: Government Printer, December 1989), pp. 23, 31, 74.

84. See, for example, the P.T.U. *News,* June 27, 1987; April 23, 1988; September 3, 1988; *Wah Kiu Yat Pao,* June 7, 1987.

85. See S.K. Lau, *Society and Politics in Hong Kong* (Hong Kong: Chinese University of Hong Kong Press, 1982), pp. 157–82.

86. These included the reform movement associated with the name of Kang Yu Wei and the revolutionary movement associated with Sun Yat-sen, the Chinese Revolution of 1911, the "War Lord" period, the "Encirclement Campaign" of Chiang Kai-shek, the Sino-Japanese War, the Chinese civil war, the establishment of the People's Republic of China, the "Great Leap Forward," and the Cultural Revolution.

87. One should also note that another aspect of transitization has been the readiness of Hong Kong people to leave Hong Kong when conditions there were unbearable (e.g., during the outbreaks of the plague in the 1890s and early 1900s, during the 1925–26 strike and boycott, and during the Japanese occupation of Hong Kong).

88. See S.K. Lau and H.C. Kuan, *The Ethos of the Hong Kong Chinese* (Hong Kong: Chinese University of Hong Kong Press, 1988), pp. 178–87.

89. Irving, E.A., "Hong Kong," in *Special Reports on Educational Subjects, vol. 14: Educational Systems of the Chief Crown Colonies and Possessions of the British Empire, Including Reports on the Training of Native Races* (London: Board of Education, 1905), p. 80.

90. Education Department, Annual Report for 1946–1947, p. 20.

91. See Lau, *Society and Politics*, p. 13.

92. The role of the late-nineteenth-century study groups in the strengthening of the reform and especially the revolutionary movement in and for China has already been noted. In the twentieth century, students (and other Hong Kong Chinese) were actively involved in the very political general strike and boycott of 1925–26, in the Kowloon City riots of the early 1950s, in the riots of 1966 and 1967, and, of course, in the late 1960s and 1970s in the Students' Movement, through which they gained representation on all the major councils of the tertiary institutions of Hong Kong. They also took a very active role in the demonstrations that greeted news of the events in Beijing in the early hours of June 4, 1989.

93. See S.Y.S. Tsang, *Democracy Shelved: Great Britain, China, and Attempts at Constitutional Reform in Hong Kong, 1945–1952* (Hong Kong: Oxford University Press, 1988).

3

Hong Kong Education in an International Context: The Impact of External Forces

Mark Bray

Introduction

An extensive literature focuses on the international flow of educational ideas. Some authors are critical and assert that education has been a tool for cultural imperialism,[1] while others focus on beneficial sides of educational innovation.[2] Most work examines flows from more developed to less developed countries, though some authors have pointed out that the reverse process can also take place.[3]

The education system of Hong Kong has of course been strongly influenced by the cultural traditions of China. However, the advent of colonization markedly changed the principal source of ideas for educational innovation. Now the colonial period is drawing to a close; but the patterns introduced under colonial rule will not be abandoned altogether.

To help analyze the nature and impact of the sources of educational innovation, this chapter commences with a historical perspective. The chapter then turns to contemporary patterns to show that although the sources of innovation remain principally Western, they are at least more diverse than before. The third section comments on probable future patterns, the most obvious of which concerns the increasing contact between Hong Kong and mainland China. The final section concludes by connecting the Hong Kong case to the broader literature on international linkages and educational development.

1. Historical Perspectives

When Hong Kong was ceded to Great Britain in 1842, it had a population of only 5,000. A few village schools existed, but their enrollment was small and, like other village schools in imperial China, the institutions imparted few skills beyond rudimentary literacy.[4]

The educational picture, like other social and economic patterns, changed abruptly with the cession. Even before the territory had been formally proclaimed a British colony, the protestant Morrison Education Society had decided to move its school from Macau to Hong Kong. The society was granted a plot of land, and opened Hong Kong's first Western-type school in 1843. In the same year the London Missionary Society established an Anglo-Chinese College with an attached preparatory school for training ministers, Roman Catholic missionaries opened a seminary, and the Anglican Church commenced plans for a similar institution. Within a few years many additional schools had been opened by these and other mission bodies.

The missionaries, of course, imported educational philosophies, curricula, and teaching methods from their countries of origin. British traditions dominated, for they shaped the views not only of several major missionary bodies but also of the government. However, Britain was not the only source of educational ideas. The Morrison Education Society school had been pioneered by an American, Dr. E.C. Bridgman; another early school was founded by the American Board of Foreign Missions; the Roman Catholic schools included institutions run by the Italian Daughters of Charity and the French Sisters of Charity; and in 1857 a German missionary, the Reverend W. Lobschied, was appointed inspector of schools.[5]

Further, although the Western model of education rapidly became dominant, it did not totally exclude Chinese traditions. The government, partly motivated by a desire to avoid the sectarian strife which was then a serious problem in England, from an early date provided grants to the local village schools. In 1847 the authorities established an Education Committee, which was instructed "not to interfere with the traditional Chinese curriculum and method except to introduce some Christian teaching on a voluntary basis."[6] The committee did not altogether follow this brief, for it immediately replaced non-Christian village teachers by ones whose outlook and methods the committee considered more trustworthy. Nevertheless, government respect for elements of the indigenous system was reflected in its Central School curriculum, which maintained the Chinese classics as a key component.

It is also worth noting that despite the rise of Western education, Chinese private schools also flourished. Endacott reports that those who could afford it preferred the traditional Chinese institutions which suffered less government interference and Western influence.[7] Interestingly, the chief objection was not so much the teaching of Christianity as the organization of schools into classes. The traditional system was very flexible, and teachers were generally available from 6:00 A.M. to 4:00 P.M. to receive pupils as they arrived.

At the same time, of course, many people were influenced by economic considerations. Thus, one of the key attractions of the Central School was that its English curriculum improved the pupils' career prospects.[8] In this respect Hong Kong differed little from other colonies.[9] Such motivation may have exasperated the more idealistic teachers, but the authorities were quite ready to exploit it. Moreover, the fact that the English language was inseparable from certain cultural values was at times readily recognized and welcomed. One obvious case arose in 1894 when Hong Kong was beset by a plague spread by unsanitary living habits. Governor Sir William Robinson responded by promoting anglicized schooling, with the aim "to elevate the Chinese people of this colony by means of English rather than Chinese teaching."[10]

It should also be noted that missionaries were not the only external individuals with wide-ranging international backgrounds. Although the majority of government officers were British, many had served in other territories and cultures. To choose just one example, Sir Frederick Lugard, governor from 1907 to 1912, had previously served in Afghanistan, India, Burma, Nyasaland, Kenya, Uganda, and Nigeria.[11]

One of Lugard's most enduring legacies was the University of Hong Kong, the justification for which went beyond the needs of the local community. Particular emphasis was placed on its importance to the development of China; consequently special efforts were made to attract students.[12] It was argued that Chinese parents in Hong Kong or on the mainland could educate their sons at the university at a fraction of the cost of sending them to Europe, and that the institution would have special advantages as "a British university on Chinese soil." Lugard's original intention got lost in subsequent decades, though there is now a possibility of returning to the spirit of this early goal.

2. Contemporary Patterns

More detailed examination of historical patterns is available elsewhere in Sweeting's chapter in this book, and it is best to turn here to more recent times. This section focuses on the background of key decision makers, the influence of external advisers, the nature of tertiary education, and the impact of overseas studies.

The Background of Key Decision Makers

In recent years the government has pursued a deliberate localization policy, and the Education Department has had a local director since 1984. However, the higher tiers of government have remained dominated by expatriates. The post of secretary for education and manpower was not localized until 1989, and the secretary still had a British deputy and two principal assistant secretaries. Above them were the British chief secretary, and the British governor. The Executive Council does have a notable proportion of Chinese members (57 percent in January 1989), and the Legislative Council even more (81 percent in January 1989). However, the proportion of expatriates at senior levels remains striking.

Moreover, although the above figures crudely classify individuals as either expatriate or local, the latter category requires closer scrutiny. The fact that individuals are racially Chinese does not necessarily imply that their personal values are markedly different from those of their expatriate colleagues. Many senior officers were educated in Western countries, and some even hold foreign passports.

This situation has important implications for the nature of decision making. The high proportion of expatriates and of Chinese with strong external links increases the decision makers' awareness of patterns in other countries. As noted by Thomas and Postlethwaite's international study,[13] this is a crucial ingredient for educational innovation. Nevertheless, in the Hong Kong context the background of the decision makers remains heavily biased, and the dominance of the West is all-pervasive. The countries of Europe, North America, and Australia are held up as role models, while the countries of the Soviet bloc, Africa, Latin America, and even most parts of Asia (with the possible exceptions of Singapore and Japan) are ignored.

Some specific examples may indicate the impact of these biases. In the curriculum sphere, the junior secondary syllabus for integrated science was based on the Scottish Integrated Science Scheme, while the social studies curriculum was influenced by a Canadian project.[14] Similarly, the structure and functions of the University and Polytechnic Grants Committee (UPGC) were based on those of the University Grants Committee (UGC) in the United Kingdom;[15] and the structure and functions of the Hong Kong Council for Academic Accreditation (HKCAA) were based on those of the Council for National Academic Awards (CNAA) in the United Kingdom.[16] Even the decision to introduce nine years' free and compulsory education was strongly influenced by prevailing patterns in Western countries. According to Cheng,[17] the decision:

> was not unrelated to conditions attached to the securing of trading rights with the European competitors. Apparently, nine-year free and compulsory education was introduced at the moment when the labour age of fourteen had put Hong Kong's international credibility at stake.

The Influence of External Advisers

The Hong Kong education system has also been heavily influenced by Western external advisers. In the sphere of manpower planning, for instance, critical inputs during the late 1970s and early 1980s were made by Professor Peter

Williams, then of the University of London.[18] Similarly, in the mid-1980s much advice to the newly emerging HKCAA was presented by Dr. S.A. Reid, former Registrar for Technology at the UK CNAA.[19] And when the University of Hong Kong established its new Department of Speech and Hearing Sciences, it invited a team from the United Kingdom to advise on courses and staffing.[20] These are just a few specific examples; many more could be given.

It is also particularly worth noting the impact of a team of advisers recruited through the Organisation for Economic Cooperation & Development (OECD) in 1981. The team was headed by Sir John Llewellyn, and in 1982 produced a document now known as the Llewellyn Report. Llewellyn himself was British, while the other team members were Australian (Dr. Greg Hancock), American (Professor Michael Kirst), and German (Dr. Karl Roeloffs). The Llewellyn Report was very influential. Among its foci were the language of instruction, access to tertiary education, special education, and the needs of the teaching service.

In one respect, however, the Llewellyn Report reduced the need for future external reviewers. It recommended that an Education Commission should be established "to bring to the Governor-in-Council consolidated advice on the needs of and priorities for the educational system as a whole and the most equitable and practicable responses to them."[21] This recommendation was implemented, and since the commission's establishment in 1984 it has produced a series of far-reaching reports.[22] Again, a high proportion of members are expatriate (35 percent in 1988), and all members have strong Western links through their own education and other affairs. However all members of the commission are resident and working in Hong Kong, and the creation of the commission has markedly altered the local advisory and decision-making system.

The Nature of Tertiary Education

Hong Kong's tertiary institutions like to think of themselves as having "international" standing. This concept is vague, but reflects strong Western biases. For example, the institutions very rarely compare themselves with ones in South Asia, Africa, or Latin America. Rather, the role model is set by North America, Europe, Australia, and New Zealand.

The existence of the University and Polytechnic Grants Committee (UPGC) has already been noted. This body is currently responsible for funding six institutions: the three universities, the two polytechnics, and the Baptist College. The body itself has a strong cultural bias, with 61 percent of its members being Westerners (August 1989). In contrast to the Education Commission, many of these Westerners were not even resident in Hong Kong. They included the director of Leicester Polytechnic (UK), a professor of English literature at the University of Leeds (UK), a professor of economics from the University of London (UK), the vice-chancellor of the University of Leeds (UK), the director of the Royal Melbourne Institute of Technology (Australia), a professor from Harvard

Table 3.1

Place of Permanent Home of Senior Staff on Terms of Service I at the University of Hong Kong

	1987–88		1988–89		1989–90	
	Number	Percent	Number	Percent	Number	Percent
Hong Kong	515	55.7	537	55.5	536	55.9
Macau	0	0.0	0	0.0	0	0.0
China	0	0.0	0	0.0	1	0.1
Taiwan	2	0.2	3	0.3	1	0.1
Elsewhere in Asia	34	3.7	35	3.6	39	4.1
United Kingdom	208	22.5	216	22.3	211	22.0
Other Parts of Europe	15	1.6	16	1.7	20	2.1
United States	48	5.2	54	5.6	48	5.0
Canada	32	3.5	33	3.4	34	3.6
Australia	43	4.7	46	4.8	52	5.4
New Zealand	13	1.4	13	1.3	12	1.3
Africa	4	0.4	4	0.4	3	0.3
Other	10	1.1	11	1.1	1	0.1
Total	924	100.0	968	100.0	958	100.0

Source: Computer files, University of Hong Kong.

Note: This table refers to staff on "Terms of Service I." Most are teaching staff, but some administrative officers are also included.

University (USA), a professor from the University of Cambridge (UK), and a former president of the New South Wales Institute of Technology (Australia).

The staffing of individual institutions is also heavily Westernized. Most obvious is the University of Hong Kong, which teaches in English and prides itself on the fact that its staff are internationally recruited. As Table 3.1 indicates, in practice international recruitment means a high proportion from the United Kingdom, with most of the remainder from other Western countries. International advertising of vacant posts is usually confined to the United Kingdom, the United States, Canada, and Australia.

The situation at the Chinese University of Hong Kong (CUHK) is different because it conducts most of its teaching in Chinese and therefore should not be expected to have so many expatriates. However, even the local staff are also Westernized in their background, and high proportions have degrees from Western universities. A similar picture may be found at the two polytechnics, the Baptist College, and the Hong Kong University of Science and Technology (HKUST). With regard to the latter, the vice-chancellor/president, Professor

Table 3.2

Place of Permanent Home of Students at the University of Hong Kong

	1987–88		1988–89		1989–90		1990–91	
	Number	%	Number	%	Number	%	Number	%
Hong Kong	8,744	98.0	8,998	97.4	9,000	97.2	9,171	96.0
Macau	5	0.1	10	0.1	7	0.1	8	0.1
China	48	0.5	78	0.8	84	1.0	112	1.2
Taiwan	1	0.0	1	0.0	2	0.0	1	0.0
Elsewhere in Asia	42	0.5	41	0.4	48	0.5	79	0.8
United Kingdom	27	0.3	24	0.3	26	0.3	33	0.3
Other Parts of Europe	6	0.1	4	0.0	10	0.1	12	0.1
United States	22	0.2	24	0.3	33	0.4	32	0.3
Canada	13	0.1	12	0.1	21	0.2	17	0.2
Australia	7	0.1	9	0.1	12	0.1	15	0.2
New Zealand	3	0.0	5	0.1	2	0.0	4	0.0
Africa	4	0.0	5	0.1	6	0.1	3	0.0
Other	3	0.0	3	0.0	1	0.0	17	0.2
Not Given	0	0.0	25	0.3	4	0.0	7	0.1
Total	8,925	99.9	9,239	100.0	9,256	100.0	9,511	99.5

Source: Computer files, University of Hong Kong.

Woo Chia-Wei, was born in Shanghai and schooled in Hong Kong, but lived and worked in the United States from 1955 to 1988—most recently as president of San Francisco State University. HKUST is making a strong effort to promote a Westernized image, and boasts a number of well-known Western academics on its council and staff. In his February 1989 newsletter, Professor Woo indicated that in order to recruit staff for the university he had "visited more than a dozen leading universities in U.S. and U.K. seeking recommendations from senior colleagues."

It may be added that when the tertiary institutions in Hong Kong aspire to be "international," they only mean international in staffing. They do not mean international in their student body, and the overwhelming majority of our students are local. This may again be demonstrated by figures from the University of Hong Kong (Table 3.2). Only 4 percent of students came from outside Hong Kong, although this figure has doubled since 1987–88, largely due to an increase in the numbers of students from the People's Republic of China. Since the other institutions use Chinese for much of their teaching, it is likely that their proportions of overseas students were even smaller.

In this connection, it is worth recalling Lugard's original aspiration that the University of Hong Kong should serve the needs of China as much as of Hong Kong, with the result that in the early years special efforts were made to recruit students from the mainland. Students also came from other parts of the region, and in 1950 still almost half the students at the University of Hong Kong came from Malaysia and Singapore.[23] In recent decades, however, the pressure of local needs has been so great that students from other countries have been excluded. The question is whether the picture will again resemble the earlier pattern. With the reintegration of Hong Kong with China, one might again predict increasing recruitment from the mainland.

Impact of Overseas Studies

The extent of local pressure on tertiary education is clearly reflected in the large numbers of Hong Kong students who study abroad. Hong Kong has been estimated to have even more tertiary students abroad than at home. Postiglione reported figures of 12,000 students in the United States, 10,000 in Canada, 4,000 in the United Kingdom, 3,000 in China, and 5,000 in Taiwan, West Germany, France and other places.[24] The total of 34,000 far exceeded the 19,000 enrolled full-time in Hong Kong's five UPGC-funded tertiary institutions. The figure for the United States was particularly startling. For every 500 persons in Hong Kong, one was enrolled at an American university. Reports in 1990 showed a further increase in the number of students studying in Canada and Australia.[25] Many people consider this situation problematic, for overseas courses are perceived as costly and sometimes of only peripheral relevance. However, the situation also has a positive side, for experience of life in other cultures has helped to make Hong Kong a more open society.

Students' choice of destination is partly determined by linguistic factors, since for obvious reasons potential students prefer to go to countries that use either English or Chinese. The chief reason why English-speaking countries receive so many more students than Chinese-speaking ones is that the Hong Kong government refuses to recognize degrees from the latter. Graduates from universities in China are reported to have difficulties in finding employment on their return to Hong Kong, and the majority work for China-affiliated organizations such as the Bank of China and Guangdong Enterprises.[26]

The number of Hong Kong people studying in China grew dramatically in the late 1980s. Jinan and Hua Qiao universities have been the two main destinations. In early 1989, eleven Chinese tertiary institutions launched a new initiative to attract Hong Kong students,[27] though Hong Kong interest in mainland institutions was subsequently reported to have dipped following the incidents in Beijing of June 4, 1989.[28]

3. The Future

The most obvious change on the future horizon concerns Hong Kong's reintegration with China. Morris's chapter in this book analyses the impact that this is having on secondary history, economic and public affairs, and government and public affairs syllabuses, and Kwo's chapter highlights the growing importance of Putonghua in the Hong Kong education system.

The dramatic plans for expansion of local tertiary education announced in the governor's 1989 opening speech of the Legislative Council[29] will reduce the need for Hong Kong citizens to go abroad for tertiary education, and in this respect will perhaps make the Hong Kong people more inward looking. However, it seems unlikely that the flow of students abroad will cease altogether. Many families still place great value on an overseas education, and political forces still are likely to make overseas links attractive.

Meanwhile, at the official level, an increasing number of delegations are traveling between Hong Kong and China, and Hong Kong's universities have special funds to promote contacts with the mainland. The refusal of the Hong Kong government to recognize mainland degrees surely will not be long lasting, and when the policy change does come it will encourage more students to study in the mainland. At the same time, it is likely that Hong Kong's tertiary institutions will take increasing numbers of students from the mainland. Current numbers are still small, but they have already shown dramatic growth during the last few years.

However, the Hong Kong government is very anxious to retain English as a key element in its education system, and is equally keen that its universities should remain institutions of "international" standing. Knowledge of the English language will continue to give Hong Kong people broad access to a wide range of cultures. The most obvious implications will be that Hong Kong will remain within the sphere of Western capitalist values, though of course the society will also have stronger sympathy for the socialist policies espoused by the mainland. If, as seems possible, China simultaneously makes a rapprochement with the Soviet Union, Hong Kong may find itself with increasing contact with that society too.

4. Conclusions

Finally, it is appropriate to return to the literature on dependency, cultural imperialism, and innovation with which this chapter commenced. While this chapter cannot explore all the implications of Hong Kong's evolving history, it is at least possible to make some broad observations.

First, it is clear that Hong Kong fits the general patterns identified by Kelly and Altbach, who observed that "in the colonial situation the school was detached from indigenous cultures in the languages and in the social values they taught. Colonial schools were set up as alternatives rather than as complements to the colonized's educational practices."[30]

Although in the early years of colonial government, the authorities did provide grants to the village schools and did include the Chinese classics in the curriculum of their own schools, the Western models rapidly proved dominant. The Western-type schools also supported the incorporation of Hong Kong into the global capitalist system and helped establish a dependency relationship.

However, although at first sight it appears that the colonization of Hong Kong separated the society from the rest of China and caused it to take a different educational path, it must also be recognized that China itself followed a similar path. Missionaries had been active in China since the sixteenth century, and although they were expelled in 1724, the door was reopened in 1844. Twelve years later the missionaries were conceded the right to work not only in the five main Chinese ports but also in the hinterland.[31] Through the missionary endeavors, Western-type schools became as firmly established in China as in Hong Kong, and the traditional schools in which the teachers merely made themselves available to pupils rather than organizing the pupils into classes gradually disappeared.

An article by Bastid entitled "Servitude or Liberation?"[32] summarizes alternative views on Chinese contact with Western education. The Hong Kong experience might perhaps be similarly entitled. However, recent years seem to have tilted the balance in a positive direction. Although at first Hong Kong was incorporated into the global capitalist system in a totally subordinate way, recent times have demonstrated the potential advantages of being part of the system. While China cut itself off from the rest of the world during the Cultural Revolution, Hong Kong remained part of the international framework. This permitted Hong Kong to prosper to such an extent that the economy has eclipsed some of those to which it was formerly subordinate. Many would contend that the school system that supported this incorporation with international capitalism was and is excessively Western; but it is arguable that this bias has paid handsome dividends.

Looking toward the future, it is obvious that Hong Kong will have increasing contact with China. On the one hand Hong Kong will probably have much to teach China, e.g., about curriculum development, teacher support, educational technology, and administrative efficiency. But on the other hand, Hong Kong can also learn from China. Two obvious spheres are in the teaching of Putonghua and in the promotion through the school system of a feeling of national identity.

Notes

1. See, e.g., M. Carnoy, *Education as Cultural Imperialism* (New York: David McKay, 1974); G.P. Kelly, "Colonial Schools in Vietnam: Policy and Practice," in *Education and Colonialism*, ed. P.G. Altbach and G.P. Kelly (New York: Longman, 1978); E.H. Berman, "Foundations, United States Foreign Policy and African Education," *Harvard*

Educational Review, vol. 49, no. 2 (1979); B. Avalos, "Neocolonialism and Education in Latin America," in *Education in the Third World*, ed. J.K.P. Watson (London: Croom Helm, 1982); Y.G.M. Lulat, "Education and National Development: The Continuing Problem of Misdiagnosis and Irrelevant Prescriptions," *International Journal of Educational Development*, vol. 8, no. 4 (1988); M. Bray, "Asian Systems of Education: Their Foundations and Cultural Biases," *Perspectives in Education*, vol. 5, no. 4 (1989).

2. See, e.g., M. Kaunda, "Post-Secondary Education by Correspondence: An African Experience," in *Correspondence Education in Africa*, ed. A. Kabwasa and M. Kaunda (London: Routledge & Kegan Paul, 1973); C. Sanger, *Project Impact* (Ottawa: International Development Research Centre, 1977); J. Zhuang and R.M. Thomas, "Educational Radio and Television: Their Development in Advanced Industrial Societies," in *Educational Technology: Its Creation, Development and Cross-Cultural Transfer*, ed. R.M Thomas and V.N. Kobayashi (Oxford: Pergamon, 1987).

3. See, e.g., S. Narullah and J.P. Naik, *A History of Education in India* (Bombay: Macmillan, 1951); A. Little, *Learning from Developing Countries: An Inaugural Lecture* (London: Department of International & Comparative Education, University of London Institute of Education, 1988).

4. N.H. Ng Lun, *Interactions of East and West: Development of Public Education in Early Hong Kong* (Hong Kong: Chinese University Press, 1984), p. 23. Sweeting (1990) presents a very illuminating account of pre-colonial education and notes that the Li-ying College and Chou-Wang-Erh Kung College had quite venerable histories. However, these colleges were in the New Territories rather than Hong Kong Island. See Anthony Sweeting, *Education in Hong Kong, pre-1841 to 1941: Fact and Opinion* (Hong Kong: Kong University Press, 1990), p. 88.

5. G.B. Endacott, *A History of Hong Kong* (Hong Kong: Oxford University Press, 1987), pp. 132–43; Sweeting, *Education in Hong Kong*, Chapter 3.

6. Endacott, *A History of Hong Kong*, p. 136.

7. Ibid., p. 141.

8. N.H. Ng Lun, *Interactions East and West*, p. 64.

9. See, e.g., Narullah and Naik, *A History of Education in India*; and P. Gifford and T. Weiskel, "African Education in a Colonial Context: French and British Styles," in *France and Britain in Africa*, ed. P. Gifford and W.R. Louis (New Haven: Yale University Press, 1971).

10. Endacott, *A History of Hong Kong*, p. 241.

11. M. Perham, *Lugard: The Years of Adventure 1858–1898* (London: Collins, 1956), p. 715.

12. B. Mellor, *The University of Hong Kong: An Informal History* (Hong Kong: Hong Kong University Press, 1980), vol. 1, p. 37; N.H. Ng Lun, *Interactions East and West*, p. 126.

13. R.M. Thomas and T.N. Postlethwaite, eds., *Schooling in East Asia: Forces of Change* (Oxford: Pergamon, 1983).

14. See Morris's chapter in this book. Also, P. Morris, "The Effect on the School Curriculum of Hong Kong's Return to Chinese Sovereignty in 1997," *Journal of Curriculum Studies* vol. 20, no. 6 (1988), pp. 511–12.

15. Government of Hong Kong, *Hong Kong 1989* (Hong Kong: Government Printer, 1989), p. 114.

16. Ibid., p. 131.

17. K.M. Cheng, "Traditional Values and Western Ideas: Hong Kong's Dilemmas in Education," *Asian Journal of Public Administration*, vol. 8, no. 2 (1986), p. 199.

18. K.M. Cheng, "The Concept of Legitimacy in Educational Policy-Making: Alternative Explanations of Two Policy Episodes in Hong Kong" (Ph.D. diss., University of London Institute of Education, 1987), pp. 186, 195.

19. S.A. Reid, "Validation: Setting the Scene," paper presented at the conference of the Hong Kong Educational Research Association, 1987.

20. University of Hong Kong, internal documents on the establishment of the Department of Speech & Hearing Sciences, 1988.

21. Sir J. Llewellyn (Chairman), *A Perspective on Education in Hong Kong: Report by a Visiting Panel* (Hong Kong: Government Printer, 1982), p. 22.

22. Education Commission, *Education Commission Report No. 1* (Hong Kong: Government Printer, 1984); *Education Commission Report No. 2* (Hong Kong: Government Printer, 1986); *Education Commission Report No. 3* (Hong Kong: Government Printer, 1988); *Education Commission Report No. 4* (Hong Kong: Government Printer, 1990).

23. B. Mellor, *The University of East Asia: Origin and Outlook* (Hong Kong: UEA Press, 1988), p. 69.

24. G. Postiglione, "International Higher Education and the Labor Market in Hong Kong: Functions of Overseas and Local Higher Education," *International Education*, vol. 17, no. 1 (1987), p. 51.

25. V. Lee, "Confidence Crisis Boosts Student Exodus," *South China Morning Post*, February 5, 1990. There were said to be 14,000 Hong Kong students in Canada, comprising the largest group of foreign students in the country. The number of new students in 1989 represented a 34 percent increase over 1988. Australia also received a sharp increase in numbers, of 48.6 percent to 4,678. Some 4,855 student visas were issued for the United States, a 15 percent increase over 1988; and the United Kingdom took 4,539 Hong Kong students in 1989 compared to 3,856 in 1988.

26. S. Leung and K.Y. Chiu, "China Graduates Face Tough Times in HK," *South China Morning Post*, August 8, 1986.

27. *South China Morning Post*, March 6, 1989.

28. J. Leung, "Students Shy from Mainland Institutes," *South China Morning Post*, February 13, 1990.

29. *South China Morning Post*, October 12, 1989.

30. G.P. Kelly and P. G. Altbach, "Introduction," in Kelly and Altbach, *Education and Colonialism*, p. 3.

31. John Cleverley, *The Schooling of China* (Sydney: George Allen & Unwin, 1985), p. 30.

32. M. Bastid, "Servitude or Liberation? The Introduction of Foreign Educational Practices and Systems to China from 1840 to the Present," in *China's Education and the Industrialized World: Studies in Cultural Transfer*, ed. R. Hayhoe and M. Bastid (Armonk: M.E. Sharpe, 1987).

Part II
Education and Politics

4

Educational Policymaking in Hong Kong: The Changing Legitimacy

Cheng Kai Ming

Introduction

Hong Kong's education has seen remarkable expansion and change in the past two decades. This has been accompanied by numerous policy discussions, mostly provoked by government documents, with the active participation of a wide range of educators. This chapter looks at how and why this occurs in a colony where the polity is still in theory an autocracy. Evidence seems to support the assertion that policymaking in education presents a typical case of how the Hong Kong government has established its own model of legitimacy which sought to compensate for its colonial status. Such a model, however, is at stake as the government has entered the transitional stage, when long-term legitimacy is no longer its concern.

The Notion of Legitimacy

The term legitimacy has been used fairly broadly in the literature of policy studies. Lipset defines the term: "Legitimacy involves the capacity of the system to engender and maintain the belief that the existing political institutions are the most appropriate ones for the society."[1]

This is in line with the Webster International Dictionary's definition, which extends the meaning of the word from legality to customs and beliefs:

> (a) the possession of title or status as a result of acquisition by means that are or are held to be according to *law* and *custom*. (b) a conformity to *recognized* principles or *accepted* rules or standards [emphasis added].

In the tradition of Weber, legitimacy has been defined as "the degree to which institutions are valued for themselves and considered right and proper."[2] Other writers define *political legitimacy* as "the quality of 'oughtness' that is perceived by the public to inhere in a political regime. That government is legitimate which is viewed as morally proper for a society."[3] Legitimacy is therefore a matter of "credibility and acceptability on the part of the modern State in its relationship to its society and its citizens."[4] Meanwhile, Dahl[5] sees that "the acquisition of legitimacy" becomes a basic task of the political leader. In the most recent edition of his famous book *Modern Political Analysis* he writes:

> Leaders in a political system try to ensure that whenever governmental means are used to deal with conflict, the decisions arrived at are widely accepted not solely from fear of violence, punishment, or coercion but also from a belief that it is morally right and proper to do so.[6]

In sum, *legitimacy* in politics is a sort of second-order objective people accept to justify the authority of the government. In this sense, a government is regarded as legitimate not necessarily because it *produces* anything "good," but more because the people *believe* that it is *doing* things in the "right" way.

From Weber to Offe to Habermas, the term *legitimacy* is used in the context of a state theory. Weber[7] talks about a normative model of *rational–legal legitimacy* as salvation to the modern state; Offe[8] refers to *legitimation problems* arising from the state's inefficiency due to its basic contradictions; while Habermas's *legitimation crisis*[9] is based on deep-rooted economic and political crises of the late-capitalist state. The theories, different as they are, concurrently identify legitimacy as an indispensable element for the state to maintain its authority. There seems to be a consensus that *legitimacy* is in the realm of value and belief, which are not always visible on the surface of the formal political structure and economic systems.

Legitimacy and the Hong Kong Government

The notion of legitimacy is particularly significant for the government of Hong Kong. Hong Kong is a British colony and "[the] Governor is the symbolic representative of the Queen's sovereignty over Hong Kong and exercises by delegation the powers of the royal prerogative."[10]

In the context that Hong Kong is a Chinese community, the appointment of the governor by the Queen of Britain contributes to a built-in legitimacy crisis in the Hong Kong polity.

As a rather developed capitalist society, there should be no doubt that Offe's contradiction of accumulation and distribution exists. However, if legitimacy is regarded as a kind of belief, climate of opinion, or culture, Offe's contradiction is not the main contributor to a *legitimation crisis* in Hong Kong. Hong Kong has achieved a very rapid economic growth in the past decades. To the amazement of many, distribution of wealth is still not so much a concern in the community. This is partly because of the expansion of social welfare and partly because of the devotion for efficiency at the expense of equity. But above all, this lack of concern about distribution of wealth is also attributable to the contrasting economic and social failures exhibited next door by mainland China during the Cultural Revolution. Hong Kong is thus said to enjoy "prosperity and stability" and the citizens seem to accept the status quo. There is little visible legitimacy problem in this respect. It could even be argued that the Hong Kong government has gained considerable "legitimacy surplus," because it is seen as "efficient" in Offe's terms.[11]

However, a legitimacy problem does arise because of the nondemocratic polity. It was only in 1982 that elected district boards were established, and 1985 saw the first elected members in the Legislative Council. Even then, decision making in major policies occured only in the Executive Council, whose members were entirely appointed by the governor and whose meetings were confidential. This nondemocracy has been identified, particularly by the intellectuals who are increasingly influenced by Western ideas, as a symbol of colonialism. Citizens in general still regard the situation as a case of "Chinese ruled by the British."

Therefore, the Hong Kong government is basically in a state of *legitimacy deficit* because it does not possess the necessary legitimacy which would otherwise come forth through election. This may easily develop into a legitimacy crisis if the government is not able to overcome the deficit. In this context, the government is prompted to be extremely careful to secure popular support in each and every step of policymaking. The situation is very different from the case in a Western democracy where the administration is extremely keen to solicit support before elections but can afford to put aside general opinions between elections.

Hence, in brief, the Hong Kong government gains its legitimacy partly because of its achievements in the economy, partly because it has been deliberate in creating citizen credibility in policymaking. The latter is done through two main approaches: the employment of expertise and consultation.

Expertise and Participation in Policymaking

Lindblom bases his conception of policymaking on the dichotomy of *efficacy versus popular control* which he sees as "the two overriding questions asked about governmental policymaking:"

> In short, a deep conflict runs through common attitudes toward policy making. On the one hand, people want policy to be informed and well analysed. On the other hand, they want policy making to be democratic, hence necessarily polit-

ical. In slightly different words, on the one hand they want policy making to be more scientific. On the other, they want it to remain in the world of politics.[12]

In other words, we may say that *expertise* and *participation* are two sides of the dichotomy. While *expertise* pertains to facts and impartiality, *participation* is related to values and interests.[13] Both are indispensable elements in policymaking.

Expertise

Expertise is taken to mean the "technical," "objective," and "scientific" methods and techniques used in policymaking. That expertise is indispensable is readily evidenced by the fact that

> Public officials, journalists, interest-group leaders and interested citizens often join in informed discussion. . . .
> [S]pecialized professional fact-finding, research, and policy analyses flourish as routine inputs into policymaking. A policymaker will ordinarily feel naked without help from both informed discussion and specialized professional studies.[14]

Expertise involves means and techniques that bring "information, thought, and analysis into the policymaking process." Lindblom labels these the "intellectual components of policymaking."[15]

That expertise becomes indispensable has a number of causes. First, modern technological change has created more new options for action and has caused rapid changes and complicated social relations. Hence, "technological change creates uncertainty and uncertainty brings about a need for experts."[16] Second, there is a strong traditional belief in knowledge and efficiency. There is an "epistemological assumption" that "knowledge is capable of achieving reasonable states of certainty."[17] Hence experts are supposed to possess the legitimacy to make policies. Third, knowledge and information pertain to facts, and facts are "objective" and therefore "impartial." This impartiality provides expertise with the legitimacy to be relied upon because it is then seen as apolitical and will not bear partisan bias.[18] Fourth, expertise provides rules for decisions. Political disputes during policymaking have to be settled by some rules of the game.[19] These rules of the game, however, are often "competition of analysis."[20]

Therefore, expertise can be employed by the state to maintain its legitimacy, and hence its authority in decision making. Legitimacy is here itself an "end," not only a "means," in state activities. The power of expertise is derived from information and impartiality.

The employment of expertise need not be a plot in hiding government motives, as many writers have implied.[21] Legitimation by expertise could well be less a matter of dishonesty than a matter of belief and convention. Expertise provides the most readily acceptable convention whereby citizens may maintain their confidence in the state.

Participation

Participation refers to the actual contribution of citizens to policymaking. We shall discuss *consultation*, a term that reflects more precisely the mode of participation in Hong Kong, bearing in mind that consultation is only one of the many modes of *participation*.[22] To be more precise, we shall look at two particular cases of consultation: advisory committees and third-party consultations.

Advisory or consultative committees are set up by the policymaker to solicit policy inputs from the community at large or its representatives. Such committees may or may not be established by legislation. If not, they are established administratively to aid policymaking. They may be either "standing" or ad hoc in nature. Members of such committees may either be elected by some parent constituency or appointed from above. The members may either represent the interest of particular interest groups, various areas of professional expertise, or ideology.[23] The most powerful committees may approve or veto a government proposal; they are almost policymakers. More often, they enjoy the legal obligation to be consulted and provide input to policymaking. In this case, their advice may receive different degrees of respect: from total acceptance to total rejection. Those committees that do not enjoy a legal status may still be consulted because they are tacitly "legitimized" for consultation.[24] Still other committees may not enjoy this "legitimization," they may have informal and unbinding dialogue with the policymaker.

There are basically two interpretations of these committees. On the one hand, they are channels of representation; on the other hand, they provide legitimacy for policymaking.

In reality, the government has grown into a bureaucracy and has its own interests to defend. There are then not only interactions among the interest groups, but also between the government sectors and the interest groups. Interaction of the latter type is even more "political." Under these circumstances, the advisory committees provide a channel for political exchange. On the one hand, the government bureaucracy needs information and support from the interest groups in making, defending, and implementing its policies. On the other hand, the interest groups need access to and influence over policymaking.[25] Advisory committees satisfy both.

In a way, the political exchange between the government bureaucracy and the interest groups can be expressed in the currency of legitimacy: the government bureaucracy gains legitimacy through accumulation of information and acquisition of support; the interest groups gain legitimacy for being involved in the policymaking process. The transaction of legitimacy takes place in the advisory committees.

In circumstances where the government has legal control over policymaking, as is the case of Hong Kong, the advisory committees may play two roles: legitimating the policies and legitimating the government. In the first role, the committees provide the government with the necessary information to formulate and implement policies with confidence. Or, in a "conspiracy" context, the government may use advisory committees to "camouflage," i.e., to legitimate a policy by "impartial" recommendation.[26] The government may also use advisory committees to delay taking a decision, to capture the support of organized interests by involving them in the policymaking process, or to "hobble" the opposition.

> Critics can be pacified by the appointment of a committee which creates the impression that something is being done when it is not, or that consultation is being taken when it is not.[27]

Gaziel has similar observations in his study of the French case.[28] There, the advisory councils play the dual role of constituting an objective appraisal of government performance and confirming the policies of the government, shielding it from criticism. One of Jennings' points is also that the committee "fulfills a political purpose in that it makes consultation amenable to control and the results more predictable."[29]

In this way, the government bureaucracy passes its policies by the endorsement of some legitimate machinery—the advisory committee—but it manages to control this machinery. Legitimation again has nothing to do with the appropriateness of the policy per se.

The second role of advisory committees pertains to what may be called "second level legitimation": the government manages to develop or is obliged to entertain a convention, or belief, that working through advisory committees is the most acceptable means of making policies. If this can be established, then the advisory committees not only legitimate the policies, but more importantly legitimate the government itself. This ideology can be developed to the extent that the government puts tremendous efforts into building this legitimacy (convention and belief that advisory committees are amenable), even at the cost of accepting some policies that may be detrimental to the bureaucracy. In this last case, the government trades benefits in specific areas for the legitimacy of its general authority.

Use of Expertise in Hong Kong's Educational Policymaking

In the Hong Kong context, *expertise* is provided by a sophisticated information base and a team of competent experts. In education, such an information base and expert team have typically contributed to policymaking in a number of manpower deliberations.

Special Committee on Higher Education: 1964–68

The Special Committee on Higher Education (SCHE) was established in 1964. It was obviously prompted by the international tide of manpower forecasting. Its interim report started with the following remark:

> Throughout the world, countries are becoming increasingly development-minded and it seems that often the key to economic expansion is the planned development of manpower resources. The most important means by which manpower resources can be developed is formal education and in particular, formal education at the higher levels.[30]

The SCHE based its methodology mainly on the British Robbins Report and the now classic work by Harbison and Myers.[31] The SCHE even thought of inviting Harbison to undertake a commissioned survey for Hong Kong.[32] The SCHE members included representatives of the two universities, senior members from the Legislative Council, and other relevant senior officials. The basic responsibility of the SCHE was to assess the demand and to design the supply of high-level manpower.

The SCHE attempted to calculate the Harbison-Myers composite index,[33] but this yielded no fruit because of lack of GNP figures. It then turned to what it called the "forecasting-manpower-needs" approach to assess the demand for "highly educated personnel."[34] By that time the results of the first general census (1961) for Hong Kong were available. Using 1961 as the base year, the SCHE tried to project the demand and distribution of high-level manpower in 1971. This projection was tested by using the government sector as a "microcosm" of the economy.[35] This projected demand was then balanced by a projected output of education. This constituted a 1966 interim report. In 1968, a second interim report was produced, which mainly included a survey of one sector of the economy—the manufacturing industry. The survey, carried out by Robert Mitchell of the Chinese University of Hong Kong, was the first of its kind in Hong Kong.[36] The Mitchell survey looked at (a) the manpower structure of all firms employing 200 or more workers and a small sample of firms employing 100 to 199 workers; and (b) the educational qualification of individuals working in these firms. The SCHE did not produce further reports.

Manpower Surveys for Industrial Training: 1967 to Date

An Industrial Training Advisory Committee (ITAC) was appointed in 1965 as a nonstatutory body to advise the governor on industrial training. In 1971, ITAC was replaced by the Hong Kong Training Council (HKTC), which was in turn replaced by a more powerful Vocational Training Council (VTC) in 1982. One of the major efforts of the ITAC, HKTC, and VTC was conducting manpower surveys in the major industries.

The surveys adopt the "employer's opinion survey" technique, which was first introduced by experts from the International Labour Organization (ILO) in 1967.[37] The surveys carry out full-population investigations as far as possible and the results are used as a basis for forecasting. An "adaptive filtering" technique is used for forecasting where mathematical models which favored more recent data yield a family of curves. The training boards for individual industries then discuss and decide on the most acceptable projection.[38] This has become a biennial exercise for each of the selected industries. Results of the survey and projection for individual industries are published, and two comprehensive reports were issued in 1977 and 1984 respectively.[39] The planning of a large range of training facilities, from the training of operatives in training centers to the training of technologists in the universities and polytechnics, is very much influenced by the survey results.

Preparation of the 1977 Green Paper: 1975–77

The preparation of the 1977 Green Paper started with a government internal Working Party on Higher Education, which was later renamed Working Party on Senior Secondary and Tertiary Education because it was found necesary to widen its terms of reference. This was a government internal interdepartmental working party with senior educational officials as its core members. Appointed in 1975, the working party produced among others an interim report in 1976 and a final report in 1977. The latter was condensed and "dressed" to become the Green Paper.[40]

The working party was the first attempt in Hong Kong to use the manpower requirements approach to plan the overall system of education. In its crucial Chapter II, "Demand and Supply," which was repeatedy rewritten, much effort was devoted to looking at the demand in terms of *student demand* ("demonstrated demand" and "student ability") and *job opportunities* ("existing occupational structure," "measured [forecast] demand," and "employment patterns and salary levels").

The working party, however, did not attempt to conduct its own survey for manpower requirements. It drew data from the Education Department, the examinations authority, HKTC, the 1976 by-census, and graduate surveys of the universities and polytechnics. The working party once thought of asking the census and statistics department to develop a mathematical model to predict the number of vacancies, but was persuaded by the experience of the HKTC that it would not be viable. While rate-of-return analysis was too difficult to carry out, the working party attempted to draw education-earnings profiles.

Later, the 1979 working group took a second look at the key issues and began to see the necessity of developing a methodology different from the HKTC approach; its exercise developed an expert team and paved the way for the review in 1980.

A Comprehensive Manpower Model: 1980–81

In 1980, the Hong Kong government established a Committee to Review Technical and Higher Education. It was a high-level advisory committee headed by Kenneth Topley, then the director of education and Hong Kong's first secretary for education-designate. It comprised fourteen members from all relevant sectors of government and the education community. The most remarkable exercise carried out by the committee was the building of a comprehensive manpower model which formed the basis of all its recommendations (in what is now known as the "Topley Report").

The committee chose, among four alternative methods, the manpower modeling approach which then materialized in two stages. Stage I was to assume the existing structure of occupation and educational levels and to arrive at a *minimum* requirement picture. In Stage II, requirements were calculated based on a future structure of occupation and educational levels.

In Stage I, there were four steps: (1) projecting total employment; (2) projecting by industries; (3) projecting by occupational groups; and (4) translating into educational levels. There is the rationale that "the nature of the Hong Kong economy and the flexibility of its labor market are such that one can safely assume that there is always full employment."[41]

Stage I found that first, the whole economy would shift away from primary production sectors and accordingly workers would shift toward higher educational qualifications. Second, comparing supply and demand, there would be a shortfall of university graduates in 1986 and 1991, but not in 1996 and 2001; however, there would be overprovision in other types of post-compulsory education. Results of Stage I were accompanied by manpower forecasts in three sectors: the civil service, the social welfare department, and the construction industry. All these pointed to the future inadequacy of high-skill manpower.

In Stage II, returning graduates from overseas were also taken into consideration. Compared with Stage I, occupational distribution within industries and educational composition of workers within occupations were changed by projection. The occupational distribution was projected after (a) a trend analysis, (b) consultations, and (c) international comparison with reference to Japan, Singapore, and Taiwan. The educational composition was replaced by the "desirable" composition based on consultations and the manpower survey conducted by the Hong Kong Training Council. Based on this desirable composition, two sets of projections were derived: a *high* projection assuming the target year as 1991 and a *low* projection assuming the target as 2001.

The second report concluded, in typical planning language:

> The shortfall of university places in 1980–86, at only about 340 a year, seems to suggest the creation of new places in existing institutions, while the anticipated shortfall after 1986 justifies the creation of a new institution. The short-

fall of technician and craft places in 1980–1986 means the need for at least one additional technical institute; to meet the shortfall in 1997–2001 requires 8 new technical institutes, or 1 new polytechnic and about 3 technical institutes.[42]

Based on these data, the Topley Report proposed that the 2 percent of the age group in degree courses should be increased to 8 percent. The nondegree courses were to be doubled. Craft courses were to be more than tripled. The report therefore proposed massive expansion in higher and technical education.

The above examples should be viewed in the context that Hong Kong is often identified as a typical free-market economy, and is hence the least desirable place for manpower forecasting and manpower planning. In reality, the mathematical models used in the VTC manpower forecasts are scrutinized by the training boards before they go to training plans, and it is not unusual for the board to modify, revert, or reject the mathematical outcome. Nevertheless, the mathematical models still provide people with the confidence that planning of vocational education is based on objective need, is impartial, and is not arbitrary. If such mathematical models were not there, the planning of training facilities might easily become an arena for interindustrial battle over resources. In other words, the manpower calculations, whether or not they yield accurate results, provide the VTC with the legitimacy to carry out the planning of its training facilities.

Likewise, the manpower models developed by the Topley committee were not employed in actual policy formulation, because the entire report did not receive consensual agreement among the various policy advisory bodies and so the recommendations were shelved. Still, it would be difficult to imagine where the policy deliberations could have started without the manpower considerations. Manpower requirements were the only criterion safely acceptable by all parties concerned, although they may still disagree upon the outcomes of the manpower calculations. The manpower models gave the committee a legitimate starting point for discussion, although that did not necessarily overcome basic divergence in interests and views.

All in all, the manpower exercises have provided a strong basis of expertise for policymaking, which has in turn given the government an impartial image as legitimate policymaker. This impartiality has helped the government shake itself of accusations of colonial bias, which is particularly effective in a Chinese community that traditionally respects rationality more than democracy. Expertise is more respectable in Hong Kong than it is elsewhere in a modern Western state. This may explain why Hong Kong has become "a planners' paradise," as is perceived by many professional educational planners who understand the situation.

Consultation in Hong Kong's Educational Policymaking

To facilitate discussion on consultation in Hong Kong's educational policymaking, it is essential to understand the basic structure of policymaking there.

The Decision-Making Structure

The governor, or the governor-in-council, is *de jure* solely responsible for making policy decisions. The governor, who is the representative of the British Queen, presides over and is advised by the Executive Council (Exco) which is *de facto* the decision-making body. The governor also presides over the Legislative Council (Legco) which makes laws and controls public expenditure. Since 1985, elected members have been introduced to the Legco. In practice, it is *de facto* a top-level advisory body and has no substantial power in educational policymaking, apart from questioning the government on its educational expenditures.

In the legal sense, the Hong Kong government is an autocracy. Nevertheless, there is an extensive network of consultation for policymaking. In 1982, there were 385 policy advisory committees established by the government.[43] These are not policymaking bodies in legal terms, but are mostly quite influential in their respective policy areas. Anyway, consultations are extensive and are not unique to education. The government is quite proud of this and regards it as the "distinctive feature of the system of government in Hong Kong."[44]

The Decision-Making Process

Apart from stage of "needs identification" which is often subtle, according to convention, policy deliberations at a macro level in Hong Kong usually involve the following steps: (a) a specially appointed committee usually invites public submissions before or during its course of deliberation; (b) after submission to the Exco, recommendations of the commissioned committee are often published, in whole or in a summary form, sometimes as a Green Paper, for public comments; (c) the recommendations are then modified, supposedly with due consideration to the public comments, and tabled at the Legco, often in the form of a White Paper, for official adoption.

There are no standard procedures for the formulation of education policies, but, until recently, the inclusion of consultation has been seen as essential. Consultation is a special feature in educational policymaking in Hong Kong. It occurs in different modes (which are discussed in an earlier study[45]) at almost all possible junctures of the policymaking process. Public consultation can be carried out by issuing a Green Paper, by inviting submissions from recognized organizations, or by discussions in regular or special consultative meetings. Public pressures developed in the mass media may also carry weight.

As examples, the 1965 White Paper was preceded by a 1963 Green Paper worked out by an overseas Education Commission. Both the commission and the Green Paper sought public submissions. The 1974 White Paper was preceded by a 1973 Green Paper which was actually a report from the Board of Education. Opinions were sought from the public both before and after the Green Paper. The

1978 White Paper followed the 1977 Green Paper. The latter sought public input both before and after its publication.

Advisory Bodies

Apart from general consultations, there are numerous ad hoc or standing committees spreading over all sectors and all levels of education to assist educational policymaking. There are, for example, standing consultative organs on preschool education, special education, private schools, and so on, and ad hoc committees on sixth form education, expatriate English teachers, preparation of a teachers' center, and so forth. These do not include the subject committees which look after curriculum development in different subject areas. In the following, we shall concentrate on the major advisory bodies which deal with overall educational policies. They are the Board of Education, the Vocational Training Council, the University and Polytechnic Grants Committee, and the Education Commission.

The **Board of Education** (BoE), appointed by the governor, is tacitly understood as representing: (a) "community leaders" who usually are unofficial Legco and Exco members; (b) major school councils (organization of schools by type); (c) major school sponsoring bodies, which usually means the major religious bodies: the Anglican Church, the Church of Christ in China, the Methodist Church and the Roman Catholic Church; (d) the Vocational Training Council; and (e) tertiary institutions. The BoE has limited policymaking power and seldom moves outside the schools sector; its chairman is, since 1972, unofficial.

The **Vocational Training Council** (VTC) comprises representatives from industry, training institutions, educational institutions, and trade unions. The VTC is virtually a policymaking body in all kinds of training and manpower preparation programs in Hong Kong. Its proposed policies are seldom opposed by the governor or the Executive Council. It has direct control over the technical education and industrial training department, which is its executive arm.

The **University and Polytechnic Grants Committee** (UPGC) was established on the British University Grants Committee model. The UPGC plays the dual role of allocating public funds on the one hand and safeguarding institutional autonomy on the other. However, the Hong Kong UPGC is unusual in that until 1986, all its academic members—eight out of fourteen—were serving members of overseas institutions. Two local representatives were added in 1985. The Hong Kong UPGC maintains a "triennium" planning system, even after the 1973–1974 recession. Thus it escapes the constraints of the government annual budgets. Until 1984, there were no "cash limits" imposed on UPGC deliberations, and as a matter of fact, UPGC proposals were seldom rejected by the government.[46] In 1980, the terms of reference for the UPGC were revised to reconfirm its policymaking functions.[47] Until very recently, the UPGC was the *de facto* policymaker of higher education in Hong Kong. The new terms of reference asked the UPGC "to keep under review in the light of the community's needs" the facilities, plans for development, financial needs, and the application of funds in university and polytechnic education in Hong Kong.

The newly established (since 1984) **Education Commission** is supposed to be a coordinating agent which oversees the overall education policies and the interface between different sectors of the system. The Education Commission is composed of representatives from the crucial government departments, as well as prominent community figures and educators. The commission has published four reports that provide only policy recommendations, most of which, however, have been adopted by the government. In fact, Report No. 1 was admitted as government policy immediately after its publication, and even the controversial recommendations in Report No. 3 were eventually taken as government policies.

Appendix B displays the position, as of 1989, of the major educational advisory bodies and their relations with the government departments.

Such advisory bodies, with different degrees of autonomy (which vary with time), play the dual role mentioned earlier. One the one hand, they help legitimate the policies made by the government, so that they appear to arise from representative opinions. On the other hand, they help legitimate the government, giving it the image of being open and impartial.

Third-Party Consultation

Third-party consultation plays such an essential part in Hong Kong's educational policymaking that it deserves separate discussion. Elements of third-party consultation are built into education policymaking where possible. Consultants include overseas experts and prominent figures in the local community.

The 1963 Green Paper,[48] also known as the Marsh-Sampson Report, was written by a two-member Education Commission appointed by the government. Marsh and Sampson, who were from Hampshire, England, paid an eight-week visit to Hong Kong in February–April 1963, and were asked to advise on the overall demand and supply of education and its finance. The White Paper[49] took the Green Paper into consideration, although it did not agree with many of the proposals.

In both the final stage of the drafting of the 1977 Green Paper and its conversion into the 1978 White Paper, Peter Williams from the University of London's Institute of Education, who had extensive experience in planning education in developing countries, was invited as external consultant. In fact, Peter Williams was also invited to be the adviser in the review exercise from 1980–81 and closely examined the manpower models developed by the Topley committee.

The institution of the UPGC is another example of third-party consultation, with interventions from prestigious overseas academics who are backed up by their international reputation and will not submit to local government pressures. Such an institution not only legitimates the government and guards it against accusations of political bias or hidden motives, its strong international composition also provides legitimacy to protect academic autonomy in local institutions of higher education. This also explains why the UPGC favors its present status as personal adviser to the governor, rather than as any part of the government machinery.

The best-known internal third-party consultations were the T.K. Ann Commission and the Rayson Huang Committee. In 1973, there was a dispute over salary between the government and the nongraduate teachers in government and government-aided schools. The dispute led to territory-wide industrial action. After the dispute was settled, a Special Commission on the Certificated Masters was appointed by the governor to (1) examine its underlying causes and (2) to advise on the measures to be taken to obviate a recurrence of such a dispute.[50] Referred to as the T.K. Ann Commission after its chairman, the committee solicited public opinions and produced the T.K. Ann Report.

The Rayson Huang Committee was set up in 1978 to investigate the controversial closure of a school run by the Catholic Precious Blood Congregation. The incident began with the public revelation of financial misappropriation by the congregation and soon developed into a confrontation between the school management and the Education Department on one side and the students, teachers, and pressure groups on the other. At the climax, there was a public students' sit-in demonstration outside the Bishop's House. The Education Department reacted by closing the school. The so-called Rayson Huang Committee invited public submissions, conducted interviews, and produced two reports.[51]

The most significant third-party consultation was of course the overall review conducted in 1981–82 by an overseas panel recommended by the OECD. The panel comprised John Llewellyn, former vice-chancellor of Exeter University and director-general of the British Council; Dr. Greg Hancock, then full-time member of the Schools Commission, Australia and chief education officer, Australian Capital Territory Schools Authority; Dr. Karl Roeloffs, former head of the Planning Division of the Federal German Ministry of Education and vice-chairman of the OECD Education Committee, now secretary-general of the Federal German Academic Exchange Service; and Professor Michael W. Kirst, Department of Education, Stanford University, California and former president of the California State Board of Education.

The panel paid two visits to Hong Kong in October 1981 and March 1982, respectively, and conducted extensive interviews with representatives from the education community. During the second visit, two unprecedented sessions were held where the panel faced the officials, in the presence of the Board of Education, representatives from more than eighty local educational bodies, and six invited educationalists from Denmark, Malaysia, Singapore, Japan, Canada, and OCED. The panel came up with a report that presented a comprehensive and critical appraisal of Hong Kong's education system. The report,[52] known as the Llewellyn Report, aroused much controversy after its publication, but on the whole its recommendations became the focus of discussion in all matters of educational policy. In fact, there was a debate in July 1983 in the Legislative Council that concluded that the report should be used as a basis for future policy deliberations.

In general, *consultation* plays an important role in the government's legitimacy in formulating education policy. In the colonial context, the general mentality is still intrinsically anti-government. Consultation improves communication between the government and the citizens, who very often feel satisfied at being heard. Consultation also provides the government with a kind of "feed-forward" which makes the government feel more confident in promulgating or implementing policies. As mentioned earlier, consultation in educational policymaking is extensive. This is part of a general policy across all sectors of public administration. Without such consultations the government lacks the means to demonstrate that it is representing and not oppressing the people. This explains the over 385 official advisory bodies established by the Hong Kong government.

Third-party consultation, which is a mix of expertise and consultation, is used quite often by the Hong Kong government, particularly in the area of education. The T.K. Ann Commission and the Rayson Huang Committee proved effective in placing the governor in an impartial position and placating the citizens who were annoyed by the government bureaucracy. The large proportion of overseas membership in the UPGC is a type of standing third-party consultation. Without such membership, the government would risk embarrassment when faced with competing demand from the different institutions. The invitation of Peter Williams to the policy exercises and the conduct of the OECD review were part of this tradition. The participation of overseas consultants in policy deliberation can easily be regarded elsewhere as an infringement of sovereignty, but has become a credit to the legitimacy of the Hong Kong government.

It is noteworthy that the Hong Kong government treasured legitimacy sometimes even at the expense of short-term benefits or convenience. A typical example was the resolution to accept the OECD review report, which proposed that the government set up an Education Commission that was not compatible with the existing policymaking mechanism.[53] As further examples, both the T.K. Ann Report and the Rayson Huang Report caused embarrassment to government departments, but have in the long run gained credibility for the government among citizens.

The Changing Legitimacy

However, the polity in Hong Kong is changing for two reasons: the context in which the existing legitimacy was established is changing, and the government's legitimacy is being threatened.

First, 1985 saw the first elected members in Legco. Election is sure to become the major means of getting into the decision-making machinery in the future. When votes in an election have become essential means of legitimacy acquisition, the role of expertise and consultation becomes subtle.

Whether expertise and consultation will remain as the basic means to maintain legitimacy in policymaking is doubtful. The respect for these techniques has been possible only because Hong Kong is a "virtual autocracy," where there is a lack of formal representation in the government.[54] The government was obliged to rely on "scientific" expertise and extensive consultation for legitimacy. "The result is a wholly undemocratic but exceptionally receptive management system."[55] The change of legitimacy may increase the emphasis on political powers and reduce the reliance on "rational" and impartial expertise or day-to-day consultation. The change in legitimacy is prompted by a process of democratization, but may reduce the direct receptiveness of the government to its client citizens. For an elected member, his legitimacy does not come from consultative committees which to him are "structurally clumsy."[56]

Second, in a way, legitimacy is a futuristic notion: a government is keen to gain its legitimacy to facilitate its future functioning. In establishing its legitimacy, a government may have to undertake painstaking, sacrificing actions, just in order to build a good future for itself. A government *without* a future is unlikely to be keen on legitimacy building. This is unfortunately the case of the Hong Kong government which, with the 1997 changeover in view, may still strive hard to maintain the prosperity and stability of the colony, but will find it difficult to succeed without making greater investment toward its own legitimacy.

The handling of the issue of university structure provided a hint of such a change. The issue grew out of the complexity in the existing system where the University of Hong Kong (HKU) took in students after Form 7 and then followed a three-year curriculum in most of the subject areas, whereas the Chinese University of Hong Kong (CUHK) admitted students after Form 6 and then followed mainly a four-year curriculum. The Education Commission Report No. 2 (1986) recommended the continuation of the present sixth-form system, which was taken by the CUHK to mean a conversion to a three-year university in the long run. This revived the long-standing battle, which started in the mid-1970s, between CUHK and proposers of the conversion. The situation was complicated in 1986 by the decision of HKU to convert to a four-year university. After a long period of silence, the Education Commission in its Report No. 3 (1988) maintained that university should admit students after Form 7. A renewed battle of words prevailed, with the academics virtually playing the role of pressure groups. Although Report No. 3 was not yet a government policy, it was commonly believed to reflect government intentions.

While the general public was not so conversant with the university structures, and many of them were not clear about the substance of the debate, the government, or more precisely, the education and manpower branch, was viewed as using high-handed measures to "oppress" the academic institutions.

Such a situation could signal the beginning of a crisis for the government's legitimacy in making educational policy. In these circumstances, criticisms that the government is trying to maintain a British system and to suppress a non-British system gained much sympathy. This is the worst thing the government would like to see, if it were keen to keep up its noncolonial image. However, developments pointed in the opposite direction. Instead of putting the issue to rational scrutiny, as it has so often done, or resorting to a powerful third party for arbitration, which had proven so effective in similar situations in the past, the branch representatives in the Education Commission came out in public in defense of the policy. This has not only intensified the government–citizen antagonism, which this government used to be so skillful in avoiding, but has also confused the public in the distinction between the Education Commission and the government, as well as spoiled the consultative image of the Education Commission. The Education Commission could otherwise become the very vehicle for third-party intervention. At the end of the episode, a decision eventually came out as part of the governor's 1989 policy speech.

In the same period, a number of important strategic policies have been announced, with little or practically no consultation among the relevant groups, nor with results of any rational deliberation to support. Among such strategic policies are the massive expansion of higher education, increasing the volume of degree education to almost three times from 1989 to 1995, and the introduction of a *direct subsidy scheme*, which in effect would release some of the schools from government dependence, if not privitize them. All these decisions were made within the government—in some cases, even the top-level advisory bodies were not consulted.

The government has apparently become preoccupied with promulgating its favored policies. In so doing, it has neglected the process in which such policies are made and legitimated. Thus, the state is putting itself into a new type of legitimacy crisis.[57]

Such a change is not surprising for a sunset government, but may be detrimental to the future of Hong Kong. The recent decision-making processes, which are likely to continue, may have set precedents for future policymaking. These precedents may undermine the entire foundations of legitimacy that the government had worked so hard to establish. They may potentially change the conventions of educational policymaking from a rational, consultative mode to one of autocracy and secrecy. The government may well succeed in forcing through the desired policies, but may in the meantime undermine the legitimacy of its policymaking bodies. The change in legitimacy will either leave the incoming government with low credibility among the citizens, or leave the new government with the ease of perpetuating bureaucratic and political manipulations in educational policies.

Notes

1. S.M. Lipset, *Political Man* (Garden City, NY: Doubleday, 1960), p. 77.
2. R. Bierstedt, "Legitimacy," paraphrasing S.M. Lipset in *Dictionary of the Social Sciences* (New York: The Free Press, 1964), p. 386.
3. R.M. Merelmann, "Learning and Legitimacy," *American Political Science Review* 60(3), (1966), p. 548.
4. H.N. Weiler, "Politics of Educational Reform," in *Innovation in the Public Sector*, ed. R.L. Merritt and A.J. Merritt (Beverly Hills: Sage, 1985), p. 185.
5. Quoted in J.F. Manley, "Neo-pluralism: A Class Analysis of Pluralism I and Pluralism II," *American Political Science Review* 77 (1983), p. 368.
6. R.A. Dahl, *Modern Political Analysis*, 4th ed. (Englewood Cliffs, NJ: Prentice-Hall, 1984), p. 53.
7. M. Weber, *The Theory of Social and Economic Organizations*, trans. A.M. Henderson and T. Parsons (Glencoe, IL: Free Press, 1947).
8. C. Offe, *Disorganized Capitalism: Contemporary Transformation of Work and Politics*, ed. J. Keane (Cambridge: Polity Press, 1985). Also C. Offe *Contradictions of the Welfare State*, ed. J. Keane (Cambridge, MA: The MIT Press, 1984).
9. J. Habermas, *Legitimation Crisis* (Frankfurt: Suhrkamp Verlag, 1973); trans. T. McCarthy (Boston: Beacon Press, 1975).
10. N. Miners, *The Government and Politics of Hong Kong*, 4th ed. (Hong Kong: Oxford University Press, 1986).
11. Offe's terms, *Contradictions*.
12. C.E. Lindblom, *The Policy-Making Process*, 2d ed. (Englewood Cliffs, NJ: Prentice-Hall, 1980), p. 12.
13. M. Carley, *Rational Techniques in Policy Analysis* (London: Heinemann, 1980), p. 12, and A.G. McGrew and M.J. Wilson, eds., *Decision Making: Approaches and Analysis* (Manchester: Manchester University Press/Open University Press, 1982), p. 3.
14. Lindblom, *Policy-Making Process* p. 13.
15. Ibid., p. 11.
16. G. Benveniste, *The Politics of Expertise*, 2d ed. (San Francisco: Boyd and Fraser, 1977), pp. 30-31.
17. M. Kogan, *Education Accountability: An Analytic Overview* (London: Hutchinson, 1986), p. 92.
18. B.G. Peters, *The Politics of Bureaucracy*, 2d ed. (New York: Longman, 1984), p. 189.
19. J.E. Anderson, *Public Policy-Making*, 2d ed. (New York: Holt, Rinehart and Winston, 1979), p. 77.
20. Lindblom, *Policy-Making Process*, pp. 30-31.
21. Benveniste, *Politics of Expertise*, p. 61; K.D. Knorr, "Policymakers' Uses of Social Science Knowledge: Symbolic or Instrumental," in *Using Social Science Research in Public Policy-Making*, ed. C. Weiss (Lexington, MA: D.C. Heath, 1977), pp. 171-72.
22. See for example S.R. Arnstein, "A Ladder of Citizen Participation," *American Institute of Planning Journal* 35(4), (1969), pp. 216-24.
23. A.P. Griffiths, "How Can One Person Represent Another?" *Aristotelian Society*, Supplement, 34 (1960), pp. 187-208.
24. M. Kogan, *Educational Policy-Making: A Study of Interest Groups and Parliament* (London: George Allen & Unwin, 1975).
25. B.G. Peters, "Insider and Outsider: The Politics of Pressure Group Influence on Bureaucracy," *Administration and Society* 9(2), (1977), pp. 191-218. Reprint in McGrew and Wilson, *Decision Making*, pp. 261-74. J.J. Richardson and A.G. Jordan, "The Policy

Process," in *Governing under Pressure* (London: Martin Robertson, 1982). Reprinted in McGrew and Wilson, *Decision Making*, pp. 275–90.

26. B. Smith, *Policy Making in British Government: An Analysis of Power and Rationality*, 2d ed. (London: Martin Robertson, 1976), p. 70.

27. Ibid.

28. H. Gaziel, "Advisory Councils in a Centralised Educational System: A Case-Study from France," *European Journal of Education* 15(4), (1980), pp. 399–407.

29. R.E. Jennings, *Education and Politics: Policy-Making in Local Education Authorities* (London: B.T. Batsford, 1977), p. 184.

30. *Special Committee on Higher Education: Interim Report* (Hong Kong Government, 1966), p. 1.

31. Ibid., p. 6.

32. Ibid., p. 4.

33. F. Harbison, and C.A. Myers, *Education, Manpower and Economic Growth: Strategies of Human Resource Development* (New York: McGraw-Hill, 1964).

34. *Special Committee*, pp. 6–9.

35. Ibid., p. 22.

36. *Special Committee on Higher Education: Second Interim Report* (Hong Kong Government, 1968).

37. D.D. Waters, "The Planning of Craft and Technician Education in Hong Kong, 1957–1982" (Ph.D. diss., Loughborough University of Technology, 1985), p. 112.

38. *Report on Technical Manpower Demand and Supply 1977–82* (Hong Kong Government, 1977).

39. Ibid.; Vocational Training Council, *Report on Demand for and Supply of Technical Manpower in the Major Industries* (1984).

40. *Senior Secondary and Tertiary Education: A Development Programme for Hong Kong over the Next Decade* (Green Paper, Hong Kong Government, 1977).

41. Quotation from an unpublished government document.

42. Unpublished government document.

43. Miners, *Government and Politics*, p. 110.

44. *The Hong Kong Education System (Overall Review of the Hong Kong Education System)* (Hong Kong Government, 1981), p. 173.

45. See K.M. Cheng, *Participatory Educational Planning: The Position of Educational Bodies in Hong Kong* (M.Ed. diss., University of Hong Kong, 1983).

46. R.C. Griffiths, "Hong Kong University and Polytechnic Grants Committee," *Higher Education* 13 (1984), pp. 545–52.

47. *University and Polytechnic Grants Committee of Hong Kong: Notes on Procedures* (Hong Kong Government, 1981), p. 1.

48. *Report of Education Commission* (Marsh–Sampson Report) (Green Paper, Hong Kong Government, 1963).

49. *Education Policy, 1965* (White Paper, Hong Kong Government, 1965).

50. *Report of the Special Commission on the Certificated Masters* (T.K. Ann Report), (Hong Kong Government, 1976), p. 4.

51. *Interim Report of the Committee of Inquiry into the Precious Blood Golden Jubilee Secondary School* (Hong Kong Government, 1978); *Final Report of the Committee of Inquiry into the Precious Blood Golden Jubilee Secondary School* (The Rayson Huang Report), (Hong Kong Government, 1978).

52. *A Perspective on Education in Hong Kong: Report by a Visiting Panel* (1982).

53. Several such episodes are analyzed in detail in K.M. Cheng, "The Concept of Legitimacy in Educational Policy Making: Alternative Explanations of Two Policy Episodes in Hong Kong" (Ph.D. diss., University of London Institute of Education, 1987).

54. Griffiths, "Hong Kong University," p. 547.
55. Ibid.
56. Remark made by Mr. Desmond Lee, see *Ming Po Daily*, December 29, 1986.
57. The crisis in legitimacy is not only limited to education. A broader view can be found in I. Scott, *Political Change and the Crisis of Legitimacy in Hong Kong* (Hong Kong: Oxford University Press, 1989).

Published Documents Reviewed

1963 Report of Education Commission (Marsh–Sampson Report) (Green Paper)

1965 Education Policy (White Paper)

1966 Special Committee on Higher Education: Interim Report

1968 Special Committee on Higher Education: Second Interim Report

1973 Report of the Board of Education on the Proposed Expansion of Secondary Education over the Next Decade (Green Paper)

1974 Secondary Education in Hong Kong over the Next Decade (White Paper)

1976 University and Polytechnic Grants Committee of Hong Kong Special Report: October 1965 to June 1976

1976 Report of the Special Commission on the Certificated Masters (T.K. Ann Report)

1977 Report on Technical Manpower Demand and Supply 1977–82

1977 Senior Secondary and Tertiary Education: A Development Programme for Hong Kong over the Next Decade (Green Paper)

1978 Interim Report of the Committee of Inquiry into the Precious Blood Golden Jubilee Secondary School

1978 Final Report of the Committee of Inquiry into the Precious Blood Golden Jubilee Secondary School (The Rayson Huang Report)

1978 The Development of Senior and Tertiary Education (White Paper)

1979 Report of the Advisory Committee on Diversification

1980 University and Polytechnic Grants Committee of Hong Kong: Notes on Procedures

1981 The Hong Kong Education System (Overall Review of the Hong Kong Education System)

1982 A Perspective on Education in Hong Kong: Report by a Visiting Panel

1984 Report on Demand for and Supply of Technical Manpower in the Major Industries

1984 Education Commission Report No. 1

1986 Education Commission Report No. 2

1988 Education Commission Report No. 3

1990 Education Commission Report No. 4

5

Preparing Pupils as Citizens of the Special Administrative Region of Hong Kong: An Analysis of Curriculum Change and Control during the Transition Period

Paul Morris

What's to come is still unsure: In delay, there lies no plenty...
—*W. Shakespeare*

In 1984, after two years of negotiations, the British and Chinese governments agreed that from 1997 Hong Kong would cease to be a British colony and would become a Special Administrative Region under the sovereignty of China. This means that many decisions are now being made in all areas, by individuals as well as by the Hong Kong government, which are based on a near certain knowledge of what will happen in the future. Unlike most other exercises in decolonization, the reversion of Hong Kong's sovereignty to the People's Republic of China (PRC) is not viewed by most of the populace as a process that will result in liberation and increased self-determination. The future is viewed with considerable uncertainty and misgivings. These concerns are exacerbated by the fact that a large proportion of the population is first or second generation migrants, many of whom have come to Hong Kong as illegal immigrants from China. The emigration of Hong Kong residents, especially to Canada and Australia, the relocation of company headquarters, and the hypersensitivity of the stock and foreign exchange markets are the most obvious examples of the "1997" effect. A number of legislative changes have also been introduced, most notably to the Public Order Ordinance, which have been interpreted as reducing the potential for open public discussion of or dissent toward Hong

Kong's political future. The critical nature of the change and the limited time period involved have highlighted and accelerated the influences on the curriculum and the mechanisms through which the curriculum is controlled. The purpose of this chapter is to analyze the impact of the return of Hong Kong's sovereignty to China in 1997 on the formal curriculum of secondary schools and to identify the mechanisms of curriculum control used to effect the influences identified.

Curriculum and Political Changes

There is an extensive literature at both the macro the micro level detailing the influence of social, economic, and political factors on the curriculum.[1] Arai and Kwong for example found that language texts used in China devoted their efforts to instilling in the young the right political attitudes to the extent of excluding their pedagogical function.[2] The texts also reflected changes in political leadership and even subtle changes in the political culture. Williams argued with reference to the United Kingdom that the main historical influences on the curriculum arose from three sources, the "old humanists," "the new industrialists," and "the Public Educators."[3] Salter and Tapper saw these ideal types as appropriate for identifying the range of interests that affect educational policymaking in the United Kingdom but suggested the need to identify a fourth group, "the state bureaucrats." The latter group is especially relevant within Hong Kong for the content and purposes of school subjects such as civics and its later derivatives—"economic and public affairs" (EPA) and "social studies"—reflect the political attitudes which were promoted by the government in different historical periods. Thus "civics," when introduced in the 1930s, was initially a response to the New Life Movement of the Nationalist government of the Republic of China.[4] It focused on providing pupils with an awareness of Hong Kong's status as a colonial territory and its role as a part of the British Commonwealth. Pupils studied in detail the role and powers of the governor and the relationship between the governments of Hong Kong and the United Kingdom. In the 1960s 'civics' was replaced by EPA and the content shifted to focus on internal topics relevant to Hong Kong. A great deal of time was spent describing how the Hong Kong government attempted to solve various social and economic problems. No mention was made of Hong Kong's colonial status nor of its links and relationships with the PRC. These curricular emphases were paralleled in the concern of the bureaucracy with regard to the registration of teachers and schools in Hong Kong. The 1930s and the early postwar period involved a great deal of activity designed to minimize the influence of the Guomindang on education while the late 1940s, 1950s and 1960s was a period in which the purpose shifted to minimizing the influence of the Chinese Communist party.[5] Since 1982, as will be seen subsequently, the political orthodoxy promoted in the school curriculum has undergone further change.

Studies that have analyzed the effect of social and political changes on the school curriculum have been primarily concerned with influences that occurred over a long time period. The influences now operating in Hong Kong are distinctive insofar as they result from an imminent political change that has served to magnify and accelerate the range of forces and interests which attempt to define the nature of the school curriculum. This provides a new basis for analyzing the influence of politics on the curriculum. Further, these changes are taking place within a system that displays varying degrees of central control over the key areas of curriculum decision making. This allows an examination of a variety of propositions concerning the relationship between the system of administrative control and the curriculum. These include Archer's assertion, based on comparative evidence, that centralized systems are characterized by the stronger direct manipulation of education for political purposes.[6] Similar propositions are put forward by Kogan and Wise.[7]

In contrast, Broadfoot and Moon have cast doubt on the view that curriculum control is broadly related to the extent of centralization of the educational system.[8] This doubt arises because of the vagueness of terms such as "centralized" and "decentralized" and because comparative analyses of specific curriculum changes suggest that they have not been primarily determined by the extent of centralization of the educational system. Moon and Ball argue that the outcome of educational change is influenced by a complex interaction between interest groups, and this cannot be explained primarily by reference to the extent of centralization of the educational system.[9] Such groups include teachers, universities, publishers, curriculum planners, parents, employers, and various overtly political bodies, all of which attempt to influence the nature and purposes of the curriculum. In contrast to their activity in the countries on which Moon and Ball focus, however, these groups are relatively quiescent in Hong Kong. Their attention has generally focused on policy problems other than the nature and purposes of school subjects, such as the language of instruction and the provision of subsidized school places.

This study also allows questions to be addressed concerning the process of decolonization and neocolonization. Specifically, a detailed examination of curriculum change in the transition period may provide evidence of attempts to promote the long-term interests of the departing colonial power.[10]

The Hong Kong Education System

The structure of the education system in Hong Kong broadly reflects the old grammar school system in the United Kingdom. Pupils start six-year primary schooling at age six and then proceed to a three-year junior secondary program. This is followed by a two-year senior secondary course ("O" level equivalent), and then those pupils who have survived take either a one- or two-year sixth form course. Tertiary education is primarily provided at present by two universities and two polytechnics. About 8 percent of the relevant age group enter this sector. The one-year sixth form serves as the matriculation course for the second university. This was established in 1963, as an attempt by the government to support the Chinese middle schools, which teach in Chinese. This situation will change in the 1990s as the impact of the "brain drain" has resulted in the introduction of a policy to expand tertiary education so that 18 percent of the relevant age group are enrolled in degree courses. It is also planned that all students will enter tertiary education after form seven.

Anglo-Chinese schools take 90 percent of pupils and officially teach in English. As is the case in many small countries, their curricula were originally imitations or adaptations of those used elsewhere. Most mainstream academic subjects in Hong Kong, such as physics, biology, history, and economics closely resemble British "O" level and "A" level syllabuses, and the junior secondary syllabus for integrated science was based on the Scottish integrated science scheme. The social studies curriculum is not U.K.-based, but is still Western, for it was influenced by a Canadian project. This dependency on foreign curricula, especially during the rapid growth of the 1960s and 1970s, was reinforced by the domination of expatriates at senior levels of the Education Department (ED) and the tertiary institutions; the use of overseas study visits by ED officials, especially to England to identify curricular trends and innovations for adoption in Hong Kong; and a reliance on visiting curriculum "experts" from the United Kingdom. The 1980s has, however, been characterized by a declining pattern of dependency. This is the result of the emergence of local issues which have had an impact on the curriculum, especially the concern over Hong Kong's political future, an increasing awareness that the centralized mechanisms for mandating curriculum change have had a limited and limiting effect on implementation, and because educational policy has increasingly focused on qualitative issues as the goals of universal primary and junior secondary education have been achieved.

The Mechanisms of Curriculum Control

While a partial and declining pattern of dependency is evident with regard to the structure of the educational system and the sources of curricula, the mechanisms for controlling curricula involve a novel combination of bureaucratic processes. These relate to three main areas of decision making, namely; the selection of the range and content of the subjects studied and examined, the provision of curriculum-wide guidelines, and the selection of textbooks that may be used in schools.

The curriculum of Hong Kong schools is controlled by two central organizations. The Curriculum Development Committees (CDC), which are administered by the government Advisory Inspectorate, are responsible for designing curricula and for approving school textbooks. In addition, the Hong Kong Examination Authority (HKEA), which is an independent statutory body, administers all of Hong Kong's public examinations and produces the syllabuses for all subjects that are publicly examined. The powers of these bodies arise indirectly from the Education Regulations[11] which state that:

> No instruction may be given by any school except in accordance with a syllabus approved by the Director.(92(1))

and:

> No person shall use any document for instruction in a class in any school unless particulars of the title, author and publisher of the document and such other particulars of the document as the Director may require have been furnished to the Director not less than 14 days previously. (92(6))

The same regulations make it clear that political education is not encouraged in schools. Thus Regulation 96 gives the director of education the power to expel any students engaged in political activities and Regulation 98 states:

> No instruction, education, entertainment recreation or propaganda or activity of any kind which, in the opinion of the Director, is in any way of a political or party political nature and prejudicial to the public interest or the welfare of the pupils or of education generally or contrary to the approved syllabus, shall be permitted upon any school premises or upon the occasion of any school activity.

In practice, schools have to study the official syllabus, and can only use those textbooks on the list approved by the Education Department's inspectorate. Both the CDC and HKEA produce syllabuses, but the HKEA syllabus is a more influential document since it determines the breadth and depth of coverage of the all-important public examinations. Further, the high economic returns for educational qualifications in Hong Kong[12] put schools and teachers under substantial pressure to obtain good examination results. This is the most pervasive influence on how the curriculum is implemented, and means that examination syllabuses and approved textbooks are the primary determinants of the content of school subjects and teaching methods.[13]

While the structure and rhetoric of the CDC appears to encourage a participative "problem-solving" strategy, the reality is that the mechanisms used to disseminate and develop curricula rely on the classic tools of bureaucratic control, namely, official directives and mandates. These take the form of the distribution of official circulars and proposed syllabuses which inform users of planned changes and invite their comments. Strong control of the subject-based Curriculum Development Committees is achieved by a variety of bureaucratic techniques which include the selection of committee members by the officials and the avoidance of any provision for full-time participation by teacher members. In practice, the teaching approaches recommended by the CDC are viewed cynically by teachers because they know that their use may not be functional for preparing students for the public examination which is controlled by the HKEA.

In contrast, the HKEA committees include a higher proportion of teachers, and the membership is not controlled by the HKEA administrators. Thus while the HKEA is also a centralized body, the influence of other groups on its decision making is much greater than is the case with the Curriculum Development Committee and the Advisory Inspectorate. This is the result of both the extent of bureaucratic control and the different functions performed by these bodies. The CDC and the inspectorate are concerned with identifying and disseminating the formal curriculum doctrine. The HKEA is concerned with determining what will be examined and how. The latter task requires a regular input from a wider variety of persons, because the authority's own staff could not carry out the task of syllabus construction, examination setting, and marking without the assistance of teachers.

The overall effect of this structure is a dual system of curriculum control which involves different degrees of bureaucratic regulation. The range of subjects studied and the textbooks used are effectively determined by the Advisory Inspectorate. Decisions related to the content of subjects are undertaken within the HKEA, which involves a wider degree of participation by other group of people, especially teachers. This pattern of control is most pervasive at those levels of the educational system in which pupils are preparing for a public examination such as the Hong Kong Certificate of Education Examination. At the Junior Secondary level there is more diversity, and the last five years have seen the development in some individual schools of new curricula. These have primarily focused on civic, social, moral and ethical education and have frequently been viewed as the responsibility of the form teacher—which means that they are not viewed as "school subjects" and involve about one period a week in the school timetable.

A separate and more recently developed mechanism for influencing the school curriculum involves the production of official guidelines for promoting a variety of interdisciplinary goals. These guidelines have been produced by the Advisory Inspectorate and have covered moral education,[14] civics education,[15] and sex education.[16] These documents indicate an official government perspective, or at least the perception of that position by the educational equivalent of what Lipsky terms "street-level bureaucrats."[17] A comparison of the moral education and civic education guidelines provides a clear indication of the effect of 1997 on at least part of the formal curriculum. The former document preceded the announcement in 1982 that the People's Republic of China intended to resume the sovereignty of Hong Kong while the latter followed it.

The Impact of 1997 on the Curriculum

Three sources of data will be used to identify the impact of the political change on the curriculum. These sources arise from the three separate mechanisms identified above for controlling and changing the curriculum, namely the production and modification of subjects through the examination syllabus, the production of curriculum guidelines, and the control of the content of school textbooks. Subsequently, an analysis will be undertaken of the School-Based Curriculum Project Scheme, which was introduced in 1988 officially to encourage curriculum initiatives from the periphery rather than from the center.

These sources influenced the curriculum in two ways. First, the decision to return the sovereignty of Hong Kong to the PRC has created pressure to prepare pupils for their future as PRC citizens. This influence has come primarily from the government, whose primary goals are to ensure minimal disruption prior to 1997 and a trouble-free handover in 1997. This task has been pursued by revising the content of school curricula to encourage pupils to understand and appreciate their Chinese cultural heritage and the workings of the political and economic system in the PRC. The second influence, which has arisen primarily from within the local community, entails an attempt to use the curriculum to increase the political awareness and involvement of the populace. This is to ensure that Hong Kong has a politically literate and active population which will allow it to function as a relatively autonomous political and economic entity after 1997. Specifically, the curriculum has been used to support attempts to promote a more representative system of government in Hong Kong.

This task, which had been largely ignored since the eventually unsuccessful attempt of the governor in the late 1940s to introduce a more representative system of government, became a matter of concern when the political future of Hong Kong was made clear in 1982 and an urgent issue following the suppression of the pro-democracy movement in China in 1989.

Examination Syllabus

An understanding of the ways that the syllabuses have changed requires an understanding of their initial content with regard to political issues and to Chinese culture. Prior to 1982, the secondary school subjects at Form IV–V level which encouraged either political awareness or which attempted to provide students with an awareness of aspects of Chinese culture were economic and public affairs (EPA), economics, history, social studies, Chinese language and Chinese history. Table 5.1 shows the school subjects and content areas that provided a basis for achieving these purposes for selected years between 1972 and 1989. It shows that the number of school subjects and the syllabus content which provided a basis for pupils to develop an understanding of political processes or of Chinese culture increased with the addition of government and public affairs (GPA) as a school subject from 1988. Further, the number and range of topics within existing subjects which required the coverage of these areas rose markedly after 1984.

Changes in the content of these subjects from 1972 to 1989 reveal a clear pattern. In the case of history, the proportion of the syllabus devoted to the study of China increased marginally from 1972 to 1984. In 1972, of the twelve topics

(text continues on page 129)

Table 5.1

The Inculusion of Political and Cultural Items in Selcected HKEA Syllabuses: 1972–1989

Economic & Public Affairs (EPA)

1972　　The 'Public Affairs' section contained fourteen topics which included the following:
(1) HK as a colony
(2) Constitution of HK
(3) Administration of HK
(4) Government and the citizen (14) U.N.O and its links with HK

Geography

The syllabus containing three sections,–A: Physical Geography,–B: Regional Geography,–and C: World Human and Economic Geography. Regional Geography included the following topics: Regional Geography: A general knowledge of the physical background of the continent of Asia as a whole. China,–Taiwan, Hong Kong, Malaysia, Singapore, Thailand, Laos, Cambodia, and Vietnam

History

Only outline study of the period after 1941 will be required. Five essay-type questions will be set for each of the three sections,–but no essay-type question will be set on the period after 1941 (A) East Asia 1793–1952 (B) Europe 1830–1959 (C) USA 1787–1960
Section A: Total twelve topics including the following:
(1) Causes and results of the First and Second Anglo-Chinese Wars
(2) The Tai Ping Rebellion; relations between China and the Western Powers, 1860–94
(4) Development of China toward a Modern State up to 1911
(6) China and Japan: their relations with each other and with the Western Powers,–1894–1914
(7) The ideas and career of Sun Yat-sen; the Chinese Revolution to 1916; the rise of the Kuomintang and the Chinese Communist party
(8) China and Japan in World War I;the Twenty-one Demands; the Versailles and Washington Conferences
(10) China and Japan in World War II; the Chinese United Front against Japan; Allied diplomacy
(11) Post-War China up to 1449: the Marshall Mission; Communist-Nationalist attempted cooperation; the Civil War

Economic & Public Affairs (EPA)

1976　　The 'Public Affairs' section contained five topics which included:
(1) Introduction to the idea of a community
(2) Government and a constitution
(3) HK's international setting—social and political links with other countries, particularly Britain and China.

Table 5.1 *(continued)*

Geography

The syllabus contains only two sections (Physical and Human Geography). The Human Geography contained six topics (a–f) which included: Section 8: Human Geography
(a) (i) Broad outlines of relief, climate vegetation of East & South East Asia and Australasia
(ii) Population distribution and location of urban centers in East and SE Asia and Australasia
(b) Rural settlement and land use
(ii) agriculture in N. China Plain
(iii) agriculture in Szechuan Basin [NB: These changes first introduced in 1975]

History

Four essay-type questions will be set for each of the three sections (A) East Asia 1860–1952 (B) Europe 1870–1960 (C) USA 1860–1963
Total ten topics including:
(l) The Self-Strengthening Movement and Foreign Relations to 1894
(2) China from the Reform Movement of 1898 to the 1911 Revolution
(3) China and Japan: their relations with each other and with the Western powers, 1894–1914
(6) World War I; Sino-Japanese Relations
(7) China after 1911: the Kuomintang,–the rise of the Chinese Communist party
(8) Japanese Nationalism: Sino-Japanese relations from the Washington Conference to 1937,–the Second Sino-Japanese War to 1945
(9) Post-War China up to 1947, Communists versus Nationalists, the Civil War

Economic & Public Affairs (EPA)

1984   The 'Public Affairs' section contained six topics which included:
(1) The HK Government: functions and policymaking (the Governor
(2) Government and the people: representative systems liberal democracies; principles and forms,–consultation with the people through official channels for the redress of grievances in HK
(5) The legal system in HK (principles of justice,–law and law making,–types of courts)
(6) HK and the outside world (the political and economic status of HK,–HK's relations with China and the UK)

Table 5.1 *(continued)*

Geography

1984   The syllabus contains the same two sections. The Human Geography involves six topics which included:
(1) General Background,–A study of thephysical environments in general of Eastand SE Asia and Australasia with a view tounderstanding their impact on human activities
    (a) the relief,–structure,–climate,–and vegetation of East and SE Asia and Australasia
    (b) The distributions of population and location of urban centers in East, SE Asia, and Australasia
(2) Agriculture and Forestry
    (d) Intensive agriculture: Sichuan Basin
(3) Minerals and Power Resources
    (a) Power resources of China
(4) Manufacturing Industries
    (b) China,–NE China,–Shanghai,–Lanchow, and Urumchi
(5) Urban Centers
    (b) Ports: Wuhan and Sydney
    (c) Capital cities: Beijing,–Canberra,–and Manila
(6) Socioeconomic and other problems
    (b) Water conservation,–irrigation,–and flood control (with special reference to Hwangho and the Snowy Mountain multipurpose schemes
    (c) Difficulties of developing the tropical rain forest (e.g.,–Indonesia) and the arid interior (Sinkiang)

    Three sections will be studied
    (A) East Asia 1870–1952
    (B) Europe 1870–1960
    (C) USA 1860–1963
    Section A: Total nine topics including:
    (l) The background to Sino-Japanese War 1894–95
    (2) China from the Reform Movement of 1898 to the Revolution of 1911
    (4) China and Japan: their relations with each other and with the Western powers 1895–1914
    (5) World War I: Sino-Japanese relations; the Washington Conference
    (6) China after 1911: the Kuomintang; the rise of the Chinese Communist Party
    (7) Japanese Militarism: Sino-Japanese relations from the Washington Conference to 1937; the Second Sino-Japanese War to 1945
    (8) Post-War China to 1949: Communists versus Nationalists to the proclamation of the People's Republic of China

Table 5.1 *(continued)*

Economic & Public Affairs (EPA)

1987 The 'Public Affairs' contained seven topics which included:
(1) The HK government: functions and policy making (the governor,–Executive Council,–Legislative Council)
(2) Local Administration (district boards,–district management committees
(3) Government and the People (representative systems liberal democracies: principles and forms
(5) Legal System in HK (principles of justice,–law and law making,–types of courts and their jurisdiction)
(6) HK and the Outside World: relationships among,–HK,China and Britain—(i) the role of the Sino-British Joint Liaison Group, (ii) emphasizing current issues, e.g. immigration, industrial and economic cooperation: the future development of HK—(i) the Sino-British agreement on the future of HK (ii) the future of HK as a Special Administrative Region

(There were no relevant changes for 1989)

Geography

1987 No change from 1984

History

No change from 1984

Government & Public Affairs (GPA)

1989 (NEW SUBJECT) This subject is available for all schools from 1989. Candidate cannot sit both EPA and GPA. A total of six topics which include:

(1) How HK is governed
 (a) the central government of HK
 (b) local administration
(2) Government and the People
 (a) fundamental rights and obligations of citizens
 (b) representative government and elections
 (c) communication,–consultation,–and the redress of grievances
 (d) mass media,–public opinion,–and interest groups
(3) Law and Justice
 (a) the rule of law and principles of justice
 (b) types of courts and their jurisdictions

Table 5.1 *(continued)*

  (6) Hong Kong and China
   (a) relationship between HK and China
    (i) HK as an industrial,–trading,–and financial center
    (ii) the Sino-British agreement on the future of HK
    (iii) the role of the Sino-British Joint Liaison Group and the Land Commission
    (iv) the idea of 'one country,–two systems' and the future of HK
   (b) political institutions of the People's Republic of China
    (i) state institutions
     –the constitution
     –National People's Congress
     –State Council
    (ii) party institutions
     –National Party Congress
     –Central Committee
     –Politburo
    (iii) relationship between party and state - their interlocking relationship at different levels - political and ideological leadership of the party over the government,–army and society
   (c) recent developments in China and their impact on HK
    (i) the Four Modernizations
    (ii) special economic zones
    (iii) special administrative regions

Geography

1989 No relevant changes

History

  (The new syllabus was first implemented in 1988). The scope of the questions will cover the period 1760–1970. At least seven questions will be set within each of the following periods:
  (a) Circa 1760–1919 (covering topics 1–11 of the syllabus)
  (b) Circa 1815–1970 (covering topics 4–14 of the syllabus)
  Topics:
  (1) The Agrarian Revolution and Industrial Revolution
  (2) The American war of Independence and Constitution
  (3) The French Revolution and Napoleon Bonaparte
  (4) The Congress of Vienna and the Congress System
  (5) The rise of nation-states in Europe
  (6) The development of Parlimentary government in Britain
  (7) The opening of China and Japan
  (8) China from the self-strengthening movement to the May 4th Movement
  (9) The rise of Japan as a world power
  (10) The Russian Revolution
  (11) World War I
  (12) Developments in major countries during the inter-war period
  (13) World War II
  (14) The contemporary world: international conflict and cooperation

in section A, eight were concerned with the history of China prior to 1949. In 1976 the ratio was seven out of ten, and in 1984 and 1987 it was also seven out of ten topics. The focus remained on the period before 1949. The 1988 syllabus has been drastically revised to focus on forteen topics in total, with no discrimination between geographic sections or time periods and with the extension of the time period to allow the study of topics up to 1970. The topics chosen focus on the political history of the establishment of statehood and political independence by the United States, the United Kingdom, France, the Soviet Union, and China. The new syllabus provides pupils with a more politicized historical framework than was previously the case, and one more relevant to Hong Kong's future.

In the case of economic and public affairs, the changes were particularly significant. Between 1972 and 1976 EPA focused on describing the processes and institutions of government in Hong Kong. The only changes evident in 1976 were the removal of the term "colony" and the specific inclusion of a topic concerned with the links between Britain and China. The 1984 syllabus saw a marked change with an increased focus on systems of government, especially those involving representation and consultation, and on the principles of law making. These themes were elaborated in the 1987 syllabus, and specific reference was made to the Joint Declaration and Hong Kong's future.

Government and public affairs was first examined as an "A" level subject in 1988, and was first examined at Certificate level in 1989. The content of the Certificate-level GPA syllabus produced by the HKEA is similar to the public affairs section of the EPA syllabus, but greater stress is placed on those concepts that are central to liberal Western democracies (the rule of law, representation, consultation, elections) and to the study of political processes in China. The genesis of the subject is itself illustrative of the effect of political change on the school curriculum. During the 1970s several attempts were made to introduce an "A" level subject in politics. These initial efforts were not fruitful as the subject was viewed by the Education Department as too specialized and unsuitable for schoolchildren who might be susceptible to undue political pressure. The Sino-British negotiations resulted in a number of public demands for increased political education. In January 1984 a legislative councilor argued that there was an urgent need for political education. In March, the director of education criticized those who had argued for the inclusion of political studies in the curriculum on the grounds that it was "too risky." He stated that there were opportunities for pupils to discuss current affairs in the existing economic and public affairs course. Later in March, a number of legislative councilors spoke of the need for political education and a motion was raised that all Hong Kong citizens should receive a true democratic education. A number of pressure groups made similar demands. In April, a representative of the Hong Kong Examinations Authority stated that they were currently considering the introduction of a new subject, GPA at "A" level. In May, the director of education stated that the government was committed to the provision of political education and that they were supportive of the university's plans to introduce GPA as an "A" level subject. Later in May, he also stated at a meeting of the Legislative Council that the Education Department was also planning to introduce GPA at Certificate level. These events indicate that the government was initially unwilling to introduce politics as a school subject but as the public demand for political education heightened, their position changed and they quickly activated the proposal for a new "A" level subject.

The nature of the influences operating through the mechanism of the HKEA have not however been uniform across subjects. The Chinese history syllabus, for example, has not, however, changed in any significant way in terms of its explicit political content. A revision of the Chinese language syllabus began in 1982, and will be introduced from 1991. The new syllabus will include as required reading a small number of texts (three out of twenty-six) originating from contemporary authors in the PRC. This is a departure from the current situation which only specifies pre-1949 texts as required reading. However, the texts from the PRC chosen for inclusion in the Hong Kong syllabus are distinctly apolitical in nature, and the change is counterbalanced by the inclusion of a similar number of texts written by contemporary Taiwanese authors.

The geography syllabus changed similarly between 1972 and 1974 in that the human geography section focused more on Asia and specifically on China. However, the syllabus remained apolitical.

Curriculum Guidelines

The curriculum guidelines on civic education, published in 1985 by the Education Department, contain the most direct attempt by the government to influence the curriculum with regard to Hong Kong's political future. It recommends that civic education be taught across the curriculum rather than in separate courses. This was a direct response by the Education Department to the concern expressed within Hong Kong over the general lack of political awareness and the need to increase that awareness if Hong Kong were to exist as a relatively autonomous part of China in the future. The suggested framework for incorporating political and cultural issues in the curriculum through civic education is shown in Table 5.2. In contrast to the EPA and GPA syllabuses, the guidelines do not specifically mention the transfer of Hong Kong's sovereignty to China in 1997. Substantial emphasis is put on developing the pupil's identification with and pride in Chinese culture. While the guidelines encourage the study of some political concepts, the greater stress is on the analysis of governmental institutions and on the rights and responsibilities of a good citizen. This focus is reflected in suggestions on teaching methods, which avoid mention of activities that might encourage political involvement. It is also in keeping with the very clear intentions of the guidelines not to disturb the status quo or to encourage radical change. At the outset it is explained that "In the light of Hong Kong's recent political development, evolution should be the watch-word and the emphasis in this guide will be on civic education as a politically socializing force for promoting stability and responsibility."

In contrast to the changes in subjects such as EPA and the introduction of GPA, the guidelines specifically avoid mention of political concepts and processes related to democracy. The justification for this position is that

> Democracy means different things to different people. As the American president Abraham Lincoln put it, it means "Government of the people, by the people, for the people." Alternatively, it may also be interpreted as a way of life in which the decision-making process is characterized by majority control. There are many brands of democracy in the political arena—some pluralistic, some centralist and various combinations of both. So education for democracy per se would be difficult to interpret. Although some basic understanding of the concept of democracy may be introduced according to the intellectual level and experience of pupils, for the purpose of these guidelines the term "civic education" will be used.

Since there is no universally accepted definition of democracy, it will be impossible to base a curriculum on it and to provide pupils with some basic understanding of the concept.

A comparison with the moral education guidelines published in 1981 is also instructive. These precepts, which have a distinctly Confucian flavor, had the potential to achieve similar aims to the civic education guidelines, for their purpose was: " . . . to develop a moral sensibility, to promote character formation and training, to encourage correct attitudes towards life, school and community."

The themes identified as appropriate to help an individual develop correct attitudes toward the community are rights and responsibilities of others, awareness and respect for other cultures, and harmony with people of other nationalities. These were to be achieved through all school subjects and by nonbook education, special functions, and school activities. The guidelines are platitudinous and vague, and, like the civic education guidelines, distinctly apolitical. They, too, encourage pupils to conform to the prevailing social system and political arrangements. The major difference between the two documents is that the latter attempts to prepare pupils for their future as citizens of China. This consideration was not influential in 1981, but was a paramount influence on the centrally controlled aspects of the formal curriculum in 1985. Thus the conditions within which the curriculum is defined changed with Hong Kong's political future.

A similar pattern emerges with the Forms I–III social studies syllabus. A revised draft syllabus was produced in 1989 by the Advisory Inspectorate of the Education Department. As a subject that is not publicly examined, the F.I–III social studies syllabus does not require any involvement by HKEA, unlike the subjects referred to in Table 5.1. Table 5.3 shows that the range of topics would

(text continues on page 136)

Table 5.2

The Inclusion of Political and Cultural Items within the Guidelines on Civic Education in Schools (Excluding Primary Schools)

	Knowledge	Attitudes	Skills
Junior Secondary	(3) *The individual and society (HK)* (a) Introduction to HK with basic knowledge of its history, its geographical setting, its people, its industrial, commercial, financial, social, and cultural development (b) How HK is governed: a brief description of the administration of HK; the importance of law and order to a community; the government and the people (c) Rights and responsibilities of a citizen: an understanding of certain basic rights, freedom, and responsibilities of a citizen: e.g.,.. *Rights* right to life right to be protected by law right to private ownership of property right to vote *Freedoms* freedom of speech freedom of worship freedom from unlawful arrest freedom of travel *Responsibilities* to be law abiding to respect the rights of others to support civic activities for the common good	Sense of belonging to HK Appreciate the cultural heritage of HK An awareness of the importance of cultural exchange Appreciate the factors that are responsible for HK's earlier success and future stability and prosperity Sense of duty to HK Appreciate the functions of the government Cooperate with the government Respect for law and order Support for common good An awareness of HK government affairs Appreciation of one's own rights in society Correct attitudes in exercising one's own rights Respect for other people's rights Be prepared to protect one's rights and those of others Appreciation of the value of freedom Appreciation of freedom of oneself and others Respect for other people's freedom Be prepared to protect one's freedom and that of other people	To identify one's relationship with HK To describe HK with a certain degree of accuracy about its history, geography, and economic development To present a good image of HK To participate in community service To think logically and rationally To evaluate the performance of government objectively Group interaction skills, e.g., discussions, debates Social and political participation skills To participate in activities in support of common good, particularly government-sponsored campaigns To express personal feelings and convictions regarding one's rights To think objectively with ability to analyze data To make decisions with consideration of consequences To express personal feelings and convictions regarding freedom To adjust one's behavior in group situations To participate in civic activities in the community

(d) Current issues: an understanding of major current issues related to the political, economic, social and cultural development of HK, e.g., representative government, district administration, trade negotiations, social and cultural services policies

(4) *The individual and the nation (China)* A basic understanding of the history of China; its geographical setting and cultural heritage; awareness of China's recent political and economic development; an understanding of HK's cultural, political, and economic link with China

(5) *The individual and the world* An understanding of HK as
(a) a cosmopolitan city (fusion of cultures)
(b) an export-oriented city (dependence on world markets)
(c) a financial center (dependence on foreign investment)
(d) a tourist center (dependence on tourists)
(e) a place to promote international understanding

Awareness of one's responsibilities
Readiness to contribute to common good and progress
Civic-mindedness

Concern for current issues
Willingness to understand current issues
Positive attitudes toward current issues with a commitment to try to solve some of the problems related to these issues

Sense of national identity and belonging
Love for the nation and pride in being Chinese
Respect for Chinese culture and tradition
Willingness to contribute toward the economic development of China
Appreciate the need for interdependence
Appreciate the importance of the role of China in maintaining stability and prosperity in HK
Appreciate the contribution of HK toward the modernization programs of China
An awareness of the latest developments in China

To show consideration for others
To acquire interpersonal relationship and social participation skills

To express personal feelings and convictions about current issues in the community
To participate in discussion of current issues
To analyze current issues objectively and be able to suggest ways of dealing with them

To identify one's relationship with China
To describe briefly the history and geography of China and particularly its latest political and economic developments
To explain the need for interdependence
To analyze and interpret information objectively

Able to understand different cultures in HK
Able to defend the case for free trade
To collect and analyze data on HK's trade and finance

Table 5.2 (continued)

The Inclusion of Political and Cultural Items within the Guidelines on Civic Education in Schools (Excluding Primary Schools)

	Knowledge	Attitudes	Skills
		Respect for different cultures Appreciate the importance of free trade Appreciate the factors that contribute to HK's financial well-being Respect for people of all races, creeds, and cultures Appreciate the importance of international understanding and goodwill	

Senior Secondary	(3) *The individual and society (HK)*
	(a) The HK government:
	  functions and policymaking
	  - need for rules and regulations
	  - types of rules in society
	(b) The government and the people
	  - representative systems under liberal democracies
	  - consultation with people
	  - major official channels for the redress of grievances
	  - informal influences on policymaking
	(c) Greater understanding of the rights and responsibilities of a citizen
	(Consumer Education; ICAC; Fight Crime)
		Greater awareness of the functions of government
		Appreciate the importance of rules and regulations in a stable society
		Appreciate the influence of rules on individual behavior
		
		Respect for equality, liberty, and rationality
		Readiness to give constructive criticism
		Appreciate the importance of these channels of communication
		Appreciate the value of informal influences on government policy
		Greater awareness of one's own rights and freedom within the limits of the laws of HK and of one's responsibilities towards the common good of the community
			Analyze and interpret information objectively
			Exercise self-control for the common good
			Relate one's behavior to the needs of the community
			
			Express personal feelings and convictions regarding liberal democracies
			Give constructive criticism
			Present a case objectively
			Identify channels for redress of grievances
			
			Express personal feelings and convictions regarding one's rights and freedom in the HK context
			Exercise one's civil rights and responsibilities
			Support and participate in community service

(d) Greater understanding of current issues related to the political, economic, social, and cultural development in HK

Greater awareness of current issues
Readiness to give constructive criticism on these issues

Analyze and interpret information objectively
Evaluate the influence of these issues on the community
Give constructive criticism

(4) *The individual and the nation (China)*
Greater understanding of the cultural heritage of China and its latest economic developments; greater understanding of HK's link with China and her role in maintaining stability and prosperity in HK

Respect for Chinese culture and tradition
Love for the nation and pride in being Chinese
Readiness to contribute towards the economic development of China
Greater awareness of the importance of interdependence of HK and China in the future

Discuss in more detail the background to Chinese culture and tradition
Analyze the factors relating to the latest economic developments in China
Explain objectively the interdependent relationship between HK and China

(5) *The individual and the world*
(a) Greater understanding of HK as
  (i) a cosmopolitan city (fusion of cultures: particularly the influence on HK's life-style)
  (ii) an export-oriented city (dependence on world markets: particularly in negotiations with our trading partners)
  (iii) a financial center (dependence on foreign investments: particularly on the value of stable and convertible local currency)
  (iv) a tourist center (dependence on tourists: particularly to maintain and improve our facilities as a tourist center)
  (v) a place to promote international understanding

Value the contribution of different cultures in enriching the life-style of HK
Appreciate the importance of free trade and the value of trade negotiations
Appreciate the importance of free market and a stable and freely convertible local currency
Respect for people of all races
Appreciate the importance of international understanding

Identify the contributions of various cultures toward the life-style of HK
Distinguish between free trade and protectionism
Gather factual information concerning money markets
Give help to tourists
Explain to others about one's own culture and appreciate that of others

(b) International understanding
  (i) world distribution of resources
  (ii) the work of the United Nations organizations
  (iii) world problems, e.g., energy crises, pollution, population

Appreciate the need for cooperation
Concern for other people
Concern for world issues

Ability to explain to others about one's own culture and appreciate that of others
Ability to analyze and evaluate information
Ability to present a well-argued case and contribute to problem solving

require pupils to focus on political and cultural issues in the original and revised syllabus. The original syllabus could best be described as a selection of topics from the mainstream social science disciplines. Very little mention was made of China and pupils were provided with a description of how the government of Hong Kong worked and their rights and responsibilities as citizens. This emphasis was similar to that in those subjects described in Table 5.1 prior to 1984. The revised syllabus contains essentially the same descriptive political orientation but specific reference is made to the joint agreement and the Basic Law. The major change occurs with the inclusion of a number of topics that provide pupils with information about China and which attempt to inculcate an awareness of and affiliation to Chinese culture and the PRC. In encouraging pupils to draw the flag of the PRC, describe the development and structure of the Chinese Communist party, study the biography of Mao Zedong, and understand the need for central planning, the revised syllabus constitutes an about-face in terms of what is viewed as acceptable content for school subjects in Hong Kong. Prior to 1982–84 such "activities" would have been viewed as contrary to Education Regulation No. 98 ("activities of a party or party political nature") and could have resulted in the closure of the school, the dismissal of the teacher, or the withdrawal of government financial support. Clearly, what constitutes acceptable politics has changed and it is the bureaucracy that decides how the education regulations should be interpreted. As with the civic education guidelines, the social studies syllabus has been revised so that pupils are prepared for and left to accept their fate as future citizens of China.

School Textbooks

With regard to the third area of curriculum decision making, namely the control of textbooks that are approved for use in schools, a similar pattern is evident. This form of influence, as with the production of curriculum guidelines, is wholly under the control of the government's Education Department. Its decisions and "suggestions" are communicated directly and confidentially to the publishers who, for commercial reasons, usually prefer to avoid publicity and make the suggested changes. As a result, this form of control is relatively private and not easily identified. Discussions with authors and publishers provide a number of examples which display the same influence evident in the curriculum guidelines. A small sample of these included the suggestions that:

- EPA and history textbooks submitted for approval in 1986 should avoid reference to Hong Kong as a British colony;
- an EPA textbook should, when discussing the Korean War, revise the phrase "North Korean armies attacked South Korea and war broke out" to read "War broke out between North Korea and South Korea";

- a geography text should delete a map that portrayed military missiles aimed by China and Russia at each other;
- a history text and school atlas should not show Tibet and Mongolia as separate countries prior to 1949.

These "suggestions" are followed by a reminder:
"N.B. The Education Department reserves the right to delete the book from the recommended Textbook List if appropriate amendments are not made."

The common element in these suggestions is the attempt to modify textbooks to ensure that China is portrayed in a favorable light. The effect has been to produce a form of self-censorship since publishers, wishing to avoid the costs of resetting a text to incorporate suggestions, have begun to edit manuscripts themselves to ensure that future amendments are not required. This is currently evident in the response of publishers to the inclusion of any references to the suppression of the prodemocracy movement in the PRC in 1989 in school textbooks. Publishers are very reluctant to include any reference to those events as they anticipate that it will be censored by the Education Department and/or could result in some form of retaliation after 1997.

The School-Based Curriculum Project Scheme (SBCPS)

This scheme was introduced by the Education Department in 1988 to encourage a movement away from center–periphery strategies of curriculum development. This initiative was portrayed as a response to criticisms of the limitations of the prevailing mechanisms of curriculum development and an attempt to develop curricula appropriate to meet the varied needs of pupils in schools. The scheme was also introduced at a time when a number of teachers had, in an attempt to develop pupils' civic and political awareness, begun to develop their own curricula in areas of civics and social education.

The purposes and the name of the scheme would, prima facie, suggest that the SBCPS would encourage greater teacher involvement in curriculum development. A consequence of this should be that the central government's influence on the curriculum would be reduced and that one could anticipate an increased focus within the curriculum on those concepts and principles that would encourage pupils to view Hong Kong as "a distinct sociopolitical entity." This would result in the introduction of curriculum changes similar to those that have been promoted through the mechanisms of the HKEA and contrary to those arising from the Advisory Inspectorate. The extent to which the liberalization and decentralization of the strategy of curriculum development will have this effect is not indicated by a detailed analysis of either the organizational details of the scheme nor of the nature of projects supported. Central control of curriculum innovation is effectively increased by a complex and new range of administrative measures. These include the way pro-

Table 5.3

The Inclusion of Political and Cultural Items in the Social Studies Syllabus: 1975–1989

The syllabus focused on the following areas: Health and Welfare, the Individual and Society, Population, Introduction to HK, Living in HK, Urbanization, Pollution and Conservation, Education, Our Neighbors, Industrialization, Law and Order, Other Regions, Structure of Our Industrial Economy, and Work and Leisure.

The following addressed political and/or cultural issues:

F.II Our Neighbors: Location and extent of China, Japan and Southeast Asian countries, e.g., Thailand, Malaysia, the Philippines, and Indonesia.

Law and Order: How H.K. is governed, structure and working of government, the legal systems, problems of law and order.

F.III The Individual and Society: Role of a citizen (rights and and responsibilities), the individual and the State (ideas of citizenship in ancient Rome and Greece). Other Regions: brief study of any two continents, sample study of one of the topics including forming activities in a commune in China.

International Cooperation and Understanding: balance of power, distribution of wealth and resources, current world problems, work of some world organizations (UN, Red Cross, etc).

1990 (Draft Revised Syllabus):

It is proposed that the new syllabus will be devised around the central theme of 'The adolescent and his world' and focus on five areas: Myself, My Family and Friends, the local community, the Chinese people, and the World. Political and cultural issues are addressed in the following topics.

The Chinese People

F.II My country and my people: Geographic background of China, cultural heritage of the Chinese people (origins of Chinese civilization, traditional culture, agricultural development, examples of Chinese contribution to world civilization).

The Local Community

F.III Political development and future of HK: Political development—How HK is governed, sources of revenue and expenditure, representative government and its future development (study the importance of direct and indirect elections). Basic Law: Principles, importance, and major content. Hong Kong in transition: Social, cultural, and political changes. (Pupils should appreciate measures to maintain HK as a major industrial, trade, and financial center, develop interest in HK's status as

Table 5.3 *(continued)*

a Special Administrative Region and its relationship with China, understand the concept of "one country two systems," understand the implications of the Sino-British Joint Agreement on HK Society in the transition period.)

Role of a citizen: Civil rights and responsibilities, communication with the government (official and unofficial channels).

The Chinese People

F.III Structure of the Chinese government: The Communist party of China, the National People's Congress, the Chinese People's Congress, the Chinese People's Consultative Conference, the State Council and Local People's Government. Pupils should be able to: trace the origin and growth of the Communist party of China, name some outstanding figures of the Communist party of China and their contribution to the rise of the party, describe the functions of the political organizations, and recognize the relationship between the different levels of the Chinese government.

Suggested activities: Collect pictures of main political figures in the PRC, prepare a chart showing the rise of the Communist party, draw a chart to show the organization and structure of the Communist party of China, prepare a biography of Mao Zedong and Zhou Enlai, draw the national flag and emblem of China, collect newspaper cuttings of activities of the chief members of the State Council, draw a political map of China.

The Chinese economy: Planned economy, modern trend of economic development in China, development of natural resources, development of heavy and light industries, and improving living standards.

Suggested activities: Discuss why it is important to plan for economic development of a country, draw a graph to show the growth in production of natural resources.

The Chinese people: Desert landscape (Xinjiang), mountain and plateau landscapes (Himalayas and Xizang Gaoyuan), Karst landscape (Guilin), agricultural landscapes (Huabei Pinyuan, Sichuan, Pearl River Delta), urban and industrial landscapes (Beijing and Shanghai).

---

jects are selected, the requirements of participants in the scheme, and the prevailing context of curriculum decision making.

(a) The Identification of Projects

The details of the scheme provided to schools made it clear that priority would be given to supporting projects that were primarily adaptive rather than creative. It was explained that

Whilst the Education Department encourages the development of school-based curriculum, it is considered essential for the projects to serve the purpose of complementing the required knowledge, concepts and skills offered to pupils in the centrally devised core curriculum.

The role of teachers portrayed by the scheme is one in which they are encouraged to produce classroom resources for use with the existing CDC curricula. The scheme will also serve to define the task of resource production, which is presently undertaken on an ad hoc and nonorganized basis as coming within the direct control and influence of the Education Department. In the first SBCPS exercise, conducted in 1988, an analysis of the nature of the projects designed for mainstream secondary schools that received support indicates that all of them involved the production of resources for use within the centrally devised curricula. No support was provided for the development of an alterative curriculum in any area.

(b) The Selection of Projects

Decisions concerning which projects will obtain grants will be made by two committees: the advisory committee and the executive committee. The advisory committee is comprised of two senior government officials and an unspecified number of lay members. The crucial executive committee, which will evaluate the applications and make recommendations to the advisory committee, is comprised of the same two officials and a number of other officials, such as subject inspectors. Therefore only members of the ED are on this crucial committee—which will be able to determine the agenda of and information provided to the advisory committee. In effect, the Education Department obtains very direct power to define what is viewed as acceptable school-based curriculum development and to determine who should receive support for school-based initiatives. A further aspect of the administration of the scheme reinforces this. The payments of the award are made in three installments, at the start, in the middle and at the end of each project. The decision to release the second and third installments will be made by one of the monitoring panels, whose membership is vaguely specified as "comprising relevant subject inspectors, together with assistance from experience teachers and heads."

Thus any project not satisfying the expectations of the central bureaucracy can effectively be terminated. The powers of the monitoring panel are therefore based on legal sanction and will place the inspectors in a very powerful position in terms of the individual teacher, for to ignore the inspectors' advice could place the resourcing and continuation of a project in jeopardy.

(c) Requirements of Participants

A teacher who is awarded a project grant will have to sign an undertaking which states that (1) the work did not interfere with his/her normal duties; and (2) the work was undertaken outside normal working hours.

These requirements, along with the direct payment of money to teachers who are involved in the scheme, will define the teacher's role in curriculum decision making as one which: (a) requires extra payment, (b) is undertaken outside normal working hours, and (c) is not part of a teacher's normal duties. This could serve to reinforce the view of the teacher as a passive transmitter of knowledge defined by someone else and is clearly antithetical to the intentions of SBCPS, which is attempting to encourage teachers to view their role as extended professionals who see curriculum development as a central part of their task.

The scheme will send a clear message to the many teachers who are already attempting to produce teaching resources that such activities are viewed as beyond their normal duties. This could have the effect of reducing the overall extent of teacher involvement in curriculum development since the vast majority of teachers will not be recipients of awards.

The SBCPS demonstrates a clear conflict between the rhetoric of policy statements and what is envisaged in practice. The scheme employs a liberal progressive rhetoric which stresses teacher participation and autonomy. Its operational practices indicate that its key features focus on hierarchy, centralization, and authority. The language of school-centered innovation is therefore being used to erect a facade to hide or disguise the realities of control and power.

The remaining question relates to the issues of intention and motivation. Two major alternative propositions can be employed to explain why the SBCPS has been developed and introduced into Hong Kong. The first proposition assumes a degree of rationality by policymakers and would interpret the scheme as a covert attempt during the sensitive political period prior to 1997 to extend central control of the curriculum at a time when there is an emergence of school-centered initiatives. Alternatively, the introduction of the SBCPS can be interpreted as evidence of the inability of bureaucracies, especially in situations where there is no countervailing power, to operate beyond a concern for the organizational factors that constitute their raison d'être, namely hierarchy, control, and authority. Evidence for the former proposition would require access to the processes and details of government policy initiatives, which are both beyond the purposes of this paper and difficult to obtain given the secrecy of the government's decision making. It is also important to recognize that any educational policy initiative can create a "Rashomon effect." The SBCPS will possibly be viewed by different groups in different ways.

From the viewpoint of the central authorities it is administratively tidy and maintains a clear hierarchy of control. From the viewpoint of teachers the scheme can be ignored if necessary and will not affect them in their day-to-day work. This will allow both parties to satisfy their own norms with a minimum of interference.

Conclusion

This study has focused on aspects of the formal curriculum of Hong Kong senior secondary schools to identify the effect on the curriculum of the impending return of Hong Kong's sovereignty to the People's Republic of China and to determine the mechanisms through which that influence operates. This allows a contribution to be made to our wider understanding of the influences on and mechanisms of controlling curricula.

Overall it has been argued that while the curriculum in Hong Kong has always been influenced by political considerations, the impending return of Hong Kong's sovereignty to China has had a marked effect on the formal curriculum of secondary schools. First, it has affected the range of subjects available for study. Second, it has influenced both the content and treatment of topics within the existing secondary school curriculum. The two specific influences identified were a distinct sino-centrification and/or politicization of some subjects. Third, the 1997 issue has resulted in the government's producing a new set of moral education guidelines under the guise of the civic education guidelines.

Three existing mechanisms of curriculum control were identified. These are: the mechanism for defining examination syllabuses for school subjects; the central production of non–subject-specific curriculum guidelines and nonexamined subjects at the F.I–III level; and the process of approving textbooks. These were distinguished with regard to the extent of bureaucratic control. The first operates through the HKEA and involves a wider range of interest groups, including school and university teachers. It was seen in some subject areas to emphasize the politicization of school subjects in an attempt to encourage the study of those concepts and principles central to the workings of a liberal democratic system. However, this influence was not uniform across subjects. The other two mechanisms emanate from within the Education Department and are an illustration of the more direct pressure of the state bureaucracy on the curriculum. These channels attempted to define the curriculum so as to minimize political awareness and to encourage pupils to identify themselves as future citizens of China. The same essential dichotomy between state control and personal freedom was also evident in the PRC during the student protests in Beijing in May and June of 1989. The students were arguing for the need for greater freedom and democracy and constructed an effigy of the Statue of Liberty to symbolize their protest. The response of the Chinese government included a number of announcements that stated that the students' actions were disloyal, unpatriotic, and inspired by foreign provocateurs. This paper indicates that the same tensions are now affecting the secondary school curriculum in Hong Kong.

A new mechanism of curriculum development and control was identified, namely the School-Based Curriculum Project Scheme. This was seen to have the potential to extend control over any attempts at school-centered innovation and to define involvement in curriculum innovation as both outside the teacher's normal role and an activity that required bureaucratic approval.

The detailed analysis of the changes that have been made to school curricula provides no support for the view that the government is attempting to alter the education system to maintain a British influence after 1997. On the contrary, the government's influence on the curriculum was an attempt to increase pupils' awareness of and pride in their Chinese cultural heritage. This was interpreted as an attempt to ensure a smooth and trouble-free period of transition prior to 1997. The tensions within and influences on the curriculum arise from essentially domestic and local concerns specific to Hong Kong as it prepares to become a Special Administrative Region of China. In methodological terms this study confirms the need for a conscientious analysis of contemporary social and economic pressures on the curriculum if we are going to develop an understanding of why curriculum change occurs. A mere description of the colonial context within which those processes operate will not suffice.

The study lends support to the view that the state bureaucracy plays a critical role in the definition of the curriculum and that it is manipulated for political purposes. Further, both the CDC and HKEA are centralized educational agencies, insofar as they perform a systemwide function, but their effect on school curricula was seen to be different. While the HKEA is in functional terms a centralized body, it does not possess the same degree of control over decision making as is the case with the CDC. This suggests that the key determinant of the extent of state control of the curriculum is not whether a centralized systemwide function is performed but rather the extent of bureaucratic control over decision making.

However, substantial caution must be exercised in deriving any generalizable propositions. First, the absence of well-organized and developed pressure groups in Hong Kong, concerned with influencing the curriculum, creates a situation in which state control is readily maintained because of an absence of alternative organized forces. Thus the conditions did not exist to test the impact of competing influences on the curriculum. However, this study's evidence of the albeit limited effect of teachers on the mechanisms controlled by the HKEA would support the view that the existence of organized interest groups is potentially a critical determinant of the direction of curriculum development. Clearly the existence of such groups is not necessarily dependent on the extent of centralization. In the case of Hong Kong, the centralized system of decision making and the absence of organized groups attempting to define the curriculum has allowed the formal curriculum to be substantially determined by the state bureaucracy.

Second, the directions operating through the HKEA on the definitions of subject content were as overtly political, if different in nature, as those arising from sources that were bureaucratically controlled. While the centrally controlled mechanisms were emphasizing the maintenance of the status quo, the other was more supportive of political change and action.

With specific regard to Hong Kong, the indications that arise in this chapter raise a number of implications for the future. Clearly Hong Kong is in a political conundrum. The 1997 issue obviously has already had a major impact on the curriculum of secondary schools. The competing pressures to develop a relatively autonomous political system and not to disturb the status quo are reflected in the school curriculum. The government has used a range of bureaucratic controls to try to ensure a trouble-free transfer in 1997, but the sources of this policy are unclear. It could have arisen from the actions of local bureaucrats, or from the pressure of the governments of China and/or the United Kingdom on the Hong Kong government. Other sources of data will be required to establish the origins of the current policy and the extent to which that policy is changed or modified in view of the suppression of the prodemocracy movement in the PRC in 1989. The initial indications are that the massacre of the students in Tiananmen Square on June 4 has encouraged a political awareness in Hong Kong which would reinforce attempts to encourage its development as a distinct and democratic sociopolitical entity. Any concern that the return of Hong Kong's sovereignty to the People's Republic of China in 1997 will result in the politicization of education are unwarranted, for it is evident that the curriculum reflects the interests of those in an influential position in Hong Kong and the impending change of sovereignty has already served to accelerate and exacerbate the political pressures on the curriculum. Further, the mechanisms of curriculum development that currently operate in Hong Kong allow the government to maintain a high degree of control over how the curriculum is defined and over any attempts at school-centered innovation. These mechanisms are currently being used and could continue to be used in the future to determine the nature of the school curriculum. A number of questions that require further analysis now arise from the changed perceptions of the Hong Kong population toward the PRC. These include the issue of whether Hong Kong the government will continue to promote the same message vis-à-vis the PRC through the secondary school curriculum in view of the population's enhanced political and civic awareness.

Notes

1. For example: J. Ben David and R. Collins, "Social Factors in the Origin of a New Science: The Case of Psychology," *American Sociological Review* 31(4), (1966); *International Perspectives in Curriculum History,* ed. I. Goodson (London: Croom Helm, 1987); J. Kwong, "Changing Political Culture and Changing Curriculum: An Analysis of Language Textbooks in the People's Republic of China," *Comparative Education* 21(2)(1985); S. Lukes, *Power, A Radical View: Studies in Sociology* (London: Macmillan, 1974); B. Salter and T. Tapper, *Education, Politics and the State* (London: Grant McIntyre, 1981), D. Schon, *Beyond the Stable State* (London: Penguin, 1973); M.F.D. Young, ed., *Knowledge and Control* (London: Collier Macmillan, 1971).
2. K. Arai, "Political Education in China: A Study of Socialization through Children's Textbooks," *Journal of North East Asian Studies* 3(2) (1984).
3. R. Williams, *The Long Revolution* (Harmondsworth: Penguin, 1965).
4. A. Sweeting, "The Reconstruction of Education in Post-War Hong Kong, 1945–

1954: Variations in the Process of Policy Making" (Ph.D. diss., University of Hong Kong, 1989).

5. A. Sweeting, *Education in Hong Kong, pre-1841 to 1941: Fact and Opinion* (Hong Kong: Hong Kong University Press, 1990).

6. M.S. Archer, *Social Origins of Educational Systems* (London: Sage, 1979).

7. M. Kogan, E. Boyle, and A. Crosland, *The Politics of Education* (Harmondsworth: Penguin, 1971); A.E. Wise, *Legislated Learning: The Bureaucratization of the American Classroom* (Berkeley: University of California Press, 1979).

8. P. Broadfoot and B. Moon, "Rhetoric and Reality in the Context of Innovation: An English Case Study," *Compare* 10(2) (1980).

9. B. Moon, "Who Controls the Curriculum? The Story of New Maths 1960–1980," in *International Perspectives in Curriculum History*, ed. I. Goodson, (London: Croom Helm, 1987); S.J. Ball, "Imperialism, Social Control and the Colonial Curriculum in Africa," *Journal of Curriculum Studies* 15(3) (1983).

10. See for example: P.G. Altbach and G.P. Kelly, eds., *Education and the Colonial Experience* (New Brunswick: Transaction Books, 1978); M. Carnoy, *Education as Cultural Imperialism* (New York: McKay, 1974).

11. Education Department, *Education Regulations*, cap. 279, section 84 (Hong Kong: Government Printer, 1971).

12. G. Psacharopoulos, "Returns to Education: A Further International Update and Implications," paper presented at the Comparative and International Education Society Meeting, Stanford University, April 1985.

13. P. Morris, "Teachers' Perceptions of the Barriers to the Implementation of a Pedagogic Innovation," *International Review of Education* 18(3) (1985).

14. Education Department, *General Guidelines on Moral Education in Schools* (Hong Kong: Government Printer, 1981).

15. Curriculum Development Committee, *Guidelines on Civic Education in Schools* (Hong Kong: Education Department, 1985).

16. Curriculum Development Committee, *Guidelines on Sex Education in Secondary Schools* (Hong Kong: Education Department, 1986).

17. M. Lipsky, *Street-Level Bureaucracy: Dilemmas of the Individual in Public Services* (New York: Russell Sage Foundation, 1980).

Part III
Education and Social Stratification

6

Egalitarianism and the Allocation of Secondary School Places in Hong Kong

Ching-kwan Lee and Tak-sing Cheung

I. Elitism vs. Egalitarianism in Educational Debates and the Transition to 1997

This chapter focuses on the debates about the reforms of the allocation of secondary school places in Hong Kong, which started in the mid-1970s and spanned the entirety of the 1980s. Initially, the reforms were aimed at minimizing the undesirable consequences of selection. But whenever allocation is involved, the issue of egalitarianism and its antonym, elitism, inevitably come to the forefront of public contentions. The ideological strife became more intensified as Hong Kong began its transition from a British colony to a Special Administrative Zone of the People's Republic of China. More specifically, the intensification of elitism and egalitarianism as the contending ideologies in the debates may be related to the political and economic situation of the transition period. Politically, the Hong Kong government has been explicit in initiating a top-down democratization process so that a viable and highly autonomous government can function and the British can withdraw with honor in 1997. Direct and indirect elections to a number of local and central governmental bodies are the clearest examples of democratization reforms. One concomitant phenomenon of a more politicized society is the emergence of a variety of interest groups. Some of these organizations are issues oriented, focusing specifically on housing, education, the environment, labor, etc. Others are quasi-political organizations that voice opinions on a plethora of public issues. Many of these champion the interests of the grass roots, whose support becomes increasingly important in view of the expansion of popular elections in the transition period. The call for more egalitarianism in educational issues can be understood as one manifestation of the democratizing political landscape of Hong Kong.

On the economic front, the brain-drain problem caused by the massive emigration of Hong Kong people, especially professionals and people in the middle levels of management, has raised concern about the quality of the education system. The quality of Hong Kong's human resources has been, and will continue to be, the mainstay of Hong Kong's economic performance. Thus, though elitism in education has in the past been associated with the British tradition, the prominence of "elitist" policies in the transition period to safeguard the quality of education may also be related to economic changes in the period. In short, the confrontation between elitism and egalitarianism in the debates on education in the 1980s can be situated in the political and economic contexts of Hong Kong's transition to 1997.

II. The Transition of Secondary Education: From an Elite to a Mass Institution

Since the early 1970s, the Hong Kong government has reversed its previous indifference toward education and started to take a more active role in reforming the educational system. The 1970s and the 1980s witnessed successive reforms of different stages of the system, and touched on both the quantity and the quality of education. Prior to the establishment of the Education Commission in 1984, the Education Department of the Hong Kong government, the formal decision-making body on educational matters, issued a number of policy papers. These included the 1974 White Paper, *Secondary Education in Hong Kong Over the Next Decade*, the 1978 White Paper, *Development of Senior Secondary and Tertiary Education*, and the White Paper *Primary Education and Pre-primary Services* in 1981. Overall, these policy papers involved two main issues: the allocation and selection mechanisms of school places and the qualitative expansion of different stages of the educational system. However, the most significant and comprehensive review of the Hong Kong education system came with the report, *A Perspective on Education in Hong Kong*, by the high-powered Llewellyn panel, on whose recommendation the government established the Education Commission. This commission, which was to offer consolidated and comprehensive advice to the government on educational matters, issued its first three reports in 1984, 1986, and 1988 respectively. Among the wide-ranging issues upon which the commission touched were the medium of instruction, Form 6 education, pre-primary school education, teachers' training, open education, and tertiary education.

With regard to secondary education, one of the main objectives of the Hong Kong government throughout the 1970s was to expand the provision of secondary school places. At first, in the 1974 White Paper, the government made it a priority to provide free education for every child for nine years, up to Form 3 (i.e., the third year of secondary education) by 1979.[1] This target was subsequently raised to include provision for more senior secondary school places, so that by 1986, 70 percent of Form 3 graduates could get senior secondary form places.[2] More recently, the first report issued by the Education Commission in 1984 envisaged universal provision for subsidized places in senior secondary education for all Form 3 leavers by 1991. It was estimated that, by that time, 85.6 percent of Form 3 graduates would proceed to Form 4 places, 9.6 percent to one-year full-time craft courses, with a 5 percent rate of provision for repetition.[3] As a result of the government's consistent effort to expand the quantity of basic education, secondary education had gradually developed from an "elite" to a "mass" institution. Whereas only less than one-third of those finishing Primary 6 were able to obtain places in secondary schools in the 1960s and 1970s, practically all Primary 6 graduates can now gain access to secondary education.[4]

During the past two decades, when secondary education made the transition to a mass institution, several controversial issues arose. These included the language of instruction, the quality of private secondary schools, and the mechanisms for selection and allocation of secondary school places. The last of these commanded the most attention since it touched on the sensitive issues of "fairness" and "equality" in educational opportunity and, implicitly, the opportunity for social mobility through educational achievement.

The following discussion traces the reforms relating to selection and allocation of secondary school places in Hong Kong and reconstructs the debates, and thus the ideological contests, that had been waged around those reforms. More specifically, in discussing the reforms on the allocation of Form 1 places, we argue that since the 1970s, as the government had gradually expanded the provision of secondary school places, the problem of selection in secondary schools had been replaced by that of allocation. However, just as full provision of places for the early 1990s was within reach, the government initiated new reforms that would recreate an elite sector out of a mass institution, necessitating a return to a new form of selection.

It will also be argued that the debates that evolved around these reforms in secondary education reflected the basic divergence between the government and its opponents on (1) the role of government in secondary education and (2) the educational principles of secondary schooling. These differences recurrently had been couched in three value-laden terms: fairness, equality, and elitism. The concepts of "fairness" and "equality" became controversial, not because of any lack of their desirability, but because there were no standard empirical referents for them. As Hyman and Brough stated, "Fairness is thus a principle that applies to the treatment of individuals; but . . . it merely characterizes the formal aspects of such treatment."[5] The same is true for equality. "The statement that equals should be treated equally and unequals unequally throws no light on what is to be done to or for equals and unequals."[6] On the other hand, the controversial nature of "elitism" stemmed from different parties' concern with its different consequences. On the one hand, elitism was thought to bring about effective and better-quality education. However, elitism was also allegedly a hurdle for the social mobility of some students. The meanings of these concepts will be elaborated in later discussions. The point here is that fairness, equality, and elitism are inextricably intertwined with each other. "[A]ny definition of fairness . . . normally involves some reference to equality of treatment,"[7] while elitism, defined as the concentration of resources for the few, is the antonym of egalitarianism, the ideology that advocates equal distribution of social resources. In short, the debates on Hong Kong's secondary education evolved around the issues of elitism and egalitarianism.

III. Allocation of Form 1 Places: The Reform

There were two major mechanisms for selecting Primary 6 students for Form 1 places before 1978 when the old system was abolished. First, there was the Secondary School Entrance Examination (SSEE) whereby Primary 6 students sat for three papers—English, Chinese and mathematics—in one afternoon. Those who scored high would be given places in schools of their high-priority choices. These better-quality, five-year places were usually in the government, aided, or subsidized sectors. Other students who did not perform as well were allocated to "bought places" in three-year private schools. The rest would either pay for themselves in private schools or enter the job market. The second mechanism of selection was the Feeder and Nominated School System (FNSS). "Feeder schools" were those receiving grants from the government, and were usually missionary schools, while "nominated schools" were those in the aided and government sectors. Both feeder and nominated schools had their own "linked" primary or secondary schools.[8] The essence of this system was to allow discretion for some subsidized, aided, and government secondary schools to select Primary 6 students from their own feeder or nominated primary schools. Therefore, the SSEE and the FNSS together made up a system of selection that was based on a mixture of merit, reflected in students' performance on the SSEE, and particularistic criteria inherent in the FNSS, ranging from the status of one's primary school to family connections with particular personnel of the school authority.

Ever since its implementation in 1962 (previously there was the Joint Primary 6 Examination), the SSEE was subjected to incessant criticism, the gist of which could be summarized as follows: First, undue pressure was exerted on Primary 6 students since their future was determined by a one-shot public examination in one afternoon. If a child failed in the SSEE, he failed forever no matter what had been his overall performance throughout his primary school career. Thus both the pressure that was generated and the validity of a one-shot test were criticized. Second, since only English, Chinese, and mathematics were tested, it resulted in an unbalanced primary education at the expense of other subjects not tested in the SSEE. Third, as students were allocated to different secondary schools according to their performance in the examination, the academically ablest students were creamed off by the "elitist" schools, perpetuating the differential standards among secondary schools. The FNSS was also criticized for its great autonomy in admitting students from its feeder or nominated primary schools, usually the most eminent ones in the territory.[9]

While the public was criticizing the undesirable SSEE and was pressing for expansion of educational opportunity for all primary-school leavers, the government was balancing the competing claims of other social and community needs.[10] Finally, in the 1974 White Paper, the government set out to provide universal, subsidized nine-year education by 1979, to abolish the SSEE, and to devise an alternative system to regulate the flow of students from primary to secondary schools. This White Paper also laid down the principles of regionalization and mixed ability intake in the allocation of secondary school places.[11] In 1976, it was announced that the last SSEE would be held in 1977 and a new system, the Secondary School Places Allocation System (SSPA) came into operation in 1978.

To highlight the essence of the reform, the main features of the SSPA system will be briefly introduced through a comparison with the replaced SSEE. First, instead of testing the students on three subjects in one public examination, the SSPA made internal assessment of students over a period of one and a half years on all subjects except physical education. This assessment was then scaled by students' performance in a centrally administered Academic Aptitude Test (AAT) on verbal and numerical reasoning. Second, whereas the SSEE made an order of merit for students in the whole territory, the SSPA introduced the device of regionalization. The entire Hong Kong territory was divided into twenty-four school areas, each of which included all primary and secondary schools in the same area, forming a school net. Five "bands" in the order of merit were formed based on the scaled internal assessment of students in the same school net. The top 20 percent of students in the same school area went to the first band in the school area, the next into the second band, and so on. The third difference with the SSEE was that instead of relying totally on merit, the SSPA allowed for a certain degree of randomization in the allocation of places. That is, although students in the first band were given the priority in allocation over students in Band 2 and below, they were not further differentiated by merit within the same band. Therefore, when schools of their first choice were oversubscribed, those places would be allocated randomly by computer. Finally, some changes were made to the FNSS: participating schools in the system retained 10–15 percent of discretionary places, plus a certain percentages of "reserved quota" for eligible students from their linked primary schools. The maximum reserved quotas for "eligible" students was reduced from 85 percent to 50 percent for feeder schools while that for the nominated schools was to remain 25 percent. "Eligible" students were those who were in either Band 1 or Band 2 and had chosen the parent schools as their first choices. The rest of the places in these schools in the FNSS would be left for open competition.[12]

Three years after the implementation of the new system of allocation, the government appointed a working party to review the SSPA. The results of the review came out in the form of a *Report of the Working Party Set Up to Review the SSPA System*, published in 1981. In July 1986, after several years of consultation, a General Administrative Circular 25/86 was issued to inform schools of a number of "enhancements" to the SSPA. Among them were the proposals to reactivate the FNSS, to increase the proportion of reserved quotas for nominated schools, and to increase the number of ability bands.[13] Although the announcements in the circular were finally shelved several months later due to severe opposition from some segments in the society,[14] both documents, i.e., the report by the working party and the circular, and the subsequent debates triggered by them revealed a great many ideological differences on secondary education held by different parties.

IV. Allocation of Form 1 Places: The Debate

The major protagonists in the debate were, on the one hand, the Education Department, principals, and teachers in the "elite" subsidized schools, mainly those affiliated with the Christian community, and on the other, various pressure and professional groups. The concrete measures that were contended included the size of the feeder quotas for schools in the FNSS, the number of ability bands, and the appropriate degree of randomization in the allocation process. The contentions on these concrete measures were based on important ideological issues. In sum, three key concepts had been recurrently brought up but had been interpreted quite differently by the two sides. These three concepts were "fairness," "elitism," and "equal educational opportunity." We shall deal with each of these.

1. "Fairness"

To the government, principals, and teachers in some well-established schools, "fairness" meant fair competition to get into schools of one's choice. According to their logic, it is unfair for good students to depend on "luck" to get into schools of their choice, while allowing less able students to benefit from "luck" to get into well-established schools that they do not deserve. A government working party was sympathetic to those who adhered to the merit principle:

> ... randomization had meant that pupils at the top of the ability spectrum had to rely on luck to get into a school of their first choice if this was a very popular school. The Working Party noted that many parents and teachers, especially those from popular feeder schools, had expressed their objections in

no uncertain terms, likening randomization to a lottery. The general view of the public seemed to be that allocation by order of merit within bands would be much fairer than randomization.[15]

It was further laid down as a principle of allocation that "the random element should be avoided if possible."[16]

Government officials from the Education Department argued, in a similar vein, that randomization went against the educational principle of different education for students of different aptitudes and inclinations.[17] The association representing teachers in subsidized secondary schools came out in support of government's stance on "fair competition":

> Given the fact that schools now have equal resources, ... and given that students can get into schools of their own choice through fair competition, the order of priority of getting into schools should then be based on students' performance in schools. Moreover, from the view point of the overall development of Hong Kong, education has to cultivate talents for the future of the local community. We strongly support the civil right of every youth to get education, while protecting their right of fair competition to get the best school places they could.[18]

In contrast, pressure groups saw "fairness" as an equal chance of getting school places, not as an equal chance to compete. Their conception of "fairness" was related to their idea of "equality of educational opportunity": since schools in Hong Kong were of different quality, and equality in quality could not be achieved overnight, "fairness" could only be achieved through devising a means to equalize chances of getting into schools of different qualities. Randomization, the best way to attain this absolute equality in opportunity was, therefore, fair. In opposition to the government's proposal to increase the number of bands and to extend the FNSS, eleven educational groups made a joint effort to denounce the proposal as depriving students of their right to fair choice of schools.[19] More specifically, the Education Action Group, the Hong Kong Professional Teachers' Union, and the Alumni Association of the Colleges of Education pointed out that the feeder school system had virtually precluded students outside the feeder school system from any chance of entry. This was because feeder parent schools enjoy discretionary quotas of 10–15 percent, in addition to reserved quotas of up to 85 percent, for eligible students from their linked primary schools. Thus, the chance of getting into these schools for nonfeeder school students would be nil.[20] Others also opposed the increase in the number of bands from five to twenty-five because the measure would raise the chance for good students to get into good schools and bad students into bad schools.[21]

2. "Elitism"

This is one of the most sensitive and ideologically charged concepts in the educational debate in Hong Kong. Pressure groups' and professional associations' attacks on government had always made use of the label of elitism, while the government remained cautious in defining its position as not "pro-elitist." The government tried hard to couch allegedly elitist policies in technical terms, i.e., in terms of effectiveness of teaching. In defending the extension of the FNSS and the introduction of more merit elements in the allocation process, both of which had been accused of "reviving elitism" in the education system, the government and its supporters from well-established schools argued for their contribution to more effective teaching. The feeder school system was beneficial to students since it provided continuity in the school environment to facilitate students in their transition from primary to secondary school. Likewise, more refined bandings would allow schools to have greater control over ability intake so as to allow for more effective teaching.[22] The Catholic Board of Education, representing 300 Catholic schools in Hong Kong, also came out in support of the report of the working party since "it's honest and faces up to the problem of falling standards."[23] Meanwhile the drawbacks of "mixed ability" intake were deemed to have created "considerable administrative and teaching problems for the schools."[24] The principal of a well-established secondary school contended that under mixed ability intake, the potential of good students who were allocated to poor schools was not allowed to develop, while students of less ability who were assigned to good schools would be destined to failure. Neither would benefit from the policy of "mixed ability."[25] In short, the government had persistently legitimized its policy as based on the principle of different education for students of different aptitudes and inclinations. The attempt to differentiate students' ability was to make education technically more effective, not more hierarchical. And since universal provision of secondary school places was guaranteed, the policies on FNSS and banding were not indications of government's total reversion to the path of elitism. At most, these were only very slight "inclinations" toward elitism.[26]

For a number of social groups, such as the Education Action Group and the Hong Kong Professional Teachers' Association, and some locally elected district board councilors, elitism meant the polarization of good and bad students.[27] Their opposition to elitism in general, and to the FNSS and increased banding in particular, was based on both educational ideology and the supposed beneficial effect of mixed ability intake. Ideologically, their principle was equal and indiscriminant education for all.[28] The FNSS and the differentiation of students' ability were deemed to undermine this principle. Moreover, the FNSS would institutionalize a system of passing down family connections with particular schools to the younger generations, perpetuating the educational privileges of the few in the elite schools. They also questioned government's deviation from the established policy of "mixed ability" as laid down in the 1974 White Paper and recommended by the Visiting Consultation Panel in 1982.[29] Technically, they saw an important advantage in mixed ability intake. The Education Action Group pointed out that "the better students, when evenly distributed among schools, could provide leadership and stimulus to fellow students who were less bright."[30] Other opponents pointed to the disadvantages of elitism, i.e., polarization of good students in good schools and bad students in bad schools. It was said that when the top-ranking students were tracked to a few eminent schools, four problems would occur: (1) for those in the elite schools, there would be less opportunity for the very best to be trained as leaders and organizers; (2) in other non-elitist schools, there was a lack of leadership and initiative by good students; (3) the motivation of the newly established schools would be dealt a severe blow since they had not yet established their status in the community and would thus be less likely to be chosen by good students; and (4) teachers in these newly established schools would be discouraged by the high concentration of less able students.[31]

3. "Equality of Educational Opportunity"

The disagreement on what constituted "fairness" and "elitism" could be linked to a third ideological difference between the two parties. The government had consistently and persistently pursued equality of educational opportunity in quantitative terms. That is, there should be equality in the opportunity to obtain a standardized and universal length of compulsory education. The government's opponents pressed for an equal quantity and quality of school places. Government policy papers kept mentioning its concern for extending the period of basic school years that was to be indiscriminately provided. What was not their concern was the equality of opportunity in getting basic education of equal quantity and quality. The commitment to guaranteeing equal quantity and uniformity in curriculum, but the omission of concern for equal quality, as reflected in the following statement: "The Government's main objective is to make available, by 1979, subsidized education for every child for nine years. . . . All children should follow a common course of general education throughout these nine years."[32] Clearly, the provision of equal quantity of education took priority over equalizing the quality of school places.

The omission of a regard for equal quality in allocating secondary school places had been the point most cited by the government's opponents. The association representing principals of subsidized primary schools argued that the existing arrangement for the provision of junior secondary school places went against the principle of equality because unequal resources were distributed among different types of schools. Subsidized schools got only 75 percent of the resources allocated to government schools; private schools got even less—only 25 percent of those of the government sector.[33] The Education Action Group's opposition to increasing the proportion of feeder quotas was also based on the idea that there was still a wide discrepancy in the quality of school places.[34] Their ideal system would be one in which every school place would be of equal quality. They are against eliminating the element of randomization, or allowing more discretionary places for some schools, since both these measures would not equalize the opportunity of getting into the better schools.

In short, when every child could be ensured a junior secondary school place, the original problem of selection (through the SSEE) became transformed into one of allocation (through the SSPA). The question was then how to allocate. In Hong Kong, there was a tension between competition by merit and mixed ability teaching. The government attempted to mix both, with a preference for introducing more merit elements, as reflected in the Review Report of the SSPA and the General Administrative Circular 25 /86. Ideologically, in the debates on the SSPA, the issues had been (1) whether a "fair" educational policy should be one that guarantees equal opportunity to compete for good schools, or equal opportunity of getting into good schools; (2) whether "elitism" meant only differentiating students by aptitudes so as to facilitate teaching or polarization of good and bad students so that different standards would be perpetuated; (3) whether "equal educational opportunity" required only the provision of equal quantity of education or the provision of equal quantity and quality of school places.

V. The Direct Subsidy Scheme (DSS): The Reform

In 1988, the third report of the Education Commission proposed the Direct Subsidy Scheme (DSS) to replace the existing Bought Place Scheme (BPS). Since the 1960s, the government had bought places from the private sector because there were insufficient places in government and aided schools to meet the demands placed on the system by the government's obligation to provide nine-year universal education. However, this Bought Place Scheme, which played the role of a convenient buffer, was found to be undesirable "to parents and students, because the places which the government secures under the scheme are generally inferior to places in government and aided schools."[35] The government noted in the report that in other developed countries, "the private schools are the prestigious ones for those who can afford, or can obtain through academic merit, a better education than that provided by the government."[36] The government's stated intention in proposing the Direct Subsidy Scheme, therefore, was to "encourage the growth of a strong private school sector, while allowing schools the maximum freedom with regard to curriculum, fees and entrance requirements."[37] The DSS would then provide a genuine, independent alternative to the public school system, thus broadening parental choice.[38]

Under the new system, schools in both the private and subsidized sectors would receive direct government grants. For those in the private sector, schools with low fees would receive the full grant for each pupil, while those who opt to charge high fees would forgo most government subsidies, although a minimum amount of grants would be guaranteed to these high-fee schools. Besides, the allocation mechanism under the new system would be correspondingly reformed. The existing SSPA would remain; however, selection by DSS schools would precede each annual exercise of the SSPA. Once selected, the parents concerned would be asked to sign a piece of paper confirming that they give up their claim to free junior secondary education. The pupils selected by the DSS would have their names deleted from the SSPA list. Others who remained in the list would then be centrally allocated as usual.[39] It was also recommended in the report that the government be allowed to allocate to the DSS schools a certain percentage of their pupils through the SSPA in the event of an unanticipated shortfall in public provision.[40] Despite widespread criticisms, which will be analyzed below, the DSS was formally approved in 1989.

VI. The Direct Subsidy Scheme: The Debate

The heated debate surrounding the Direct Subsidy Scheme saw the recurrence of themes associated with previous reforms as well as the emergence of new issues, such as the relationship between education and social mobility.

Although the DSS was a key measure of the government's reform for the existing private sector, critics saw the plan's most immediate effect to be on the existing aided school sector. They predicted that only the best and most popular schools would have the confidence to join the DSS, under which schools would not be guaranteed student enrollment, but would be granted a high degree of autonomy. Moreover, since these schools would be given a free hand to select students and set their own school fees, it was feared that elite schools would become the privilege of students from well-off families. Moreover, when the proposed measures would come into effect, the SSPA, instead of being the only means of allocating students, would coexist with admission procedures devised by individual DSS schools. The debates invoked by the DSS were therefore no longer focused on the internal mechanisms of the SSPA (e.g., banding and feeder quotas, etc.). The concern now became focused on the relations between the public and the private school sectors, between education and the larger social structure. Although the same concepts entered the debates, new meanings were attached to them.

1. "Fairness"

To the critics of government policy, a "fair" educational system was (1) one in which every student had equal opportunity of getting into the school of their choice, and (2) which would provide opportunity for social mobility. We have seen the first meaning of fairness being expressed in the debate on the SSPA, particularly in their insistence on the use of randomization in allocating school places. The second element of fairness had not been an issue before the DSS proposal, possibly due to the effective functioning of the educational system as a mobility channel. Now this was questioned under the DSS. The Education Action Group worried that "the government's intention is to upgrade the already reputable schools to 'super' institutions for the rich," and there would be the possibility that the scheme might "prompt the schools to charge higher fees, and thus deprive students from families with less financial means the chance to study there."[41] The DSS was unfair precisely because it produced unequal opportunity for educational and social mobility. Lower-class students, even if they were academically capable, might not be able to attend prestigious but expensive schools. This would in turn hamper their chance of advancing to higher education and thus of attaining social mobility. On the other hand, students from the upper-middle stratum would easily perpetuate their social positions by virtue of their economic resources and/or family connections with elite schools. Instead of promoting social mobility, education under the new system would serve to perpetuate social inequalities. Therefore, the Hong Kong Professional Teachers' Association argued that the DSS would undermine the function of education in promoting interclass mobility. The social consequence of the DSS would be class polarization, social unfairness, and social instability.[42] In short, to these critics, the fairness that the DSS provided was only "market fairness," which could only be enjoyed by those with economic and political means.[43]

The government did not make any specific statement on how fair the DSS would be. However, the Education Commission made it clear that there would be a graded system of subsidies, so that "schools with low fees would receive the full grant for each pupil," while those who opt to charge very high fees would forgo most government subsidies.[44] Moreover, as mentioned, the government did not see the DSS as undermining its commitment to provide universal nine-year education, since there would be guaranteed places for those students who, for various reasons, would be outside the DSS sector. The government's self-perceived role seemed to be that of an umpire, to monitor that everyone followed the rules of the game, to ensure that competition among schools and students would be fair and to guarantee that a minimum amount of education would be provided.

2. "Elitism"

In the previous debates, "elitism" meant to the critics the polarization of academically able students in good schools and bad students in bad schools. This time, one of the accusations against the DSS was again elitism, with an expanded meaning of the term "elite." In the previous debates, the elite consisted mainly of those who were academically more capable. Opponents objected to concentrating these able students in good schools. The danger of this type of polarization persisted under the DSS, which would grant schools autonomy to select students. However, what critics worried more about was that a new elite would emerge from well-off families who could afford the unregulated school fees charged by prestigious schools. Elitism here meant the polarization of well-off students and those of lesser financial means. Elite schools, then, critics predicted, would become an "aristocratic" privilege, monopolized and inherited by a few. This was allegedly the main evil of the DSS. Thus, under the DSS, a new school hierarchy in secondary education would emerge: the few prestigious schools could choose to admit the ablest and/or the most well-off, while other schools would cater to students who would be less well-off. The meaning of nine-year universal education would be altered. It would only be applicable to students considered to be less competitive than those who could get into the private schools.[45] This scenario was likened to that in the 1950s, and the DSS was therefore branded as a policy that "regressed to the old route of elitism."[46]

In response, the government and its supporters defended the DSS in terms of the merits of school autonomy, market competition, and parental choice. They also repeated the old argument that students had different aptitudes and suitability for different kinds of schools. A lecturer of education supported the government's position in arguing that "If we agree that mentally retarded children should be provided with special schools, why could we not accept some excellent schools for excellent students?"[47] They also rejected the analogy with elitism in the 1950s since the DSS was premised on the fact that every schoolchild had been guaranteed a school place of sufficient quality.[48] A newspaper supported the government's stance, emphasizing the freedom of choice provided by the DSS: "The big difference between the old elitist system and the new proposals is that before, everyone was scrambling for a few school places. Now parents are being told 'you can choose' specialist education if you want it. It may be for a school that teaches in Mandarin, or a school that includes ballet."[49]

3. "Equal Opportunity in Education"

As in the previous debates, the views of the two sides toward "fairness" and "elitism" reflected another implicit but often-mentioned concept in educational debates in Hong Kong—that of equal educational opportunity. The government believed its essential role was to provide everyone an equal opportunity to get an equal amount of education. Since this had been realized, the introduction of some market mechanism in the form of the DSS could be justified. On the contrary, critics envisioned a broader role for the government—one that should guarantee equal opportunity in getting equal quantity and quality of school places, so that the function of education in promoting social mobility would be ensured.

VII. Summary and Discussion

We have chosen to focus on one of the most controversial aspects of reforms in secondary education in Hong Kong—reforms in the selection and allocation of students. We have traced the development of various changes in these policies over the past two decades. The overall direction of change, as discussed in the previous pages, was that the government had gradually increased the proportion of students able to attend five-year secondary education. Consequently, the original problem of selecting students through the SSEE was replaced in 1978 by the problem of allocation through the SSPA, when all Primary 6 graduates could get junior secondary places. The planned abolition by 1991 of selection mechanisms at the end of Form 3 was consistent with this government policy of providing sufficient places for all Form 3 leavers, and replacing all selective mechanisms with allocative ones. However, just as full provision of secondary school places could be envisioned by 1991, the government initiated a policy shift. The DSS reintroduced a selective mechanism and an elite sector in secondary education would be recreated. Despite the charge of the revival of elitism, it is important to point out that the selection devices implemented by individual schools under the DSS would coexist with, not replace, the centrally administered allocation through the SSPA. Therefore, the anticipated elite sector would only be a subset, albeit a more prestigious one, within the mass institution of secondary education that would be universally available.

We have also analyzed the controversies underlying these policy changes. Two camps of opinion and values on these educational reforms were identified. The major protagonists included the government and well-established schools on the one side and some groups of progressive educationists in society on the other. An important qualification must be made to this scenario: these were only the two most vocal actors. They by no means represented all shades of opinions in the society. We must recognize the groups that were left out of the discussion: the unorganized and diffuse population of students and parents, the less outspoken pressure groups and educational associations, and most of the business community. Within this delimited framework, two opinion camps had been identified, each adhering to quite different ideologies about secondary education. In short, they had divergent views on two issues: the role of government in secondary education and the educational principles appropriate for secondary schools. First, the government considered its priority in secondary education to be a guaranteed minimum amount of universal education. On the other hand, critics of the government considered that ensuring equal quality of school places was as important as ensuring an equal amount of universal education. This was the perennial dispute that resulted in the reforms of the SSPA. Second, once universal provision of secondary school places was realized, the government adopted a more limited role in secondary education, so as to allow for more school autonomy, parental choice, and market competition among schools. Hence the DSS. Pressure groups and opponents, however, wanted the government to adopt a more active and interventionist stance to ensure that secondary education could fulfill the function of promoting social mobility. For them, education should not be viewed as a market transaction, where the relation between the producer (the school) and the consumer (the parents) could be unregulated. The government must prevent any discriminatory measures against students who had less resources to compete in the market. Hence the opposition to the DSS.

Moreover, each side adhered to very different educational principles of secondary schooling. The government insisted on having some competition by merit among students and among schools. Competition by merit was not only fair, but differentiation of students according to ability also would be conducive to effective teaching. Their principle was different teaching to students of different aptitudes. Others were against using any competition to differentiate students by ability or other ascribed status. They contended that secondary education was too early for such competition, which should be postponed until the exit point of secondary schooling, i.e., at the Certificate Examination in Form 5. Within secondary schools, mixed ability was the appropriate arrangement.

To understand these differences, we must take the perspectives of both sides. The government looked at education as one among the many social services it had to provide. Its perspective was that of balancing competing claims on limited financial resources, and of balancing the manpower need of the economy with the educational aspirations of the people. While in the past, the most urgent demand of the population was the universal provision of basic education, the affluent society of Hong Kong in the 1980s had the additional aspiration toward better quality education, particularly among the middle classes. On the other hand, for the progressive educationists, education was always the primary, if not the only, concern. Since their constituencies were mainly composed of the grass roots, these groups were against any elitist educational policies that would undermine the interests of the lower strata in society. In the final analysis, their stance was one of "egalitarianism."

Despite competing opinions on the selection and allocation of secondary school places, the views of the Hong Kong government usually prevailed over those of its opponents. Concession, like the withdrawal of the circular to reform the SSPA, was possible, though not institutionally guaranteed. The lack of any institutionalized power for pressure groups prevented them from exerting an effective challenge to any policy that the government staunchly supported. The DSS was one such instance. Thus although the debates were intense, the actual content of the reforms was, to a large extent, shaped by how decisive the government chose to be on any particular issue.

However radical the progressive educationists' demands seemed to be, the equality of educational opportunity they asked for was limited to equal access to the same amount of educational resources, both tangible and intangible, instead of equality of results. Equality of results had been the focus of attention in the pursuit of equal educational opportunity in the West in general and in the United States in particular.[50] Equality of educational opportunity carried with it strong moral legitimacy. However, it might conflict with other social goals.[51] The tension between maintaining quality and equality in education had been found in China, the United States, Italy, and other countries in the 1960s.[52] It is our opinion that if there is a rich reservoir of manpower but a strikingly unequal distribution of educational resources, more consideration should be given to equality in the formulation of educational policies. However, if social mobility is already very active and if the society is confronting a brain-drain problem, the concern with quality of education should gain priority over equality in education. In the case of Hong Kong, the proportion of working-class children among university students, a very good indicator of the extent of social mobility through education, had been over 70 percent for the Chinese University of Hong Kong and only slightly lower for the University of Hong Kong.[53] Nevertheless, this excludes the larger number of Hong Kong students that attain their university education overseas, the majority of whom are middle class. Meanwhile, as Hong Kong makes its transition to 1997, there is an acute brain-drain problem, particularly in the professional and middle managerial strata. Seen in this light, it seems justified for the Hong Kong government to put greater emphasis on the issue of quality instead of equality in formulating educational policies.

Notes

We are grateful to Dr. Joseph T. F. Lau for his critical comments on the early drafts of this chapter and to Mr. Ting-hong Wong for his research assistance.

1. Hong Kong Government, *White Paper: Secondary Education in Hong Kong over the Next Decade* (Hong Kong, 1974).
2. Hong Kong Government, *White Paper: The Development of Senior Secondary and Tertiary Education* (Hong Kong, 1978).
3. Education Commission, *Education Commission Report No. 1* (Hong Kong, 1984).
4. Education Department, *Annual Summary* (Hong Kong, 1964–86).
5. R. Hyman and I. Brough, *Social Values and Industrial Relations: A Study of Fairness and Equality* (Oxford: Basil Blackwell, 1975), p. 8.
6. M. Ginsberg, *On Justice in Society* (Harmondsworth: Penguin, 1965), p. 7.
7. Hyman and Brough, *Social Values*, p. 5.
8. The historical origin of the feeder and nominated school systems can be traced back to 1956, when the grant-in-aid schools joined the allocation system based on the then Joint Primary 6 Examination, in exchange for the government's giving them discretion to allocate a proportion of their own places. Such an arrangement was extended to some aided schools and government schools later, forming the nominated school system by 1973. See Working Party, *Report of the Working Party Set Up to Review the Secondary School Places Allocation System* (Hong Kong, 1981).
9. *Wah Kiu Yat Pao*, Hong Kong, March 20, 1976; *Tai Kung Pao*, Hong Kong, April 26, 1975.
10. Hong Kong Government, *White Paper*, 1974, para. 1.8.
11. Ibid., para. 2.7.
12. Education Department, *General Schools Circular No. 101/76*, Hong Kong, August 6, 1976.
13. Working Party, *Report*.
14. *Wah Kiu Yat Pao*, November 18, 1986.
15. Working Party, *Report*, para. 6.4.
16. Ibid., para. 6.13.
17. *Wah Kiu Yat Pao*, August 31, 1986.
18. *Tai Kung Pao*, September 20, 1986.

19. *Wah Kiu Yat Pao*, August 26, 1986.
20. *Wen Wai Pao*, Hong Kong, September 1, 1986, and August 5, 1986; *Wah Kiu Yat Pao*, August 27, 1986.
21. *Wah Kiu Yat Pao*, August 13, 1986.
22. *Ming Pao, Hong Kong*, August 9, 1986.
23. *South China Morning Post*, Hong Kong, May 4, 1981.
24. Working Party, *Report* , para. 6.1.
25. *Wen Wai Pao*, October 31, 1986.
26. *Ming Pao*, August 9, 1986.
27. *Tai Kung Pao*, September 16, 1986.
28. *Wah Kiu Yat Pao*, September 26, 1986.
29. *Tai Kung Pao*, August 5, 1986.
30. *South China Morning Post*, October 20, 1986; *Wah Kiu Yat Pao*, August 13, 1986.
31. *Tai Kung Pao*, August 5, 1986; *Wen Wai Pao*, August 24, 1986.
32. Hong Kong Government, *White Paper*, 1974, para. 2.2.
33. *Wah Kiu Yat Pao*, September 20, 1986.
34. *Tai Kung Pao*, September 16, 1986.
35. Ibid., para. 4.12b.
36. Ibid., para. 4.10.
37. Education Commission, *Education Commission Report No. 3* (Hong Kong, 1988), para. 4.22.
38. Ibid., para. 4.64.
39. Ibid., para. 4.56.
40. Ibid., para. 4.64a.
41. *Hong Kong Standard*, Hong Kong, August 1, 1988.
42. *Wah Kiu Yat Pao*, September 14, 1988.
43. *Hong Kong Economic Journal*, Hong Kong, July 2, 1988.
44. Education Commission, *Report No. 3*, 1988, para. 4.62.
45. *Tai Kung Pao*, June 20, 1988.
46. *Ming Pao*, May 4, 1988.
47. *Tai Kung Pao*, June 13, 1988.
48. *Ming Pao*, May 4, 1988.
49. *Hong Kong Standard*, May 23, 1988.
50. J. Coleman, "The Concept of Equality of Educational Opportunity," *Harvard Educational Review* 38 (1968):7–22.
51. F. Oppenheim, "The Concept of Equality" in *International Encyclopedia of the Social Sciences* 5, ed. David Sills (1968):109.
52. T. S. Cheung, "The Zig-zag Course of Educational Development in Mainland China over the Past Three Decades," *Ming Pao Monthly* 14, 10 (1979):107–13.
53. W. K. Tsang, "Equality of Educational Opportunity in University," *The Chinese University Educational Journal* 13, 1 (1985):10–27.

7

The Schooling of Girls in Hong Kong: Progress and Contradictions in the Transition

Grace C.L. Mak

Hong Kong's economic success is closely wedded to its acclaimed industrious and high-caliber labor force, and education has increasingly become a major yardstick of measurement of the quality of the labor force. In the last four decades Hong Kong has been part of the worldwide trend in educational expansion. This has been accompanied by a rise in the educational attainment of the population as a whole. Women and the lower classes, previously disadvantaged in access to schooling, have benefited from the expansion. However, has full educational equality between the sexes been realized? How does social class background influence a daughter's educational chances? How does increased educational attainment affect women's labor force participation? Does investment in education for females yield the same earnings as for males? How does the transition to 1997 affect women's participation in education and the economy?

These are among the questions that this chapter aims to address; it will investigate the extent to which women have taken advantage of educational expansion in Hong Kong, how their education articulates with the labor market, and if and how changes in both are taking place during the transition. Beginning with a brief history of girls' schooling in Hong Kong up until 1950, it will then examine changes in females' access to education in the light of major points of expansion that have occurred since, along with the implications of the imminent return of Hong Kong's sovereignty to China for women's education. The second half of the chapter looks at the relationship between women's educational attainment and occupational outcomes. It will be argued that women have generally benefited from the educational expansion. However, in spite of a nonsexually discriminatory educational policy, inequality still exists, especially at the upper end of the educational ladder. While vertical segregation is decreasing, horizontal segregation remains a serious problem. The concentration of females in "traditionally feminine" disciplines has led to an overrepresentation of women in occupations perceived to be suitable for females and underrepresentation in "traditionally masculine" professions. Although the female labor force is larger and better educated than before, the economic return on educational investment is lower for women than for men. The labor shortage problem, accentuated by the economic boom and brain drain, has opened up employment to women as a reserve labor force. However, traditional gender roles mediate this participation and act to prevent many women from realizing their full potential.

A Brief History of Girls' Schooling in Hong Kong

Although Hong Kong is predominantly a Chinese society, girls' schooling here has taken a different course than in China, where females' share of educational provision was meager. Significant change came only after liberation.[1] In the heyday of the colony, diverse influences of the church, British education, and Chinese education coalesced into the educational system of Hong Kong.[2] In the nineteenth century, girls were already present in the schools. In 1870 they represented a small proportion (8.5 percent) of children attending school.[3] While still only a small proportion of the school-aged children attended school (9,500 out of 33,868)[4] in 1900, the proportion of girls among children attending school had grown to 41.3 percent.[5] Throughout the 1930s, girls' enrollment had hovered in the neighborhood of a third of the total.[6] Their representation grew further in the late 1940s—in 1946–47 it was 43.4 percent,[7] while in 1948–49, reflecting demographic changes, it declined to 39.1 percent of the total school enrollment.[8]

As for coeducation, the Education Ordinance of 1913 stipulated that boys and girls under twelve years of age could attend coeducational schools and those over had to attend single-sex schools.[9] This trend continued over the next twenty-five years. The director of education reported in 1938 that the education system in Hong Kong was in general not coeducational.[10] However, by 1948 coeducation had become the rule rather than the exception.[11]

Underlying a seemingly impartial educational policy for boys and girls, there was bias in practice. Girls were segregated by language stream. Those in government schools were mainly channeled into the vernacular stream. Anglo-Chinese schools, which taught in English and promised a brighter occupational prospect, were for boys. The reason given was an absence of social demand for Anglo-Chinese schools for girls. The Report of the Committee on Education in April 1902 stated that "the education of girls in the colony should follow the lines indicated for boys as a general rule," but went on to say that there was no need to set up Anglo-Chinese schools for girls, since boys acquired English for business purposes and such a stimulus was absent in girls.[12] Differential investment in boys and girls was also demonstrated in the amount of educational grant money available for them. In 1903 a grant was paid at the rate of $40 per annum for each boy and $35 for each girl in Anglo-Chinese grant-in-aid schools. For the vernacular stream, the grant amount was $35 per annum for each boy and $14 for each girl.[13] The pattern remained the same for the following twenty-five years.[14]

In higher education, the University of Hong Kong (HKU) was founded in 1911 but did not start admitting girls until 1921.[15] Females initially made up a small percentage of enrollment. In 1922–23, they accounted for only 1–1.5 percent of the student body.[16] However, the number soon began to increase. By 1933, it had grown to 10 percent,[17] and by 1950, 29 percent.[18] Nevertheless, these women were unevenly distributed in the disciplines. In 1928–33, about two-thirds were in the arts and a third in medicine. Very few were in the science faculty, and even fewer in engineering.[19] This pattern persisted for many years.

Educational Expansion and Its Impact on Girls' Enrollment since 1950

Not until the early 1950s did education in Hong Kong begin to expand on a significant scale. This was mainly due to the influx of refugees from China after the Communist Revolution. The estimated population of Hong Kong in 1949 was 1.86 million. By 1959 it had soared to 2.97 million.[20] The sex composition of the population had also changed. Before, Hong Kong was predominantly male. Men worked there and supported their families in China. After 1949, whole families moved to Hong Kong. The sex ratio (number of males per thousand females) was 1,844, 1,580, and 1,348 in 1911, 1921, and 1931 respectively. In 1961 it was 1,056 and has remained stable since.[21]

In general there has been a rise in the educational attainment of the population since 1961 (see Table 7.1). Women's gains have been significant. As Table 7.2 suggests, of those that had received education at upper secondary, matriculation, and tertiary non-degree levels in 1961, about a third were female. By 1986, the proportion had climbed to about 48 percent. Similarly, comparable figures on degree education increased from a fifth in 1961 to a third in 1986.

Educational expansion in Hong Kong came in stages. In the 1950s and 1960s, the focus was on the primary level, and in the 1970s, on the secondary level. Compulsory primary education became a reality in 1971, and in 1978 it was extended to nine years of education. In the 1980s, the focus shifted to higher education.[22] An analysis of enrollment trends of females by level of education may shed light on the impact of educational expansion on gender equality.

Primary and Secondary Education

The tradition of a relatively high percentage of girls in primary schooling continued into the 1950s (see Table 7.3). The increase in proportion of females was gradual, and not a direct result of the introduction of compulsory education.

Table 7.1

Percentage of Whole Population: Educational Attainment by Sex, 1961–1986

Educational attainment	1961 M	1961 F	1971 M	1971 F	1981 M	1981 F	1986 M	1986 F
No sch/kg	13.7	24.8	10.3	18.2	8.2	13.9	7.6	12.5
Primary	26.7	18.5	26.0	21.9	20.2	16.5	17.5	15.1
Lower sec.	5.8	2.8	6.5	4.3	10.3	7.2	10.5	7.2
Upper sec.					8.7	7.3	9.7	9.3
Matriculation	4.1	2.2	6.7	4.4	2.1	1.3	2.8	2.3
Tertiary nondegree					0.9	0.9	1.1	1.1
Degree	1.1	0.3	1.3	0.4	1.8	0.7	2.2	1.1
Total	51.4	48.6	50.8	49.2	52.2	47.8	51.4	48.6

Source: Census and Statistics Department, *Hong Kong Annual Digest of Statistics 1987*, p. 199.

However, the two compulsory education acts did have a positive effect on enrollment in general. In 1971, 92.3 percent of those aged 5–9 and 89.6 percent of those aged 10–14 were attending school, as compared to 99.3 percent and 98.8 percent in 1986.[23]

Tertiary Education

Through the 1950s and until the early 1960s, women's enrollment at HKU stayed at about 25 percent. A boost came in 1963 with the founding of the Chinese University of Hong Kong (CUHK).[24] In that year women made up 31 percent of undergraduates at HKU and 36.3 percent at CUHK.[25] In general, women's share of university education has been increasing ever since. It reached a record high of 42 percent in 1988.

A grant-and-loan scheme introduced in 1969 provided support for needy students admitted to both universities.[26] Many believed that widened female access owed much to this scheme. Our data suggest otherwise. It is true that financial aid has extended university education to those from families of humble means.[27] For example, in 1977–78, 48.7 percent of the students at CUHK received grants and 70.1 percent received interest-free loans.[28] However, the grant-and-loan scheme did not seem to have a direct impact on women's enrollment relative to men's. On the contrary, the proportion of women dropped by a percentage point per year from 1970 to 1973 and again in 1975. The assistance scheme acted

Table 7.2

Percentage of Females Relative to Whole Population by Level of Educational Attainment, 1961–1986

Educational attainment	1961	1971	1981	1986
No sch/kg	65	64	63	62
Primary	41	46	45	46
Lower sec.	33	40	41	41
Upper sec.			46	49
Matriculation	35	40	38	45
Tertiary non-degree			50	49
Degree	21	24	28	33

Source: Calculated from Table 7.1.

more to change the social class rather than sex composition of the student body. Nevertheless, like their male counterparts, female university entrants benefited from this scheme. A study suggested that in the 1970s' cohort, there were proportionally more females from the lower classes than in the 1960s' cohort.[29]

Social class interacts with gender in women's access to university. Female students generally came from a higher socioeconomic background. The 1955–56 survey by Maunder et al. revealed that the average annual family income of female students was $23,600, a significant departure from $14,800 for male students.[30] The pattern persists. In the late 1970s and early 1980s, female students at CUHK came from better-off families than their male counterparts.[31] In poor families, sibling order may overcome daughters' disadvantages. Younger daughters may have as much opportunity as their brothers in schooling.[32]

Women's gains have been less evident in distribution by discipline than in overall enrollment. Women have entered new disciplines as they were added to university programs. Their presence has strengthened in the social sciences, business studies, and law. Despite this improvement, gender segregation continues. Statistics on enrollment in university faculties by sex in 1988 gives the latest picture. At HKU, women made up 68 percent of those enrolled in arts, 55 percent in law, 44 percent in social sciences, 31 percent in architecture, 19 percent in medicine, 18 percent in dental studies, 15 percent in science, and a mere 3 percent in engineering.[33] This distribution pattern was similar at CUHK, where women represented 77 percent of those enrolled in arts, 68 percent in social sciences, 62 percent in business administration, 26 percent in medicine, and 24 percent in science.[34] In the less "traditionally feminine" disciplines, such as business administration and architecture, women have fared considerably better.[35] However, they remain a minority in dentistry, medicine, science, and especially engineering.

Table 7.3

Women as a Percentage of Those Enrolled in Education by Level, 1950–1988*

Year	Primary	Secondary	University undergraduate
1950	40.0	34.9	29.0
1951	N.A.	35.3	28.6
1952	N.A.	36.0	27.5
1953	N.A.	37.2	26.0
1954	N.A.	37.0	25.7
1955	N.A.	37.5	N.A.
1956	N.A.	37.3	26.1
1957	N.A.	38.6	N.A.
1958	43.8	38.4	23.5
1959	44.0	38.5	25.4
1960	44.4	39.2	24.3
1961	44.9	39.6	26.5
1962	45.3	39.7	27.4
1963	45.8	40.2	33.5
1964	46.1	41.1	35.6
1965	46.5	42.1	35.8
1966	46.8	42.2	36.3
1967	47.2	42.3	36.1
1968	47.2	43.2	34.4
1969	47.3	43.3	34.1
1970	47.4	42.9	33.3
1971	47.7	43.5	32.2
1972	48.0	44.6	31.7
1973	48.0	44.2	31.0
1974	48.0	45.4	30.5
1975	47.9	46.1	29.6
1976	47.9	46.7	31.2
1977	48.0	48.8	31.9
1978	N.A.	N.A.	33.2
1979	N.A.	N.A.	34.3
1980	47.9	50.3	34.6
1981	47.9	50.8	34.3
1982	47.7	51.0	35.0
1983	47.8	50.7	35.3
1984	47.7	50.5	36.1
1985	47.7	50.4	37.8
1986	47.7	50.2	39.5
1987	47.9	49.8	40.8
1988	48.0	50.1	42.2

*The figures from which these percentages were calculated were taken at different points of the academic year and may not precisely match the calendar year. However, they are given in the right order to show enrollment trends.

Sources: 1959–67 figures for primary and secondary education: Census and Statistics Department, *Hong Kong Statistics 1947–1967*, p. 184; 1950–67 figures for university education: Education Department, relevant years; 1968–76 figures: Education Department, annual reports. The primary and secondary education figures do not include evening school enrollment. 1977–88 figures: Census and Statistics Department, *Hong Kong Annual Digest of Statistics*, relevant years.

Statistics on sex differences in other tertiary institutes are not as detailed as those for the two universities. Figures suggest a similar pattern of segregation—for example, the proportion of women in the student body of the Hong Kong Polytechnic in 1978 through 1982 was 18.9 percent, 21.8 percent, 20.9 percent, 21.7 percent, and 22.4 percent respectively.[36] Such low percentages can be attributed to the programs offered. Women were concentrated in design, languages, social work, and business management, but not in engineering and the applied sciences, which are major divisions at the Hong Kong Polytechnic.[37]

Teacher training at the non-degree postsecondary level has long been a major outlet for female secondary school leavers. In Hong Kong there are four such institutes, called colleges of education. Their graduates teach in the primary and lower secondary panels. It has always been deemed "suitable" for women to be primary schoolteachers, and colleges of education have always been female-heavy. Even in the 1950s and before, when few women were in postsecondary education, women as a rule outnumbered men in training colleges, as they were called then.[38] They are still the majority (over 70 percent).[39] Again, there is gender segregation by program within the institutes. Programs specializing in technical education tend to attract male students and those in kindergarten education female students.[40] This reflects and perpetuates segregation in the teaching force, which will be discussed later.

The above enrollment figures reveal a lower transition rate of females than males from secondary to tertiary education. The reason for this is unclear. One explanation is parental bias. The superior position assigned by traditional Chinese culture to sons continues in a modern society like Hong Kong. Asked if they would choose to send a son or a daughter to university if they could only afford to send one, most parents in Lai's sample indicated they would send the son, although a smaller number said they would send the elder or the more academically suitable one regardless of gender. Very few indicated they would send the daughter.[41]

The next few years will see a radical expansion in tertiary education. To remedy Hong Kong's severe brain-drain problem, the number of first-year first-degree places will be more than doubled, from 7,000 in 1990 to 15,000 in 1995. By 1995, 25 percent of the youth in the relevant age group will be enrolled in tertiary education.[42] How females will take advantage of this expansion is yet to be studied.

Overseas Education

The higher education scenario is incomplete without addressing the flow of students abroad. Limited places in tertiary institutions in Hong Kong make it necessary for many school leavers to go abroad for further studies.[43] The value of overseas education grows as 1997 approaches, for it promises not only credentials but also possibilities for residence in the host country. Most Hong Kong students abroad are enrolled in postsecondary institutions, but some are in secondary or primary schools. Their average age when leaving Hong Kong is declining, reflecting a growing anxiety to seek an escape route. Studying abroad is expensive. Many in Hong Kong have the perception that parents prefer to send sons abroad and keep daughters behind. Available data suggest that females do better than expected. For example, they made up 27 percent, 28 percent, and 29 percent of Hong Kong students in tertiary education in the United Kingdom in 1984–85, 1985–86, and 1986–87 respectively.[44] They were 34 percent, 35 percent, 36 percent, 37 percent, 38 percent, and 40 percent of Hong Kong students working toward a bachelor's degree in Canadian universities in 1983, 1984, 1985, 1986, 1987, and 1988 respectively.[45] The Australian figures are even higher. Women represented 37 percent, 42 percent, and 46 percent of Hong Kong students undertaking full-fee and subsidized courses in higher education and postsecondary education in Australia.[46] The figures reveal rising proportions of females relative to males in the flow of Hong Kong students going abroad. These figures roughly resemble comparable figures on local universities, suggesting that parents do not necessarily discriminate against daughters in overseas education more than in local higher education.

Articulation between Women's Education and Their Labor Force Participation

Rising educational attainment has enabled more women to enter the labor force. However, greater equality between the sexes in education has not led to parallel equality in employment. This section examines remaining areas of inequality to see if they may change in the labor market situation in the approach to 1997.

Both the male and female labor force participation rates have been rising, but the female rate has been rising faster. In 1988 the labor participation rate for males was 80 percent, as opposed to 79.4 percent in 1979, while corresponding figures for females are 48.2 percent in 1988 and 43.8 percent in 1979.[47] As with the labor force in general, working women in Hong Kong are better educated than before.[48] Education appears to have facilitated women's entry into the job market. In 1981, 66.3 percent of college or university educated women were working, as compared to 47.9 percent of those with secondary education, 34.9 percent of those with primary education, and 23.2 percent of those with kindergarten or no education.[49]

Table 7.4 provides statistics on the sex composition of the labor force in 1986. Of those gainfully employed, about 40 percent were female. With some exceptions, the percentage distribution of women roughly coincided with the profile of the entire labor force. However, segregation becomes obvious when we examine each occupational category. The disparity was particularly pronounced in clerical work and management. Women accounted for about two-thirds of clerical workers but less than a fifth of administrative and managerial workers.

Table 7.4

Composition of Sex-Specific Labor Force by Industry, 1986

Industry	Labor force		% Composition		% Distribution	
	Total no.	% total	M	F	M	F
	2,643,273	100.00	62.41	37.59	100.00	100.00
Professional, technical, and related workers	220,528	8.34	56.72	43.28	7.58	9.61
Administrative and managerial workers	95,417	3.61	83.14	16.86	4.81	1.62
Clerical and related workers	385,587	14.58	41.42	58.58	9.68	22.73
Sales workers	309,059	11.69	69.13	30.87	12.95	9.60
Service workers	429,389	16.24	62.68	37.32	16.32	16.13
Agricultural workers and fishermen	50,150	1.90	65.18	34.82	1.98	1.76
Production and related workers, transport equipmt. operators, and laborers	1,143,280	43.25	66.59	33.41	45.15	38.44
Armed forces and unclassifiable	9,863	0.37	88.43	11.57	0.53	0.11

Source: Calculated from Census and Statistics Department, *Hong Kong Annual Digest of Statistics 1989*, p. 33.

Women are also unevenly represented on the hierarchy within professions. Here we look at two major occupational outlets for educated women: teaching and the civil service. Teaching is one of the earliest professions that admitted women. In 1938, 45 percent of teachers in primary and secondary schools were female.[50] Teaching continued to attract women—writing in 1960, Engel maintained that three-quarters of the female arts graduates had entered teaching since 1956.[51] However, taken as a whole, women serve mainly at the base of the teaching force. In 1987, 99 percent of the kindergarten teachers, 75 percent of the primary schoolteachers, 51 percent of the secondary schoolteachers, and 28 percent of teachers at the postsecondary level were female.[52] In the civil service, women are concentrated in secretarial, typing, and clerical grades. In 1981 they made up 24.6 percent of the civil service but only 4.9 percent of directorate posts.[53]

Women may have to be better educated than men to fill the same post even in the civil service, which is supposedly nondiscriminatory. In Lai's sample of civil servants at the upper-middle ranks and above, 72.9 percent of women had at least a university degree, compared to 59.2 percent of men.[54] However, on the whole it takes women longer to be promoted. A 1980 study by Burns reveals that men were five times more likely than women to achieve senior status in the civil service. The reasons given can be grouped into three categories: women are tied down by domestic duties; they lack the drive to compete with male counterparts; and they suffer from discrimination in education, work, and society.[55]

Preference for males may reduce the effect of education on women's entry to the professions. For example, in the late 1970s and early 1980s, about one out of five architecture students at HKU was female, but of the female architects that graduated, only 5 percent eventually entered the trade.[56] Evidence by Fung confirms reports of female architects being discriminated against when seeking employment or starting their own business. The reason cited is that architecture is a twenty-four-hour profession and incompatible with the schedule of married women. In management, employers also favor males, as shown in Ho's analysis of recruitment advertisements for managerial positions in Hong Kong.[57] Even when women have entered management, they are mostly placed in peripheral and supplementary positions, such as those in public relations and personnel, or in less tradition-bound fields, such as communications, marketing, advertising, and computer operations.[58] A positive aspect is that, as both Ho and Ting-Chao point out, proportionally more women are entering management.

The same amount of education brings higher economic returns to men than to women. A 1977 survey by the Hong Kong Productivity Centre reveals that male matriculants and university graduates earn a higher monthly income than their female counterparts.[59] Recent census data show that at every level of educational attainment, proportionally more women are in the lower income brackets than in the upper brackets. For example, in 1986, 29 percent of the working population with a tertiary degree education were women, but only 19 percent of them were in the top three income groups, and 54 percent were in the bottom three.[60]

Anxiety about the future of Hong Kong is rapidly changing the psyche and behavior of its working population. Idealism and commitment are sacrificed to quick success. This becomes all the more evident when job seekers have more choice in a hungry labor market. The brain drain and the recent economic boom have coalesced to intensify the labor shortage.

Educated professionals have an edge to emigrate as skilled workers. While in general the professions on the priority lists of receiving countries are male-dominated, some of them are female-dominated. This somewhat upsets the conventional order of occupational prestige. For example, nurses and social workers, although heavily female and low on the hierarchy of professions, are among the categories that Canada and New Zealand currently prefer. Medical doctors (who are predominantly males) do not enjoy a similar advantage in the case of Canada and Australia. Engineers are at the bottom of the Canadian immigration priority list.[61] This has in turn affected choice in further education. Emigration preference has resulted in an increase of applications, from both females and males, for admission to nursing schools.[62] The feminization of certain trades may be attributed partially to brain drain. An example is Chinese-language journalism. It pays poorly and cannot attract highly educated talent. Reporters are now overwhelmingly female, possibly because men have turned to more lucrative jobs. Teaching also suffers from staff shortages.

Emigration has in some cases changed the economic relations of couples. A new family situation has taken shape whereby the husbands come back to Hong Kong for high-paying jobs, leaving wives and children behind in the host society. They fly between family and work and are dubbed "spacemen." This is a modern version of the pre-1949 situation where husbands came to work in Hong Kong and frequently visited their families in China. In such cases, wives, previously working or not, become the sole head of family. They cannot work and are economically dependent.

On the other hand, the labor shortage resulting from rapid economic growth is changing women's entry and distribution in occupations. Housewives are urged to take jobs as factory workers, saleswomen, and cashiers. The phenomenon of middle-aged women in fast food stores and convenience stores is rather recent. Women with some education and knowledge of English find entry to junior white-collar work as telephone operators and clerks. It is not as yet clear if female staff find less discrimination in promotion to positions that face competition from males. The move of Hong Kong-owned manufacturing, especially its labor-intensive segments, to neighboring China is likely to affect women most, since they are concentrated in unskilled factory work.

Women in Chinese Hong Kong

This chapter has argued that while women in Hong Kong have taken advantage of widened access to education and work, the equality drive in work force participation still lags behind that in education. Covert discrimination is still alive in institutions[63] and in the family.[64] Traditional values also reduce the role of educational attainment as a facilitator of women's participation in the public sphere. The Chinese woman as self-sacrificing mother and obedient wife remains an ideal to many in Hong Kong, and has prevented many women from realizing their full potential. Even the minority of successful women in employment and politics, who obviously are not frustrated in their ambition, appear to be uneasy about their achievement. In public, they emphasize their paramount commitment to their families, as if to soften their competitive image.[65] The present situation of the territory is unlikely to change such attitudes, although increasing numbers of men and women are equally keen to equip themselves with education and work experience.

How 1997 will affect women's status in Hong Kong is seldom discussed, largely because of the perception that Hong Kong women have won the battle for equality[66] and that the problem no longer exists. The return of Hong Kong to Chinese rule is unlikely to eliminate present sex inequalities or to rekindle interest in the issue. While women's status has greatly improved in China, women's liberation has never been high on the state's agenda.[67] Neither the Hong Kong government nor the Xinhua News Agency, the *de facto* Chinese consulate in Hong Kong, view women's issues as a priority. Therefore, with little enthusiasm from society in general, the few feminist groups in Hong Kong are unlikely to receive encouragement from the future government.

Notes

1. For an account of women's schooling in China, see G. Mak, "People's Republic of China," in *International Handbook of Women's Education,* ed. G. Kelly (Westport, CT: Greenwood, 1989).

2. D.W. Vikner, " The Role of Christian Missions in the Establishment of Hong Kong's System of Education" (Ed. D. diss., Teachers College, Columbia University, 1987), chap. 3.

3. Calculated from Edward A. Irving, "The System of Education in Hong Kong" (Xerox copy at the University of Hong Kong library from *Great Britain Board of Education Special Report on Educational Subjects,* vol. 14, 1905), p. 94.

4. Ibid., p. 70.

5. Calculated from ibid., p. 94. The 1870 and 1900 figures excluded Queen's College, a prestigious boys' college. Otherwise the percentages of girls would be lower.

6. Calculated from Education Department, Hong Kong, *Annual Reports 1936–37,* p. 11; *1937–38,* p. 9; *1938–39,* p. 13 (Hong Kong: Government Printer, n.d.).

7. Calculated from Education Department, *Annual Report 1946–47,* p. 57. This figure includes evening school enrollment.

8. Calculated from Education Department, *Annual Report 1948–49,* p. 71. This figure does not include evening school enrollment.

9. Yau Yuen, *A Historical Study of the Educational System of Hong Kong* (Hong Kong: Progressive Education Publishers, 1948), p. 42. (In Chinese.)

10. Education Department, *Annual Report 1938–39,* p. 12.

11. Education Department, *Annual Report 1948–49,* p. 22.

12. Irving, "System of Education," p. 100. This referred to government schools.

13. Yuen, *Historical Study,* p. 58. Currency in HK$.

14. Ibid.

15. I. Cheng, "Women Students and Graduates," in *University of Hong Kong: The First 50 Years, 1911–1961,* ed. B. Harrison (Hong Kong: Hong Kong University Press, 1962), pp. 148–49.

16. Ibid., p. 150.

17. Ibid., p. 152.

18. Calculated from Education Department, *Annual Report 1951–52,* p. 101.

19. The first female engineering student at HKU was enrolled in 1923. Cheng, "Women Graduates," p. 149.

20. Census and Statistics Department, Hong Kong, *Hong Kong Statistics 1947–1967* (Hong Kong: Government Printer, 1969), p. 40.

21. Census and Statistics Department, *Hong Kong Annual Digest of Statistics 1989* (Hong Kong: Government Printer, 1990), p. 11.

22. Y. Fung, "Education," in *Hong Kong in Transition,* ed. J. Cheng (Hong Kong: Oxford University Press, 1986).

23. Census and Statistics Department, *Annual Digest 1989,* p. 202.

24. Three colleges merged and were upgraded to become the government-funded Chinese University of Hong Kong.

25. Calculated from Education Department, *Annual Report 1962–63,* pp. 23, 49. There

THE SCHOOLING OF GIRLS IN HONG KONG   179

have been proportionally more females at CUHK than HKU—e.g., in 1988 women made up 52 percent of the student population at CUHK but only 33 percent at HKU. One explanation is that HKU offers engineering programs that are predominantly male, and CUHK does not as yet. Engineering is the second largest faculty at HKU, after arts, in terms of enrollment.

26. Mark Bray, "Student Loans for Higher Education: The Hong Kong Experience in International Perspective," *Higher Education* 15 (1986):343–54.

27. W.F. Maunder et al., "Survey of Student Life," *Journal of the Economics Society* (HKU) (1958):11–68.

28. The Chinese University of Hong Kong, *Vice-Chancellor's Report. A New Era Begins, 1975–78*. (Hong Kong: Chinese University of Hong Kong, n.d.), p. 31.

29. G. Mak, "Development and Women's Access to Higher Education: A Comparative Study of the People's Republic of China and Hong Kong," paper presented at the CUHK Conference on Gender Studies in Chinese Societies, Hong Kong, 1989.

30. Maunder et al., "Survey," pp. 20–21.

31. Wing Kwong Tsang, "Equal Opportunity in University Education in Hong Kong," *Education Journal* (CUHK) 13, no. 1 (1985): 10–27. (In Chinese.)

32. S.L. W. Tang, "The Differential Education Attainment of Children: An Empirical Study of Hong Kong" (Ph.D. diss., University of Chicago, 1981).

33. Calculated from Census and Statistics Department, *Annual Digest 1989*, p. 211.

34. Ibid.

35. Ibid.

36. Education Department, *Annual Report 1977–78*, pp. 77–81; *1978–79*, pp. 66–69; *1979–80*, pp. 70–71; *1980–81*, pp. 59–60; *1981–82*, pp. 60–61.

37. Ibid. See enrollment in these divisions.

38. For instance, in 1947–48, 35 female and 14 male students were enrolled in Northcote Training College, and 27 females and 19 males in the Rural Training College. In 1955, a total of 144 females and 98 males were enrolled in Northcote and Grantham Training Colleges. See Education Department, *Annual Report 1957–58*, p. 5; *Annual Report 1954–55*, p. 108.

39. Calculated from Census and Statistics Department, *Annual Digest 1989*, p. 208.

40. Ibid.

41. May-ling Wong Lai, "Civil Attitudes towards Women in Hong Kong" (M. Soc. Sc. diss., University of Hong Kong, 1982), p. 23.

42. Address by the Governor, Sir David Wilson, at the Opening of the 1989–90 Session of Legislative Council on October 11, 1989.

43. The number of students who had left the territory to study abroad soared from 5,982 in 1972–73 to 9,910 in 1986–87. In 1986–87 the major host countries were the United Kingdom (4,240), Canada (3,023), the United States (1,946), and Australia (701). See Education Department, *Annual Summary 1986–87*, p. 56.

44. Calculated from the British Council, *Statistics of Students Abroad in the United Kingdom 1984–85, 1985–86*, and *1986–87* (London: The British Council, 1987, 1988, and 1989).

45. Calculated from statistics supplied to this author by Employment and Immigration, Canada (Ottawa) in March 1990.

46. Calculated from Department of Employment, Education and Training, Canberra, Australia, "Private Overseas Students Statistics" for the years 1987, tables 2, 5; 1988, tables 2, 5; and 1989, tables 3, 5, respectively.

47. Census and Statistics Department, *Annual Digest 1989*, p. 31.

48. Suk-Ching Ho, "Women's Labor-Force Participation in Hong Kong, 1971–1981," *Journal of Marriage and the Family* 46 (1984):947–54.

49. Ibid.
50. Yuen, *Historical Study*, p. 59.
51. J.M. Engel, "Higher Education for Women in Hong Kong and Scope of Employment for Highly-Educated Women," *Journal of Education* (HKU), no. 18 (1960):10.
52. Calculated from Census and Statistics Department, *Annual Digest 1989*, p. 213.
53. Lai, "Civil Attitudes," p. 1.
54. Ibid., p. 19.
55. John Burns, "Representative Bureaucracy and the Senior Civil Service in Hong Kong," *Hong Kong Journal of Public Administration* 2, no. 1 (1980): 5. This argument is confirmed in Daniel C.C. Tang, "An Evaluation of the Career Patterns and Attitudes of Upper Middle Civil Servants in Hong Kong" (M. Soc. Sc. diss., University of Hong Kong, 1982).
56. Julia Fung, "Women and Architecture—A Budding Romance," *Asian Architect & Builder* 9, no. 5 (1980):17–22.
57. Suk-Ching Ho, "Women Managers in Hong Kong: A Content Analysis of the Recruitment Advertisements," *Equal Opportunities International* 4, no. 2 (1985):30–33.
58. Theodora Ting-Chau, "Women Executives in Hong Kong," *Hong Kong Manager* 16, no. 1 (1980):8–12.
59. Cited in Suk-ching Ho, "The Era of the Female Managers: Looking Back and Looking Forward," *Hong Kong Manager* 17 (1981), p. 9.
60. Calculated from Census and Statistics Department, *Hong Kong 1986 Bi-Census Main Report*, vol. 2 (Hong Kong: Government Printer, 1987), pp. 72–73.
61. See *The Emigrant* 5 (May 1990), pp. 39–40 for current occupational priority lists set by major immigrant countries. This periodical has appeared in the last two years and specializes in emigration information.
62. See, e.g., *Ming Bao*, April 24, 1990, "Sharp Rise in Application for Admission to Nursing Schools as a Means to Emigrate." (In Chinese.)
63. For example, school girls are socialized to become "feminine" and channelled to "female" academic disciplines; working women suffer from employers' preference to promote males, and staff prefer male bosses.
64. For example, in poor families daughters work to help financially and sons are major recipients of family benefits. See Janet W. Salaff, *Working Daughters in Hong Kong* (Cambridge and New York: Cambridge University Press, 1981). Also, in families mothers shoulder most housework and child care. See *Ming Bao* March 4, 1990, "Hong Kong Men Seldom Participate in Housework." (In Chinese.)
65. See, e.g., *South China Morning Post*, 15 October, 1989, "Women Break Through." The term "successful career women" implies a disapproval of women who made it to the top but are perceived to lack feminine charm and to have failed as mothers and wives.
66. This author is dubious. For example, women are weak in political participation. Most of the few high-profile women politicians in Hong Kong's decision-making bodies are government-appointed. Women's participation and success rates in political elections are very low. See Association for the Advancement of Feminism, *Survey of Women's Community Participation in Hong Kong* (Hong Kong: Association for the Advancement of Feminism, 1985), and Chi Kie Wan, "Political Participation of Women in Hong Kong" (B. Soc. Sc. thesis, University of East Asia [Macau], 1985).
67. For an analysis of changes in women's status in China, see, among others, Elisabeth Croll, *Feminism and Socialism in China* (London: Routledge & Kegan Paul, 1978); Phyllis Andors, *The Unfinished Revolution of Chinese Women 1948–1980* (Bloomington, IN: Indiana University Press, 1983); and Margery Wolf, *Revolution Postponed: Women in Contemporary China* (Stanford: Stanford University Press, 1985).

Part IV

Educational Issues:
Language and Labor

8

Cantonese, English, or Putonghua—Unresolved Communicative Issue in Hong Kong's Future

Herbert Pierson

Introduction

During Hong Kong's transition away from British colonial rule to full Chinese sovereignty in 1997, a number of salient sociopolitical concerns remain unresolved. One such persistent issue is language and communication.[1] Hong Kong operates, at least superficially, as a multilingual society where English and Cantonese, currently functioning in separate domains, coexist with one another. However, with the imminent takeover of the territory by mainland China, it would appear that Putonghua (Mandarin), China's official language, will emerge as a potentially strong rival to both Cantonese and English.

Because of growing economic links between Hong Kong and mainland China, Kwo[2] reports that efforts to learn to speak Putonghua are increasing. Some observers[3] contend it is almost axiomatic that after the Chinese takeover in 1997, a natural and quick solution to the language problem will evolve. A policy of Putonghua replacing English as the language of administration will enable Putonghua, which only functions marginally at present in the territory, quickly to surpass both English and Cantonese in prestige and importance. This could result in an unusual sociolinguistic situation of having two high languages and one low language in a single community. Putonghua would become the language of politics and administration; English the language of technology, commerce, and finance; and Cantonese the language of the family and intimacy.

Before the tragic events of June 4, 1989, it was possible to believe that the territory's sociopolitical future could be negotiated and settled amicably and reasonably in the spirit of the Sino-British Joint Declaration on the Question of Hong Kong, initialed by Britain and China in 1984. This agreement assured the territory that its socioeconomic structure would remain unaltered for the first fifty years after the territory comes under mainland Chinese governance and jurisdiction in 1997. The agreement even made provisions to allow the territory a certain amount of freedom in the educational and linguistic domains.[4]

With no official guidance coming either from the present British colonial government or the mainland Chinese authorities, it is conceivable that language and communication matters will evolve or drift as they have in the past, and continue on in this way for the next fifty years. However, the Tiananmen Massacre, the economic decline that has recently hit China, the disharmony and acrimony that have resurfaced during the writing of the Basic Law, the mini-constitution for Hong Kong, and the current tense, almost hostile, relations between China and Great Britain make it less clear that many sociopolitical issues, not the least being language and communication issues, can be negotiated and settled amicably and rationally before or even after 1997.[5]

A direct consequence of this uncertainty is that the politically sensitive citizenry of Hong Kong, who have traditionally "voted with their feet," are doing so in greater numbers. Thus, there is concern about a brain drain as some of the territory's best-educated citizens emigrate or prepare to emigrate. According to government estimates, in 1989 approximately 42,000 people emigrated to Australia, Canada, and the United States. Many of these Hong Kong emigrants are among the territory's most linguistically talented.[6]

This chapter will attempt to shed light on the language and communication issues facing the people of Hong Kong by presenting and discussing research data that examine students' personal attitudes and beliefs on the communicative choices facing them. The chapter will proceed by first looking at the Chinese dialects of Hong Kong and then commenting on the present and future prospects for English in Hong Kong. This will be followed by a review of some studies on language attitudes, both toward English and Putonghua, but with special concentration on student attitudes toward learning Putonghua. The data will then be discussed with some preliminary recommendations about planning the teaching of Putonghua in preparation for the 1997 takeover.

The Chinese Varieties of Hong Kong

Although the Hong Kong government has legislated[7] that English and Chinese are the official languages of the territory, English is the language of the upper echelons of government administration, the medium of instruction in most secondary schools and postsecondary institutions, and the language of the law courts. However, with the establishment of such groups as the Bilingual Law Advisory Committee, steps are being taken to see that laws are published in both Chinese and English. Chinese was only recently accorded the status of an official language in the Official Languages Ordinance of 1974, and then only after a language campaign was waged by politically active members of the community. Even though Cantonese is by far the most widely spoken variety of Chinese in Hong Kong and the vernacular, the ordinance did not specify any particular variety of Chinese, only Chinese.

In relying on the term "Chinese," there is an inherent ambiguity and imprecision. Chinese can refer to Cantonese, the dialect of Canton (Guangzhou) and the prosperous Canton delta, and the mother tongue of most Hong Kong Chinese. It can also refer to Putonghua, the national language of China, or to modern standard Chinese, the written language. In addition, it can refer to the dozens of regional and village varieties of Chinese that are spoken in Hong Kong. Although Cantonese is the vernacular of Hong Kong and of many overseas Chinese communities, as a communicative medium it is not as socially prestigious as Putonghua. Putonghua is both the official language of mainland China and also of Taiwan, where it is called Mandarin. It is estimated that Putonghua and its mutually intelligible varieties are spoken as a native tongue by 72 percent of the population in mainland China, primarily the inhabitants of Northern China. It embraces the dialects of Beijing, Nanjing, and Siquan.[8]

Hong Kong has been able to resist the inexorable pull of Putonghua for a number of reasons. First of all it lies within the reaches of those areas of the Canton delta in South China where older regional dialects are diffused and preserved in the domain of friendship and family.[9] Since liberation in 1949, the authorities in China have tried to transform this linguistic situation by making Putonghua available to speakers of minority dialects in remote villages by means of schooling, mass media, and a language reform policy that has seen the standardization of pronunciation and the simplification of Chinese characters. There are, however, indications that this language program has met with only moderate success in South China after nearly forty years of effort.[10] For example, in the metropolitan district of Guangzhou (Canton) in South China, Putonghua as a medium of instruction is confined to certain "key point" schools, while the remaining schools use Cantonese as the main instructional medium.[11] In spite of the fact that people are taught to read in Putonghua, Cantonese, precisely because it is their mother tongue, is the usual medium at home, at work, and in social situations.

An added sociohistorical factor for the tenacious hold of Cantonese on Hong Kong stems from the almost 150 years of British rule. Hong Kong's decades of political, economic, and social development as a British Crown Colony, cut off from the direct political control of a succession of mainland Chinese regimes, has undoubtedly reinforced the present independent development in language and communication. Even with the growth of the China trade and the enhancement of China's international political prestige, regional linguistic loyalties in Hong Kong have not declined significantly, allowing Cantonese to remain firmly entrenched as the vernacular of Hong Kong.

However, it should be noted that there was a brief period in Hong Kong's recent history where Putonghua experienced a mini-revival. This was a result of the chaos in China after World War II and the ensuing civil war in China, which compelled Hong Kong to receive wave after wave of mainland Chinese immigrants in the early 1950s. These immigrants not only brought their capital and possessions, but also their native Chinese dialects, which for many of them was Putonghua. For a brief period Putonghua songs had great popularity and many films were released in Putonghua. Putonghua was even introduced as a formal subject in school, and students were allowed to take it as a half-subject in the Certificate examination. The revival was fleeting indeed. As the Putonghua-speaking immigrants became assimilated, it was Cantonese that became the mother tongue of their offspring. By 1965, Putonghua as an examinable subject in public examinations was deleted.

This has not been an altogether surprising development because subsequent waves of immigrants have their cultural roots in the villages and countryside of the Canton delta where Cantonese or its local varieties flourish. Added to this was the fact that the British colonial administrations in Hong Kong have seldom provided, until recently, any substantial institutional support for Putonghua tuition. It should be noted that even though Putonghua is not a dialect intelligible to the general public of Hong Kong, as 1997 approaches, Putonghua, not Cantonese, is often used at official functions alongside English, especially when mainland Chinese officials are in attendance.

Different Dialects

Although the Cantonese and Putonghua are dialects belonging to the same Sino-Tibetan language group, Cantonese differs significantly from Putonghua in syntax, lexis, and phonology. Cantonese is a tonal language with 9 tones and 20 initial and 53 final sound segments. Putonghua, by contrast, is a tonal language with 4 tones and 22 initial and 38 final sound segments.[12] In general one can say that the written language, i.e., the Chinese characters, is basically the same everywhere in Chinese, and the differences between the written language in Beijing, Taipei, Shanghai, and Hong Kong lie fundamentally in the pronunciation. However, since liberation the mainland Chinese authorities have adopted a simplified type of Chinese characters in which certain strokes have been eliminated. This makes it easier for ordinary people to write and thereby promotes literacy. Nevertheless, the ubiquity and basic uniformity of the written language in Chinese communities has given literate Chinese, speaking diverse regional dialects, the ability to communicate with one another. The written language is a mode of communication that has helped unify the Chinese people and promote the unity of the culture.

Kalgren[13] has suggested that the present form of written Chinese, along with its Northern pronunciation system, is a relatively recent linguistic development and that there is sufficient linguistic evidence to support the notion that Cantonese is one of the contemporary Chinese dialects most closely resembling ancient Chinese in both pronunciation and structure. If this proposition is true, then Cantonese is the "daughter dialect" most closely related to the ancient "mother dialect" of China. Today, because of the differences between Cantonese and Putonghua, a Cantonese-speaker learning to communicate in Putonghua is learning what can be described as "half a foreign language."

Education Department Input

As a result of the increasing contact between China and Hong Kong in recent years, the Hong Kong government has in a modest way begun to promote Putonghua by making it available as a subject—first in primary schools in 1986, and in secondary schools in 1988. This has been accomplished through the Education Department's encouragement of Putonghua classes, either during school hours or as an extracurricular activity, by providing the schools with financial incentives. For example, in 1988 HK$335 was allotted for primary students and HK$445 for secondary students. In addition, Putonghua has become a component in the teacher training facilities under the jurisdiction of the Education Department, i.e., the Institute of Language in Education (ILE) and the colleges of education. Up until May 1989, 940 primary and 436 secondary schoolteachers have received some training in the teaching of Putonghua.[14]

The Education Department has developed provisional syllabuses for primary and secondary school Putonghua, which have been distributed to the schools. Nevertheless, the time available in the present school system that can realistically be given to Putonghua tuition is no more than a token one hour per week. This is a problem perceived by the language specialists in the Education Department who in a recent report on language improvement plans urged that more research be done to ameliorate the situation: " . . . the introduction of Putonghua into schools highlights the need in Hong Kong for a review of language use and likely needs in order to have a clearer picture of the roles and the likely requirements for various languages in Hong Kong."[15]

The fact that this eighty-eight page official report on language improvement policy devotes only two pages to concerns about the teaching of Putonghua is significant in itself.

The Training of Local Putonghua Teachers

There is, however, a growing public commitment to promote Putonghua by training local teachers in the dialect and instructing them in language teaching methodology. This has been mainly the responsibility of the Institute of Language in Education (ILE), an Education Department structure established to do language research and to train and retrain language teachers. The ILE was established in 1982 and one of its stated responsibilities is to enable teachers to enhance their proficiency in Cantonese, Putonghua, and English.

Within the ILE there are two main divisions, Chinese and English. The Chinese division comprises three sections, one of which is responsible for Putonghua. This section has a staff strength of nine officers, including a vice-principal, a senior lecturer, and seven lecturers. Many of these lecturers are not native speakers of Putonghua, but rather local teachers who have gained Putonghua proficiency by attending courses offered either by the government or private organizations. While the ILE needs to recruit good competent Putonghua lecturers, it is hampered in hiring them because of regulations requiring lecturers to have both a recognized university degree and a good command of Putonghua. In spite of these limitations, the section has the ability to certify 500 Putonghua teachers a year.

This is accomplished through organizing a fundamental Putonghua course with the stated objective of enhancing "participants' awareness of Putonghua through the training of listening and spoken skills."[16] In addition, the section has run Putonghua extension courses. Between September 1987 and June 1988, the ILE supervised 247 primary and secondary schoolteachers who were studying in a Putonghua proficiency course. In the summer of 1988, it organized a five-day Putonghua methodology course with 227 participants. The course covered such areas as the classroom teaching of Putonghua, language materials development, micro teaching, reference materials for teaching, and the design of Putonghua exercises.

Official Commitment to Putonghua

The Education Department's efforts to promote Putonghua are modest indeed when compared to the daunting task of making Putonghua a full subject in the education system. An ideal time to have initiated such a program might have been in the mid-1970s, right after the Hong Kong government had made Chinese an official language of Hong Kong. This was a period when the local citizenry was exceedingly conscious of Chinese as the "mother tongue" and would have been more inclined to accept this added curricular burden because of its connection with ethnic consciousness and general Chinese patriotism. Another ideal period for promoting Putonghua in the schools might have been in the late 1970s, when China's "open door" policy began. At that time Hong Kong people, many of them students, went on extensive tours all over mainland China where Putonghua was an indispensable tool for getting to know the real China.

In the past decade the Education Department's pronouncements about Putonghua have been stronger than its investment of resources. In an official report dating back to 1981, it stated that:

the time is right to consider the teaching of Mandarin, to put Hong Kong in the mainstream of Chinese cultural and economic development. . . . The teaching of Mandarin (or Putonghua) and its use as the medium of instruction are at present very restricted, but the Education Department is planning a pilot scheme to introduce Putonghua as a teaching subject in a limited number of schools.[17]

This plan was endorsed by a panel of "visiting experts" headed by Sir John Llewellyn, a former director-general of the British Council. Their report suggested that:

> Putonghua be offered as a publicly financed by extra-curricular (Saturday or after normal school hours), and therefore optional, supplement for those who wish to enroll from P3/4 onwards... from F1 ... by the end of FIII are receiving ... their instruction in each language, with Putonghua continuing to be an option which can be built into secondary time-tables as well as being offered on an extra-curricular basis at public expense.[18]

With this objective in mind, the Education Department did in fact carry on an experimental pilot scheme on teaching Putonghua in schools. It was completed in 1984 and the results of this pilot research were reported to be favorable and encouraging. This resulted in another pilot scheme started in 1984 at the secondary level and completed in 1987. This also reported positive, satisfactory results. The Education Commission, which was established around this time, was given these results and made the following recommendation in their official reports:

> Putonghua should continue to option for inclusion into the secondary school time-table or as an extra-curricular activity at public expense.[19]
>
> More schools should be encouraged to teach Putonghua either during school hours or as an extra-curricular activity.[20]

Present Status of Putonghua

According to a current Education Department reports,[21] 473 primary schools, or 67 percent of the total, offer Putonghua in the school curriculum, while 353 schools, or 50 percent, are offering Putonghua as an extracurricular activity. At the secondary level, 133 schools, or 27 percent, offer Putonghua in the formal curriculum and a further 207 schools, or 42 percent, offer Putonghua as an extracurricular activity. These programs are served by 1,653 trained teachers of whom 1,122 are engaged in primary school teaching and 531 in secondary school teaching. In addition to these programs, Putonghua tuition is organized by Hong Kong's tertiary institutions and private language centers.

Present and Future Status of English

Although Hong Kong has a population approaching 6 million, of whom 98 percent are Chinese and mostly speaking Cantonese as their mother tongue, English is the official language of the colony. There are no precise figures on what proportion of the population can function in English. Even though the citizens of Hong Kong are increasingly proud of their Cantonese heritage, they accept, with few exceptions, the reality of English being the language of government administration, the law courts, and a virtually compulsory subject in the schools. The influence of English is manifest in the colonial education system where English, not Chinese, is the main medium of instruction in 94 percent of the secondary schools[22] (however, the extent to which English *actually* functions as the medium of instruction is questionable). Yet in order to attain a place in one of Hong Kong's highly competitive tertiary institutions, a candidate has to demonstrate in examinations some degree of communicative competence in English. Besides this institutional support for English, there is significant mass media support for English coming from such enterprises as two major local English-language newspapers, four radio stations, and two TV stations, broadcasting in English.

English has gained dramatically in importance during the postwar years as the colony has transformed itself from a small *entrepôt* trading center to a hub of international trade and commerce. The need for English has grown with the territory's development as a commercial, financial, and exhibition center as well as a trading and manufacturing base in which worldwide telecommunication links have developed with extraordinary rapidity. Hong Kong is also a regional headquarters for many multinational corporations who conduct their day-to-day operations in English. A survey of candidates taking the prestigious Institute of Linguists final diploma indicated that, on the job, English was used 66.86 percent of the time, Cantonese 31.82 percent of the time, and Putonghua 1.3 percent of the time.[23]

English, therefore, can be rightly viewed as one of Hong Kong's many assets, similar perhaps to a valuable natural commodity. Many people believe that after the Chinese takeover in 1997, the value of this commodity will decline or be in serious jeopardy as the official status, which English now holds, is replaced by or shared with Putonghua. This issue causes such nervousness that some commentators suggest that the continuing status and function of English in the community is a partial guarantee that the territory will remain free and autonomous because it will operate as China's eyes on the outside world.[24]

In recent years there has been concern about the English standards in Hong Kong.[25] A report by a local publisher and even an inaugural professorial lecture with the ominous title of "The Worst English in the World" have sounded some alarms about general English standards.[26] Whether the standards are falling has not yet been seriously and methodically researched, nor has the research question been clearly and precisely defined. However, with the steady growth in the territory's economy in the past decade, there is a perception among business leaders that the number of English speakers needed for the demands of commerce and industry is insufficient if the territory is going to maintain its competitive position as an important international financial and commercial center in

Asia.[27] A commercially financed "Language Campaign" has been mounted to publicize the fact that the territory needs a steady supply of staff with bilingual competence.

Attitudinal Research on Language and Communications

For over a decade there have been a number of language attitude studies conducted in Hong Kong with the purpose of analyzing the mutual impact of English and Chinese communication and culture on each other. Most of the studies have investigated secondary and tertiary level students with the purpose of evaluating the factors that have contributed to achievement or underachievement in English. A survey published in 1975 indicated that there were attitudinal problems related to English communication.[28] Although the subjects in this survey considered English to be an important academic subject, they also reported uneasiness about communicating in that language. At the same time these subjects reported pride in Chinese culture and had a negative evaluation of Western culture and English-speaking people.

A "matched guise" communication study published in 1976 indicated that subjects using Cantonese-speaking guises were evaluated significantly higher on character traits such as kindness, trustworthiness, honesty, sincerity, humility, and friendliness, while those communicating in English-speaking guises were evaluated significantly higher on such character traits such as attractiveness, wealth, intelligence, and kindness.[29] A study of the relationship between language attitudes and English communicative competence pointed to a series of ambivalent attitudinal orientations toward English and Western people.[30] Again there was a stated desire to learn to communicate in English, but at the same time there were suggestions of ambivalence and antipathy toward Chinese communicating in English.

On the basis of this research one would have expected face-to-face communication research studies would have exposed ambivalent and possibly even hostile reactions to English-language communication and Western culture. This was not indicated in a communication study conducted on sixty-four female undergraduates with the assistance of Chinese and Western interlocutors. The subjects perceived the Western interviewers to be more natural and confident than the corresponding Chinese interlocutors.[31] The absence of antipathy toward communication in English with the Western interlocutors was partially explained by pointing out that the subjects participating in this study were undergraduates majoring in the English language and literature at one of Hong Kong's two public universities. Because of this academic training one would presume a receptiveness to outgroup cultures and communication styles.

A series of communication studies based on the social psychological model of *group vitality*[32] were undertaken to assess the position of the two languages and cultures in contact. A pilot Hong Kong Chinese version of the Subjective Vitality Questionnaire (SVQ), the research instrument developed from this model, was administered to a small group of undergraduates. The results were mixed. For example, the subjects perceived that Westerners were prouder of their cultural history and more highly regarded in Hong Kong than the Chinese. At the same time, however, they considered that the Chinese language was more highly regarded internationally than English. Follow-up studies using the SVQ on both Chinese and Western subjects in Hong Kong have suggested that societal orientations toward language and ethnicity are fluid.[33]

Study of Attitudes toward Putonghua

The Putonghua communication research now discussed emerges from the previously cited studies on the sociolinguistic alignment of English and Chinese. However, this time the element of decolonization and the transition to Chinese sovereignty was taken into account. The research question was to probe the impact of making Putonghua a compulsory subject in the secondary school curriculum, implying that it would become a medium of communication in education.

The research was set up as part of a public examination in English language for postsecondary school students. In this examination the students were asked to write an essay in which they were to react to a hypothetical situation of Putonghua being introduced as a compulsory subject in secondary school. It was not specified how this would be implemented or whether it was even feasible. The subjects were simply asked to comment on a future introduction of Mandarin in secondary schools. The term *Mandarin* rather than *Putonghua* was used in the question because it was felt that Putonghua could be construed as a politically loaded term, suggesting a bias toward Beijing. The term Mandarin is traditional and politically neutral.

Underlying the hypothetical situation in the question was the juxtaposition of Putonghua to Cantonese and English, and by extension the juxtaposition of mainland Chinese culture to the local hybrid Hong Kong culture. The data were collected and analyzed ever mindful of Fishman's profound insight that the language of communication is invariably a potent symbol of ethnicity among heterogeneous cultural groups in contact, "the quintessential symbol of ethnicity."[34] It was hypothesized that Putonghua, which is neither the mother tongue of most Hong Kong people nor the vernacular of Hong Kong, would nevertheless emerge as an irresistible symbol of Chinese ethnicity, and that reactions to Putonghua as a communication medium would expose in part the internal dispositions individuals in Hong Kong have toward China. In addition, there was an attempt to gauge the intensity of Putonghua as a focus for ethnic consciousness and its strength to transcend and transform the open and outgoing cultural orientation that is a key characteristic of Hong Kong Chinese ethnolinguistic vitality.

The subjects involved in this research were academically successful Form VI students (12th grade) between seventeen and eighteen, who had already been provisionally accepted in one of Hong Kong's two highly competitive publicly financed universities. Their selection for university entry was based on a set of public examinations taken a year before, which entitled them to an admission interview by a selection committee of one of the faculties at the university. It was decided to use this stratified sample of students because it was supposed that they would articulate better in English the social and political realities facing Hong Kong than their nonacademic counterparts.

To obtain these data about attitudes toward communication and ethnicity, the candidates were instructed to write a letter of approximately 350 words to an English-language newspaper in Hong Kong, discussing one of the following topics:

1. Introduction of compulsory Mandarin in the secondary school curriculum;
2. Construction of a nuclear power plant in Daya Bay, only forty miles north of Hong Kong;
3. Censorship of TV programs;
4. A new tax on soft drinks.

To determine the English standard of the students, the examination papers were first analyzed and graded according to predetermined criteria by qualified language instructors. The standard was deemed acceptable, with less than 2 percent of the 1,600 candidates unable to reach the predetermined proficiency standard set by the official examining board. Each script contained approximately 350 words. The overall quality of the student writing varied from highly literate to incoherent. Although the researchers were expecting about 25 percent of the candidates to write on the issue of compulsory Mandarin, more than 50 percent chose to write on this subject, indicating how important the issue was for the student writers.

From the nearly 800 examination scripts written on the topic of compulsory Mandarin, 100 were randomly chosen to constitute the research corpus. By means of content analysis, these scripts were analyzed to determine attitudes toward language, especially Putonghua. The individual protocols were analyzed by two research assistants whose task it was to identify references pertaining to language. It was assumed that the spontaneous English prose of the subjects would reveal insights into their present attitudes toward language and by extension toward ethnolinguistic values and identity.

In analyzing the contents of the corpus, 377 items were identified as being either directly or indirectly related to Putonghua. As indicated in Table 8.1, the items were spread over five main categories: (1) Communicative need; (2) Political exigency; (3) Sociocultural attractiveness; (4) Instrumental demand; and (5) Educational/linguistic need. These were defined as follows:

Communicative need:
Those items in the corpus dealing with Putonghua as a vehicle of communication with either other Chinese or foreigners, and its spread throughout the world at large. These items take into account the fact that Putonghua is the main medium of communication with mainland Chinese contacts.

Political exigency:
Those items that were connected with the political reality of the imminent Chinese takeover of Hong Kong. Here can be found repeated references to the year 1997, the national language, Chinese sovereignty, citizenship, and contact with the political authorities of China.

Sociocultural attractiveness:
Those items in the corpus that reflected a loyalty to Putonghua in its function as the language of China, a sense of shame for not being fluent in it, and a stated desire to master it in order to be fullfilled as a Chinese. There are also references to Putonghua as the mother tongue.

Instrumental demand:
Those items in which Putonghua is perceived as a practical communicative tool, a prerequisite for career advancement or as a means of engaging in the profitable China trade. It is instrumental in the sense described by Gardner and Lambert in their work on language motivation.[35]

Educational/linguistic need:
Those items in the corpus that referred to the use of Putonghua in education and its linguistic impact on written Chinese communication.

Examples of these items can be found in the Appendices.

Discussion

Table 8.1 presents a simple breakdown of the 377 Putonghua items. Although the task given to the subjects required them to comment on the compulsory introduction of Putonghua in the school curriculum, only 15 percent of the items identified from the corpus directly mentioned language in education. Fourteen percent of the Putonghua items mentioned practical issues such as career prospects and commerce. Twenty percent of the items in the corpus mentioned the communicative function of Putonghua in general, while another 24 percent mentioned the political value of Putonghua. More than one quarter of the items in the corpus referred to sociocultural values inherent in Putonghua communication, suggesting that Putonghua does elicit a strong sense of ethnic consciousness.

From the preliminary content analysis, it would appear that the Cantonese-speaking subjects were affirming their Chinese ethnic identity as well as accommodating themselves to the sociopolitical reality of eventual mainland Chinese

Table 8.1

Attitudes toward Putonghua

Area	Number	% of total
1. Communicative	77	20
2. Political	92	24
3. Sociocultural	99	26
4. Instrumental	51	14
5. Educational/linguistic	58	15

control over Hong Kong, which has been termed by one observer as "decolonization without independence."[36] While both areas are of interest, the affirmation of Chinese identity is more congruent with previous ethnolinguistic research.[37]

In the present data Hong Kong Cantonese-speaking subjects often referred to Putonghua as their mother tongue and expressed shame and incompleteness if they were unable to communicate in it. The mention of Putonghua elicited feelings of ethnic consciousness, which conceivably transcend the strong attraction that the hybrid Hong Kong Chinese culture holds. This can be noted in examples of the generally negative or neutral categorizations of Cantonese made by native Cantonese-speakers:

1. Cantonese can't be used in formal writing.
2. Cantonese is *only* a dialect.
3. Cantonese sounds coarse.
4. Cantonese is not a national language.
5. Cantonese has a bad influence on Putonghua.
6. Cantonese is the form of language in Guangzhou.
7. Cantonese is a less formal language, which makes it difficult for us to express our ideas in writing.
8. Cantonese is just a dialect, not officially recognized.
9. Cantonese is vague, undefined, and rough.
10. Cantonese is a dialect impractical to use outside of Guangdong Province and even of limited use there.
11. Cantonese is insufficient as it is only a dialect.

There is some linguistic irony about these points of view because Cantonese is, according to Forrest, probably the variety of Chinese most closely related to ancient Chinese, the source of all of China's present-day varieties.[38] One can only speculate that these Cantonese-speaking subjects are affirming their Chinese ethnic identity through the mediation of Putonghua, at the temporary expense of their true mother tongue, Cantonese.

What these data also indicate is an apparent general lack of antipathy toward

Putonghua. In fact, only one item in the selected 100 protocols suggested that Cantonese (i.e., Cantonese-speakers) should not be forced to learn Putonghua. This should be contrasted with studies of attitudes toward the English language cited earlier in this paper where antipathy and ambivalence toward English has been reported. Any expression of antipathy toward English in these protocols was limited, perhaps because English was not the central issue in the writing task. Only a few of the protocols mentioned the English language. References to English were generally practical or neutral, as can be seen from these examples:

1. English should remain compulsory as it is a world language.
2. Because of colonial influence, English seems easier to write.
3. Putonghua should not replace English as Hong Kong is an international place.
4. Written and spoken English are the same.
5. Learning English decreases chances for learning Chinese.
6. It is a shame that English is more fluent than Chinese.

It appears that when the language in question was Putonghua, the reactions of our Cantonese-speaking subjects were uniformly positive and favorable. Even though there are significant linguistic differences between Putonghua and Cantonese, the subjects did not emphasize the fact that Putonghua is still a foreign language for them. Fishman's insights about language and ethnicity are particularly pertinent for interpreting the processes underlying these results when he states that "language is not only code but Code. For the ethnicity experience language is much more than merely communication just as ethnicity is much more than mere life."[39]

Putonghua in itself evidently signifies "Chineseness," Chinese values, and Chinese ethnic consciousness to these students, comparable to the way English probably signifies Western cultural values to the same group of subjects. However, the surprising aspect of these attitudes is that Putonghua is not their real mother tongue, but the national language of the temporarily separated mother country. Our subjects do not belong to the mother country in any legal or political sense, but certainly on the spiritual and emotional level they do. Hong Kong's political and cultural separation from the mother country might in fact make this loyalty and longing for the mother country even more poignant.

Implications for Language Planning

As long as Putonghua remains on the periphery of the school curriculum, it is going to be difficult to maintain an acceptable level of seriousness among Hong Kong students studying the language. Hong Kong students, like students the world over, are practical. If a subject does not affect their academic results, invariably they are going to pay less attention to it. One way to motivate students to study Putonghua seriously is to build in a true reward structure, because enthusiasm in the form of patriotism and the desire to communicate with China has its limitations. For any large-scale Putonghua program to be successful in Hong Kong, it must be treated as much as possible like an ordinary examinable core subject in the school syllabus. However, the students, especially secondary students in Hong Kong, are already shackled by an inordinately heavy workload, and the addition of another core subject, albeit the dialect of the mother country, might exacerbate the increasing dysfunction of the educational system. One government official has suggested that lack of a favorable linguistic environment is the reason why there appears to be no compulsion or zeal for Putonghua tuition in the schools.[40] To break this deadlock there probably needs to be a massive overhaul of the education system which would rationalize the entire primary and secondary language curriculum in preparation for 1997. In the present political climate, that seems most unlikely.

At present, one possible way to promote interest in Putonghua in the schools might be to make it the medium of instruction for some of the core Chinese subjects in the syllabus. This would provide students with more exposure to the language, which is one of the reasons given for the lack of progress and sustained motivation in its adoption.

Conclusion

Linguists such as Bauer[41] are inclined to believe that Putonghua will replace English, and presumably Cantonese, to become the language of power and the official language of government. Everybody will be required to learn it. Whether this is what will happen after the Chinese takeover of the territory in 1997 is still uncertain. However, it might be to the advantage of the citizens of Hong Kong to master the language of their new masters, otherwise the political and linguistic alienation that is keenly felt by a good portion of the population under the British colonial rule will have little chance of subsiding.

If the results of these studies, particularly the Putonghua study, reflect the attitudes of most young people today toward language and communication, there are grounds to rationalize and formulate an educational policy that would support the introduction of a formal Putonghua syllabus in the secondary school system. If approached rationally and sensitively, motivation problems such as have been associated with learning English as a second language in Hong Kong could be minimized. In this period of transition from British sovereignty to Chinese sovereignty, educational policy should ensure that the young people of Hong Kong are equipped for their responsibilities as citizens of what will become a Special Administrative Region of China. It would seem that communicative competence in Putonghua as well as English would be a substantial investment in making the Cantonese-speaking community of Hong Kong, in the words of the tired local cliché, "stable and prosperous" after 1997.

Appendices

Appendix A: Communicative Area

1—Mandarin is widely used in China and Asian countries
2—communications with foreigners, usually use Mandarin instead of Cantonese
3—increasing interaction with China
4—better communication → improvement → prosperous Hong Kong
5—communicate with other Chinese in the world
6—help communication (travel, film show)
7—increasing contact with China; a trend
8—Mandarin as a united language can avoid conflicts between Chinese living in different areas of China
9—to communicate with people in China and overseas
10—useful for communication in various parts of China
11—communicate with Chinese
12—helps when traveling in China and meeting Chinese overseas
13—Mandarin-speaking relatives
14—enthusiastic foreigners
15—more contact with Chinese people after 1997

Appendix B: Political Area

1—after 1997, civil servants will be required to speak Mandarin
2—China sovereignty
3—may become an international language since China will grow stronger and more influential
4—China sovereignty
5—Sino-British Agreement
6—necessary to have knowledge of the official language of the People's Republic of China
7—main language in China
8—nationality will be well defined → must understand official language
9—aids communication with Chinese officials
10—national language
11—pave way for future of Hong Kong after 1997
12—essential for communication between Hong Kong people and Chinese government
13—good citizens should know the language of the government
14—national language of China
15—political

Appendix C: Sociocultural Area

1—mother tongue
2—shameful that foreigners speak Mandarin better
3—mother tongue
4—can know more Chinese civilizations and customs
5—a big joke if do not know Mandarin when Hong Kong is returned to China
6—Chinese should know Mandarin
7—mother tongue
8—we must respect our language and culture
9—shameful if can't speak language of Chinese
10—mother language
11—help to understand and appreciate Chinese literature
12—ashamed of understanding English version better than Mandarin version in radio
13—English is accepted as compulsory subject; now Mandarin is "our" language
14—being learned by many foreigners
15—shameful if can't speak national language

Appendix D: Instrumental Area

1—a basic requirement of most new jobs
2—only way to get better job after 1997
3—job opportunity is greater if one knows Mandarin
4—help to get a better job after 1997
5—increase job opportunities
6—people who speak Mandarin highly favored by commercial firms
7—may be required to speak Mandarin if you wish to become government official
8—trade with China
9—necessary for trading with China
10—trade with China
11—business with China
12—business activities with China
13—trade and commerce development
14—improved and further enhanced our trading relation with China
15—commercial and industrial benefits

Appendix E: Educational/Linguistic Area

1—easy to learn
2—help students to relax from hard work

3—should be learned in primary schools
4—raise Chinese standard, therefore more elegant
5—may lower Chinese standard even more, therefore confuse even more the mix of Cantonese, Chinese, and English
6—education should be started in primary schools
7—to raise Chinese standard of local students
8—related to our written Chinese language
9—enhance student's ability in composition and comprehension
10—learning Mandarin helps students a lot in Chinese writing skills
11—improve our standard in Chinese language
12—improved our Chinese writing standard
13—compensate effects of English on written Chinese
14—spoken → written
15—improves standard of Chinese and writing ability

Notes

1. E. Lau, "A Language Problem," *Far Eastern Economic Review* 37:7 (1988):34.
2. Ora Kwo, "Language Education in a Changing Economic & Political Context: The Teaching of Putonghua in Hong Kong Schools." Paper presented at the First Hong Kong Conference on Language, and Society (1989).
3. See R. Lord, and B. T'sou, *The Language Bomb* (Hong Kong: Longman Books, 1985), and R. Quirk, "Speculations on the Future Role of English in Hong Kong and the Implications for Educational Policy," in *Future Directions in English Language Teacher Education*, ed. V. Bickley (Hong Kong: Institute of Language in Education, 1986).
4. *Sino-British Joint Declaration on the Question of Hong Kong* (Hong Kong: Xinhua News Agency, 1984).
5. See Ian Burma, "The Last Days of Hong Kong," *The New York Review of Books* 37:6 (April 12, 1990): 41–46; K. Rafferty, *City on the Rocks: Hong Kong's Uncertain Future* (New York: Viking, 1990); and W. Shawcross, *Kowtow!* Chatto Counterblast, no. 6 (London: Chatto Counterblast, 1990).
6. B. Basler, "English Language Follows Empire Out of Hong Kong," *New York Times* (April 16, 1989).
7. D. Roberts, ed., *Hong Kong 1990* (Hong Kong: Government Information Services, 1990).
8. J. De Francis, *The Chinese Language* (Honolulu: The University of Hawaii Press, 1984).
9. R. Li, *The Language Atlas of China* (London: Longman Books, 1988).
10. T.L. Tsim, "English Proficiency in Hong Kong," manuscript, 1989.
11. G.S. Fu, and P.T. Iu, "Language Attitudes and the Social Order in Hong Kong after 1997," Applied Linguistics Association of Australia, Occasional Paper no. 10 (1988):135–49.
12. D. So, "Implementing Mother Tongue Education amidst Societal Transition from Diglossia to Triglossia in Hong Kong," *Language and Education*, 3:1 (1988):29–44.
13. B. Karlgren, *The Chinese Language* (New York: The Ronald Press Company, 1949).
14. Hong Kong Education Department, "Report of the Working Group Set Up to Review Language Improvement Measures," Hong Kong, (1989), p. 58.

15. Ibid.
16. Hong Kong Education Department, "Institute of the Language in Education Annual Report," Hong Kong (1989), p. 7.
17. Government Secretariat, Hong Kong Government, "The Hong Kong Education System," Hong Kong (1981), p. 127.
18. Hong Kong Education Department, "A Perspective on Education in Hong Kong: Report by a Visiting Panel," Hong Kong (1982), p. 26.
19. Hong Kong Government, *Education Commission Report No. 1*, Hong Kong (1984), p. 47.
20. Hong Kong Government, *Education Commission Report No. 2*, Hong Kong (1986), p. 20.
21. Hong Kong Education Department, "Education Bulletin," Ref. No. 1/4466/69/04/89, (1989).
22. So, "Implementing Mother Tongue Education," pp. 29–44.
23. B. Blomfield, and H.D. Pierson, "A Survey of Language Use in Hong Kong" (Special Report, The Institute of Linguists Education Trust, Hong Kong Regional Society, 1987).
24. B. Basler, "English Language."
25. T.L. Tsim, "English Proficiency."
26. R. Harris, "The Worst English in the World: An Inaugural Lecture from the Chair of English Language," Hong Kong University (1989).
27. W. Purves, "Chairman's Statement to Shareholders by W. Purves, Chairman, at the Annual General Meeting on 9 May 1989," Hong Kong Bank (1989).
28. G.S. Fu, *A Hong Kong Perspective: English Language Learning and the Chinese Student*, University of Michigan: Comparative Education Dissertation, Series 28 (1975).
29. R. Lyczak, G.S. Fu, and A. Ho, "Attitudes of Hong Kong Bilinguals towards English and Chinese Speakers," *Journal of Cross-Cultural Psychology* 7 (1976):425–36.
30. H.D. Pierson, G.S. Fu, and S.Y. Lee, "An Analysis of the Relationship between Language Attitudes and English Attainment of Secondary School Students in Hong Kong," *Language Learning* 30 (1980):289–316.
31. H.D. Pierson and M. Bond, "The Impact of Interviewer Language on the Perceptions of Chinese Bilinguals," Occasional Paper No. 96, Social Research Centre, The Chinese University of Hong Kong (1981).
32. See H. Giles, R.Y. Bourhis, and D.W. Taylor, "Towards a Theory of Language in Ethnic Group Relations," in *Language, Ethnicity and Intergroup Relations*, ed. H. Giles (New York: Academic Press, 1977); and P. Johnson, H. Giles, and R.Y. Bourhis, "The Viability of Ethnolinguistic Vitality: A Reply to Husband and Khan," *Journal of Multilingual and Multicultural Development* 4 (1983):255–69.
33. See H.D. Pierson, H. Giles, and L. Young, "Intergroup Vitality Perceptions during a Period of Political Uncertainty: The Case of Hong Kong," *Journal of Multilingual and Multicultural Development* 8 (1987):451–60; and L. Young, H. Giles, and H.D. Pierson, "Sociopolitical Change and Perceived Ethnolinguistic Vitality," *The International Journal of Intercultural Relations* 10 (1986):459–69.
34. J. Fishman, *Language and Ethnicity in Minority Sociolinguistic Perspective* (Philadelphia: Multilingual Matters Ltd., 1989).
35. R.C. Gardner and W.E. Lambert, *Attitudes and Motivation in Second Language Learning* (Rowley, MA: Newbury House, 1972).
36. S.K. Lau, *Decolonization without Independence: The Unfinished Political Reforms of the Hong Kong Government* (Hong Kong: Institute of Social Studies, 1987).
37. M. Bond, "Language as a Carrier of Ethnic Stereotypes in Hong Kong," *Journal of Social Psychology* 125 (1985):53–62.

38. R.A.D. Forrest, *The Chinese Language* (London: Faber and Faber, 1965).
39. J. Fishman, *Language and Ethnicity*.
40. B. Fong, "No Compulsion for Students to Learn Putonghua," *South China Morning Post*, May 21, 1987.
41. R. Bauer, "The Hong Kong Cantonese Speech Community," manuscript, University of Hong Kong, Center of Asian Studies, 1984.

9

The Teaching of Putonghua in Hong Kong Schools: Language Education in a Changing Economic and Political Context

Ora W.Y. Kwo

The debate on the medium of instruction in Hong Kong schools has a long history. The most heated part of the debate has concerned the balance between English and Chinese;[1] but part of the debate has focused on the nature of Chinese, which has many spoken forms of which some are mutually unintelligible. Among those who argue that Chinese deserves a stronger place in the curriculum, there is still disagreement about *which* Chinese. One side in this argument supports Cantonese, which is the most widely spoken form of Chinese in Hong Kong. The other side favors Putonghua, the official language of the People's Republic of China. Advocates of Putonghua highlight potential political, economic, and educational benefits from increased emphasis on the language, and note that Putonghua will become increasingly important during the period up to 1997 and after the reunification of Hong Kong with China.

This chapter explores these arguments and examines their practical implications. It begins by examining in more detail the rationales for stronger emphasis on Putonghua in the school system, before turning to the nature of present educational provision. The third section outlines the main options open to policymakers at both institutional and territory-wide levels, and is followed by comments on the desirability and feasibility of these options. Finally, the paper concludes with an overall appraisal.

1. The Rationales for Stronger Emphasis on Putonghua

The three principal rationales for stronger emphasis on Putonghua in Hong Kong schools are political, economic, and educational. The rationales should not necessarily be accepted without consideration of counterarguments, but are nevertheless worth summarizing.

(a) The Political Rationale

The political rationale may be stated quite simply: that Putonghua is already needed for official negotiations with China and will become even more important after 1997. Hong Kong is expected to be administered as a Special Administrative Region from 1997 until at least 2047, but political contact with the rest of China can only expand. The leadership of China cannot realistically be expected to learn Cantonese, so it is up to the people of Hong Kong to learn Putonghua.

Observers in Hong Kong have reached this conclusion on their own, but have been nudged along by strong views in China itself. For example, when in 1986 the Hong Kong government launched a scheme to encourage the use of Cantonese in local schools, Yang Xun, a ministry of education official in China, greeted the policy with the declaration that Hong Kong was "moving backwards."[2] He suggested that Hong Kong risked becoming "a minority area," and that students would be disadvantaged when trying to enter universities in China. Yang's remarks were described as personal rather than official, but their implications were not lost on a wide segment of Hong Kong society. The *South China Morning Post* presented a strong editorial:[3]

> It has taken years of pressure and discussion for the Education Department to embark on its present course of encouraging the vernacular. It must seem unfair to those civil servants who have quietly laboured to formulate this policy for a senior mainland official to enter the debate and add his comments, thus risking a revival of the whole debate.
>
> Unfortunately for those civil servants, Mr. Yang has an important point. We would recommend a fresh look at the subject. Putonghua and English are the languages which Hong Kong should be stressing.

Similar views were later presented by Dominic Chu, chairman of the Secondary Schools Section of the Diocesan Schools Council. He declared that "Hongkong Chinese risk being isolated by the vast Putunghua [sic] speaking population in mainland China and Taiwan if they continue to adhere to Cantonese."[4]

(b) The Economic Rationale

The economic rationale parallels the political one. China's open-door policy has boosted trade with Hong Kong, and speakers of Putonghua have strong advantages in business. In 1987, Hong Kong's re-export trade was over six times its 1977 level, and as much as 80 percent of the trade involved China.[5] The volume of direct trade has also expanded dramatically, partly because of the growth of processing activities being subcontracted in China by Hong Kong manufacturers. As many as one million Chinese workers may be involved in one way or another in this activity; and the corollary of Hong Kong investment in China is equally impressive investment by China in Hong Kong. It is true that much of this economic activity is with China's Guangdong Province, where Cantonese is widely spoken. However, increasing trade links are also developing with the rest of China, and the need for fluency in Putonghua can only be expected to grow.

Advocates of Putonghua would also point to the volume of trade with other Putonghua-speaking countries (though outside China the language is more often called Mandarin). Thus, while China is by far the largest source of Hong Kong's imports, it is followed in third place by Taiwan and in sixth place by Singapore.[6] Those two countries are also major destinations for Hong Kong's re-exports, and in Singapore's case, for Hong Kong's direct exports. Although English is also widely spoken in Singapore, knowledge of Mandarin, it is argued, is an added facilitator for trade.

(c) The Educational Rationale

There is a general concern about the standard of written Chinese in Hong Kong schools,[7] and at least some educators propose the general introduction of Putonghua to help improve the situation. The problem, it is suggested, arises partly because the discrepancy between spoken Cantonese and written Chinese hinders the writing of good Chinese prose. Children can certainly learn to write good Chinese without knowing Putonghua, but the task is difficult.

For those who have never learned Cantonese, this point perhaps requires elaboration. A child learning to write a simple sentence such as "Kéuih deih gàm yaht hóu aan sìn ji faàn ùk ké"[8] ("They will come home very late today") would have to say to himself "Tà muhn gàm tïn hán máahn chòih wuih gà" before writing

他們今天很晚才回家

To arrive at this sentence, the child must learn that certain characters must be inserted, deleted, or replaced to create an acceptable written phrase.

Emphasizing this point, there is a strong tendency for Cantonese speakers to write a kind of Chinese that is considered either odd or totally incomprehensible to Putonghua speakers. Wong's[9] survey found that even teachers made common errors in such terms as:

English	(Hong Kong) Chinese	(China) Chinese
desk	書枱	書桌
ball-pen	原子筆	圓珠筆
ruler	間尺	尺
eraser	擦紙膠	橡皮
blackboard duster	粉擦	板擦
classroom	班房	教室

It is argued that Hong Kong students would find it easier to write good standard Chinese if they were taught Putonghua.

A further educational question relates to practices at the university level. Hong Kong's two existing universities currently use varying degrees of English and Cantonese. The choice of Cantonese rather than Putonghua limits contacts with and presumably acceptability by China. Johnson proposed a trilingual approach for the University of Hong Kong, which would permit Cantonese as the language of oral exchange among students and a significant proportion of staff, Putonghua as the oral medium for links with China, and "International English" for external links.[10] Although made in the context of the University of Hong Kong, Johnson's proposals might be equally valid in the other institutions of higher education.

In making the proposals, Johnson assumed that the student population would remain largely Cantonese-speaking. Yet if students were an elite from all over China, Putonghua would certainly receive more emphasis. The trilingual policy would require language ability as a prerequisite for university entry, since devoting time and resources to basic language proficiency would unreasonably detract from other studies and thus would lower standards. Enrollment of university students from other parts of the People's Republic of China would create a need for local students to learn Putonghua too.

2. Existing Putonghua Provision in the Educational System

In almost all Hong Kong schools, Cantonese is the medium of instruction for classes in Chinese and Chinese history. It is also the principal language of instruction in other subjects, even in many so-called Anglo-Chinese schools.[11] The Education Commission has recommended that schools be encouraged to teach Putonghua either during school hours or as an extracurricular activity,[12] but only two schools currently use it as the medium of instruction in all subjects (except English language itself).

Between 1981 and 1984, the Education Department conducted a pilot scheme at the primary school level to help assess the role of Putonghua in the curriculum. On the basis of the scheme the department produced a provisional Putonghua syllabus for primary schools, released in September 1986, and a recommended booklist, released in March 1987. The government reported later in 1987 that 310 of the 874 public-sector primary schools were offering Putonghua as an independent subject, and that a further 181 were promoting the language through extracurricular activities.[13]

In 1984, the Education Department also launched a pilot scheme in 51 secondary schools. In mid-1987, 62 secondary schools outside the pilot scheme were already offering Putonghua within the formal curriculum, and another 46 were promoting it on an extracurricular basis. In aggregate, approximately 50 percent of primary and secondary schools were teaching at least some Putonghua.[14]

Recent years have also witnessed growth of training for teachers of Putonghua. The Chinese University of Hong Kong introduced a course for trainees to study as a minor subject in 1983, and currently has a quota of 20 students. The innovation was paralleled in 1986 by the University of Hong Kong, which has a similar enrollment in a comparable course. Since 1986, preservice training has also been provided as an elective subject in the three colleges of education, which had a 1987 enrollment of 144 students. The Education Department's Institute of Language in Education also offered teacher training, particularly with an in-service emphasis. By 1989, 940 primary and 436 secondary teachers had been trained to teach Putonghua.[15]

Recent years have also brought rapid growth of adult education classes. For example, classes at the University of Hong Kong Language Centre are now over three times their size in the early 1980s, and comparable increases have been recorded at the Chinese University of Hong Kong and among various volunteer organizations.[16] Further short courses are run by the Adult Education Section of the Education Department.[17]

3. The Options for Development

If one accepts the need for further development of Putonghua, it becomes necessary to identify appropriate strategies. For policymakers at both the school level and in the territory as a whole, the basic options are to offer Putonghua:

1. only as an extracurricular activity;
2. as an independent optional subject in the main curriculum;
3. as an independent compulsory subject in the main curriculum;
4. as part of the Chinese language curriculum;

5. as the medium of instruction for Chinese language and Chinese history;
6. as the medium of instruction in all subjects except English.

These options could be implemented in both primary and secondary schools, according to the philosophy of the authorities concerned and the background and existing skills of their pupils.

To some extent the options may be considered a series of stages. Thus introduction of Putonghua as an extracurricular activity could be considered an initial stage that leads later to Putonghua as an independent optional subject, as a compulsory subject, and finally as a medium of instruction. However, it is not essential to see the options as stages, for the language could be offered as both an extracurricular activity and a subject on the main curriculum. Similarly, a school could easily go straight to Putonghua as an optional subject and need not offer it as an extracurricular activity.

4. Appropriate Future Development

The choice of option at any particular time must reconcile desirability with feasibility. The two dimensions are considered here in turn.

(a) Desirability

The first section of this chapter presented the arguments for more Putonghua in Hong Kong schools; but how much is "more," what form should it take, and to what types of students should it be made available?

(i) The Viewpoint of Individual School Authorities

For authorities operating individual schools, the nature of priorities depends on personal philosophies. The proprietors of the Kiangsu Chekiang Primary School and the Sun Fong Chung Primary School, which are already dedicated to Putonghua education, believe in total immersion from the first day. In contrast, the proprietors of the Chinese International School feel that Chinese lessons should be taught in Cantonese for pupils for whom that is the mother tongue until the end of Primary 3, but in Putonghua from Primary 4. The majority of other schools follow neither of these models.

Most primary schools are particularly unwilling to make Putonghua the medium of instruction because, quite accurately, they consider Cantonese to be the mother tongue, and for pedagogic reasons favor at least initial instruction in that language. There is substantial professional literature to support this view.[18] The mother-tongue argument is less strong at the secondary level because the pupils are older. However, secondary school proprietors must grapple with the demands of the market place which, at least for the time being, places much more stress on English than on Putonghua.

In most cases, therefore, a more acceptable option is to teach Putonghua just as a subject in the main curriculum. The main question before policymakers then becomes what subject it should displace. To many people, the answer is to teach through Putonghua rather than Cantonese in at least some Chinese lessons, and thus only to displace Cantonese. Others would allocate lessons to Putonghua in the "residual" number of periods not covered by the Education Department's recommended timetable.[19] At primary level, for example, the official timetable contains only 33 lessons per week, whereas half-day schools actually have 38 lessons per week and full-day schools have 40. Allocation of the extra lessons to Putonghua would be at the expense of religion, ethics, moral education, or whatever else the school might decide to use the time for.

Opinion is divided on the matter of compulsion. It is favored by such educators as Szeto Wah, chairman of the Professional Teachers' Union,[20] but opposed by others. Some policymakers recommend compulsion from the first day in Primary 1, following the model in China; others recognize constraints in the crowded curriculum and recommend compulsion only from Primary 4. At the other end of the scale, compulsion is not generally favored after Form 3. By this time, it is assumed that students who have studied Putonghua in earlier years will have an adequate grasp of the language. Also, the demands of subject specialization militate against compulsory Putonghua in Form 4 and after.

Whether Putonghua is made compulsory or voluntary, school authorities must of course devise their policies only after finding out what their pupils know already. Secondary schools are likely to find wide diversity, corresponding to the range of institutions from which their pupils are drawn. In this situation, a good case exists for separate "topping up" classes for pupils with weak abilities or inadequate previous tuition. Without this separate provision, other pupils would be likely merely to repeat work that they had already covered. This would waste time and resources, and could also lead to boredom and a counterproductive attitude toward the subject. "The worst education policy," as one educator puts it, "is to treat all students as having alike potential and to try to devise a system to mould them like making mooncakes."[21]

(ii) The Viewpoint of Official Policymakers

So far, the role of policymakers in the territory as a whole has been restricted to facilitation and encouragement rather than compulsion. In 1987, when asked in the Legislative Council whether the government intended to make Putonghua compulsory, the secretary for education and manpower replied that "as a matter of principle, we do not make any specific subject compulsory."[22] However, in the changing political and educational climate, such a principle might not remain forever fixed.

Meanwhile, no school-focused policies should be introduced without prior consideration of alternative ways through which society's needs can be met. Hong Kong already has a strong tradition of out-of-school language learning to meet the demands of commerce and other needs. Motivation in such classes is greatly enhanced by the direct benefits that learners can identify for themselves, and curricula can be adapted to specific needs. It is therefore arguable that society's needs could be met much more efficiently in this way than by compulsion at the school level. Unless stronger arguments for compulsion emerge, the government would be well-advised to restrict itself to a facilitating role.

(b) Feasibility

(i) Supply of Teachers

The most obvious constraint on Putonghua development is a shortage of trained teachers. By refusing to recognize the qualifications of teachers from the People's Republic of China and from Taiwan, the Hong Kong government closes a major avenue of supply. This policy may be changed in the future, but for the present it necessitates reliance on local staff.

The second section of this paper pointed out that teacher training has already expanded dramatically, and a government goal is to have trained 2,600 teachers by 1992. If this goal is achieved, the government declares, it will enable all primary and secondary schools to introduce Putonghua if they wish.[23] The accompanying statement omitted indication of the underlying assumptions on the number of schools expected to teach the subject or on the extent of that tuition. Nevertheless, the figure suggests rapid quantitative progress.

The question turns to quality and to the ways that the authorities can cater to the wide range of needs and levels. The teaching methodology course run by the Institute of Language in Education lasts only 12.5 hours, and thus is rather limited in scope.[24] Likewise, the institute's follow-up refresher courses cover only two to three sessions. The teacher training offered by the universities is also only at the minor-subject level. There seems a clear need for courses that allow teachers to train thoroughly. As to the general situation in schools, the standard of teaching is variable. A recent government report[25] points out that because there is no recognized standard of proficiency in Putonghua set for teachers, the decision as to whether particular teachers may or may not teach Putonghua is left to the discretion of school principals.

The importance of adequate staffing is also emphasized by the situation in China. Fu and Iu[26] observe that despite the official emphasis on Putonghua, many schools in Guangdong province continue to use Cantonese. Only Guangzhou's key-point schools—those selectively identified to become the city's premier institutions—are said to use Putonghua as the medium of instruction, while other schools use Cantonese. The success of key-point schools is to a large extent attributed to their ability to recruit teachers from universities where

Putonghua is the medium of instruction.[27] Few Hong Kong schools can expect to be better off than the non–key-point schools in Guangdong, especially as long as the government refuses recognition of degrees from Taiwan and China.

(ii) Motivation

The absence of Putonghua in many Guangdong schools is also, of course, partly due to lack of motivation. If that problem exists in China, it is likely to be much worse in Hong Kong, for relatively few opportunities currently exist for use of Putonghua in everyday Hong Kong life. Opportunities will undoubtedly increase during the coming years, but the government should not overestimate this trend. Hong Kong already has extensive exposure to the English language, but for many pupils the impact of this exposure seems very limited.

Nevertheless it is worth noting several new initiatives. First, since February 1988 the RTHK radio station has broadcast a two-hour program in Putonghua every afternoon from Monday to Friday. Second, since August 1988 the Examinations Authority has offered an oral and written test of proficiency in Putonghua. It is chiefly aimed at candidates of Form 3 level and above, and is open to the public. The authority also has plans for a test of higher proficiency. Third, a number of schools have developed their own ways to increase motivation. Interschool Putonghua recorded storytelling competitions are reported to be one successful strategy to improve motivation.[28]

5. Conclusions

This chapter has outlined the case for increased attention to Putonghua in Hong Kong schools and has presented the principal options open to policymakers. The overall situation is rather haphazard, with different schools operating a wide range of programs, and mostly doing so in isolation from each other. One reason for this neglect has been the preoccupation with the debate on Cantonese versus English. It has been widely assumed that increased use of Cantonese in Hong Kong classrooms is the first step toward increased exposure to Putonghua. This certainly is logical insofar as the pressure for mother-tongue teaching has increased the supply of Chinese-language textbooks. However, further steps to develop Putonghua have not been thought about very carefully.

In the past, the government has chiefly preferred to leave decisions on the language of classroom instruction to market forces. Since 1986 it has taken a more decisive stand, and has been actively promoting Cantonese. In recent years, active provision has also been made for Putonghua, particularly in teacher training, syllabus preparation, and guidance on reading lists. Recommendations have recently been made[29] concerning long-term language planning in education, cooperation and exchange of information with other Cantonese-speaking communities in Southeast Asia, and a minimum standard of proficiency in Putonghua for teachers. It is arguable that all these issues deserve further attention. Leaving development of Putonghua to market forces might not be desirable. There is a need for substantial planning and for more detailed guidance on the implementation.

Notes

1. See, e.g., N.L. Cheng et al., *At What Cost? Instruction through the English Medium in Hong Kong* (Hong Kong: Shum Shing Co., 1973); Gail Schaefer Fu, "Bilingual Education in Hong Kong: A Historical Perspective," *Working Papers in Language and Language Teaching: 1* (University of Hong Kong: Language Centre, 1979); Keith Johnson, "Language Policy in Education in Hong Kong," *Asian Journal of Public Administration*, vol. 5, no. 2 (1983); Ora Kwo and Mark Bray, "Language and Education in Hong Kong: New Policies but Unresolved Problems," *RELC Journal*, vol. 18, no. 1 (1987); Robert Lord and Helen N.L. Cheng, eds., *Language Education in Hong Kong* (Hong Kong: The Chinese University Press, 1987).

2. *South China Morning Post*, July 22, 1986.

3. Ibid.

4. *Hong Kong Standard*, April 13, 1987.

5. Government of Hong Kong, *Hong Kong 1988: A Review of 1987* (Hong Kong: Government Printer, 1988), p. 13.

6. Ibid., p. 343.

7. Government of Hong Kong, *Education Commission Report No. 1* (Hong Kong: Government Printer, 1984); Government of Hong Kong, *Education Commission Report No. 2* (Hong Kong: Government Printer, 1986).

8. The Yale System of romanization is used. For explanation of the symbols, see Parker Po-fei Huang, *Speak Cantonese* (New Haven, Yale University: Far East Publications, 1977).

9. Pui-kwong Wong, "Chinese and Putonghua: A Combined Subject or Two Separate Subjects in a Society where There Are Three Languages but Only Two Written Codes?" paper presented at the conference of the Institute of Language in Education, Hong Kong, 1987. (In Chinese.)

10. Keith Johnson, "Medium of Instruction: Policies and Options," *Interflow*, University of Hong Kong, Issue 49 (1986).

11. Keith Johnson, "Bilingual Switching Strategies: A Study of the Modes of Teacher-Talk in Bilingual Secondary School Classrooms in Hong Kong," *Language Learning and Communications*, vol. 2, no. 3 (1983); Kwo and Bray, "Language and Education in Hong Kong: New Policies but Unresolved Problems," *RELC Journal*, vol. 18, no. 1 (1987).

12. Government of Hong Kong, *Education Commission Report No. 1*, p. 47.

13. Government of Hong Kong, *Hong Kong Hansard: Reports of the Sittings of the Legislative Council of Hong Kong*, vol. 2 (Hong Kong: Government Printer, 1987), p. 1624.

14. Ibid., pp. 1624–25.

15. Government of Hong Kong, *Report of the Working Group Set Up to Review Language Improvement Measures* (Hong Kong: Government Printer, 1989), p. 58.

16. Yat-shing Cheung, "A Survey of the Motivation in Learning and the Practical Use of Putonghua," *Institute of Language in Education Journal*, vol. 3 (1987), pp. 35–36. (In Chinese.)

17. Government of Hong Kong, *Hong Kong Hansard*, p. 1625.

18. See, e.g., UNESCO, *The Use of Vernacular Languages in Education* (Paris: UNESCO, 1951); A. Babs Fafunwa, "Education in the Mother Tongue: A Nigerian Experiment," *West African Journal of Education*, vol. 19, no. 2 (1975); Ayo Bamgbose, ed., *Mother Tongue Education: The West African Experience* (London: Hodder & Stoughton, 1976).

19. Government of Hong Kong, *The Hong Kong Education System* (Hong Kong: Government Secretariat, 1981), pp. 253–55.

20. Wah Szeto, "Teaching Putonghua," *Asiaweek* (September 6, 1987), p. 78.

21. L.K. Ng, letter to the *South China Morning Post*, October 17, 1986.

22. Government of Hong Kong, *Hong Kong Hansard*, p. 1625.

23. Ibid.

24. Ibid., Annex IV.

25. Government of Hong Kong, *Report of the Working Group*, p. 59.

26. Gail Schaefer Fu and Pui-to Iu, "Language Attitudes and the Social Order in Hong Kong after 1997," paper presented to the conference of the Association Internationale de Linguistique Appliqué, Sydney, 1987.

27. Pui-to Iu cited in Gail Schaefer Fu, "The Hong Kong Bilingual," in *Lanugage Education in Hong Kong*, eds. Robert Lord and Helen N.L. Cheng (Hong Kong: The Chinese University Press, 1987), p. 45.

28. *Hong Kong Standard*, March 3, 1988.

29. Government of Hong Kong, *Report of the Working Group*, p. 59.

10

Educational Expansion and the Labor Force

Glenn Shive

Introduction

The Hong Kong government's formulation of the need for the expansion of upper levels of the educational system has been stated in terms of three demands:

- student demand for tertiary education;
- the proportion of students capable of meeting the demands of the academic standards which the course requires; and,
- the likely manpower demand for persons of a good general education or with special qualifications, and the capacity of the economy to provide satisfactory and rewarding employment for such highly educated people.[1]

These may be contrasted with the demands for educational expansion identified in sociological conflict theory. In his revision of Weberian conflict theory, Randall Collins identifies three demands as shaping the development of educational systems:

- the demand of individuals for practical skills;
- the demand of status groups and social classes for cultural capital; and,
- the demand of state bureaucracies for social control.[2]

Conflict theory posits three lines of societal division—economic, organizational-political, and cultural—as meshing together in such a way that the strength of economic classes and the power of organizational politicians will be greater in proportion to their relative possession of cultural resources. In this form of interpretation, ethnic, national, religious, or other cultural divisions can influence forms of social struggles into patterns much more complex than those simply emerging along class lines. Educational expansion is viewed as part of the larger social process of the structuralization of social classes, status cultures, and bureaucratic power structures.

Sociological conflict theory, with its emphasis on economic, organizational-political, and cultural divisions in society, provides a way of thinking about the context of the situation facing higher education and the labor force in Hong Kong's transitional period. This chapter reviews some of the major aspects of this situation and concludes by noting issues that sociological conflict theory raises for the future relationship between educational expansion and the labor force.

Hong Kong Higher Education: Toward the 1990s

At the beginning of the 1980s, university degree places in Hong Kong were available to only 2 percent of the relevant student population. In the decade that followed, this figure increased to 8 percent. Throughout most of the 1980s, the University of Hong Kong with its three-year program and the Chinese University of Hong Kong with its four-year program were the only two degree granting institutions. By the end of the 1980s, other postsecondary institutions such as the Hong Kong Baptist College, the Hong Kong Polytechnic, and the City Polytechnic of Hong Kong were permitted to upgrade some of their diploma/certificate courses to degree level. This trend will continue in the 1990s as the new Hong Kong University of Science and Technology opens its doors, and Lingnan College begins to offer degree places. In the meantime, the rest of the postsecondary sector continues to expand, including teacher training and nursing colleges, technical institutes which offer some postsecondary level technician courses, and the new Open Learning Institute, which offers distance learning programs and part-time courses.[3]

By the early 1980s Hong Kong had entered the ranks of the newly industrialized territories of the world. Though most of its young people remained in school through the upper secondary level, it only offered a small percentage of university degree places. The limited university sector has been explained by a number of factors, including the government's concern with credential inflation and the diploma disease that had afflicted other developing societies, the colonial status of Hong Kong with the potential for university student activism, and the British tradition with its emphasis on elite higher education.[4] Hong Kong would not have been able to continue limiting the number of university degree places were it not for the availability of overseas higher education degree places. By the late 1980s Hong Kong had about 35,000 of its young people enrolled in overseas degree places, a figure far beyond the 15,000 within the territory.[5]

Another way of containing the public demand for more education was to greatly expand upper secondary level technical education. This acted to relieve some of the pressure on the system, although it created a situation in which middle-class students denied entrance to Hong Kong's universities could still obtain costly overseas university education while working-class students of an equal academic standard were left only with the option of attending local technical institutes. Earning a technician qualification leaves working classes behind their wealthier counterparts when the latter return to Hong Kong from overseas. Women were at a particular disadvantage, since they were less encouraged to go overseas, while if they stayed in Hong Kong they would not attend technical institutes (nor universities) in as great a number as their male counterparts.[6]

Access to higher degree places is still regulated through a heavily examination-based selection system. This, and the specialized nature of Hong Kong higher education, has contributed to a narrow form of personal educational development. The University of Hong Kong had proposed offering a foundation year to create a more liberal education for Hong Kong students, and, at the same time, allow them more time to raise their standard of English. However, this proposal was defeated when the Education Commission moved to standardize university admissions, which, in effect, limited university education in Hong Kong to three years.[7]

Given the educational attainment of the population, and Hong Kong's level of economic development, the expansion rate of university places during the 1980s was still modest by international standards. It was not until November 1989 that new higher targets were set in accord and with the governor's speech, which indicated that one out of four students would find a place in postsecondary education by 1996, and the number of degree places would be increased to 16 percent of the relevant age group.[8]

The magnitude of the expansion is reflected in the fact that the present university staffing numbers will have to double by 1996. This executive decision to expand was arrived at without the usual consultative process among education groups, associations, and unions. The consultative process had long been used as a way of ensuring legitimacy; however, it began to seem that the government was no longer as concerned with legitimacy.[9] This decision has been referred to as "crisis management," because it followed on the heels of the June 4 incident, and was made mainly for two reasons: to build confidence and to compensate for the tremendous emigration of talented people from Hong Kong.[10]

In the fall of 1990 Hong Kong had places for 7,000 first-year first-degree places, or only about 7 percent of the age group. That number will expand to 15,000, which would allow places for about 16 percent of Hong Kong's secondary school graduates. The total enrollment of the five government-funded institutions in Hong Kong for 1990–91 academic year was 38,545.

Hong Kong University	8,150
Chinese University of Hong Kong	8,025
Hong Kong University of S & T	0
Hong Kong Polytechnic	13,500
City Polytechnic of Hong Kong	8,000
Hong Kong Baptist College	3,000

The projected total enrollment for the system in 1994–95 is 58,270.[11] That means a growth of nearly 20,000 students. Hong Kong University, for example, has set itself the target of 11,500 total enrollment in 1994–95, of which 9,114 (79 percent) will be undergraduates and 2,386 will be graduate students (1,386 of whom will do taught degrees and 1,000 will do research degrees). Even if the increase in first-degree places levels off after 1995, the natural growth building in the system would take the University of Hong Kong to about 12,275 places by 1997–98. The growth at Chinese University of Hong Kong is comparable.

By 1997 education leaders in Hong Kong hope to have a higher education student enrollment, including expanded graduate programs, of 67,000 per year. This would accommodate about 25 percent of its secondary school leavers each year. The director of one of Hong Kong's polytechnics estimated that if Hong Kong tertiary institutions kept to an overall 1:11 student teacher ratio, they would need 2,500 new faculty by 1995 to keep up with the growth in student numbers.[12] This figure does *not* take into account staff lost to emigration and retirement. The secretary of education and manpower, Mr. Yeung Kai-yin, expects that Hong Kong will need 4,000 extra faculty in the next four years to staff the expansion.[13] Many of these additional faculty would have to come from outside Hong Kong. Hong Kong institutions have an average of about 20 percent of their staff recruited from overseas. After a period of localization, the tables have turned as more recruitment for vacant positions is done overseas.

Some senior academics will be invited south from the People's Republic of China. This will be politically if not always academically important for Hong Kong. The Chinese prime minister, Mr. Li Peng, already made the offer to the governor of Hong Kong, Mr. David Wilson, that China was prepared to allow mainland professionals to work in the territory.[14] The main obstacle is Hong Kong's strict immigration laws. American-trained faculty from Taiwan will also be prime recruitment targets. Britain has a surplus of academics, but their colonial advantage is weakening. Yet Commonwealth systems still articulate better with Hong Kong's. Strong efforts will be made to lure Hong Kong graduates of American universities back to the territory.

Within a British system of tertiary education, the Hong Kong University of Science and Technology (HKUST) will have many features of an American university. Dr. Woo Chia-wei, the former head of San Francisco State University, is its president. He has recruited over twenty deans and department heads, many from the United States, and American-trained Chinese academics from Taiwan and mainland China. These twenty are now recruiting the 1,000 faculty they wish to have in place by October 1991. The HKUST will have colleges of science, engineering, business and management, and general studies (including divisions of humanities and social sciences). Each will have graduate divisions and research departments. The medium of instruction will be English. With a strong emphasis on research and graduate programs, HKUST is championing the cause for Hong Kong's new emphasis on research and development in service of high technology industry for the twenty-first century.[15]

Educational Expansion at Different Levels

In 1979 a special high-level committee was appointed by the governor to examine the factors that had contributed to the growth of the economy and to advise on how the process of diversification of the economy could be facilitated through "the modification of existing policies or the introduction of new policies."[16] A major section of the report dealt with education and training. Although it gave its strongest support to expanding vocational and technical education, the report is important because it tied economic development directly to educational expansion.

By 1979 the Hong Kong education system already had a universal system of primary education and was for the first time able to offer all primary school leavers a free place leading to three years of secondary education. In the same year it was announced that attendance would be compulsory for those nine years of schooling. This rapid expansion of primary, lower and upper secondary education was achieved with almost no expansion at the tertiary level.[17]

Primary Education. The 1965 White Paper ensured that universal primary education would be achieved by 1971. In the process, private primary schools, with the exception of a few elite schools, were closed or came under the control of government. In this way, the government not only ensured quality education but also a standardizing of the schools.

Junior Secondary Education. The 1965 White Paper recommended that between 15 percent and 20 percent of those completing primary education should receive subsidized secondary education. In 1970 it was decided that a further major expansion was necessary, and steps were taken to increase the provision of FI to FIII places to 50 percent of the age group. This reached 100 percent by the end of the decade.

Senior Secondary. At the same time that junior secondary education was expanding, the government began to provide subsidized places for senior secondary school students. The 1974 White Paper established an allocation system which eventually led to 40 percent of the 15–16 age group being provided with subsidized places in the public sector by 1979. The 1978 White Paper moved the target to 60 percent by 1981 and to 70 percent by 1986. Meanwhile, by 1988, about 80 percent of the age group were enrolled in senior secondary education, if not by government subsidy, then by their own financing.

Tertiary Education. It is difficult to explain how a society undergoing such a rapid educational expansion coupled with an extraordinary economic growth can successfully keep a lid on tertiary expansion, unless one examines the nature of state control over education. After having achieved nine years of universal education, with an additional more than 70 percent of the age group in senior secondary education, Hong Kong was still only accommodating about 2 percent of its relevant student age group with degree places. Had it not been for the ease with which overseas places were secured, this policy would have been a failure.

Technical Education. Only recently has vocational-technical education moved from being a peripheral phenomenon to a thriving sector of the education complex in Hong Kong. Academic education was the prevailing type of schooling for most of Hong Kong's history. Hong Kong achieved its industrialization without a heavy reliance on vocational-technical education. To the contrary, it was a heavy dose of academic secondary education that coincided with Hong Kong's rapid development. In contrast to China, Hong Kong never planned a heavy reliance on vocational-technical education to help it succeed with industrialization. Moreover, the growth of high technology industrialization in Hong Kong has led simply to a higher number of jobs in that industry rather than a higher proportion of high-tech jobs. The expansion of technical education provides a partial explanation for how Hong Kong released the pressure to expand its tertiary level degree places. It pushed ahead with this expansion against both the reluctance of the population to send children to technical schools and the knowledge that came from international experience concerning the questionable benefit of vocational-technical education. The expansion of technical institutes was rapid between 1976 and 1985. This trend continues to the present.[18]

International Education

Hong Kong has a strong tradition of overseas study. As a British colony, Hong Kong has for many years sent aspiring youth off to boarding schools and universities in the United Kingdom. Many scholarships and subsidies financed this flow, at least until the United Kingdom introduced the full fees policy in the early 1980s. Local secondary schools were well articulated with the UK tertiary system, and staffed by many expatriates from Britain. American universities have hosted about 10,000 or more Hong Kong students during most of the 1980s. Most have returned and taken jobs in the private sector economy, leaving the governmental posts for local graduates. Hong Kong has at least 50,000 alumni from American universities.[19]

Table 10.1
Full-Time Enrollment by Level of Education and Type of Institution

Level/Type	1979	1980	1981	1982	1983	1984	1985	1986	1987	1988	1989
Primary											
Government and aided	472,198	472,513	471,627	476,384	480,678	480,074	480,268	479,635	482,253	483,232	483,191
Private	70,129	67,747	65,496	62,074	59,178	56,146	54,635	52,358	52,056	51,805	51,259
Secondary and matriculation											
Government and aided	197,953	203,461	212,491	293,420	302,187	311,377	318,965	330,630	338,638	347,417	355,349
Private	265,845	265,514	252,432	166,191	151,182	136,436	125,556	117,128	109,391	96,484	82,946
Colleges of education											
Government	1,121	1,314	1,732	2,196	2,519	2,774	2,614	2,573	2,435	2,355	2,351
Technical institutes											
Government	2,978	2,921	3,516	3,676	4,955	6,248	5,846	7,980	10,415	11,296	11,853
Approved postsecondary	6,622	7,449	7,543	7,377	7,084	4,634	4,789	5,253	5,426	5,230	5,049
Polytechnics and Baptist College											
Government subvened	6,682	7,547	7,625	7,506	8,200	10,231	11,406	13,674	14,845	16,337	18,346
Universities											
Government subvened	9,315	9,661	9,908	10,295	10,615	11,307	11,915	12,321	12,890	13,254	13,786

Source: Hong Kong Annual Digest of Statistics, 1990 Edition.

Table 10.2

Enrollment in Technical Institutes by Type of Course

Type of course	1979	1980	1981	1982	1983	1984	1985	1986	1987	1988
Full-time	2,978	2,921	3,516	3,676	4,955	6,248	5,846	7,980	10,415	11,296
Part-time day	7,920	8,931	10,096	10,275	10,334	10,718	12,223	13,142	13,876	14,157
Part-time evening	12,711	14,827	16,245	21,183	24,739	25,107	26,319	28,160	28,397	28,702
Total	23,609	26,679	29,857	35,134	40,028	43,373	44,388	49,282	52,688	54,155

Returning college graduates from overseas constitute the best technology transfer program in the world. Hong Kong's international work force has been leavened year after year by the ideas, skills, and outlook that returning students have put to work in this dynamic economy. The laissez-faire government has wisely imposed very few constraints on student mobility or the migration of talent. Living in a major transportation and communications hub of East Asia, returned professionals remain in easy contact with new trends and ideas developing overseas.

Study abroad has served Hong Kong families and companies very well. Student visas issued in the early months of 1990 have risen over the comparable period of 1989 by 100 percent to Canada, 40 percent to Australia (which had already been rising sharply), and 30 percent to the United States. Reflecting the anti-British feeling that is growing in the colony, student visas to the United Kingdom have, if anything, declined in 1990 over 1989. To counter this trend, the British government is increasing the scholarship funding available to Hong Kong students by 10 percent. Hong Kong is the single largest supplier of foreign students to British universities and polytechnics. Educators in the United Kingdom have expressed chagrin to the British Council and to the government that in response to disappointment over the meager Nationality Package, Hong Kong students are voting with their feet. Had the British government granted the right of abode to a broad swath of Hong Kong people, British higher education would have blossomed with new Hong Kong students who would have found their futures there.

Hong Kong has about the same number of students in local higher education as in overseas higher education. If one assumes that on average each of 11,000 Hong Kong students in the United States spends about US$17,000, then Hong Kong is paying the United States economy US$187 million a year. Higher education is a major and growing export to Hong Kong, and to all of East Asia, where American deficits are staggering. Hong Kong families probably pay out over US$500 million each year to the United States, United Kingdom, Australia, and Canada for offshore tertiary education. This is just one of the channels of capital outflow that will grow in the approach to 1997.

In the past, there was so much demand for further education that local and offshore options did not compete with one another. With the growth of indigenous capacity through the expansion plan, local and overseas institutions will have to compete to some extent, especially for the best students. Local higher education is cheaper, one stays close to family and home culture, and jobs are easier to get upon graduation.

The Hong Kong Labor Force and Emigration

The diaspora of Hong Kong talent comes just as the Hong Kong economy is making the transition from dominance in manufacturing to new dynamism in

Table 10.3
Educational Attainment of Hong Kong's Labor Force, 1989

Level	Percent
No schooling	5.3
Primary education	28.2
Secondary and matriculation	53.2
Postsecondary/Technical-Vocational	7.4
First degree	5.9

Source: General Household Survey—June 1989, Census and Statistics Department.

the services sector. Hong Kong's GDP grew at a compounded rate of over 8 percent per year during the last two decades. Forty percent of China's exports go out through Hong Kong, which has become the eleventh largest trading nation and fourth largest financial center in the world. The United States has US$7 billion invested in Hong Kong, which is twice its investments in the People's Republic of China, and the United States does US$16 billion of trade with the tiny territory.

With no natural resources, Hong Kong's single economic asset is people. Even without the brain drain, Hong Kong would have a labor shortage. The out-migration of talent exacerbates the problem just as Hong Kong shifts toward a more high-technology, information-based service economy. The critical ingredient for this kind of economy is highly trained human resources. Because of a lack of natural resources, an educated labor force is essential to Hong Kong's economic success. In mid-1989, the Hong Kong labor force was composed of 2,757,800 persons, which constitutes 47.9 percent of the population. The male and female participation rates are 79 percent and 46.6 percent, respectively. It is a full-employment economy. Moreover, there have been widespread labor shortages in many sectors of the economy during recent years. Unemployment is 1.4 percent, and underemployment is 0.8 percent. The median age of the labor force is 34 years. More than half of the employed persons have a secondary education, 7.4 percent have a postsecondary education, and 5.9 percent are degree holders.[20] Professionals, technicians, and related workers constitute 7.4 percent of the labor force, while 3.8 percent are administrative and managerial workers. The median monthly earnings of professionals, administrators, and managers (HK$9,432) are more than double that of all employed persons (HK$4,362). (A small but significant percentage of professionals and managers earn less than HK$4,500 per month).[21]

Since 1987 the emigration of talented members of the work force has quickened. In 1988, there were 45,800 persons who emigrated, and in 1990 the figure reached 55,000. Some estimate that the figure will reach 70,000 per year by the mid-1990s.

According to the government's 1990 comprehensive manpower survey, of the

Table 10.4
Occupational Distribution of Hong Kong's Labor Force, 1989

Type	Percent
Professional	7.4
Administrative and managerial	3.8
Clerical	18.7
Sales	12.3
Services	16.9
Agricultural and fisheries	1.3
Production	39.5

Source: April to June 1989, General Household Survey, Census and Statistics Department.

2.86 million manpower stock required by the beginning of 1997, 29 percent will have to be filled by returning students; 37 percent by existing stock; 28 percent from local graduates and 5 percent from returning emigrants and new immigrants to Hong Kong. During the period, the government estimates that outflow as a result of overseas studies will reach 118,400 and emigration 427,000.[22]

This emigration trend has most serious consequences for a number of occupational groups, including lawyers, judges, system analysts, programmers, accountants, auditors, medical doctors, dentists, nurses, midwives, engineers, architects, surveyors, and general and production managers. Those that emigrate are typically young and well educated. They are likely to be professionals, administrators, and managers. The departures of these people "reduce efficiency, lower productivity of those who remain, result in a massive loss of human capital, and cause an outflow of capital from Hong Kong."[23]

Right of Abode

The Hong Kong government received far less than the expected number of applications for United Kingdom passports in the first round of its new right of abode scheme. Of the 50,000 passports being offered, 13 percent of the passports will be held back until closer to 1997. Hong Kong's 3,500 lawyers will be issued 323 passports, its 12,500 accountants will be allocated 1,615 passports, the 57,300 engineers will contend for 3,230 passports, 10,300 journalists and information professionals will share 1,938 passports, 44,700 doctors, nurses, pharmacists, and other medical professionals will get only 2,584 passports among them, and the 82,700 educators will scramble after the 2,907 passports allocated to them. These are thin reeds with which to stem the brain drain.

The United States is considering its own immigration package for Hong Kong prior to 1997. Congressmen Solarz and Porter sponsored legislation that will increase Hong Kong's annual passport quota from 5,000 to 20,000. Instead of requiring immigrants to enter the United States within the usual four months, this

Table 10.5
Occupation of Emigrants, 1988

Type	Percent
Professional	33.6
Administrative and managerial	16.2
Clerical	13.4
Sales	13.1
Service	10.6
Production	9.0
Other	4.0

Sources: Census and Statistics Department, Consulates, High Commissions.

law will extend the time limit to 2002 as an incentive for key people to remain in Hong Kong through the transition.

But Beijing's leaders cast doubt over even these modest efforts to encourage Hong Kong professionals to stay. They announced that after 1997 such passports from Britain or anywhere else may not be considered valid travel documents. Hong Kong recipients of foreign passports would have to first apply to renounce their Chinese citizenship before they could use foreign passports to leave Hong Kong. Beijing also insisted that local people with foreign passports would not enjoy consular protection in Hong Kong after 1997. Beijing's tough stand on passports is an attempt to scare off efforts from Britain and other countries to offer "insurance policy passports" to Hong Kong people in tacit recognition that the PRC could not be trusted to manage the little capitalist colony well. The PRC would not allow Hong Kong people with foreign passports to occupy key governmental positions. Perhaps Beijing would not mourn the loss of critical professionals if the only way they would stay in Hong Kong after 1997 was by virtue of a foreign passport to serve as an insurance policy. In any case, China has begun to assert itself as the manager of Hong Kong's foreign relations, including consular affairs, after 1997.

Brain Drain and the Hong Kong Diaspora

Employers have looked to some of their emigrating staff to return to Hong Kong after securing foreign passports. Personnel officers in multinationals in Hong Kong are working openly with their employees to help solve "their 1997 problem." But so far the return rate is less than 10 percent. One inhibitor of return is the limited capacity of international schools in Hong Kong to give children of returned emigrants a Western-style education. Of those who have returned, less than one-third stated an intention to stay beyond 1997.[24]

One researcher of the brain drain estimates that if things settle down in China and the economy in Hong Kong continues to prosper, the annual rate of emigra-

Table 10.6
Long-Term Movement of Residents before 1996

Year	Overseas students	Returned students	Emigrants	Returned emigrants	Total net outflows
1989–91	44,400	27,620	152,000	15,716	153,064
1992–96	74,000	52,260	275,000	24,140	272,600
1989–96	118,400	79,880	427,000	39,856	425,664

Source: A Statistical Projection of Manpower Requirements and Supply for Hong Kong (1990).

Table 10.7
Projected Balance of Manpower, 1996

Educational level	Supply	Needed	Balance
Lower secondary or below	1,516,500	1,459,600	56,800
Upper secondary	666,100	715,700	–49,600
Sixth form	164,000	187,500	–23,500
Technical/vocational education (craft)	35,900	32,700	3,300
Technical/vocational education (technical)	118,900	113,800	5,000
Non-degree tertiary education	144,300	126,900	17,300
First degree and above	214,600	224,000	–9,400

Source: A Statistical Projection of Manpower Requirements and Supply for Hong Kong (1990).

tion could be about 75,000 people per year between 1990 and 1994.[25] By 1995, however, another surge could begin as people scramble to leave in the last two to three years before June 30, 1997. If this is true, Hong Kong could lose about 700,000 people, or nearly 13 percent of its population of 5.5 million. At least one-quarter of these would be considered important to the economy and the vital functioning of the society.

A more optimistic scenario would plot a steady line at about 60,000 emigrants per year for the next five years, with a final surge in 1995. This pattern would yield a total loss to emigration of about 550,000 people, or 10 percent of the population. However, if foreign countries expand their immigration quotas for Hong Kong, and/or China reverts to chaos in the post-Deng era, these numbers could go significantly higher.

Table 10.8
Functional Core of Hong Kong's Labor Force, 1989

	Percent	Number
Core	4.7	130,200
Non-Core	95.3	2,629,600

Source: April to June 1989, General Household Survey, Census and Statistics Department.

Table 10.9
Educational Attainment of Functional Core, 1989

Educational level	Percent
Primary	3.9
Secondary and Matriculation	30.2
Postsecondary/Technical-Vocational	16.2
First degree	49.6+

Source: April to June 1989, General Household Survey, Census and Statistics Department.

The government's first comprehensive manpower survey reveals that the number of jobs in the professional, technical, and managerial sectors—the worst hit by emigration—will increase by about 26 percent between 1988 and 1996. This means that Hong Kong, already severely affected by the brain drain, will have to find 93,400 more professionals, technical experts, and managers before 1996. Many of these jobs can only be filled by people with degrees or higher qualifications. However, the survey shows there will a shortfall of 36,700 persons with first-degree qualifications in 1996. Combined with an expected surplus of 27,300 postgraduates, this leaves a total shortfall of 9,400 persons with degrees or higher qualifications.[26]

The Functional Core of the Labor Force

The key to the success of the "one country, two system" arrangement is economic prosperity. Hong Kong will have to sustain its steady economic growth up to and after 1997 in order for it to be able to continue to make significant contributions to China's economic development, particularly in the south. Economic prosperity creates economic opportunities that can attract Hong Kong people to stay in Hong Kong, or return to the territory.

In order for the economy to remain prosperous, it must maintain a core of key people. Without this functional core, there would be a loss of efficiency, lower productivity of subordinates, a loss of human capital, and an outflow of capital (HK$12.4 billion in 1988). This functional core of the labor force can be deter-

Table 10.10

Projected Size of Functional Core, 1989–1997 (in thousands)

Growth	1989	1990	1991	1992	1993	1994	1995	1996	1997
High	130.2	141.9	154.8	168.8	184.2	200.9	219.2	230.1	260.8
Medium	130.2	139.8	149.9	160.3	171.0	182.1	193.6	205.5	217.8
Low	130.2	138.8	147.4	156.0	164.5	173.3	181.9	190.5	199.1

Source: General Household Survey, 1982–1989; Civil Service Personnel Statistics, 1982–1989.

mined in a number of ways. It constitutes 3–10 percent of the employees of a firm. They are relatively well paid (HK$12,500 and above per month), and constitute the mid- to upper levels of management and professional and technical groups. It is this group that is so highly represented among the emigrants.[27]

This functional core accounts for 3.8 percent of all those employees in the private sector (96,180), and 18.3 percent of the civil service (33,983). Thus, the 1989 functional core accounts for 130,200 individuals (4.7 percent of the total labor force). Given the general rate of growth of the labor force each year, the size of the functional core is expected to grow to be 6.6 percent by 1997. The functional core of the labor force has increased from 2.8 percent in 1982 to 4.7 percent in 1989. The projection by 1997 will be between 199,000 and 261,000. Therefore, a conservative estimate is that in 1989, 96,200 people were in the functional core and that by 1997, that figure will be 193,000. This corresponds to a family total of 356,000 and 714,000 respectively.[28]

Conclusion

The 1990s will be a dynamic period for higher education in Hong Kong. The traditionally small number of university places will increase rapidly, thus further expanding opportunities for the working class in Hong Kong. However, acquiring a tertiary level education will also encourage some to use it as a basis to acquire the right of abode overseas. As the Senior Legislative Councilor Allen Lee Peng-fei stated, "some graduates will use their new skills as bargaining chips to gain overseas passports."[29] Moreover, whether or not the rapid expansion of local higher education will discourage Hong Kong residents from choosing to enroll in overseas universities instead is also questionable due to the uncertainty surrounding the quality of the expanded tertiary education sector in Hong Kong. Also, there is apprehension as to whether or not there are a sufficient number of high standard students to enter tertiary institutions. In addition, there is already a problem of recruiting qualified staff to fill the large number of teaching vacancies in tertiary institutions.

Moreover, the heavily British-influenced character of Hong Kong institutions of higher education will further strengthen the growing differentiation in the status culture of Hong Kong. Lau Siu-kai and Kuan Hsin-chi have already noted the ethos of the Hong Kong Chinese that has developed since World War II and the dual identities that this ethos reflects.[30] Such factors can drive a wedge into the social structure by fostering a bifurcated status culture, one tied to British colonialism, and the other tied to the new Chinese sovereignty.

A mostly English-language system of university education when posed against a Chinese-speaking society has a potential to be divisive. The secondary schools are planning to implement a scheme that will stream most students into Chinese-medium education, with a small group of approximately 20–30 percent in English-medium education where most university recruitment will take place. This may intensify the divisiveness created by the United Kingdom's right of abode scheme, in which 50,000 British passports will be issued to Hong Kong residents.

Nevertheless, without the right of abode scheme, the Hong Kong economy would likely suffer a serious blow. Thus Hong Kong finds itself in a quandary wherein it will be easy to acquire either stability or prosperity, but acquiring both at the same time will be difficult.

Notes

We would like to acknowledge the assistance of Mr. Andy Yung Man Sing in the preparation of this chapter.

1. *The Development of Senior Secondary and Tertiary Education*, White Paper (Hong Kong: Government Printer, 1978).

2. Randall Collins, "Some Comparative Principles of Educational Stratification," *Harvard Educational Review*, vol. 47, 1977, pp. 1–27.

3. See, for example, *Hong Kong 1990* (Hong Kong: Government Printer, 1990), and yearbooks for 1981–89.

4. See Gerard Postiglione and Shui Lai Hung, "Educational Expansion in Hong Kong: Contradicting Modes of Explanation," *Educational Research Journal*, vol. 1 (1986): 95–99; Gerard Postiglione, "Higher Education and the Labor Market in Urban Hong Kong," in *Planning and Development in Open Coastal Cities*, ed. L.Y. Choi, K.W. Fong, and Y.W. Kwok (Hong Kong: Center of Urban Studies and Urban Planning of the University of Hong Kong, 1986).

5. See Gerard Postiglione, "International Higher Education and the Labor Market in Hong Kong: Functions of Overseas and Local Higher Education," *International Education*, vol. 17, no. 1 (1987): 48–54; also, Jay Henderson, "Hong Kong Students Flood U.S.," in *South China Morning Post*, April 27, 1986, p. 19.

6. See Grace Mak, "The Schooling of Girls in Hong Kong," chapter 7 of this book.

7. *Education Commission Report Number 3* (Hong Kong: Government Printer, 1988).

8. See Sir David Wilson, Governor of Hong Kong, Speech on Higher Educational Expansion, November 1989.

9. Cheng Kai Ming, "Educational Policymaking in Hong Kong: The Changing Legitimacy," Chapter 4 of this book.

10. See "Academic Hits Out at Crisis Intervention," *South China Morning Post*, November 5, 1989.

11. Universities and Polytechnics Grants Committee Annual Report, 1990.

12. John Clark, Address to the Conference on Management of Higher Education, Hong Kong Polytechnic, February 19–20, 1990.

13. Yeung Kai-yin, Speech by the Director of Education and Manpower.

14. Daphne Cheng, "Mainland Offer to Ease Work Shortage," *South China Morning Post*, May 9, 1990.

15. *Newsletter of the Hong Kong University of Science and Technology*, April 1990.

16. *Report of the Advisory Commission on Diversification* (Hong Kong: Government Printer, 1979), p. 2.

17. *The Hong Kong Education System* (Hong Kong: Education Department, 1981).

18. See Census and Statistics Department, *The Hong Kong Annual Digest of Statistics* (Hong Kong: Government Printer, 1989); also, *Enrollment Survey*, Statistics Section (Hong Kong: Government Printer, 1989).

19. The Institute of International Education, unpublished data.

20. *General Household Survey: Labor Force Characteristics*, Quarterly Report, 1982–89 (April to June Quarters) (Hong Kong: Government Printer).

21. See Paul Kwong, Pak-wai Liu, and Stephan Tang, *Functional Core of the Labor Force: Toward the Retention of Key Personnel in Hong Kong* (Hong Kong: December, 1989).

22. Hong Kong Government Manpower Survey, 1990, unpublished.

23. Kwong et al., *Functional Core of the Labor Force*.

24. "Emigrant Return Rate Only One in Ten," *South China Morning Post*, April 22, 1990.

25. Paul Kirkbride, Sara F.Y. Tang, and Gilbert Ko, *Emigration from Hong Kong: Evidence from Professionals* (Hong Kong: Institute of Personnel Management, 1989).

26. Hong Kong Government Manpower Survey, 1990, unpublished.

27. Kwong et al., *Functional Core of the Labor Force*.

28. Ibid.

29. "Talent Threat: The Biggest Threat to the Economy," *South China Morning Post*, May 8, 1990.

30. Lau Siu-kai and Kuan Hsin-chi, *The Ethos of the Hong Kong People* (Hong Kong: The Chinese University of Hong Kong Press, 1988).

Part V

Comparative Perspectives: One Country, Two Educational Systems

11

Pressure for Educational Excellence in China: Implications for Education in Hong Kong

W.O. Lee

The Excellence Movement

In 1983, the United States published *A Nation at Risk*, which set out the educational crises that the country was facing, but at the same time inaugurated the excellence movement in the eighties. The awareness of educational crises and the urge for educational excellence does not seem to be a U.S. patent, however. Many other countries, such as Japan, are experiencing similar crises and have expressed similar concern for promoting excellence in education.[1] And it seems pertinent to apply this perspective in studying recent educational development in China.

If "a nation at risk" is an expression of the contemporary feelings of the Americans, it is not difficult to see that such a crisis consciousness also prevails in China. The only difference is that, while the United States is afraid of losing her prominence in the international theater, China is afraid of remaining backward.

Backwardness and excellence are contradictory concepts, yet they best represent the paradoxical consciousness of the people in modern China. On the one hand, the Chinese are backwardness-conscious, but on the other hand they are equally excellence-conscious. It is not difficult to observe the concerns over backwardness in China. Deng Xiaoping, for example, is among the outspoken many who voiced the necessity of recognizing the country's backwardness. "We must recognize our backwardness, because only such recognition offers hope," he said in a speech in 1978.[2] The CPC Central Committee also publicly deplored the fact that managerial personnel fell far short of the country's expectation in terms of knowledge, expertise, and attitudes toward work.³ Concomitantly, studies reporting backwardness of the country proliferated. For instance, the Shanghai Revolutionary Committee's 1977 study showed that about 70 percent of the college graduates of the year failed the middle-school-level tests in mathematics, physics, and chemistry. In 1981, the nationwide basic knowledge tests given to middle-level science and technology engineers and workers who graduated in 1975 also revealed that a large batch of college graduates were of low standard, as those who failed comprised nearly 50 percent of the candidates.⁴ Moreover, worries over the country's backwardness were even manifested in the charges against the "Gang of Four," whose greatest crime, among others, was that of bringing about sabotage in education, thus causing a decline in the level of knowledge, retarding the development of a whole generation of young people, and above all, resulting in a widening gap between China's level of science and education and that of the rest of the world.⁵

It is interesting to note that ten years after Deng's speech, at the Thirteenth CPC National Congress held in 1987, the notion of the primary stage of socialism in China was put forth, and this notion well reflects the backwardness–excellence paradox. As a government publication says,

> In short, the primary stage of China's socialism is one in which we shall gradually put an end to poverty and backwardness.... It is a stage in which, by introducing reforms and exploring new methods, we shall establish and develop socialist economic, political and cultural structures that are full of vitality. Lastly, it is a stage in which the people of the whole country will rise to meet the challenge and work hard to bring about a great rejuvenation of the Chinese nation.⁶

Bringing about "a great rejuvenation of the Chinese nation" is indeed a deep-seated yearning of the Chinese people who are at present obsessed by the current state of backwardness. Not only expressed in the newly created notion of the primary stage of socialism, such desire was also reflected in the "China in the year 2000" research projects launched in 1983. In 1985, a number of project reports were produced. A report titled "General Strategy for Advancing Towards the Year 2000" emphasized that "striving for gigantic achievements in the fifteen years before 2000" should be a major target for China, although the perceived achievements would only be initially aimed at catching up.⁷

Education for Excellence

To avert backwardness and the stigma attached, the country was more than ready and indeed anxious to initiate extensive reforms. And the significant role of education has been reiterated over and over during the last decade. "We must improve the quality of education and raise the level of teaching in the sciences, social sciences and humanities," Deng said at the Fifth National Conference on

Education Work in 1978.[8] At a National Education Work Conference in 1985, Deng also stated that "the quantity and quality of our intellectuals have become increasingly important in determining whether our nation is strong or weak. If a huge nation with one billion people could boost its education, its tremendous superiority in human resources would never be matched by any other country." If the country paid attention to the development of education, China would approach the level of the developed nations by 2049.[9] "We must actively develop pre-school education, consolidate and raise the level of junior middle education, reorganize and reform senior middle education, make great efforts to develop professional and technical education, and actively wipe out illiteracy," the Sixth Five-Year Plan (1981–1985) stressed.[10] "[W]e must combat all ideas and practices that belittle science and technology, the cultivation of intellectual resources and the role of intellectuals," the CPC Central Committee also asserted in its 1984 document on Economic Reform.[11] Again, "the improvement of technologies and the cultivation of intellectual resources" remained one of the three priorities of the Seventh Five-Year Plan.[12]

With this concern and awareness, a series of educational reforms was launched. The view that education is a key to achieving the four modernizations of China was endorsed in the 1978 constitution, and was also emphasized in the National Science Conference and the Fifth National Education Work Conference of that year.[13] Moreover, "education and science" was officially announced as one of the three key strategic factors for the country's development in the Sixth Five-Year Plan.[14] And in the Seventh Five-Year Plan, investment in education was increased immensely to 116 billion yuan, as compared to 67 billion yuan in the last plan; the amount of increase was well over 70 percent.[15] The significance of achieving universal and compulsory education was openly addressed in the 1982 constitution and the clear goal of providing a nine-year compulsory and universal educational system was expressed in the 1985 Decision on Educational Reform.[16] Also, the development of secondary education was considered a key area of reform, and vocationalized secondary schools were introduced.[17]

While the universalization of basic education was considered important, the pressure for excellence was equally conspicuous. Basic education is indeed a means of generating "a continued flow of talents which can help raise the scientific and cultural level of the Chinese nation as a whole."[18] And all this has a clear-cut goal—the building of a "modern, powerful, socialist state" in order to "effectively consolidate the socialist system."[19] To achieve this, Deng asserted that special efforts must be made to "nurture talent and break with routine ways of discovering, selecting and training outstanding people."[20] To cater to this goal, there was a full-fledged reorientation of the school system. The unified college entrance examination, the key-point school system, and the two-track school system were all reinstated. Associated with these policies are the notions of efficiency and quality.

The restoration of the unified entrance examination was considered important as a means of selecting quality and talented students:

> First, the quality of the students enrolled has been generally improved, and this is a fact generally acknowledged by all institutions of higher learning. Second, the new students enrolled by universities are those who are morally, intellectually and physically sounder than others.... In other words, it is relatively accurate to select talented students through college entrance examinations.[21]

The key-point school system, by definition a system designed for the gifted, the talented, and the able, was fully instituted. The concept "education for the able" came to be increasingly important, and it emerged as the major thrust of the Fifth National Education Work Conference in 1978. In 1980, Jian Manxiang was appointed minister of education to foster "a new ethos of academic excellence."[22] With such an orientation, the "key" schools emerged as institutes admitting the brightest and best of the younger generation, who were to be taught by the most talented teachers in a most favorable learning environment.[23] In contrast to the generally low standards of students, the keypoint school graduates are remarkably successful, as the best key-point schools could achieve a 90 percent or even higher rate of admission to tertiary institutes. This is remarkable in view of the fact that on average less than 5 percent of all senior-middle graduates in the whole country could proceed to higher educational institutes in 1982.[24]

If key-point schools are for the brightest, so are the tertiary institutes. The limited proportion of senior-middle graduates eligible for higher education illustrates the fact. This results in intense competition in which those qualified to sit for entrance examinations are strictly defined, for example, to be an unmarried senior middle-school graduate under twenty-five years of age or with an equivalent amount of education.[25]

Moreover, there is abundant evidence that the development of science and technology has been of great concern in post-Mao China. For example, Deng pointed out clearly that the development of science and technology is the key to achieving the four modernizations. And the universalization of basic education is considered important as "basic to the training of scientific and technical personnel."[26] The 1985 "Decision on Educational Reform" stressed the importance of establishing a system of technical education from primary to senior levels.[27] This viewpoint was echoed by "China's Education in the Year 2000," a research paper of the "China in the Year 2000" project. As stressed in the paper, the development of technical education constituted one of the three key strategic educational reforms; the other two were concerned with the implementation of nine-year compulsory education and the development of full-time higher education.[28] In 1987, the Thirteenth Party Congress once again set top priority for the development of scientific, technological, and educational undertakings.[29]

Concerns for science and technology development can also be seen in the intensity of discussion in newspapers and journals. Looking into *Chinese Education News* [*Zhongguo Jiaoyu Bao*], for instance, it was found that between 1985 and 1987, the ratio of the articles concerned with natural sciences and technology to those concerned with social sciences and humanities was 6 to 1.[30] The strong emphasis on progress in science and technology has led to the technical intellectuals gaining increasing significance in the country's administration. Many of them are recruited to high official positions, and they have increased their involvement in environmental affairs.[31] To promote scientific and technological development, an organization for promoting inventions was established in 1985 and prizes for scientific achievements were set up.[32] "Science parks" were established in Shenzhen, Guangzhou, and Shanghai, new high-tech industrial zones were set up in Beijing and elsewhere, and numerous research centers in various fields were also established.[33]

As reflected in the education sector, a host of specialized senior middle schools were established—variously known as polytechnic colleges, secondary specialized schools, vocational and technical schools, and secondary professional schools. The proportion of vocational and technical school students in senior middle schools rose sharply from 5 percent in 1978 to 40 percent in 1987.[34] And there have been suggestions to raise the proportion to 60 or even 70 percent.[35] In the higher education sector, the proportion of students majoring in science and technical subjects also comprised about 40 percent of the total student population. In contrast, humanities students comprised on average about 6 percent during 1977–87. In Shanghai in 1984, the ratio of science and technical students to humanities students was 7 to 3.[36]

To further improve the scientific and technical level of the country, China was eager to adopt an "open-door" policy. The significance of this policy was well expressed in Deng's speech at the National Conference on Science in 1978:

> Backwardness must be recognized before it can be changed. One must learn from those who are more advanced before he can catch up with and surpass them. . . . Science and technology are part of the wealth created in common by all mankind. Every people or country should learn from the advanced science and technology of others. It is not just today, when we are scientifically and technologically backward, that we need to learn from others. Even after we catch up with the most advanced countries, we shall still have to learn from them in areas where they are particularly strong.[37]

In order to learn from the advanced countries, to catch up and eventually to surpass them, China was actively engaged in exchange programs. During the Sixth Five-Year Plan (1981–1985), more than 36,500 Chinese government-sponsored students and visiting scholars went abroad for advanced studies and/or research in sixty-three countries.[38]

The year 1985 saw another landmark in the development of education. The publication of the *Reform of China's Educational Structure: Decision of the*

CPC Central Committee inaugurated an age of decentralization in education.

> The Central Committee holds that, to avert the above-mentioned [backward] condition, we must start with reforming the educational structure and proceed systematically. To reform the management system, while reinforcing management at a macro level, we are determined to simplify the administrative system, release power, and extend autonomy for running schools.[39]

As a result, the responsibility for the universalization of basic education was left to local governments. They could make their own decision in major restructuring of education, and they would have only a few rules to observe. What is most important is that the decision particularly emphasized the extension of autonomy in the higher education institutes. This suggests that the government realizes the necessity of developing an open and flexible policy to encourage creativity, and also considers important the relevance of educational policies to particular circumstances. The adoption of a flexible policy has particular significance and implications. As Suttmeier states, "the increasing institutional diversity offers a key indicator of change in China."[40]

Flexible Policy: Special Economic Zones

Following the adoption of the "open-door policy" at the Third Plenum of the CPC Eleventh Central Committee in 1978, the Special Economic Zone (SEZ) policy was promulgated in 1980. The basic thrust of the policy was of course economic development. This SEZ policy was in fact an application of the New Economic Plan (NEP) of Lenin, who maintained that the socialist system will not be jeopardized by concessions to foreign capital, but, on the contrary, the realization of socialism will be fostered by such compromises and flexibility. However, the Chinese version of the NEP philosophy took an extra step forward. While the NEP concession policy was meant to be a temporary measure, China on the other hand regarded it as a long-term strategy. As Thomas Chan et al. remarked, "The Chinese, including Deng himself, have argued that the time for the abandonment of NEP-like measures in China is a long way off. It has even been said that Lenin's NEP is an absolutely necessary path for eventual socialist construction, and that as such it should last for a long time and should not be treated just as a temporary retreat before aggression."[41]

While the basic intention of the policy is economic development, the basic strategy is flexibility. This is, *ipso facto*, underscored by the term "special." By special, it officially refers to "special economic policies, brisk economic provisions and special economic management systems, which are different from those of [the] island."[42] The idea of flexibility is more explicit in another statement: "Its special economic zones are being special because they adopt a more flexible policy than other parts of the country in drawing in foreign funds for economic development."[43] Although initially and basically the SEZs are areas designated for experimental economic programs, given that different sectors of a society are interrelated, it seems a corollary that the experimental development programs will be extended to other sectors. Such an intention is revealed in a statement by Wu Nansheng, head of the Guangdong provincial SEZ administration: "The SEZs are a testing ground for integrated development in infrastructure, regulation and law, industrial projects, construction, tourism and foreign investments."[44]

Referring to the Shenzhen SEZ, Chan, Chen, and Chin also point out that experiment and development are not confined to industry alone, but also cover various other sectors such as agriculture, animal husbandry, tourism, commerce and services, real estate, and science and education.[45] This is well expressed in the official Shenzhen report of China's Urban Reform Series. According to the report, "since the beginning of the Shenzhen special economic zone, systematic and all-round reforms have been carried out boldly."[46] The report includes 129 essays, denoting reforms in nearly every social and economic sphere in the region, of course including education. With respect to educational reform, the report states:

> A fundamental change in the SEZ has already taken place. Firstly, primary and secondary school education has been popularized.... Secondly, secondary and higher education is progressing rapidly. The SEZ had no higher education before. Now, it has Shenzhen University, Shenzhen Educational Institute, Shenzhen Normal School and Television and Broadcasting University. And it is making preparations to set up China's Experimental University.... Thirdly, adult education has witnessed rapid development.... Fourthly, means of teaching has gradually been modernized. A number of advanced audio-visual educational equipment has been imported and efforts have been made to popularize education with electrical audio-visual aids. The quality of education has thus been greatly improved.... The education in Shenzhen is following the SEZ construction and developing by leaps and bounds in the process of reforms so as to bring up more talented personnel earlier....[47]

The establishment of Shenzhen University should be noted especially. Founded in 1983 with the aid of foreign capital and many joint enterprises, the university is "a new-type comprehensive university" characterized by distinguished breakthroughs. It is the first Chinese university to adopt a system of academic credits, with both required and elective courses. Such a system allows ambitious students to take more courses each semester in order to graduate in four instead of five years, while slower students can take six years. Another breakthrough is that students are allowed to change their major or even transfer to another university after their first year. Moreover, the university has taken the lead in abolishing the traditional job assignment practice. Shenzhen University students have to apply for their own jobs on graduation, although the university will make recommendations in certain cases. On the administration side, the presidential responsibility system has been introduced. The president is in charge of the management of the school and is fully responsible to the governments of the province and the municipality rather than to the Party Committee, while the Party Committee is confined to taking charge of the Party's affairs. And the separation of the teaching administration from the Party's affairs is regarded as evidence of depoliticization in the region.[48] Depoliticization in the SEZs is considered important, as a major strategy of the zones is to invite foreign investments which are essential for the realization of their modernization. And the Chinese government has to emphasize depoliticization to assure the foreign investors.[49] Not only are the staff given more autonomy, but so also are the students. The report stresses that "students are encouraged to manage their own affairs and educate themselves, so as to abolish the old closed-type education with too much supervision of and rigid restrictions on students."[50]

The establishment of Shenzhen University thereby offers an illustration of the flexible policy and is a conscious breakthrough from the traditional practice, namely, politicization and "closed-type education." All this points to one goal—generating a new breed of talented personnel which is "the key to the success of the four modernizations and also to the success of the SEZ construction."[51]

It should be noted that the bold experimentations and successes of the SEZs were officially recognized, and other regions were called upon to learn from them. "The SEZs are leaders of affluent areas and they provide new scientific technologies and advanced management experience to inland China."[52]

Further Flexibility: Special Administrative Region

China's policy toward Hong Kong is in fact an extension of the SEZ policy. The signing of the Joint Declaration on the Question of Hong Kong by the Chinese and British governments in December 1984 affirmed the fact that China will resume sovereignty over Hong Kong in July 1997. Concomitantly with the signing of the declaration, China resolved to designate Hong Kong as a Special Administrative Region (SAR) under the principle of "one country, two systems," and in accordance with the provisions of Article 31 of the PRC constitution, which stipulates that "the state may establish special administrative regions when necessary." According to the "one country, two systems" principle, the socialist system and policies shall not be practiced in the Hong Kong SAR and Hong Kong's capitalist system shall remain unchanged for fifty years.[53] Applying the notion of the primary stage of socialism, this further extension of the flexible policy is considered essential for perfecting socialism and achieving modernization.[54]

According to the Basic Law of the Hong Kong SAR, which was promulgated in April 1990 by the Chinese government, the SAR is to exercise a high degree of autonomy and enjoy executive, legislative, and independent judicial power

(Article 2). Regarding education, Chapter VI of the Basic Law stipulates:

> On the basis of the previous educational system, the Government of the HKSAR shall, on its own, formulate policies on the development and improvement of education, including policies regarding the educational system and its administration, the language of instruction, the allocation of funds, the examination system, the system of academic awards and the recognition of educational qualifications.
>
> Community organizations and individuals may, in accordance with law, run educational undertakings of various kinds in the HKSAR. (Article 136)
>
> Educational institutions of all kinds may retain their autonomy and enjoy academic freedom. They may continue to recruit staff and use teaching materials from outside the HKSAR. Schools run by religious organizations may continue to provide religious education, including courses in religion.
>
> Students shall enjoy freedom of choice of educational institutions and freedom to pursue their education outside the HKSAR. (Article 137)

Hong Kong Education in China's Eyes

That China is willing to permit great flexibility with regard to Hong Kong elucidates Hong Kong's special significance to China. Politically, the treatment of Hong Kong will be a stepping stone as well as a testing ground for the future treatment of Taiwan. Economically, China gains one-third of its foreign exchange earnings via Hong Kong. And above all, in terms of China's urge for modernization and its open-door policy, Hong Kong as an international city will offer a most favorable environment for China to absorb the state-of-the-art foreign technology expertise. With respect to the pursuit of excellence in education, Hong Kong will undoubtedly have a role to play.

In fact, China's interest in studying Hong Kong has long been established. Numerous research centers or institutes for Hong Kong and Macau Studies have been set up since 1980. For example, a Hong Kong and Macau Studies Centre was established by the Academy of Social Sciences of China (at Guangzhou) in 1981, and another one by the Shanghai Academy of Social Sciences in 1982. A third appeared in 1983, set up by the Shenzhen Provincial Party Committee. In the same year, Zhongshan University established its Hong Kong and Macau Research Institute. Also, the Hong Kong and Macau Studies Centre at Guangzhou started to publish "Newspaper Clippings on Hong Kong and Macau's Economy," and the newly established center at Shenzhen published "Hong Kong and Macau News." In 1984, the Guangzhou Academy of Social Sciences established a special center for studying Hong Kong and Macau history. South China Normal University also set up a center for studying Hong Kong and Macau's economy.

Moreover, Hong Kong and Macau studies were carried out extensively by various departments and institutes, including the Beijing University Economics Department, Fujian Academy of Social Sciences, East Asia Research Institute, Guangzhou Institute of Foreign Trade, Guangzhou Institute of Foreign Languages, Guangzhou Academy of Social Sciences Research Institute, and the Shenzhen University SEZ Economic Research Institute.[55]

The publication records of these research institutes and centers are impressive. Between 1980 and 1986, Zhongshan University alone published 246 articles, of which 216 were actually published during 1984–86. These articles cover a wide range of areas, including Hong Kong's demography, history, economy, education, politics, law, geography, ecology, and intellectual thought and literature.[56] Hong Kong's economic development has attracted the most attention.

A quick scrutiny of these works suggests that Chinese scholars regard Hong Kong as a place of prosperity and wonder, and there is much for them to learn from the territory, although they are also aware that Hong Kong is by no means free of problems. Typical opinions expressed in these writings are directed toward Hong Kong's long history; Hong Kong's well-developed economy and role as an important financial center in the Asia-Pacific region; Hong Kong's remarkable economic achievements; its modernized and advanced infrastructure, facilities, and technologies; its skilled and hard-working labor force; and its legal system's protection of property rights.[57] The fact that Hong Kong's economy could take off and join Asia's Big Four at the very time that China was experiencing a recession has attracted attention among Chinese researchers.[58]

There is similar admiration with respect to education. As the mainland editors of *Hong Kong Higher Education* say:

> Hong Kong today has already developed an atmosphere of respecting knowledge and talents. This is a significant sign of social development. Albeit there exist various conflicts and problems in the higher education sector, from its development, we can indeed find out a great deal about its successes and experience from which we can learn. For example, concerning how to build up a close link between higher education and social and economic development how to make the two boost each other, the formulation of educational policies, the management of higher education, and the implementation of open education, Hong Kong has already developed relevant regulations, systems and ordinances, and has materialised the principles of democracy and efficiency. Today, our country is still at the primary stage of socialism. We have to, under the conditions of socialism, "achieve what many capitalist countries have already achieved, i.e. industrialization, and the commercialization, socialization and modernization of production." Through the principle of "one country, two systems," we will realize the country's unified thought and practice. These theories can help us objectively to compare, analyze and study Hong Kong's experience of higher education, and this will help us promote our present extensive educational reforms.[59]

In 1986, at the Second Symposium on the Guangdong-Hong Kong Relationships toward the 21st Century, the achievements of education in Hong Kong were again mentioned:

> In respect of education, Hong Kong has regarded education as an important means of promoting economic competitiveness and commercial development. This is worth-noting.... On the basis of universal education, Hong Kong set out to improve the quality of secondary education, for example, running computer courses, paying great attention to technical education, increasing applied and technical subjects in junior secondary curriculum to 25–30 percent, setting vocational training projects for Form 3, Form 4 and Form 5 school-leavers, etc. All these practices are what we should draw lessons from....[60]

Indeed, there are reasons for Hong Kong to be highly regarded in the area of educational development. While China was exerting strenuous effort to promote the universalization of education in the eighties, Hong Kong had already achieved the provision of nine years free and compulsory education by the late seventies. While China's illiteracy still stood at 26 percent in 1990, Hong Kong had already reduced illiteracy to 23 percent early in 1970 and to 11 percent in 1990. Although educational expenditures in China, as a proportion to total public expenditures, rose dramatically from 4.2 percent in 1975 to 8.1 percent in 1986, Hong Kong's proportion remained relatively very high at 21 percent and 19 percent in the respective years.[61] While teachers in China generally suffer from low status and salaries, Hong Kong teachers are much more respected and their salaries compare favorably with other occupations, and are even relatively higher than those in major European cities.[62] While educational level does not guarantee an increase of income in China—hence the prevalence of the notion "education is useless"—in Hong Kong, the higher up the educational ladder, the higher the level of income, hence education is generally much valued in the society.

It is no wonder that Lei and Chen, after reviewing education in Hong Kong, Macau, and Guangzhou, drew the conclusion that, with respect to the universalization of education, the implementation of technical education, the expansion of higher education, the extension of various forms of education (including formal and informal education), and the adoption of modern teaching methods, "Hong Kong provides examples and experience of providing the kind of education that caters to the needs of the society.... To make education a better service for economic development, and to make the superiority of socialism more distinguished, we must also develop education in a way to meet the needs of the society."[63]

Implications for Hong Kong's Educational Development

The above review elucidates how China, not unlike many other countries, has demonstrated an urge to drive toward excellence vis-à-vis a sense of crisis in education, and/or, a sense of backwardness. This concern, among other factors, has contributed to the restoration of the key-point school system and the national college entrance examinations, the emphasis on education for modernization, and hence technical education. Moreover, as a strategy for realizing the four modernizations, China has introduced a range of flexible policies, including the open-door policy as manifested in the scholar and student exchange programs with foreign countries, decentralization, the establishment of SEZs and depoliticization in these regions, and the "one country, two systems" policy. Further, the emergence of the notion of the primary stage of socialism offers theoretical justification for the adoption of these policies. The provision of theoretical justification, if it means anything at all, demonstrates China's determination to realize these goals.

With reference to Hong Kong, the application of the "one country, two systems" policy suggests not merely an additional example of the flexible policy, but also explains the disproportionate significance of Hong Kong in view of its small size. Coupled with the consideration that official documents (such as the Joint Declaration and the Basic Law) tend to reiterate the guarantee that Hong Kong is going to retain its autonomy, it seems a corollary that Hong Kong's present systems, including the educational sector, will not be subject to drastic changes after 1997 and that Hong Kong will play a significant role in China's future development. This is indeed a fantasized version of Hong Kong's future. As Yee purports,

> In our fantasized SAR well into the 21st century, Hong Kong would be the most modern and international part of China, a distinction that must be constantly maintained and enhanced.... With Hong Kong's world-class infrastructure, such as being a world leader in cargo container terminals, financial, communications and international networks, the fear aired now and then of Shanghai and other ports surpassing Hong Kong seems quite unlikely.... Our fantasized Hong Kong would be a bustling, vital, international center with claims to greatness in major sectors.[64]

Nevertheless, such a fantasized optimistic view does not seem to match the actualities. From the onset of the drafting of the Basic Law, it has become increasingly clear that the Chinese authorities have attempted to exert influence and control over the transition toward 1997. "[T]he organization and membership of the Basic Law Drafting Committee, the drafting of its constitution, and the controversy over the phrase 'domestic consultations' in its draft constitution, and the authority of its executive committee and the procedures governing the revision of its constitution all demonstrated the PRC authorities' intention to control this supposedly unofficial, voluntary organization," says Joseph Cheng.[65] Moreover, it has been pointed out that the extent of autonomy provided in the Basic Law is questionable[66] and that the future political system provided in the Basic Law in many ways resembles the present colonial system of government in terms of the substantial power endowed to the chief executive who is to be appointed by and accountable to the central government rather than the legislature.[67] After all, Hong Kong is a unique case of decolonization, for it is decolonization without independence.[68]

All these considerations suggest that the "one country, two systems" principle offers nothing more than an ostensible picture of a future autonomous Hong Kong. As Ting says, "Instead of providing a legal foundation for the autonomous region, the Basic Law enables the central authorities to exercise supreme power in the case of necessity. It limits the scope of powers enjoyed by the HKSAR, but no provisions are available in the Chinese Constitution to check upon the exercise of power by the CPG."[69] If so, the extent of the flexible policy applied to Hong Kong is equally questionable. What is more, the June 4 incident seems to have made all hopes fade.

However, if what has happened in China over the past decade has any historical meaning at all, if the aforementioned urge for advancing toward modernization and excellence in China has shown any consistency at all, and if there is any sincerity about the adoption of a flexible policy, then, it seems unreasonable to assume that the "one country, two systems" policy is only an ostensible measure. In light of historical perspective, China's intention to modernize the country will continue, and thus so will the open-door policy. And China must remain open if she wishes to take advantage of the new international division of labor.[70] Just a few months after the June 4 incident, an official document reemphasized the significance of expanding the open-door policy:

> Adopting the open-door policy is our country's long-term unchanged policy.... The past decade of openness has brought about great achievements in commercialization and economic and skills exchange. Experience proves that the open-door policy as set by the Third Plenum of the CPC Eleventh Central Committee is entirely correct.... The economic difficulties that we are facing are not due to the open-door policy. On the contrary, our openness is not enough....[71]

Moreover, a recent issue of *Outlook* [*Liaowang*] has stressed that "there is no return from the reform and open policy."[72] The significance of the open-door policy as reasserted in these official publications is further testified by recent attempts of the Chinese leaders to pay official visits to a number of foreign countries, and Party General Secretary Jiang Zemin's offer to be interviewed by the American Broadcasting Corporation. Further, it has been suggested that Premier Li Peng is moving away from economic orthodoxy, and will restore reforms, restimulate the economy and become pragmatic.[73] Concerning these attitudes Suttmeier says,

> [I]f China wants to reap a harvest of symbolic and material benefits from doing things that the scientific communities of few other countries can do, must it not

recognize and reward the talents and dedication of its technical intellectuals?...
The achievements of China's scientists in superconductivity (and their discoveries in other areas) thus raise complex questions about the type of society China wishes to become.... The China of 1989 is a most unhappy place, and in the near term, it is unlikely to become happier. Ideological conflicts and elite power struggles are likely to impose serious costs on a society that is already beset by serious economic difficulties. The underlying issues of modernization which China has been confronting during the past decade have not changed, however, and central to these remains the constitution of science. While some in China ... may wish to recast the constitution more in terms of the pre–Cultural Revolution formula, ... many elements of reform will remain, and some of the mistakes of reform will be corrected.[74]

The Chinese government's recent reiteration of the significance of the "Double Hundred" principle seems to affirm this observation. And it is interesting to note that the aforementioned "learning" document also reasserts the significance of education in a way entirely reproducing what has been said over the past decade:

Our country is situated at the primary stage of socialism, and our major task is to develop the productive force of society. What is most important now is to realize the second goal of our economic development, i.e., doubling our GNP by the end of this century.... [T]o guarantee that our country's economy is developing steadily, we should fully recognize the paramount significance of developing the education enterprise.... That education is a major means of developing human intelligence and human quality and is a determining factor of developing modern society has become increasingly clear.

Since the founding of our country, our educational development has made great strides, especially in the decade following the Third Plenum of the CPC Eleventh Central Committee. However, we must clearly understand that our education enterprise on the whole is still backward, ... we must enhance our sense of urgency and responsibility in developing education, we must make up our mind to solve our problems, and to strive hard to avert the backwardness of our education. This is in concert with the long-term benefits of our economic construction and social development.[75]

Returning to the case of Hong Kong, assuming that China's interest in modernization remains, China's concern for upgrading education persists, China's open-door policy continues, and China's SEZ policy is still an important strategy for economic reforms, the "one country, two systems" policy, no matter how vague, will affirm Hong Kong's contribution to future economic and educational reforms in China. It is unrealistic to expect that the educational system of Hong Kong will remain unchanged for fifty years, for society changes, and so does the educational system. Nor is it easy to predict what kind of change will take place in the educational system, even if we assume that the system will gradually conform to the Chinese system, for different reforms have been taking place in various parts of China.[76]

However, it is certain that education bears a twofold function in society, conservative as well as creative. The conservative function mirrors the characteristics of a particular society at a particular time. In this respect, as Hong Kong is having close ties with China, and in view of the increasing influence of China over Hong Kong, it is conceivable that Putonghua will be taught increasingly in schools, and some schools may even adopt Putonghua as the medium of instruction. Regarding the curriculum, elimination of anti-socialist elements in textbooks will be required. With regard to its creative function, educational change will contribute as a leading force of social change. To operate this function effectively, Hong Kong should make a conscious effort to raise its educational standards, to continue its present educational reforms, and to increase its international linkage, so as to offer impetus and examples for future economic and educational development in China. Thus, China's commitment to excellence or nonexcellence will have strong implications for the future of Hong Kong and China. As Margaret Ng said in a recent review:

> Hong Kong's increasing affluence makes the demand for higher standards inevitable, and the means to attain them available.... Unless China develops phenomenally in the next six or seven years, this disparity of standards will continue to exist,... and this disparity will result in an erosion of standards in Hong Kong.[77]

In view of the intermittent complaints about the slow pace of educational development that appear in official Chinese publications, such as *Outlook*, and in view of the fact that the economic contribution of Hong Kong to China is recognized, if Hong Kong could make good use of the creative function of education, it should certainly have an important role to play in terms of experimentation and pioneering reforms in education that can contribute to the future development of both Hong Kong and China.

Notes

I would like to express my gratitude to John Biggs, R.W. Marsh, and R.F. Goodings.

1. See W.O. Lee, "The Search for Excellence and Relevance in Education: Japan's Fourth Educational Reform Proposal," *British Journal of Educational Studies* XXXIXC (1) (February 1991): 17–32.

2. Deng Xiaoping, *Selected Works of Deng Xiaoping* (Beijing: Foreign Languages Press, 1984), p. 53.

3. *Decision of the Central Committee of the Communist Party on Reform of the Economic Structure* (Hong Kong: Joint Publishing Co., 1984), p. 28.

4. Robert E. Klitgaard, *Elitism and Meritocracy in Developing Countries* (London: The John Hopkins Press Ltd., 1986), p. 29.

5. *Beijing Review*, no. 2, January 13, 1978, p. 15.

6. *The 13th Party Congress and China's Reform* (Beijing: Beijing Review, 1987), p. 25.

7. Wang Hsueh-wen "Communist China's Educational Reforms: An Analysis" in

Changes and Continuities in Chinese Communism, vol. 2, *The Economy, Society, and Technology*, ed. Yu-ming Shaw (Boulder: Westview Press, 1988), p. 390.

8. *Deng Xiaoping: Speeches and Writings* (Oxford: Pergamon, 1987), p. 119.

9. Peter Mauger, "Another Great Leap Forward?" *The Times Educational Supplement*, July 12, 1985, p. 11.

10. *The Sixth Five-Year Plan of the People's Republic of China for Economic and Social Development* (1981–1985) (Beijing: Foreign Languages Press, 1984), p. 206.

11. *Decision of the Central Committee of the Communist Party on Reform of the Economic Structure*, p. 30.

12. China's Economic Reform Studies Association [Zhongguo Jingji Gaige Yanjiuhui], ed., *Dialogues on Reform and Open Policies* [*Gaige Yu Kaifang Duihualu*] (Beijing: Jingji Kexue Chubanshe, 1987), p. 3.

13. Barbara Gasper, "Keypoint Secondary Schools in China: The Persistence of Tradition?" *Compare* 19, 1 (1989): 5–20; Pauline Chan, "Education in the People's Republic of China: Tradition and Change" in *Equality and Freedom in Education: A Comparative Study*, ed. Brian Holmes (London: George Allen and Unwin, 1985), p. 181.

14. *The Sixth Five-Year Plan of the People's Republic of China*, p. 14.

15. James M. Ethridge, *Changing China: The New Revolution's First Decade, 1979–1988* (Beijing: New World Press, 1988), p. 181.

16. Ibid., p. 195.

17. John H. Hawkins, "The People's Republic of China," in *Schooling in East Asia: Forces of Change*, ed. R.M. Thomas and T. Neville (Oxford: Pergamon Press, 1983), pp. 144–45.

18. *Deng Xiaoping: Speeches and Writings*, pp. 48–49.

19. Ibid., p. 41.

20. Ibid., p. 49.

21. Cited by Klitgaard, *Elitism and Meritocracy*, p. 30.

22. Gasper, "Keypoint Secondary Schools," p. 10.

23. Ibid., p. 10.

24. Börge Bakken, "Backwards Reform in Chinese Education," *The Australian Journal of Chinese Affairs* (19/20), 1988, p. 136.

25. Klitgaard, *Elitism and Meritocracy*, pp. 23–24.

26. *Deng Xiaoping: Speeches and Writings*, pp. 41, 49.

27. Reform of China's Educational Structure: Decision of the CPC Central Committee [Zhonggong Zhougyang Guanyu Jiaoyu Tizhi Gaigede Jueding], *People's Daily*, May 19, 1985.

28. See Wang Hsueh-wen, "Communist China's Educational Reforms," p. 391.

29. *The 13th Party Congress and China's Reform*, p. 63.

30. Cuilin Xiao, "China's Open-door Policy in Education: A Content Analysis of the Chinese Education Newspaper," *Compare*, vol. 18, no. 2, 1988, p. 164.

31. Richard P. Suttmeier, "Reform, Modernization, and the Changing Constitution of Science in China," *Asian Survey*, 24(10), October 1989, pp. 1010–11.

32. *White Paper on Science and Technology No. 1: Directory of China's Policies on Science and Technology* [*Kexue Jishu Baipishu Diyihao: Zhongguo Kexue Jishu Zhengce Zhinan*] (Beijing: Xinhua Chubanshe, 1986), pp. 85–87.

33. Suttmeier, "Reform, Modernization," p. 1008.

34. Ethridge, *Changing China*, p. 189.

35. Xu Mingdi, Xu Jianquan, and Guo Sile, "An Experimental Reform in China's Primary and Secondary School Systems" [Guonei Zhongxiaoxue Xuezhi Gaige Shiyan], *The Chinese University Education Journal*, 14, 2 (December 1986): 97.

36. Hao Keming et al., *A Study of China's Higher Education Structure* [*Zhongguo*

Gaodeng Jiaoyu Jiegou Yanjiu] (Beijing: Renmin Chubanshe, 1987), pp. 142–43, 167.

37. *Deng Xiaoping: Speeches and Writings*, p. 45.

38. Huang Shiqi, "Contemporary Educational Relations with the Industrialized World: A Chinese View," in *China's Education and the Industrialized World*, ed. Ruth Hayhoe and Marianne Bastid (Armonk, NY: M.E. Sharpe, 1987), p. 244.

39. *Reform of China's Educational Structure*.

40. Suttmeier, "Reform, Modernization," p. 1008.

41. Thomas Chan, E.K.Y. Chen, and Steve Chin, "China's Special Economic Zones: Ideology, Policy and Practice" in *China's Special Economic Zones: Policies, Problems and Prospects*, ed. Y.C. Jao and C.K. Leung (Hong Kong: Oxford University Press, 1986), p. 98.

42. R.D. Cremer and K.Y. Choy, *From Shekou Industrial Zone to the Opening of Coastal China—The Emergence of Zoning as a National Economic Strategy for Development* (Macau: Chinese Economic Research Centre, University of East Asia, 1988), p. 3.

43. "Beijing Review" Special Feature Series, *China After Mao* (Beijing: Beijing Review, 1984), p. 144.

44. Cited by Cremer and Choy, *Shekou to Coastal China*, p. 11.

45. Chan, Chen, and Chin, "China's Special Economic Zones," p. 91.

46. Lu Zufa et al., eds., *China's Urban Reform: The New Look of Shenzhen Special Economic Zone*, China's Urban Reform Series (Hong Kong: Economic Information and Agency and The Red Flag Publishing House, 1985), p. 10.

47. Ibid., p. 208.

48. Ibid., p. 228; cf. Peter Mauger, "China Breaks with Tradition," *The Times Educational Supplement*, August 3, 1985, p. 8.

49. C.Y. Chang, "Bureaucracy and Modernization: A Case Study of the Special Economic Zones in China," in *China's Special Economic Zones: Policies, Problems and Prospects*, ed. Y.C. Jao and C.K. Leung (Hong Kong: Oxford University Press, 1986), p. 120.

50. Lu et al., *China's Urban Reform*, p. 299.

51. Ibid., p. 208.

52. *People's Daily*, 29 March 1984, cited by David K.Y. Chu and Kwan-yiu Wong, "Modernization and the Lessons of the Special Economic Zones" in *Modernization in China: The Case of the Shenzhen Special Economic Zone*, ed. Kwan-yiu Wong and David K.Y. Chu (Oxford: Oxford University Press, 1985), p. 214.

53. *The Basic Law of the Hong Kong Special Administrative Region of the People's Republic of China* (Hong Kong: The Consultative Committee for the Basic Law, 1990), pp. 5–6.

54. Gao Guang et al., *Studies of Class Structure in China's Primary Stage of Socialism* [*Zhongguo Shehuizhuyi Chuji Jieduan Jiezi Jiegou Yanjiu*] (Beijing: Zhonggong Zhongyang Dangxiao Chubanshe, 1988), p. 197.

55. "The Present State of Studies of Mainland China on Hong Kong and Macau" [*Neidi Duiyu Gangao Yanjiu Gaikuang*], *The Studies of Hong Kong and Macau* [*Gangao Yanjiu*], 1/2, 1986, pp. 4–5.

56. "Articles on Hong Kong and Macau Studies," *The Studies of Hong Kong and Macau*, 3/4, 1986, pp. 133–39.

57. See Gan Changqiu, *A Textbook of Hong Kong's Economy* [*Xianggang Jingji Jiaocheng*] (Guangzhou: Zhongshan University Press, 1989), pp. 22, 40, 526; Lu Tongseng and Pei Haolin, *Studies on the Economies of Taiwan and Hong Kong* [*Taiwan Xiangang Jingji Yanjiu*] (Zhenjian: Nongcun Duwu Chubanshe, 1989), pp. 309–10; Zheng Deliang, *A Preliminary Study of Hong Kong's Economic Problems* [*Xianggang Jingji Wenti Chutan*] (Guangzhou: Zhongshan University Press, 1987), pp. 2–25, 47–53; and Zhongshan University Economics Department, *Studies on Hong Kong's Economy*

[*Xianggang Jingji Kaocha*] (Guangdong: Guangdong Renmin Chubanshe, 1985), pp. 2–9.

58. Bu Donxin, " 'One Country, Two Systems' and Academic Exchange between Guangdong and Hong Kong" [*Yiguo Lianzhi Yu Yuegang Guanxi Xueshu Jiaoliu*], *Social Sciences in Guang Dong* 2 (1986): 2–25.

59. Lei Qiang et al., *Hong Kong Higher Education* [*Xianggang Gaodeng Jiaoyu*] (Guangdong: Guangdong Gaodeng Jiaoyu Chubanshe, 1988), pp. 2–3.

60. Bu, " 'One Country, Two Systems,' " p. 22.

61. UNESCO figures excerpted in Cheng Kai Ming, *Educational Planning, Administration and Management in Asia and Pacific: A Regional Study*. Working document for the International Congress on Planning and Management of Educational Development, Mexico, March 26–30, 1990, pp. 85–86.

62. See Cheng Kai Ming, "Financing Education in Mainland China: What Are the Real Problems?" *Issues and Studies*, March 1990, pp. 55–60; *Perspectives on Education in Hong Kong* [*Xianggang Jiaoyu Mianmian Guan*] (Guangzhou: Guangdong Renmin Chubanshe, 1988), p. 107.

63. Lei Qiang and Chen Lijun, "Developing Intelligence in Guangzhou and Macau by means of Hong Kong's Experience" [*Cong Xianggang Zhili Kaifa Kan Suiao Zhili Kaifa de Tujing*] *The Studies of Hong Kong and Macau* 3–4 (1986): 125.

64. Albert H. Yee, *A People Misruled: Hong Kong and the Chinese Stepping Stone Syndrome* (Hong Kong: API Press, 1989), pp. 235–36.

65. Joseph Y.S. Cheng, "The Draft Basic Law: Messages for Hong Kong People" in *The Draft Basic Law of Hong Kong: Analysis and Documents*, ed. Hungdah Chiu (Maryland: University of Maryland School of Law, 1988), p. 10.

66. Ibid., pp. 20–24; Albert C.Y. Ho, "Autonomy" in *The Basic Law and Hong Kong's Future*, ed. Peter Wesley-Smith and Albert Chen (Hong Kong: Butterworths, 1988), pp. 303–8; and Ting Wai, "What Will the Basic Law Guarantee?—A Study of the Draft Basic Law from a Political and Comparative Approach," in *The Draft Basic Law of Hong Kong: Analysis and Documents*, ed. Hungdah Chiu (Maryland: University of Maryland School of Law, 1988), pp. 55–64.

67. *Basic Law*, Articles 45, 48 and 50. See also Joseph Cheng, "Draft Basic Law," p. 47 and Lau Siu-kai, *Basic Law and the New Political Order* (Hong Kong: Centre for Hong Kong Studies, The Chinese University of Hong Kong, 1988), p. 15.

68. See Lau Siu-kai, *Decolonization without Independence: The Unfinished Political Reforms of the Hong Kong Government* (Hong Kong: Centre for Hong Kong Studies, The Chinese University of Hong Kong, 1987).

69. Ting, "What Will the Basic Law Guarantee?" p. 79.

70. Kwan-yiu Wong and David K.Y. Chu, "Export Processing Zones and Special Economic Zones as Locomotives of Export-led Economic Growth" in *Modernization in China: The Case of the Shenzhen Special Economic Zone*, ed. Kwan-yiu Wong and David K.Y. Chu (Oxford: Oxford University Press, 1985), p. 24.

71. *Learning Document for the Fifth Plenum of the CPC Thirteenth Central Committee: Questions and Answers* [*Xuexi Shisanjie Wuzhong Quanhui Wenjian: Wenti Jieda*] (Beijing: Falu Chubanshe, November 1989), pp. 159–61.

72. *Outlook* [*Liaowang*], April 2, 1990, p. 6.

73. Robert Deffs, "Hardliners Hit Back," *Far Eastern Economic Review*, May 10, 1990, pp. 8–9.

74. Suttmeier, "Reform, Modernization," pp. 1012, 1015.

75. *Learning Document*, pp. 125–26.

76. See Xu, Xu, and Guo, "Experimental Reform."

77. Margaret Ng, "Report on CAAC Crash Bodes Ill for Future," *South China Morning Post*, August 14, 1990.

12

On the Characteristics, Strong Points, and Shortcomings of Education in Hong Kong: A Mainland Chinese Educator's View of Education in Hong Kong

Li Yixian

Hong Kong will be returned to China in 1997. It is part of Chinese territory and more than 95 percent of its population is Chinese. Hong Kong has been a British colony for more than one hundred years due to various historical reasons. Its social system is capitalist and its education has a strong colonial color; however, this colonial color has diminished on a large scale in the past ten years.

Beginning in the 1960s education in Hong Kong began to expand and develop very rapidly. This author visited the colony on three occasions to observe the educational system. As a mainland Chinese educator, my views and understanding of education are based on a different perspective than those of an educator from a developed country. Some of my ideas are in agreement with those in Hong Kong educational circles; however, it is impossible for me to have as deep and thorough understanding of the subject as does a long-time educator from Hong Kong. This is exactly the reason for writing this chapter. Education in Hong Kong includes many issues—in this chapter, I will only deal with a few of them.

Characteristics of Education in Hong Kong after the Sino-British Declaration

According to this joint declaration, Hong Kong will be returned to China in 1997 and the Chinese government will carry out the special "one country, two systems" policy. Education in Hong Kong consequently will have the following characteristics:

A. Systems and Policies on Education in Hong Kong to Be Decided by the People

The declaration ensures that after 1997, the previous educational system in Hong Kong will be maintained in the Hong Kong Special Administrative Region (SAR). The Chinese government will not interfere. The Hong Kong SAR will be autonomous and make its own policies regarding culture, education, and technology, including the educational system and its management, the allocation of the education budget, the language of instruction, the examination and degree systems, degree recognition, and technical qualifications. All schools, including those that are organized by religious and social groups, will be autonomous and free to hire faculty members from outside the SAR and to choose their own textbooks. Students will also enjoy the freedom of choosing schools and going to school outside the special zone.[1]

During the transitional period before June 30, 1997, the British government is responsible for administrative management in Hong Kong, including education.

Many educational groups, university professors, lecturers, and personnel in educational circles have made quite a few proposals and suggestions on educational issues that need to be developed in order to make a smooth transition possible. The author of this chapter recognizes the following issues:

1. Educational Goals

A primary question is how to formulate educational goals, clarify the direction of education, and train personnel to manage Hong Kong. The present educational goals in Hong Kong are far too narrow. "Education in Hong Kong is mainly a way to reach economic and occupational goals."[2] The educational policy that the Hong Kong government has been trying to implement seems to focus only on the training of skilled workers, technicians, and manpower for the labor market. Secondary school students study solely for the purpose of getting a degree or degree recognition. They lack an ideal sense of the nation and are bereft of creative ability.

2. Citizen Education

It is important to increase a sense of social and national responsibility and reinforce education in morals. The educational system in Hong Kong has always stressed education in and examination of knowledge, while ignoring its citizens' moral education, such as their views on life, love of the country and nation, as well as education in proper social behavior. The Hong Kong Education Department has only recently issued guidelines on civics education.

3. Language Medium of Instruction

How to teach in the mother tongue, popularize standardized Chinese (Putonghua), and continue to reinforce English language teaching are matters that need to be resolved.

4. Reform in the Length of Schooling, Course Work, and the Examination System

Unification of the educational system in preparatory courses for postsecondary education is an important goal. In this regard, the Hong Kong Education Commission issued its No. 2 Report on September 16, 1986, in which it suggested that under the premise of maintaining the length of secondary education, preparatory courses should be unified into a two-year comprehensive course and the previous examinations should be replaced by an "Intermediate-Level Examination." As a response to this report, the University of Hong Kong agreed to convert to a four-year program by adding a foundation year. The Hong Kong Education Commission issued the No. 3 Report on June 16, 1988, which mainly discussed the length of sixth-form education and resulted in proposals that would lead to a three- rather than four-year system of university education. As for reform of course work and the examination system, many Hong Kong experts in education have already come up with various criticisms and suggestions that will help students achieve all-around development.

5. Reinforcement of Scientific Research in Universities and Development of Various Academic Activities

Hong Kong's prosperity in commerce and finance make it a truly international city, but in areas of academics and scientific research, Hong Kong does not enjoy international status. Its academic studies in education, scientific research, and publications are not even as good as those on Taiwan. Thus it is very important to determine how to build its international status in specialized fields of education and academic studies as well as in scientific research.

6. Revision of the Education Ordinance

The present education ordinance and the educational regulations in Hong Kong were made in 1952 and revised in 1958 and 1971. They achieved a standardized educational system and made possible its scientific management. But there are quite a few points that are not reasonable and result in maintainence of a colonial atmosphere. These improper, antidemocratic, and colonial-like regulations need to be reexamined and revised when Hong Kong returns to China in 1997.

B. Education in Hong Kong as a Bridge between Mainland China and the Western World

Due to historical reasons, Hong Kong enjoys a close relationship with advanced

Western countries. Many of the professors and lecturers in Hong Kong studied abroad and earned master's or doctoral degrees there and have maintained connections with the Western world. Universities and colleges in Hong Kong have also invited scholars from Western countries to teach in the territory. All these contacts that help Hong Kong absorb Western knowledge and experience are exactly what mainland China lacks. This author expects educational scholars in universities and colleges in Hong Kong to continue to maintain and develop their close relationships abroad after 1997.

Hong Kong, as an international city located on the Chinese border, functions as a bridge between mainland China and the Western world. This function includes two aspects: one is to connect the Chinese hinterland and the Western world, through an exchange of culture, scientific technology, and education. The second is to evaluate objectively the strong and weak points both in China and the Western world, in order to assist educational reform in the Chinese hinterland.

The Chinese-English bilingual system is very important to education in Hong Kong. The deterioration of the level of Chinese-English education in the colony is of real concern. There is no problem with the bilingual ability of the older generation who received a good education. But the proficiency in English of present-day students in Hong Kong is decreasing. One education official pointed out that only 20 percent of the students are able to understand courses taught in English. According to survey results on English proficiency issued by the Education Department, more than 40 percent of lower secondary school students are unable to achieve minimum requirements. English has become an international language, and its mastery is important for maintaining international ties in academics, education, technology, commerce, and finance as well as in many other areas involving Hong Kong and the rest of the world. The key point is how to maintain and develop the good tradition of learning English in Hong Kong's schools.

On the other hand, although Chinese is the mother tongue, the Chinese proficiency of students in Hong Kong is low due to the fact that the policy of teaching Chinese in Hong Kong is always to "lay more emphasis on English and less on Chinese." Both the comprehension level of Chinese and Chinese writing ability are low. Language is not only a very important tool and means of communication with other people, it also represents the nation's culture, the structure of thought, and overall state of mind. If Chinese students in Hong Kong are not familiar with Chinese culture and language, it would be impossible either to eliminate colonial influence or to reach the goal of connecting China to the rest of the world. Of course, it is not possible or necessary for all people in Hong Kong to be literate in both Chinese and English. However, because it is required in their work, bilingual practice should be intensified among primary and secondary school teachers. And, due to requirements in academic research, teachers and scholars in universities need to be good at both languages and play an important role between the Chinese hinterland and the Western world.

Educational and Social Development in Hong Kong

In the past decades, especially since the 1960s and 1970s, Hong Kong's rapid social and economic development is world renowned. Education in Hong Kong has also been developing rapidly since the 1960s.

A. Development in Education Results from Economic and Social Development

At the end of the 1960s, Hong Kong entered a stage of unprecedented prosperity. Economic development provided the material conditions for the development of education. Indeed, the vigorous development of education is mainly promoted by the economic and social consequences of Hong Kong's development, while the development of education is a major part of the colony's social development.

The education White Paper issued in 1965 outlined a goal of implementing free elementary education by 1971. This plan was realized on schedule, and in 1978 it became possible to offer free education to all children through the first nine years of schooling. Thus in a period of thirteen years, nine-year free education was realized. At present, secondary school education in Hong Kong has basically been popularized, which is a great achievement in educational development. Professional education and adult education in Hong Kong have also been developed.

B. The School System and Examination System Serve the Sole Purpose of University Admission and Selection

Most secondary schools in Hong Kong are pure grammar-style (*Wenfashi*) schools that serve only to prepare students for university entrance, but do not prepare them very well to enter society. They do not aim at developing capable personnel for society nor do they train the students to adapt to social life and to make a living. Yet only a small percentage of secondary school graduates are able to enter university each year.

Many educational scholars in Hong Kong are critical of the pure grammar-style schools in Hong Kong. Dr. Zheng Zhaozhen pointed out early in 1952: "The pure grammar-style school education only shows its good effect for entering university.... The Education Department should design courses that are useful to the majority of people from the point of view of society."[3]

The examination system was set up solely for the purpose of passing the university entrance examination. The numerous subjects covered and the number of separate exams are simply horrible from the point of view of a mainland Chinese educator. It is torture for the youngsters and affects their overall development. The frequent exams result in the burden of additional homework and pressure. Students study to take exams and ignore courses that have nothing to do with the exams, thereby losing the possibility of developing in a thorough and active way.

C. Vocational Training

The percentage of students entering vocational and technical schools is not yet 10 percent of grammar-style school students, while the percentage of grammar school graduates entering university is also less than 10 percent. Apart from the 10,000 students who leave Hong Kong to study abroad each year, the rest of the students all need to have occupational training. From the perspective of a mainland educator, occupational training work in Hong Kong is done well. There is a Vocational Training Council (set up in 1982) in Hong Kong and its responsibility is to offer an overall industrial education and training system that supplements the need of economic development by promoting, developing, and implementing training plans, as well as establishing and managing several technical institutes and industrial training centers. Courses are also offered to skilled workers and technicians, which serves the same purpose as the occupational training programs offered by private companies. The author has visited this kind of school where there are all types of equipment and flexible teaching methods are practiced. The length of schooling varies—the shortest term is four weeks and the longest is several years. Some are day schools and some are evening school. There is a great variety of courses, including engineering, business, and service, as well as diploma and certificate courses with ample apprenticeship training.

There are various kinds of training committees under the Vocational Training Council that are responsible for overseeing and supervising training, designing new training plans, and opening and managing training centers. Thus, occupational training in Hong Kong is based on a calculation of manpower requirements which guarantees a mutually supportive process of occupational training and economic development. In this regard, the Chinese hinterland should learn from Hong Kong. But at present there are an insufficient number of technical colleges and industrial training centers in Hong Kong. The ratio of qualified applicants to full-time vacancies is 10:1. This indicates the shortcoming of the grammar-style schools that are only for the purpose of university entrance. It also indicates that education in Hong Kong needs to be improved in terms of further adapting itself to the needs of economic development.

D. Relatively Ample Educational Funds for Modern Educational Equipment and School Buildings

Following advanced capitalist countries, Hong Kong considers education as part of social welfare. Expenditures on education are always the highest or next highest item in the total annual budget in Hong Kong, constituting approximately 18 percent of total expenditures. The educational budget expenditure and the various student educational fees on average are high compared with other Asian countries. Of course, they are still low compared with most of the Western

European countries. Apart from the government's educational budget, there are also educational funds from community groups which are encouraged by the Hong Kong government to open schools, thereby increasing the overall expenditure on education.

Compared to schools in mainland China, Hong Kong universities and polytechnics as well as primary and secondary schools are generally better equipped. There are financial regulations in primary and secondary schools to guarantee the purchase of books and instruments, the provision of physical training facilities, and the repair of school buildings. Given the fact that (as the common saying goes) "A Piece of Land Is a Piece of Gold in Hong Kong," a school with one outdoor playground and one indoor playground as big as a basketball court is in a fairly good situation though not compared with student playgrounds in mainland China.

Development in Education for Teacher Training

The quality of teachers is key to the development of education. Hong Kong has rich experience in this area.

A. Concentrating on Teachers' Qualifications and Training Teachers to Be Professionals

Teachers are an important factor in the development of education. The quality and quantity of teachers directly affect the proficiency of educational work in schools, which determines whether or not a school will succeed. With the development of the economy, the Hong Kong government now pays more attention to building up a teacher corps with appropriate degrees and teaching experience. There is a whole set of strict regulations regarding the qualities of teachers in which teachers are classified as either degree-holding or non-degreed.

B. In-service Training System for Teachers

All teachers in Hong Kong, including both day and evening teachers, must have teacher training. They are now given various ways of acquiring this training: Teachers with a non-teaching university degree can apply for the two-year part-time teacher training program either at the University of Hong Kong or the Chinese University of Hong Kong and get a postgraduate certificate in education. "Employed" teachers who do not have a university degree can apply for the two-year program in a teacher training college to take in-service courses.

Teachers who are admitted to teaching courses are given favorable conditions, in terms of day-release time, by the schools where they work. There is a set of strict regulations regarding teachers' attainment of a degree and training in Hong Kong; this would be worthwhile for China to learn and follow, though there are no specialized teachers' universities and colleges in Hong Kong as there are in China.

C. Salary and Welfare System for Teachers

The salary of both elementary and secondary school teachers (not including private school teachers) is determined by the same salary rule as for public workers in Hong Kong. There are altogether fifty-one different ranks, each with its own salary scale. The Education Department decides on the starting ranking according to the teacher's degree, as well as deciding on each teacher's monthly salary. The salary of teachers in universities and polytechnics is higher than those in secondary schools. This is also decided according to the degree and is based on a salary scale chart.

The salary of teachers in Hong Kong is considered to be medium-high as compared with other lines of work. It is higher than that of public workers who are at the same rank. It is also higher than that of the teachers in most Asian cities and in large cities in some European countries. The teaching profession in Hong Kong is stable due to teachers' good economic and social status, although there is growing concern that many teachers are leaving Hong Kong in anticipation of 1997.

Many teachers in China do not have the required degree and many do not even have a teaching certificate. The concept that teachers are professionals has not been established in China; their salary is excessively low, even lower than that of unskilled and uneducated physical laborers. Thus, Hong Kong's experience is valuable and significant for China.

But Hong Kong teachers have their own problems: namely a heavy work burden. Secondary school teachers work 30 to 34 hours per week and elementary teachers 32 to 36 hours per week, plus the additional time as class teachers, including extracurricular instruction work. This time burden hinders the improvement of teaching quality and teacher-student rapport. Teachers in China do more than teachers in Hong Kong in terms of communicating with students and caring for their development in various ways.

The same problem exists within universities and polytechnics in Hong Kong. There are certain quotas in junior and senior teachers' positions in every school. If the quotas are filled, teachers who want to be promoted have to wait for the senior teachers to retire or resign. This causes the problem that many qualified teachers remain in inferior positions over a long period of time anxiously waiting for vacancies in superior positions, all of which affects their enthusiasm.

Autonomy of Universities and Colleges

This is a very important topic in the development and reform of higher education. How have the universities and colleges in Hong Kong done in this area?

A. The Realization of Autonomy of Hong Kong Universities

Autonomy in universities is required by their social function and their academic activities. Students trained by universities and colleges are not only required to have knowledge, but must also possess a democratic conscience. Dr. Wang Gungwu, Vice-Chancellor of the University of Hong Kong, once said that a university, on the one hand, "can train young people who have received higher education and who are qualified for professional and management work." For these young people, "what they have benefited from at the university is not the practical knowledge regarding geography, mechanical engineering or other subjects, but a trained brain which enables them to seek truth relying on their imagination, to know how to deal with society, to judge the feasibility of objects and to make wise decisions." In this way they become "the future pillars of society."[4] Dr. Ma Lin, former Vice-Chancellor of the Chinese University of Hong Kong, said: "For an independent and autonomous society, universities are the laboratory and workshop that create the future. We can see from today's society the results of past efforts by universities; we can also see from today's society the future development of that society."[5] Thus, a democratic society requires the formation of a democratic conscience through autonomous universities and colleges. Ever since the (European) Middle Ages, the world historical development of universities is a history of their striving for independence and campus autonomy.

Dr. Rayson Huang, former Vice-Chancellor of the University of Hong Kong, stated precisely the issue regarding independence and autonomy for universities and colleges: "The University needs two things in order to continue to produce these leaders. The first is independence, the vital element in any intellectual achievement. The freedom that we have always had, to select students, to appoint staff, to decide what to teach and how to teach it, is very precious to us. It is also essential for [a] healthy community."[6] Many wise personnel in Hong Kong have expressed strong demands regarding the autonomy of universities. Dr. Thomas H.C. Lee of the Chinese University of Hong Kong stated that due to the fact that the nature of universities is "not the same as that of the government . . . if universities are limited in terms of teaching and administration by regulations made by the Hong Kong government bureaucracy, it would be impossible for them to carry out their educational responsibilities."[7] Academic freedom is closely linked with university autonomy.

B. The Basic Category of University Autonomy in Hong Kong

The Hong Kong Universities and Polytechnics Grants Committee (UPGC) once listed the five major issues regarding university autonomy in its Notes on Procedures in 1980. They are freedom to: 1) hire faculty members; 2) choose students; 3) control course content and academic standards; 4) make research plans; and 5) allocate and use university funds.

These freedoms are guaranteed by the "University Ordinances" that are part of Hong Kong's laws. Universities and colleges have autonomous control and have become relatively independent bodies according to the rights regulated in the form of law.

C. Scholarly Autonomy

University autonomy requires universities and colleges to manage schools in accordance with regulations of university academic activities. Scholars in universities and colleges, that is, professors and lecturers, have the most say in terms of management of academic activities. Thus, university autonomy eventually produces "scholarly autonomy."

Many professors are involved in administrative affairs. Among members of the educational administration committee—the highest organization that is in charge of teaching, scientific research, and other academic activities on campus—almost all are scholars in the university. Professors and lecturers become members of various kinds of specialized committees either on the university, college, or departmental level, to study and decide on the activities regarding teaching and academic research of the whole campus through elections. This embodies the ideal of scholarly autonomy.

D. The Relativity of University Autonomy

"Autonomy" is the opposite of "being controlled." Absolute autonomy, complete separation from the outside world, is impossible. It is the same with universities and colleges in Hong Kong, where autonomy is based on control by law. This is obvious. The administrative power of the government also controls and directs university autonomy. This can be seen from the allocation of educational funds and general educational policy. Also, university autonomy is influenced by the supervision of outside campus academic organizations. The establishment of academic majors and courses must gain recognition from the internationally relevant academic organizations which are responsible for approving the levels of proficiency achieved in such courses, thereby increasing the school's reputation.

Viewed from the outside, it most often appears that there is an identity between the government-managed "administrative direction" and the university-managed "academic direction." This aspect of Hong Kong's universities is important and deserves further study.

Notes

1. *Sino-British Joint Declaration on the Question of Hong Kong* (Hong Kong: Xinhua News Agency, 1984), p. 17.

2. *A Perspective on Education in Hong Kong*. Report by a Visiting Panel, 1982, [n.p.], pp. 34, 75.
3. "The Policy and Future of Education in Hong Kong," in *Hong Kong Educational Perspectives*, comp. Hong Kong Professional Students' Union of the Chinese University of Hong Kong (Hong Kong: Wide Angle Publishing House, 1952), p. 13.
4. Wang Gungwu, "Commencement Speech," University of Hong Kong, 1988.
5. Ma Lin, "Commencement Speech at the 34th Session," Chinese University of Hong Kong, 1986.
6. Rayson Huang, "Commencement Speech at the University of Hong Kong," 1984.
7. Thomas H.C. Lee, "One Characteristic of the Financial System of Professional Education in Hong Kong," Chinese University of Hong Kong, School of Education, manuscript.

13

Education in Hong Kong and China: Toward Convergence?

Julian Y.M. Leung

The most perplexing questions facing Hong Kong's educational future concern the potential for increasing integration between various parts of the educational systems of Hong Kong and the rest of China. Given the successful levels of cooperation and integration that the two economic systems have experienced, and the growing association of education with economic concerns such as human capital development, the question of educational integration is well posed. Moreover, the cultural foundations of education in Hong Kong already share a Confucian heritage with the rest of China. Where then does one begin such an analysis? As the chapters of this book have highlighted, there are a number of examples of how such integration is already happening in language teaching, in political studies, in history, etc., and this is further amplified as academic exchange relationships become increasingly more pronounced. This final chapter attempts to explore this issue by noting three pairs of forces at work during the transition: insulation and interdependence; decolonization and neo-colonization; and internationalization and indigenization.

Insulation and Interdependence

The promulgation of the Basic Law at the National People's Congress in March 1990 signifies Hong Kong's formal entry into a period of real transition. The Chinese government expects all parties to contribute toward a smooth transfer of sovereignty in 1997, including those whose major concern is with education in Hong Kong. Yet the concept of "one country, two systems" is by itself a source of ambivalence that will constantly affect the relationship between Hong Kong and the rest of China. For instance, Chinese leaders like Deng Xiaoping have repeatedly stressed that Hong Kong should be governed by patriotic Hong Kong people who support the sovereignty of the PRC.[1] Yet Jiang Zemin, the Chinese Communist party general secretary, used the analogy "river water and well water should not mix," to indicate that the Chinese socialist system should not be subjected to subversive interference from Hong Kong, especially prodemocracy activities.[2] Thus one reading of these messages is that the two political systems should be kept insulated from each other. But how can one be patriotic if one's concern for the country's democratic development is considered a subversive activity? The application of the concept of "one country, two systems" in Hong Kong's educational transition has been met with ambivalence. Section six of the Basic Law stipulates that Hong Kong will keep all her unique educational features intact, including the existing structure of schooling, academic freedom, and language policy.[3] The underlying rationale, that education is merely the superstructure that rests on Hong Kong's economic foundation, defines education's function strictly in terms of its service to a capitalist economy. Educational changes in Hong Kong will be made by local educators in response to Hong Kong's economic changes. But does the preservation of status quo education in Hong Kong mean that the two educational systems should be insulated from each other as are the two political systems? Will the specific ideological and structural differences between education systems of Hong Kong and the PRC remain insulated from one another? How then can future academic exchanges and bilateral cooperation be increasingly deepened?

A closer examination of the two educational systems reveals that there are important similarities (see Appendix E). For example, both are highly centralized in administration and curriculum development. Both have an early differentiation of pupils and narrow specialization, with pronounced separation between the arts and sciences, with social science given low priority. Both have an overemphasis on higher education at the expense of primary schooling and preschooling. Above all, Hong Kong is basically a Chinese community having a strong cultural identity with mainland China. Indeed, mainland educators visiting Hong Kong have observed that Hong Kong preserves most of the Confucian traditions in education—such as obedience to the school authority, obedience to the enforced school regulations, and high esteem for success on examinations. Existing evidence indicates that a kind of benevolent interdependence between education in Hong Kong and China has developed and will be strengthened in the future. Historically, Hong Kong has been a center of cultural interchange between China and the West. Since the early nineteenth century Hong Kong has contributed to China's modernization, as evidenced by the production of "bicultural and bilingual middlemen."[4] It is seldom remembered that the University of Hong Kong was established in 1911 to serve China's modernization.

As Hong Kong's economy has become closely tied to the Chinese economy in recent years, the academic linkage between Hong Kong and the PRC has correspondingly become closer. There is a growing number of mainland Chinese students being enrolled for higher degree studies in Hong Kong's tertiary institutions. Correspondingly, mainland Chinese tertiary institutions recruit hundreds of Hong Kong students every year, particularly in the fields of medicine, Chinese literature, law, and engineering. Other forms of academic linkages are flourishing. Examples include a part-time diploma in Chinese law, which is jointly offered by Shu Yan College and the People's University in Beijing. Also, the Biotechnology Institution of the Chinese University of Hong Kong developed specific cooperation with Shanghai counterparts to disseminate biotechnical innovations in Hong Kong and internationally. There are many other examples. Hong Kong has already tapped the talent of mainland Chinese professionals, many of whom arrive in Hong Kong as legal immigrants and are absorbed by local industries as mid-level technicians or even engineers although their academic qualifications may not be formally recognized. They also form the backbone of Putonghua teachers in Hong Kong. A mini "Silicon Valley" has been set up in Shenzhen with a powerful Hong Kong electronics group to further research and development for Hong Kong. Chinese institutions of higher education are eager to sell their research results to Hong Kong industries. The newly established University of Science and Technology of Hong Kong will undoubtedly see joint research and development with Chinese institutions as one of its major tasks.

In the light of rapid expansion of higher education in Hong Kong and the brain drain, the Hong Kong Education Commission has advocated that short-term contracts be offered to mainland Chinese scholars.[5] At the same time, the PRC actively uses Hong Kong as a workshop for learning Western management skills. Through different foundations set up by patriotic Hong Kong industrialists, numerous training courses have been organized for Chinese bankers, international traders, hotel managers, and mayors. The Beijing-Hong Kong Academic Exchange Centre is working to promote technology transfer between Hong Kong and mainland Chinese higher institutions. The State Education Commission sends secondary school principals and teacher trainers to the Hong Kong University for short- and long-term training, primarily because in addition to its proximity, Hong Kong best demonstrates how a Chinese community adopts Western educational philosophies and practices. Moreover, as W.O. Lee has described in his chapter, educational development in Hong Kong is a "model of excellence" in terms of its contribution to economic development.

To insulate Hong Kong and mainland China is economically impossible, as Hong Kong's economy is already strongly integrated with that of China. Political insulation just implies minimal commitment to mainland Chinese politics so that Hong Kong can survive in a better way. In the field of education it is expected that a kind of educational interdependence, mutually beneficial and complimentary for both Hong Kong and the PRC, will develop throughout the transition period. On the other hand, it is hoped that the Hong Kong educational system will maintain its uniqueness and independence.

Decolonization and Neo-colonization

The literature on colonial education abounds with eulogistic, apologetic, or accusative discussions on the the nature and impact of colonial education. Among the stereotyped accusations of colonial legacies are the creation of: (a) a privileged, Westernized elite divorced from the aspiration of the indigenous majority, especially the rural masses; (b) citizens unsure of their real identity or caught between two cultures; (c) an unchangeable administrative bureaucracy; (d) a belief system hostile to the indigenous culture, such as a Eurocentric, academic curriculum that overlooks manual work and the mother tongue; (e) a racially segregated schooling system based on "divide and rule"; and, (f) a "culture of silence" with low political aspirations.[6] It is common to find Hong Kong educators attributing educational problems such as juvenile deliquency and underinvestment in preschool education to the evils of "colonial education" often without any in-depth analysis.

Watson identifies three distinct features of British colonialism in education.[7] First, the British played the role of the "reluctant colonizers" who adopted a "laissez-faire" educational policy and tolerated indigenous education. Second, there was no common colonial educational policy due to the regionalization of policymaking in London. The strength of the personality of individual governors decided educational policy in the colonies. Third, Britain was prepared to hand over power to the colonized people after World War II. Thompson adds that the British educational mission is to train leaders during colonial rule and make the unequal equal during decolonization.[8] Local researchers who study the development of education in Hong Kong since 1840 share a similar viewpoint. Ng Lun Ngai Ha asserts that educational development in Hong Kong is not an uncritical transfer of content and system from the metropolitan country. The underlying forces of change that shaped Hong Kong's educational development were the social composition and attitude of the local Chinese community, the political conditions in China, and Britain's changing policy toward the Chinese government.[9] Anthony Sweeting (chapter 2) also argues that the major forces of change originate locally and that decolonization began by mid-century.

Decolonization is a collective and individual adventure that involves both structural and cultural changes. Indeed, after the chief Chinese UN delegate announced that Hong Kong should not be categorized as a colony in 1973, the Hong Kong government had undertaken measures to decolonize Hong Kong. For example, Chinese was made a parallel official language with English and Hong Kong inhabitants were deprived of the right of abode in Britain. The urge for civic education in the early 1980s could be interpreted as a "conscientization" process to equip the young people of Hong Kong for their responsibilities as citizens of the future Special Administrative Region. Paul Morris (chapter 5) identifies several government-initiated curriculum changes for inculcating stronger national identity with China among school pupils in the period of transition from British sovereignty to Chinese sovereignty. Herbert Pierson (chapter 8) believes that the promotion of Putonghua, which was intitated by the government, can be a useful means to overcome the political and linguistic alienation produced by British colonial rule. The Hong Kong government has also encouraged the use of Chinese (Cantonese) as a medium of instruction in schools by subsidizing the publication of Chinese textbooks and appointing additional Chinese language teachers. Examination rules have been revised to allow pupils to take subject examinations in Chinese at all levels without any indication of the use of language mode in the certificates. All these can be counted as decolonization or "domestication" measures to encourage a smooth integration with the mother culture when Hong Kong returns to China in 1997.

However, other educational policies can be interpreted as measures of neo-colonialism. For example, in 1988 it was argued that the existing 6+5+2+3 British model of schooling should be replaced by a 6+6+4 model in line with the dominant world trend and particularly with the mainland Chinese system. In June 1988, the Education Commission Report No. 3 reinforced the existing model of education. Accordingly, the Chinese University has to take students from a two-year matriculation course and abandon the four-year university structure. A local scholar cited this decision as a British conspiracy imposing an outdated British model of education on the future Hong Kong SAR for the purpose of extending British influence until 2047.[10] Similarly, the Hong Kong Education Commission's decision in May 1990 to introduce streaming of primary school graduates according to their language proficiency in Chinese and English could be seen as a major setback on the promotion of "mother-tongue" education because 20–30 percent of all pupils, those capable of following an English-medium secondary schooling, will become the future elite.

The decolonization-neo-colonization dichotomy can become a bone of contention during the transition period. Transition toward 1997 will not be trouble-free. In a time when the Sino-British relationship becomes strained, the Chinese government perceives every British action as conspiratorial, as exemplified by her attacks on the Right of Abode issue and the Bill of Rights. In April 1990, the Hong Kong government announced the proposal to remove the textbook approval system, which originated in 1930 to ensure that school textbooks are not subjected to Communist influence. This could be interpreted as a government decision to relax its political control over education and a step toward democratization. However, the suggestion was attacked in a leftist newspaper as a way of weakening the authority of the future SAR government.[11]

Ironically, it is the Basic Law that has guaranteed the continuation of the educational system and practices erected by the British colonial regime. It legitimizes the continued postcolonial influence of the British on the educational system's policies as well as the intellectual life of the educated. Moreover, the general public opts to support the colonial legacies. Parental choice of English-medium education, rather than government decree, is the greatest barrier to full-scale implementation of Chinese-medium education. Parental sentiment has led the teachers of one excellent Chinese-medium school to vote to switch back to English-medium instruction.[12]

In general, what teachers worry about is that after 1997 they may be compelled to switch to educational practices along the mainland Chinese model. Any measure to decolonize existing practices will be received with panic. After the June 4 crackdown of the pro-democracy movement, there is less likelihood that local Chinese inhabitants will become extremely nationalistic and anti-British as their predecessors had been in the 1920s and 1960s. The postcolonial impact of Britain on Hong Kong's educational system and policies as well as the international outlook of the local inhabitants will definitely persist, although such a phenomenon is labeled by Altbach and Kelly as a sympton of neo-colonialism.[13]

Internationalization and Indigenization

A number of forces have acted to both facilitate and stifle the international influence on Hong Kong's educational development. For example, due to the colonial status of Hong Kong, international organizations such as the World Bank and UNESCO, which have traditionally played a role in shaping education in developing societies, have had a negligible impact on educational developments in Hong Kong. Nevertheless, while Hong Kong's educational system has been most heavily influenced by that of the United Kingdom, it has also developed an expansive international character. The educational community is composed of an increasing number of those who have attended universities in Canada, the United States, Australia, and even Japan, although the leadership in the government Education Department is still a product of predominantly British-style education. Most of Hong Kong's elite schools are strongly influenced by the British system. This includes the University of Hong Kong, which favors recruitment from the United Kingdom and the Commonwealth for its overseas staffing. All this has contributed to the insular character of much of Hong Kong elite education. Only the reality of China's staunch Communist-dominated system on Hong Kong's border has prevented a strong reaction against the British-dominated character of much of Hong Kong education.

Heavy doses of overseas investment and technology transfer in Hong Kong have created opportunities to deepen the influence of Americans, Japanese, Australians, and continental Europeans. Aside from having their own international secondary schools in Hong Kong, these countries sponsor many Hong Kong students for overseas study, and when they return to Hong Kong they are often recruited by the respective national firms. However, the influence of these groups on the structure and content of the Hong Kong educational system remains minimal.

Nevertheless, there have been new efforts to internationalize education. The severe brain drain has seriously crippled the localization of tertiary teachers and administrators. A large amount of recruitment is likely to be international, ending up with many posts being filled by foreign-passport holders. A large expatriate-staffed tertiary education sector may come to be viewed as contradictory to the expectation of Hong Kong people administering Hong Kong. At the same time, the increasing number of expatriates, including returned emigrants, in Hong Kong has created a growing demand for international schooling. Those lining up for emigration also put their children in international schools as preparation. The Sino-British Land Commission has set aside an area for the development of a school which is hoped to be the first of many that will internationalize education in Hong Kong. This sixth-form international school, the Lo Po Chun United World College, would draw students from overseas, as well as offer international qualifications to local pupils. The school would be independently operated, and would offer the international baccalaureate diploma.[14]

Opposite the internationalization pole of the dichotomy is indigenization. This force pulls Hong Kong in the direction of its inherent character as a unique Chinese society. Indigenous forces, as part of the culture and identity that Hong Kong has built up over several decades, have acted to anchor the educational system. Such forces not only moderate the forces of internationalization, but also temper the influence of contemporary mainland culture. If decoupled from the United Kingdom and from traditional Chinese culture, the Hong Kong indigenous educational power base may quickly disintegrate. Therefore, after 1997 it is likely that there will be a growing tension between internationally sponsored and Chinese-sponsored education. This could potentially lead, at the very least, to a controversy-bound transition process, or even to a crisis of Western education in Hong Kong.

An Uncertain Future

The capacity of Hong Kong education to adapt to the transition will be greatly determined by the degree to which it justifies its existence within the "one country, two systems" framework. Three questions remain: First, will Hong Kong's economy continue to prosper so that its educational superstructure will still be considered as contributory to growth? Second, will the internationalization and democratization of Hong Kong's schooling system be tolerated by the Chinese government? Third, will the Chinese government pressure the Hong Kong educational system to inculcate "patriotism" to prepare patriotic Chinese inhabitants to administer the Hong Kong Special Administrative Region?

Notes

1. Deng Xiaoping, "Maintain the Prosperity and Stability of Hong Kong," *The Birth of the Basic Law* (Hong Kong: Wen Wei Publishing Co., 1990), p. 185.
2. *People's Daily*, January 21, 1990.

3. *Basic Law of the Hong Kong Special Administrative Region of the People's Republic of China*, February 1990.

4. K.C. Fok, *Lecture Notes on Hong Kong History* (Hong Kong: The Commercial Press, 1990).

5. R. Fan, "Opportunities and Challenges of the Experience of Higher Education," *Wah Kiu Yat Pao*, May 14, 1990.

6. M. Carnoy, *Education as Cultural Imperialism* (New York: David McKay, 1984); P. Freire, *Pedagogy of the Oppressed* (London: Penguin, 1971); P.G. Altbach and G.P. Kelly, *Educational Colonialism* (New York: Longman, 1978).

7. K. Watson, "Colonialism and Educational Development," in *Education in the Third World*, ed. K. Watson (London: Croom Helm, 1982).

8. AR.Thompson, *Education and Development in Africa* (London: Macmillan, 1981).

9. Ng, L.N.H. *Interactions of East and West: Development of Public Education in Early Hong Kong* (Hong Kong: Chinese University Press, 1984).

10. M.K. Chan, "Full Scale Restoration of British Education," *The British Sunset in Hong Kong* (Hong Kong Economic Journal, 1989), pp. 42–52.

11. "The Textbook Approval System Shound Not Be Removed," *Wen Wei Pao*, April 11, 1990.

12. *Ming Pao Daily News*, June 19, 1990.

13. Altbach and Kelly, *Education and Colonialism*.

14. "Site Set Aside for Unique International College," *South China Morning Post*, April 1990.

Appendices

Appendix A: Education System of Hong Kong (developed by Leung Kam Fong and adapted by Chen Kai Ming; originally produced by William C.W. Pang) — 274

Appendix B: The Policymaking and Administrative Bodies of Education (developed by Cheng Kai Ming) — 275

Appendix C: Chronological Framework (developed by Anthony Sweeting) — 276

Appendix D: Chronology of Important Documents Regarding Hong Kong Education (developed by contributions from Anthony Sweeting, Cheng Kai Ming, and Gerard Postiglione) — 282

Appendix E: A Comparison of the Educational Systems of the PRC and Hong Kong (developed by Julian Y.M. Leung) — 285

Appendix A: Education System of Hong Kong

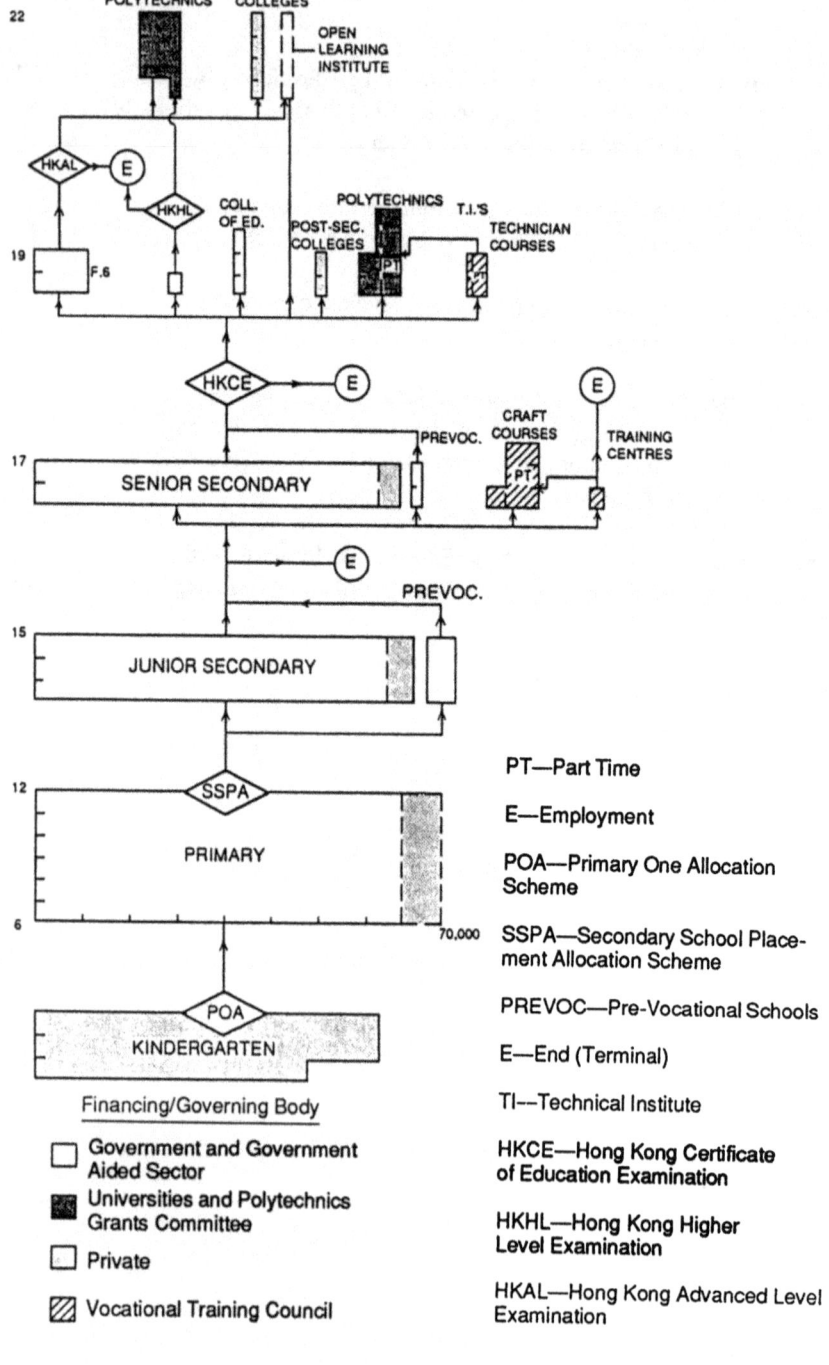

PT—Part Time

E—Employment

POA—Primary One Allocation Scheme

SSPA—Secondary School Placement Allocation Scheme

PREVOC—Pre-Vocational Schools

E—End (Terminal)

TI—Technical Institute

HKCE—Hong Kong Certificate of Education Examination

HKHL—Hong Kong Higher Level Examination

HKAL—Hong Kong Advanced Level Examination

APPENDIX B   275

Appendix B: **The Policymaking and Administrative Bodies of Education**

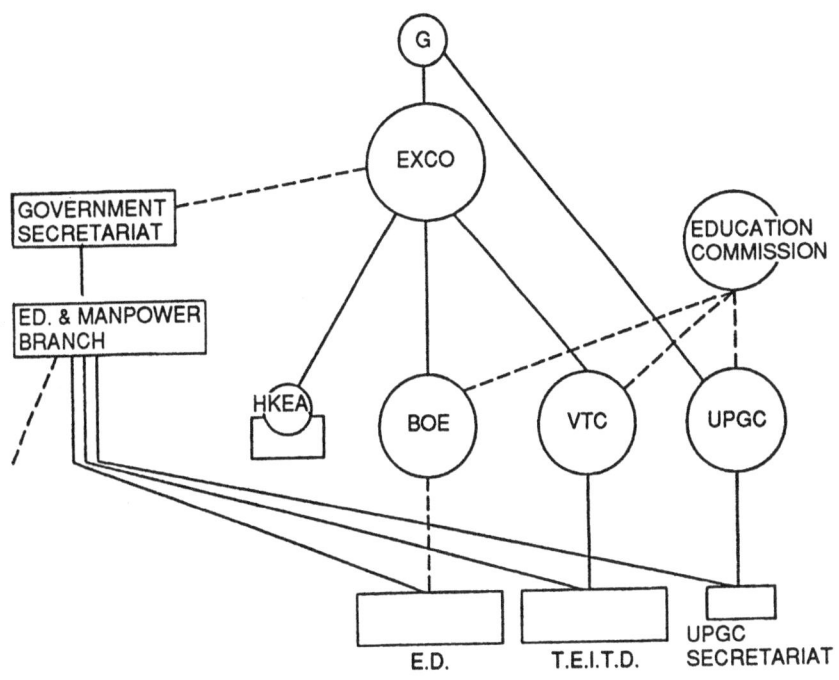

G—Governor
EXCO—Executive Council
HKEA—Hong Kong Examinations Authority
BOE—Board of Education
VTC—Vocational Training Council
UPGC—Universities and Polytechnics Grants Committee
ED—Education Department
TEITD—Technical Education Industrial Training Department

Appendix C: **Chronological Framework**

1075 Li-ying College was founded at Kam Tin in about this year by Deng Fuxie, a native of Jiangxi Province. The college became famous for its large library.

1259 According to extant documents, the first degree holder who had been born in the region later known as Hong Kong was Huang Shi. He earned the degree of *Jin-shi* in this year.

1664 The government post of county director of studies was allowed to lapse until 1678, a direct result of the forced evacuation of the coastal area (1660–1669) by the Manchu authorities.

1754 Jiang Shi-yuan of Tai Po received the degree of *Jin-shi* and became well known throughout southern China for his literary accomplishments.

1789 Deng Ying-yuan, a local calligrapher, passed his military examination, the *Ju-ren*. He later built the So Lay Yuen Study Hall at Shui Tau Tsuen in Kam Tin.

1840 The Sin Sui Study Hall in San Uk Tsuen, Fanling, was constructed. Today it possesses some of the finest wood carvings in the New Territories.

1842 In the Treaty of Nanjing, signed on August 29, China ceded the island of Hong Kong to the United Kingdom.
  The Morrison Education Society School opened on November 1. This was the first Western-style school on Hong Kong island.

1843 China and Britain ratified the Treaty of Nanjing, establishing Hong Kong as a colony of the British Crown in perpetuity.
  Four to six new Chinese schools opened to cater to the children of the incoming population of artisans and shopkeepers.
  Anglicans, Roman Catholics, and Non-Conformist missionaries began negotiating with the colonial authorities for land in order to open schools. Various denominational schools were founded in the next few years. Their fortunes fluctuated; the Morrison Education Society School, for example, had to close in 1849. Other early schools associated with the endeavors of Christian missionaries included Ying Wa College, St. Paul's College, the Asile de Sainte Enfance, the Diocesan Native Female Training School, the West Point Reformatory, and St. Saviour's College.

1847 The governor of Hong Kong received Colonial Office approval of his 1845 request to provide financial assistance to existing Chinese schools. He then appointed an investigating committee which identified three schools worthy of assistance. The government authorized a grant of HK$10 per month and issued rules to these schools (in Victoria, Aberdeen, and Stanley). A Committee of Supervision (generally known as the Education Committee) was appointed. The number of schools that the Hong Kong government supported and the amount of the support gradually increased.

1860 The Education Committee was replaced by a stronger Board of Education. One of the Board's members, Dr. James Legge, drew up a scheme for the reorganization of government-supported schooling. This entailed the concentration of government assistance for education in the urban area into a new "central" school, where English would be taught more effectively under a headmaster especially recruited in Britain. The board endorsed the scheme. In the following year, it received the approval of the Hong Kong government and a recruitment exercise commenced.

In the same year, China ceded the Kowloon peninsula to Britain. There was little British-sponsored educational activity in Kowloon until 1868 when two government-assisted schools were established there.

1862 The Government Central School opened in Gough Street. Its first headmaster was Mr. (later Dr.) Frederick Stewart. Stewart was also appointed inspector of the other government schools.

1865 The Board of Education was dissolved and its functions assumed by Frederick Stewart who was now referred to as head of the Education Department.

1873 Frederick Stewart introduced the first Grant Code, which offered a grant-in-aid to schools founded by voluntary (mainly missionary) associations on condition that they were public elementary schools with an average attendance of not less than twenty and that they would offer purely secular education for not less than four consecutive hours daily. The enactment of this Grant Code stimulated still further the public controversy which had begun in the late 1860s between "secularists" and supporters of religious education. By the end of the year, all Roman Catholic schools had withdrawn from, or refused to enter, the scheme.

1879 The revised code for the grant-in-aid scheme, largely based on suggestions from the Roman Catholic Bishop Raimondi and enthusiastically espoused by the Roman Catholic Governor, Sir John Pope Hennessy, was enacted. This simply deleted the words "elementary," "secular," and "consecutive," and removed the average attendance condition. With the religious question solved in this way, Roman Catholic schools now entered the scheme.

1882 The Education Commission, appointed by Sir John Pope Hennessy in 1880, reported shortly after Hennessy's final departure from Hong

Kong. The commission dismissed Hennessy's idea of elevating the Central School into a "collegiate institution" but supported the opening of five new "district schools" (the new name for village schools), arguing that the great need of the majority of the population was for a sound elementary education and that the government should not establish an institution that would be mainly for the advantage of the wealthy members of the community. The commission also condemned the continued existence of a separate Normal School, which had been set up with Hennessy's approval in 1881, claiming that, through a pupil-teacher scheme, the Central School could resume responsibility for training the limited number of teachers required.

1902 A small Education Committee, appointed a year earlier to review education in Hong Kong, produced its report. It recommended that "what education is given should be thorough, and that better results will be obtained by assisting to enlighten the ignorance of the upper classes of Chinese than by attempting to force new ideas on the masses of the people." The secretary of state queried the principle of concentrating on the education of an elite, claiming that "it would need very strong grounds to justify withholding Government assistance to a large native community such as exists in Hong Kong, thereby presumably excluding the very poorest from the benefits of education." The recent lease of the New Territories (1898) tended to strengthen this argument.

1913 The Hong Kong government enacted its first education ordinance. Influenced by the urge to eradicate Chinese political propaganda from schools within Hong Kong territory, the ordinance provided for the registration and supervision of private schools, as well as those maintained or assisted by the government. Its immediate effect was that the head of the Education Department (renamed director of education in 1909) assumed responsibility for over 500 schools and 11,000 pupils.

1926 The Government Vernacular Middle School (later renamed Clementi Middle School) was founded. This reflected the growing demand for vernacular education in Hong Kong which was at least partly stimulated by the May Fourth Movement in China. It also served as a response to the anti-British feelings so current during the general strike and boycott of 1925–26.

1935 Edmund Burney, a visiting inspector from Britain, produced his *Report on Education in Hong Kong*. The report criticized the small proportion of public expenditure that the Hong Kong government devoted to primary education in Chinese. It also provided a detailed list of recommendations on subjects ranging from educational administration and language policy to the need for physical education and intelligence testing. The Hong Kong government officially adopted the Burney Report as its education policy blueprint.

1942 In February, a two-month course for teachers was organized by Japanese Occupation authorities. In May, the first schools to open since the invasion of December 1941 began classes. In the next three years, responsibility for education was undertaken by a section of the Civil Affairs Bureau in conjunction with the District Bureaux and the Chinese Representation Committee. Compulsory education was discussed, but not implemented, and by the end of the war, largely because of the huge drop in Hong Kong's population, school attendance had declined markedly.

1945 Schools began to reopen from September onward, most of the earliest being grant schools, several of which were conducted by Irish or Italian religious bodies and had been allowed to operate during the Occupation. The Policy Directive for the British Military Administration (September 1, 1945–April 30, 1946) was brief. It focused mainly (and understandably) on quantitative matters and was clearly influenced by Burney. Even after the return of civil government on May 1, 1946, quantitative concerns predominated during an era of postwar reconstruction and Cold War friction. The renewed and accelerating influx of immigrants from China added to the problems and the sense of emergency, though it was some time before the Hong Kong government accepted that social services (including education) for a population which might be transient was part of its responsibility. Political tensions vis-à-vis China contributed to the strengthening of the director of education's powers to control schools (mainly through revisions to the education ordinance in 1948 and 1952 and the establishment of a "Special Bureau" within the Education Department charged with "Counter-Communist activities").

1954 The director of education's seven-year plan for a rapid expansion of primary school places represented a considerable advance over targets put forward in the ten-year plan (under discussion at the end of the 1940s) and over the recommendations of Mr. N.G. Fisher, the chief education officer from Manchester who had been invited to visit Hong Kong toward the end of 1950, in his *Report on Educational Expenditure in Hong Kong*. It also marked the Hong Kong government's acceptance of its responsibilities for the education of the children of immigrants.

1965 After restructuring, especially with regard to entry ages at different levels of schooling and length of courses, provoked criticism, and a visiting commission (by two local government officials from the United Kingdom) stimulated further debate about education, the Hong Kong government produced a policy statement. The White Paper on *Educational Policy* declared that one major objective was to achieve universal primary education by 1971 by means of increasing the number of places in government and aided schools as rapidly as possible and by introducing a scheme of subsidizing places in selected private schools.

1971 The government announced that "the aim of providing an aided primary school place for every child in the age-group seeking it had been achieved." Measures were therefore taken to ensure that primary education was universal, free, and compulsory.

Government spokesmen argued that interest in improving the quality of education was evinced by the beginning of educational television broadcasts to schools, the drafting of a constitution for a new Curriculum Development Council, and the decision to amalgamate the two Certificate of Education Boards to pave the way for the introduction of a single Certificate of Education examination in which subjects could be taken in either Chinese or English. Education pressure groups, which began proliferating in the late 1960s and early 1970s, gained support and publicity when contesting such claims.

1978 From September, junior secondary education (up to the end of secondary Form 3 or the pupil's fifteenth birthday) became free and compulsory for the vast majority of pupils (mainly except those studying in private international schools). Some public comment within Hong Kong doubted the wisdom of introducing free junior secondary education at this time. There was, however, quite widespread support for one of the consequences of the change: the abolition of the secondary school entrance examination.

Demonstrations by pupils of the Precious Blood Golden Jubilee Secondary School during May and June brought to light not only financial malpractice at the school itself, but also allegations about the lack of communication between the government Education Department, the school authorities, and the teachers and pupils.

To achieve an overview of the series of specific policy discussion papers [green papers] and policy statements [white papers] that appeared in the 1970s or were about to appear in the early 1980s, the government decided to launch an "overall review of education."

1982 An international panel of visitors had been appointed in June 1981 in close consultation with the OECD, and began visits to schools, government offices, other educational agencies, and pressure groups in October 1981 and March 1982. The panel of visitors (also known as the Llewellyn Commission after its chairman) delivered its report to the Hong Kong government in November, although it was not released to the public until May of the following year. The commission defined Hong Kong's current problem as "the balancing of competing demands for meeting quantitative shortfalls against qualitative improvement," endorsed criticisms of the lack of participation in policymaking by practicing educators, arguing that the system seemed overadministered but underplanned, and recommended the establishment of a permanent Education Commission to coordinate policy, advise the governor, and produce planning reports.

1984 The government announced the setting up of an Education Commission to coordinate, consolidate, and give advice on education in Hong Kong.

The Draft Agreement between the Governments of the People's Republic of China and the United Kingdom on the Future of Hong Kong stipulated that the educational system of Hong Kong would remain unchanged after 1997, when China would resume sovereignty over the territory.

1987 An Expatriate English Language Teacher Pilot Scheme was introduced by the government Education Department to evaluate the effects on the schools of having at least two English teachers whose first language was English. The scheme reflected concern about declining language standards, especially in English, since the rapid quantitative expansion of secondary schooling in the late 1970s.

Sustained public discussion began toward the end of the year about the educational connotations of the brain drain which was beginning to affect Hong Kong as growing numbers of the well-educated sought to obtain foreign passports as a form of insurance for themselves and their families against the possible effects of the Chinese resumption of authority over Hong Kong.

1990 The Expatriate English Language Teacher Pilot Scheme was declared a success by the Education Department but attracted criticism from some local teachers, students, and parents.

A proposal by a working group that had been established by the Education Department that pupils should be streamed into schools according to their language skills, with no more than 30 percent being permitted to study in English-medium schools, stimulated considerable (mainly critical) public discussion.

Further debate concerned government assistance at the chronological extremes of schooling, preschool and tertiary education. Some critics claimed that the government was not doing enough to support kindergarten education and that the large increase in tertiary education places (to enable one in four of the age-group to gain a tertiary education place) was unnecessary and/or politically motivated.

Appendix D: Chronology of Important Documents Regarding Hong Kong Education

Report of the Investigating Committee of 1847 on the Chinese Schools of Hong Kong, in W. Lobscheid, *Few Notices on the Extent of Chinese Education and the Government Schools of Hong Kong; with remarks on the history and religious notions of the inhabitants of this island*, 1859.

"The New System prepared by the Rev Dr Legge," *Hong Kong Government Gazette*, 1861, pp. 106–7.

Report of the Education Commission appointed by His Excellency Sir John Pope Hennessy, KCMG . . . to consider certain questions connected with Education in Hong Kong, 1982.

Report of the Education Committee, signed by A.W. Brewin, Ho Kai, and E.A. Irving, 1902.

"An Ordinance to provide for the registration and supervision of certain schools" (The Education Ordinance), *Hong Kong Government Gazette*, August 8, 1913, pp. 344–48.

E.A. Irving, *The Educational System of Hong Kong* (Hong Kong: Government Printer, 1914).

E. Burney, *Report on Education in Hong Kong*, 1935, published on behalf of the Government of Hong Kong by the Crown Agents of the Colonies.

N.G. Fisher, *Report on Educational Expenditure in Hong Kong*, 1950.

Report of the Committee on Higher Education (the "Keswick Report"), 1952.

Report of the Committee on Technical Education and Vocational Training (the "Burt Report"), 1953.

W.I. Jennings and D.W. Logan, *On the University*, October 1953.

Report of the Fulton Commission, tabled at the Legislative Council, April 1963.

Statement on Government Policy on the Re-organization of the Structure of Primary and Secondary Education, 1963.

Report of the Education Commission, 1964 (by R.M. Marsh and J.R. Sampson).

The White Paper on *Educational Policy*, 1965.

Special Committee on Higher Education: Interim Report, 1966.

Special Committee on Higher Education: Second Interim Report, 1968.

Hong Kong 1970: Address by His Excellency the Governor Sir David Trench to the 1970–1971 Session of the Hong Kong Legislative Council on 1st October, 1970, 1970.

Report of the Board of Education on the Development of Secondary Education in Hong Kong over the next decade (the Green Paper), 1973.

The White Paper on *Secondary Education in Hong Kong over the next decade*, 1974.

The Report on the Certificated Masters' Dispute (the "T.K. Ann Report"), 1976.

The Green Paper on *The Further Development of Rehabilitation Services in Hong Kong*, 1976.

University and Polytechnic Grants Committee of Hong Kong Special Report: October 1965 to June 1976 (1976).

The White Paper on *Integrating the Disabled into the Community*, October 1977.

The Green Paper on *Senior Secondary and Tertiary Education: A Development Programme for Hong Kong over the Next Decade*, November 1977.

The Report on the Precious Blood Jubilee School Dispute (the "Rayson Huang Report"), October 1978.

The White Paper on *Senior Secondary and Tertiary Education*, October 1978.

Report of the Board of Education's Committee on Sixth Form Education, June 1979.

Report of Advisory Committee on Diversification, 1979.

The Green Paper on *Primary Education and Pre-Primary Services*, April 1980.

University and Polytechnic Grants Committee of Hong Kong: Notes on Procedures, 1980.

Government Secretariat (1981) The Hong Kong Education System (Overall Review of the Hong Kong Education System).

The White Paper on *Primary Education and Pre-Primary Services*, July 1981.

A Perspective on Education in Hong Kong: Report by a Visiting Panel (the "Llewellyn Report"), dated November 1982, but not released to the public until May 1983.

The Education Commission Report No. 1, October 1984.

University and Polytechnic Grants Committee of Hong Kong: Report January 1983 to December 1984 (1985).

The Education Commission Report No. 2, August 1986.

The Education Commission Report No. 3, June 1988.

Report of the Working Group on Sixth Form Education, July 1989.

Report of the Working Group set up to review Language Improvement Measures (Education Department), December 1989.

The Education Commission Report No. 4, November 1990.

The School Management Initiative, March 1991.

Appendix E: A Comparison of the Educational Systems of the PRC and Hong Kong

	PRC	Hong Kong
Pupil population	220 million	1 million
Educational goals	Explicitly political—education is to serve proletarian politics, to produce faithful supporters of the Chinese road of socialism and modernization	Apolitical—all-round development of pupils and to fulfill manpower needs
Structure of school system	predominantly 6+6+4	6+5+2+3
Ideological orientation	Socialist and paternalistic	colonial–capitalist and individualistic
Span of universal compulsory education	9-year, partially implemented	9-year, fully implemented
Curriculum control	highly centralized	highly centralized
Curriculum development	state-monopolized and controlled, dominated by academics	government-led but with greater degree of participation by principals and teachers
Curriculum uniformity	highly standardized syllabus and textbooks	uniform syllabus but allows diversities in textbooks
Curriculum arrangement	highly academic and compartmentalized; lacks diversity	academically oriented but recently vocationalized and diversified
Degree of differentiation	streaming after 16+, strong orientation toward science	streaming after 16+, strong academic orientation
Medium of instruction	Chinese for Han-Chinese	90 percent English (in policy, but less in practice)

Selected References

Altbach, P.G., and Kelly, G.P., eds. (1973). *Educational Colonialism*. New York: Longman.
Altbach, P.G., and Kelly, G.P., eds (1984) *Education and the Colonial Experience*. New Brunswick, NJ: Transaction Books.
Anderson, J.E. (1979). *Public Policy-making*. 2d ed. New York: Holt, Rinehart and Winston.
Andors, Phyllis (1983). *The Unfinished Revolution of Chinese Women 1948–1980*. Bloomingdale,: Indiana University Press.
Arai, K. (1984). Political Education in China: A Study of Socialization through Children's Textbooks. *Journal of North East Asian Studies* 3(2).
Archer, M.S. (1979). *Social Origins of Educational Systems*. London: Sage.
Arnstein, S.R. (1969). A Ladder of Citizen Participation. *American Institute of Planning Journal* 35(4): 216–24.
Articles on Hong Kong and Macau Studies (1986). [Zhongshan Daxue Gangao Yanjiu Chengguo Suoyin] (1986). *The Studies of Hong Kong and Macau* [Gangao Yanjiu] (3/4):133–39.
Association for the Advancement of Feminism (1985). *Survey of Women's Community Participation in Hong Kong*. (In Chinese) Hong Kong: Association for the Advancement of Feminism.
Avalos, Beatrice (1982). Neocolonialism and Education in Latin America. In *Education in the Third World*, ed. Keith Watson. London: Croom Helm.
Bailey, S.F. (1983). *The Hong Kong Polytechnic: The First Ten Years*. Hong Kong: Hong Kong Polytechnic.
Bakken, Börge (1988). Backwards Reform in Chinese Education. *The Australian Journal of Chinese Affairs* (19/20): 127–63.
Ball, S.J. (1984). Imperialism, Social Control and the Colonial Curriculum in Africa. In *Defining the Curriculum: Histories and Ethnographies*, ed. Ivor F. Goodson and Stephen J. Ball. London: Falmer.
Bamgbose, Ayo, ed. (1976). *Mother Tongue Education: The West African Experience*. London: Hodder & Stoughton.
Barnett, K.M.A. (1964). Hong Kong before the Chinese: The Frame, the Puzzle and the Missing Pieces. Lecture delivered on 18 November 1963, *Journal of the Hong Kong Branch of the Royal Asiatic Society* 4: 42–67.
Basic Law of the Hong Kong Special Administrative Region of the People's Republic of China (1990). Hong Kong: The Consultative Committee for the Basic Law.

Basler, B. (1989). English Language follows empire out of Hong Kong. *The New York Times*, April 16.
Bastid, Marianne (1987). Servitude or Liberation? The Introduction of Foreign Educational Practices and Systems to China from 1840 to the Present. *China's Education and the Industrialized World: Studies in Cultural Transfer*, ed. Ruth Hayhoe and Marianne Bastid, Armonk, NY: M.E. Sharpe.
Bauer, R. (1984). The Hong Kong Cantonese Speech Community. Manuscript, Centre of Asian Studies, University of Hong Kong.
Bell, L.A. (1988). School as an Organization: A Reappraisal. In *Culture and Power in Educational Organizations*, ed. Adam Westoby. Milton Keynes, London: Open University Press, 3–14.
Ben David, J., and Collins, R. (1966). Social Factors in the Origin of a New Science: The Case of Psychology. *American Sociological Review* 31(4).
Bentley, M.W. (1988). Language, Culture, and Education in Hong Kong before 1941. Seminar paper at the Center of Asian Studies, University of Hong Kong, 10 November 1988.
Benton, G. (1983). *The Hong Kong Crisis.* London: Pluto Press.
Benveniste, G. (1977). *The Politics of Expertise.* 2d ed. San Francisco: Boyd and Fraser
Berman, Edward H. (1979). Foundations, United States Foreign Policy and African Education. *Harvard Educational Review* 49(2).
Bierstedt, R. (1964). Legitimacy. In *Dictionary of the Social Sciences.* New York: The Free Press, p. 386.
Blomfield, B., and Pierson, H.D. (1987). A Survey of Language Use in Hong Kong. Special Report, The Institute of Linguists Education Trust, Hong Kong Regional Society.
Boli, J.; Ramirez, Franscisco O.; Meyer, John W. (1986). Explaining the Origins and Expansion of Mass Education. In *New Approaches to Comparative Education*, ed. Philip G. Altbach and Gail P. Kelly. Chicago: University of Chicago Press.
Bond, M. (1985). Language as a Carrier of Ethnic Stereotypes in Hong Kong. *Journal of Social Psychology* 125: 53–62.
Bray, Mark (1986). Student Loans for Higher Education: The Hong Kong Experience in International Perspective. *Higher Education* 15: 343–54.
Bray, Mark (1989). Asian Systems of Education: Their Foundations and Cultural Biases. *Perspectives in Education* 5(4).
Brimer, A., ed. (1985). The Effects of the Medium of Instruction on the Achievement of Form 2 Students in Hong Kong Secondary Schools. Study conducted by a team of researchers in the Faculty of Education in the University of Hong Kong and the Education Department of the Hong Kong Government, December.
Brimer, Allan, and Griffin, Patrick (1985). *A Study of Mathematics Achievement in Hong Kong.* Hong Kong: The Centre of Asian Studies, University of Hong Kong.
British Council (1987–1989). *Statistics of Students Abroad in the United Kingdom 1984/85, 1985/86, 1986/87.* London: British Council.
Broadfoot, P. (1980). Rhetoric and Reality in the Context of Innovation: An English Case Study. *Compare* 10(2).
Bu Donxin (1986). One Country, Two Systems and Academic Exchange between Guangdong and Hong Kong [Yiguo Lianzhi Yu Yuegang Guanxi Xueshu Jiaoliu]. *Social Sciences in Guangdong* (2):20–25.
Bullivant, B. (1981). *The Pluralist Dilemma in Education: Six Case Studies.* Sydney: Allen and Unwin.
Burma, Ian (1990). The Last Days of Hong Kong. *The New York Review of Books* 37 (6):41–46.

Burney, E. (1935). *A Report on Education in Hong Kong*. Hong Kong: Noronha.
Burns, J.P. (1980). Representative Bureaucracy and the Senior Civil Service in Hong Kong. *Hong Kong Journal of Public Administration* 2(1).
Burns, J.P., and Scott, I. (1984). *The Hong Kong Civil Service: Personnel Policies and Practices*. Hong Kong: Oxford University Press.
Burns, J.P., and Scott, I. (1988) *The Hong Kong Civil Service and Its Future*. Hong Kong: Oxford University Press.
Carnoy, Martin (1974). *Education as Cultural Imperialism*. New York: David McKay.
Carnoy, Martin (1985). *The State and Political Theory*. Princeton: Princeton University Press.
Carley, M. (1980 *Rational Techniques in Policy Analysis*. London: Heinemann.
Castells, Manuel (1986). *The Shek Kip Mei Syndrome: Public Housing and Economic Development in Hong Kong*. Hong Kong: Center of Urban Studies and Urban Planning, January.
Census and Statistics Department, Hong Kong (1969). *Hong Kong Statistics 1947–1967*. Hong Kong: Government Printer.
Census and Statistics Department, Hong Kong (1978–1990). *Hong Kong Annual Digest of Statistics*. Hong Kong: Government Printer.
Census and Statistics Department, Hong Kong (1987). *Hong Kong 1986 Bi-Census Main Report Vol. 2*. Hong Kong: Government Printer.
Chan, Ming K., and Kirst, Michael (1986). Hong Kong: The Political Economy of Education. In *Education, Recession, and the World Village*, ed. F. Wirt and G. Harmon. London/Philadelphia: Falmer Press.
Chan, Ming K. (1989). Full Restoration of British Style Education. In *The British Sunset in Hong Kong*. Hong Kong: Hong Kong Economic Journal Press, pp. 42–52.
Chan, Pauline (1985). Education in the People's Republic of China: Tradition and Change. In *Equality and Freedom in Education: A Comparative Study*, ed. Brian Holmes. London: George Allen and Unwin, pp. 178–208.
Chan, Thomas; Chen, E.K.Y.; and Chin, Steve (1986). China's Special Economic Zones: Ideology, Policy and Practice. In *China's Special Economic Zones: Policies, Problems and Prospects*, ed. Y.C. Joa and C.K. Leung. Hong Kong: Oxford University Press, pp. 87–104.
Chang, C.Y. (1986). Bureaucracy and Modernization: A Case Study of the special Economic Zones in China. In *China's Special Economic Zones: Policies, Problems and Prospects*, ed. Y.C. Jao and C.K. Leung. Hong Kong: Oxford University Press, pp. 105–23.
Chen, Edward E.K.Y. (1983). *Multinational Corporations, Technology, and Employment*. London: Macmillan Press.
Cheng, Daphne (1990). Mainland Offer to Ease Work Shortage. *South China Morning Post*, May 9.
Cheng, Irene (1962). Women Students and Graduates. In *University of Hong Kong: The First 50 Years, 1911–1961*, ed. B. Harrison. Hong Kong: Hong Kong University Press.
Cheng, Joseph Y.S. (1986a). The Changing Political Culture of the Hong Kong Chinese. In *Hong Kong in Transition*, ed. Joseph Cheng. Hong Kong: Oxford University Press.
Cheng, Joseph Y.S. (1986b). *Hong Kong in Transition*. Hong Kong: Oxford University Press.
Cheng, Joseph Y.S. (1988). The Draft Basic Law: Messages for Hong Kong People. In *The Draft Basic Law of Hong Kong: Analysis and Documents*, ed. Hungdah Chiu. Baltimore: University of Maryland School of Law, pp. 7–48.
Cheng Kai Ming (1983). Participatory Educational Planning: The Position of Educational Bodies in Hong Kong. M.Ed. dissertation, University of Hong Kong.
Cheng Kai Ming (1986). Traditional Values and Western Ideas: Hong Kong's dilem-

mas in Education. *Asian Journal of Public Administration* 8(2).

Cheng Kai Ming (1987). The Concept of Legitimacy in Educational Policy-Making: Alternative Explanations of Two Policy Episodes in Hong Kong. Ph.D. Dissertation, University of London Institute of Education.

Cheng Kai Ming (1988). Educational Policy-Making in Hong Kong. Working paper, Department of Education, University of Hong Kong.

Cheng Kai Ming (1990a). *Educational Planning, Administration and Management in Asia and the Pacific: A Regional Study*. Working document for the International Congress on Planning and Management of Educational Development, Mexico, 26–30 March.

Cheng Kai Ming (1990b). Financing Education in Mainland China: What Are the Real Problems? *Issues and Studies*, March: 54–75.

Cheng, N.L. et al. (1973). *At What Cost? Instruction through the English Medium in Hong Kong*. Hong Kong: Shum Shing Co.

Cheng, T.C. (1939). Changes in Local Vernacular Schools. *Hong Kong University Journal of Education*, January: 46–52.

Cheng, T.Y. (1982). *The Economy of Hong Kong*. Hong Kong: Far East Publications.

Cheung, T.S. (1979). The Zig-zag Course of Educational Development in Mainland China over the Past Three Decades. *Ming Pao Monthly* (Hong Kong) 14(10):107–13.

Cheung Yat-shing (1987). A Survey of the Motivation in Learning and the Practical Use of Putonghua, *Institute of Language in Education Journal* [in Chinese], vol. 3.

China after Mao (1984). Beijing Review Special Feature Series. Beijing: Beijing Review.

China's Economic Reform Studies Association [Zhongguo Jingji Gaige Yanjiuhui], ed. (1987). *Dialogues on Reform and Open Policies* [*Gaige Yu Kaifang Duihualu*]. Beijing: Jingji Kexue Chubanshe.

Chinese University of Hong Kong (n.d.). The Vice-Chancellor's Report, *A New Era Begins, 1975–78*. Hong Kong: The Chinese University of Hong Kong.

Ching S., and Sweeting, A.E. (1979). Pre-School or Prep-School? The Dilemma of Kindergarten Education in Hong Kong. Privatley published pamphlet.

Ching, S., and Sweeting, A.E. (1988). The Marriage of Chinese Cultural Tradition with Modern Kindergarten Practice in Hong Kong: A Question of Compatibility. Paper delivered to the International Conference on Chinese Cultural Tradition and Modern Education. The Chinese University of Hong Kong, October.

Choi, Frank (1988). Education Report Criticized for Promoting Elitist System. *Hong Kong Standard*, October 25.

Choi Po King (1988). Cultural Identity and Colonial Rule: The Hong Kong–China Connection. Paper presented at the Chinese University of Hong Kong, Conference on Chinese Cultural Tradition and Modern Education, November 7.

Chu, David, K.Y., and Kwan-yiu Wong (1985). Modernization and the Lessons of the Special Economic Zones. In *Modernization in China: The Case of the Shenzhen Special Economic Zone*, ed. Kwan-yiu Wong and David K.Y. Chu. Oxford: Oxford University Press, pp. 208–17.

Church, Robert (1976). *Education in the United States: An Interpretive History*. New York: The Free Press.

Civil Service Branch (1986). *Civil Service Personnel Statistics*. Hong Kong: Civil Service Branch, Government Secretariat. Mimeo.

Clark, John (1990). Address to the Conference on Management of Higher Education, Hong Kong Polytechnic, February 19–20.

Cleverley, John (1985). *The Schooling of China*. Sydney: George, Allen & Unwin.

Clignet, R. (1984). Damned If You Do, Damned If You Don't: The Dilemmas of Colonizer-Colonized Relations. In *Education and the Colonial Experience*, ed. Philip G. Altbach and Gail P. Kelly. New Brunswick, NJ: Transaction Books.

Coleman, J. (1968). The Concept of Equality of Educational Opportunity. *Harvard Educational Review* 38: 7–22.
Collins, Randall (1977). Some Comparative Principles of Educational Stratification. *Harvard Educational Review* 47.
Connolley, W., ed. (1984). *Legitimacy and the State*. Oxford: Basil Blackwell.
Cremer, R.D., and Choy, K.Y. (1988). *From Shekou Industrial Zone to the Opening of Coastal China—the Emergence of Zoning as a National Economic Strategy for Development*. Macau: Chinese Economic Research Centre, University of East Asia.
Croll, Elisabeth (1978). *Feminism and Socialism in China*. London: Routledge & Kegan Paul.
Crozier, M. (1964). *The Bureaucratic Phenomenon*. London: Tavistock.
Dahl, R.A. (1984). *Modern Political Analysis*. 4th ed. Englewood Cliffs, NJ: Prentice-Hall.
Decision of the Central Committee of the Communist Party on Reform of the Economic Structure (1984). Hong Kong: Joint Publishing Co.
De Francis, J. (1984). *The Chinese Language*. Honolulu: The University of Hawaii Press.
Deffs, Robert (1990). Hardliners Hit Back. *Far Eastern Economic Review*, 10 May: 9–10.
Deng, Xiaoping (1984). *Selected Works of Deng Xiaoping*. Beijing: Foreign Languages Press.
Deng Xiaoping (1987). *Speeches and Writings*. Oxford: Pergamon.
Deng Xiaoping (1990). Maintain the Prosperity and Stability of Hong Kong. *The Birth of the Basic Law*. Hong Kong: Wen Wei Publishing Co.: 185
Department of Employment, Education and Training, Canberra, Australia (1987–1989). *Private Overseas Student Statistics*.
Education Commission (1984). *Education Commission Report No. 1*. Hong Kong: Government Printer.
Education Commission (1986). *Education Commission Report No. 2*. Hong Kong: Government Printer.
Education Commission (1988). *Education Commission Report No. 3*. Hong Kong: Government Printer.
Education Commission (1990). *Education Commission Report No. 4*. Hong Kong: Government Printer.
Education Department Triennial Survey (1958–61).
Education Department (1971). *Education Regulations*, cap. 279, section 84. Hong Kong: Government Printer.
Education Department (1976). *General Schools Circular No. 101/76*. Hong Kong, August 6.
Education Department (1981a). *Report of the Working Party Set Up to Review the Secondary School Places Allocation SSPA System*. Hong Kong: Government Printer.
Education Department (1981b). *General Guidelines on Moral Education in Schools*. Hong Kong: Government Printer.
Education Department (1983a). *Report of the Allocation of Senior Secondary School Places— 1981–83 Cycle*. Hong Kong: Government Printer.
Education Department (1983b). *Report of the 1983 Junior Secondary School Assessment*. Hong Kong: Government Printer.
Education Department (1985a). *Guidelines on Civic Education in Schools*. Hong Kong: Government Printer.
Education Department (1985b). *Report of the Working Group Set Up to Review the Secondary School Place Allocation System*. Hong Kong: Government Printer.
Education Department (1986a). *Guidelines on Sex Education in Secondary Schools*. Hong Kong: Government Printer.

Education Department (1986b). *Report of the Working Party on the Review of the JSEA System*. Hong Kong: Government Printer.
Education Department (1989a). *Report of the Working Group Set Up to Review Language Improvement Measures*. Hong Kong: Government Printer.
Education Department (1989b). *Institute of the Language in Education Annual Report*. Hong Kong: Government Printer.
Education Department (1989c). Education Bulletin, Ref. No. 1/4466/69/04/89.
Education Department (1989d). *Report of the 1989 Junior Secondary Assessment*. Hong Kong: Government Printer.
Education Department (1989e). *Report of the Working Group on Sixth Form Education*. Hong Kong: Government Printer.
Education Department (relevant years). *Annual Summary*. Hong Kong: Government Printer.
Endacott, G.B. (1987). *A History of Hong Kong*. Hong Kong: Oxford University Press.
Engel, J.M. (1960). Higher Education for Women in Hong Kong and Scope for Employment for Highly Educated Women. *Journal of Education* (University of Hong Kong) (18):9–13.
Ethridge, James M. (1988). *Changing China: The New Revolution's First Decade, 1979–1988*. Beijing: New World Press.
Fafunwa, A. Babs (1975). Education in the Mother Tongue: A Nigerian Experiment. *West African Journal of Education* 19(2).
Fagerlind, Ingemar, and Saha, Lawrence J. (1983). *Education and National Development: A Comparative Perspective*. Oxford: Pergamon Press.
First, R. (1970). *The Barrel of a Gun: Political Power in Africa and the Coup d'Etat*. London: Allen Lane.
Fishman, J. (1989). *Language and Ethnicity in Minority Sociolinguistic Perspective*. Philadelphia: Multilingual Matters.
Fok, K.C. (1990). *Lecture Notes on Hong Kong History*. Hong Kong: The Commercial Press.
Fong, M.Y. (1974). *The First Hundred Years of Hong Kong Education*. Hong Kong: China Learning Institute. (In Chinese.)
Forrest, R.A.D. (1965). *The Chinese Language*. London: Faber and Faber.
Freire, P. (1971). *Pedagogy of the Oppressed*. London: Penguin.
Fu, G.S. (1975). *A Hong Kong Perspective: English Language Learning and the Chinese Student*. University of Michigan: Comparative Education Dissertation, Series 28.
Fu, G.S. (1979). Bilingual Education in Hong Kong: A Historical Perspective. Working Papers in Language and Language Teaching. Language Centre, University of Hong Kong.
Fu, G.S. (1987) The Hong Kong Bilingual. In *Language Education in Hong Kong*, ed. Robert Lord and Helen N.L. Cheng. Hong Kong: The Chinese University Press.
Fu, G.S., and Iu, Pui-to (1987). Language Attitudes and the Social Order in Hong Kong after 1997. Paper presented to the conference of the Association Internationale de Linguistique Appliqué, Sydney.
Fu, G.S. and Iu, P.T. (1988). Language Attitudes and the Social Order in Hong Kong after 1997. Applied Linguistics Association of Australia, Occasional Paper No. 10: 135–49.
Fung, Julia (1980). Women and Architecture—A Budding Romance. *Asian Architect and Builder* 9(5):17–22.
Fung Yee Wang (1986). Education. In *Hong Kong in Transition*, ed. Joseph Y.S. Cheng. Hong Kong: Oxford University Press.
Gan Changqiu (1989). *A Textbook of Hong Kong's Economy [Xianggang Jingji Jiaocheng]*.Guangzhou: Zhongshan University Press.

Gao Guang et al. (1988). *Studies of Class Structure in China's Primary Stage of Socialism* [Zhongguo Shenhuizhuyi Chuji Jieduan Jiezi Jiegou Yanjiu]. Beijing: Zhonggong Zhongyang Dangxiao Chubanshe.
Gardner, R.C., and Lambert, W.E., (1972). *Attitudes and Motivation in Second Language Learning*. Rowley, MA: Newbury House.
Gasper, Barbara (1989). Keypoint Secondary Schools in China: The Persistence of Tradition? *Compare* 19(1):5–20.
Gaziel, H. (1980). Advisory Councils in a Centralised Educational System: A Case-Study from France. *European Journal of Education* 15(4):399–407.
Gibbons, John (1982). The Issue of the Language of Instruction in the Lower Forms of Hong Kong Secondary Schools. *Journal of Multilingual and Multicultural Development* (3): 117–28.
Gifford, Prosser, and Weiskel, Timothy (1971). African Education in a Colonial Context: French and British Styles. In *France and Britain in Africa*, ed. Prosser Gifford and Wm. Roger Louis. New Haven: Yale University Press.
Giles, H.; Bourhis, R.Y.; and Taylor, D.W. (1977). Toward a Theory of Language in Ethnic Group Relations. In *Language, Ethnicity and Intergroup Relations*, ed. H. Giles. New York: Academic Press.
Ginsberg, M. (1965). *On Justice in Society*. Harmondsworth: Penguin.
Giroux, Henry A. (1983). Theories of Reproduction and Resistance in the New Sociology of Education. *Harvard Educational Review* 53:257–93.
Goodson, I., ed. (1987). *International Perspectives in Curriculum History*. London: Croom Helm.
Griffiths, A.P. (1960). How Can One Person Represent Another? *Aristotelian Society*, Supplement, 34: 187–208.
Griffiths, R.C. (1984). Hong Kong University and Polytechnic Grants Committee. *Higher Education* 13: 545–52.
Guldin, Gregory (1977). Overseas at Home: The Fujianese of Hong Kong. PhD. dissertation, University of Wisconsin at Madison.
Habermas, J. (1973, trans. 1975). *Legitimation Crisis*. Trans. T. McCarthy. Frankfurt: Suhrkamp Verlag. Boston: Beacon Press.
Hao Keming et al. (1987). *A Study of China's Higher Education Structure* [Zhongguo Gaodeng Jiaoyu Jiegou Yanjiu]. Beijing: Renmin Chubanshe.
Harbison, F., and Myers, C.A. (1964). *Education, Manpower and Economic Growth: Strategies of Human Resource Development*. New York: McGraw-Hill
Harris R. (1989). *The Worst English in the World: An Inaugural Lecture from the Chair of English Language*. Hong Kong: Hong Kong University.
Hawkins, John H. (1983a). The People's Republic of China. In *Schooling in East Asia: Forces of Change*, ed. R.M. Thomas and T. Neville. Oxford: Pergamon, pp. 137–88.
Hawkins, John H. (1983b). *Education and Social Change in the People's Republic of China*. New York: Praeger.
Hayes, J. (1977). *The Hong Kong Region, 1850–1911: Institutions and Leadership in Town and Countryside*. Hamden, CT: Archon.
Henderson, Jeffrey (1987). Hong Kong: High Technology Production and the Makings of a Regional Core. In *Global Option: Society, Space, and the Internationalization of High Technology Production*, ed. J. Henderson. London: Croom Helm.
Henze, Jurgen (1987). Educational Modernization as a Search for Higher Efficiency. In *China's Education and the Industrialized World*, ed. Ruth Hayhoe and Marianne Bastid. Armonk, NY: M.E. Sharpe.
Ho, Albert C.Y. (1988). Autonomy. In *The Basic Law and Hong Kong's Future*, ed. Peter Wesley-Smith and Albert Chen. Hong Kong: Butterworth, pp. 294–308.

Ho Suk-ching (1981). The Era of the Female Managers: Looking Back and Looking Forward. *Hong Kong Manager* 17: 8–11.

Ho Suk-ching (1984). Women's Labor-force Participation in Hong Kong, 1971–1981. Journal of Marriage and the Family 46: 947–54.

Ho Suk-ching (1985). Women Managers in Hong Kong: A Content Analysis of the Recruitment Advertisements. *Equal Opportunities International* 4(2):30–33.

Hong Kong Government (1974). *White Paper: Secondary Education in Hong Kong over the Next Decade*. Hong Kong: Government Printer.

Hong Kong Government (1978). *White Paper: The Development of Senior Secondary and Tertiary Education*. Hong Kong: Government Printer.

Hong Kong Government (1979). *Report of the Advisory Commission on Diversification*. Hong Kong: Government Printer.

Hong Kong Government (1981). *The Hong Kong Education System*. Hong Kong: Government Secretariat.

Hong Kong Government (1982). *A Perspective on Education in Hong Kong: Report by a Visiting Panel*. Hong Kong: Government Printer.

Hong Kong Government (1984) *A Draft Agreement between the Government of the United Kingdom of Great Britain and Northern Ireland and the Government of the People's Republic of China on the Future of Hong Kong*. Hong Kong: Government Printer.

Hong Kong Government (1985a). *Hong Kong: 1984*. Hong Kong: Government Printer.

Hong Kong Government (1985b). *Universities and Polytechnics Grants Committee of Hong Kong: Interim Report for 1985–88*. Hong Kong: Government Printer.

Hong Kong Government (1985–90). *Vocational Training Council: Annual Reports*. Hong Kong: Government Printer.

Hong Kong Government (1987). *Hong Kong Hansard: Reports of the Sittings of the Legislative Council of Hong Kong*. Session 1986/87. Hong Kong: Government Printer: 2 (20 May).

Hong Kong Government (1988). *Hong Kong 1988: A Review of 1987*. Hong Kong: Government Printer.

Hong Kong Government (1989). *Green Paper: The 1987 Review of Developments in Representative Government*. Hong Kong: Government Printer.

Hong Kong Government (1990a). *Universities and Polytechnics Grants Committee Annual Report*. Hong Kong: Government Printer.

Hong Kong Government (1990b). *Hong Kong 1990: A Review of 1989*. Hong Kong: Government Printer.

Howe, Christopher (1983). Growth, Public Policy, and Hong Kong's Relationship with the People's Republic of China. *China Quarterly* 95:512–33.

Huang Rayson (1984). Commencement Speech, University of Hong Kong.

Huo Guoqiang (1988). *Xianggang zhongxue gailan*. Xianggang: Xianggang zhonghua jidujiao qingnianhui.

Hyman, R., and Brough, I. (1975). *Social Values and Industrial Relations: A Study of Fairness and Equality*. Oxford: Basil Blackwell.

International Standing Conference for the History of Education, Volume 1 (1986). Introduction, Development and Extension of Compulsory Education. Conference Papers for the 8th Session, Parma, Italy, September 3–6.

Irving, E.A. (1905a). The System of Education in Hong Kong. Photocopy from Great Britain, Board of Education Special Report on Educational Subjects 14, pp. 61–132.

Irving, E.A. (1905b). Hong Kong. In *Special Reports on Educational Subjects*. Vol. 14 of *Educational Systems of the Chief Crown Colonies and Possessions of the British Empire, Including Reports on the Training of Native Races*. London: Board of Education.

Jao, Y.C. (1983). Hong Kong's Role in Financing China's Modernization. In *China and Hong Kong: The Economic Nexus*, ed. A.J. Youngson. Hong Kong: Oxford University Press.
Jao, Y.C.; Leung Chi-keung; Wesley-Smith, Peter; and Wong, Siu-lun (1985). *Hong Kong and 1997: Strategies for the Future*. Hong Kong: Centre of Asian Studies, University of Hong Kong.
Jennings, R.E. (1977). *Education and Politics: Policy-making in Local Education Authorities*. London: B.T. Batsford.
Johnson, Keith (1983a). Language Policy in Education in Hong Kong. *Asian Journal of Public Administration* 5(2).
Johnson, Keith (1986). Medium of Instruction: Policies and Options. *Interflow* 49, University of Hong Kong.
Johnson, P.; Giles, H.; and Bourhis, R.Y. (1977). The Viability of Ethnolinguistic Vitality: A Reply to Husband and Khan. *Journal of Multilingual and Multicultural Development* 4:255–269.
Jurgen, Henze (1987). Educational Modernization as a Search for Higher Efficiency. In *China's Education and the Industrialized World*, ed. Ruth Hayhoe and Marianne Bastid. Armonk, NY: M.E. Sharpe, pp. 252–70.
Karabel, Jerome, and Halsey, A.H., eds. (1977). *Power and Ideology in Education*. New York: Oxford University Press.
Karlgren, B. (1949). *The Chinese Language*. New York: The Ronald Press Company.
Kaunda, Martin (1973). Post-Secondary Education by Correspondence: An African Experience. In *Correspondence Education in Africa*, ed. Antoine Kabwase and Martin Kaunda. London: Routledge & Kegan Paul.
Kelly, Gail P. (1978). Colonial Schools in Vietnam: Policy and Practice. In *Education and Colonialism*, ed. Philip G. Altbach and Gail P. Kelly. New York: Longman.
Kelly, Gail P. (1984). Colonialism, Indigenous Society, and School Practices: French West Africa and Indo-China. In *Education and the Colonial Experience*, ed. P.G. Altbach and G.P. Kelly. New Brunswick, NJ: Transaction Books, pp. 9–32.
King, Edmund (1984). Chinese Educational Development in Comparative Perspective. *Comparative Education* 20(1):165–81.
King, K. (1985). Open and Closed Universities: North and South. In *Current Developments in Higher Education: Proceedings of a Symposium Organized by the Society of Hong Kong Scholars*. Hong Kong: Longman.
Kirkbride, Paul; Tan, Sara F.Y.; and Ko, Gilbert (1989). *Emigration from Hong Kong: Evidence from Professionals*. Hong Kong: Institute of Personnel Management.
Klitgaard, Robert E. (1986). *Elitism and Meritocracy in Developing Countries*. London: The Johns Hopkins Press.
Knorr, K.D. (1977). Policymakers' Use of Social Science Knowledge: Symbolic or Instrumental. In *Using Social Research in Public Policy-making*, ed. C. Weiss. Lexington, MA: D. C. Heath, pp. 165–82.
Kogan, M. (1975). *Educational Policy-Making: A Study of Interest Groups and Parliament*. London: George Allen & Unwin.
Kogan, M. (1980). *Relationship between Educational Policy, Planning and Politics*. Paris: OECD. Mimeograph.
Kogan, M. (1986). *Education Accountability: An Analytic Overview*. London: Hutchinson.
Kogan, M., Boyle, E.; and Crosland, A. (1971). *The Politics of Education*. Harmondsworth: Penguin.
Kracke, E.A. (1957). Religion, Family and Individual in the Chinese Examination System. In *Chinese Thoughts and Social Institutions*, ed. John K. Fairbank. Chicago: University of Chicago Press.

Kwo, Ora (1989). Language Education in a Changing Economic and Political Context: The Teaching of Putonghua in Hong Kong Schools. Paper presented at the First Hong Kong Conference on Language and Society.

Kwo, Ora (In press). Language Priorities in a Changing Political Context: The Teaching of Putonghua in Hong Kong Schools. *Journal of Multicultural and Multilingual Development.*

Kwo, Ora, and Bray, Mark (1987). Language and Education in Hong Kong: New Policies but Unresolved Problems. *RELC Journal* 18(1).

Kwok, D.M. (1988). Language Attitudes and Tri-Lingual Oral Learning during Hong Kong's Countdown toward being a Post-Colonialistic Region of China. Paper presented at the First Hong Kong Conference on Language and Society. April.

Kwong, J. (1985). Changing Political Culture and Changing Curriculum: An Analysis of Language Textbooks in the People's Republic of China, *Comparative Education* 21(2).

Kwong, Julia (1988). *Cultural Revolution in China's Schools.* Stanford: Hoover Institution.

Kwong, Paul; Liu Pak-wai; and Tang, Stephan (1989). Functional Core of the Labor Force: Toward the Retention of Key Personnel in Hong Kong. Hong Kong: Economics Department, Chinese University of Hong Kong, Manuscript.

Lai Wong May-ling (1982). Civil Attitudes towards Women in Hong Kong. M. Soc. Sc. dissertation. University of Hong Kong.

Lau, E. (1988). A Language Problem. *Far Eastern Economic Review* 37 (7):34

Lau Pui-king (1986). Economic Relations between Hong Kong and China. In *Hong Kong in Transition,* ed. Joseph Y.S. Cheng. Hong Kong: Oxford University Press, pp. 235–67.

Lau Siu-kai (1982). *Society and Politics in Hong Kong.* Hong Kong: The Chinese University of Hong Kong Press.

Lau Siu-kai (1987). *Decolonization without Independence: The Unfinished Political Reforms of the Hong Kong Government.* Hong Kong: Institute of Social Research Center.

Lau Siu-kai (1988). *Basic Law and the New Political Order.* Hong Kong: Centre for Asian Studies, The Chinese University of Hong Kong.

Lau Siu-kai (1990). "Decolonization without Independence and the Poverty of Political Leaders in Hong Kong. Hong Kong: The Chinese University of Hong Kong, Hong Kong Institute of Asian Pacific Studies, Occasional Paper No. 1.

Lau Siu-kai and Kuan Hsin-chi (1986). The Changing Political Culture of the Hong Kong Chinese. In *Hong Kong in Transition,* ed. Joseph Y.S. Cheng. Hong Kong: Oxford University Press.

Lau Siu-kai and Kuan Hsin-chi (1988). *The Ethos of the Hong Kong Chinese.* Hong Kong: The Chinese University of Hong Kong Press.

Law, K.C.D. (1979). A History of Adult Education in Hong Kong: An Analysis of Role, Scope, and Change from 1955–1975. Ph.D. dissertation, Florida State University.

Learning Document for the Fifth Plenum of the CPC Thirteenth Central Committee: Questions and Answers *[Xuexi Shisanjie Wuzhong Quanhui Wenjian: Wenti Jieda]* (1989). Beijing: Falu Chubanshe, November.

Lee, M.K. (1982). Emerging Patterns of Social Conflict in Hong Kong Society. In *Hong Kong in the 1980s,* ed. Joseph Y.S. Cheng, Hong Kong: Summerson Eastern Publishers.

Lee, W.O. (1989). The Search for Excellence and Relevance in Education: Japan's Fourth Educational Reform Proposal. *British Journal of Educational Studies* 39(1):17–32.

Lei Qiang et al. (1988). *Hong Kong Higher Education [Xianggang Gaodeng Jiaoyu].* Guangdong: Guangdong Gaodeng Jiaoyu Chubanshe.

Lei Qiang and Chen Lijun (1986). Developing Intelligence in Guangzhou and Macau by Means of Hong Kong's Experience [Cong Xianggang Zhili Kaifa Kan Suiao Zhili Kaifa de Tujing]. *The Studies of Hong Kong and Macau* (3–4):116–31.
Lethbridge, H.J. (1979). *Hong Kong: Stability and Change.* Hong Kong: Oxford University Press.
Leung, Stanley, and Chiu Kit-Ying (1986). China Graduates Face Tough Times in HK. *South China Morning Post,* 8 August.
Li, R. (1988). *The Language Atlas of China.* London: Longman Books.
Lindblom, C.E. (1980). *The Policy-making Process.* 2d ed. Englewood Cliffs, NJ: Prentice-Hall.
Lipsky, M. (1980). *Street-Level Bureaucracy: Dilemmas of the Individual in Public Services.* New York: Russell Sage Foundation.
Little, Angela (1988). Learning from Developing Countries: An Inaugural Lecture. Department of International and Comparative Education, University of London Institute of Education.
Liu, Wing-kei Spencer (1990). The Role of Teachers as a Political Force in the Period of Transition: A Case Study of the Professional Teachers Union. Master's thesis, University of Hong Kong.
Llewellyn, Sir John (Chairman) (1982). *A Perspective on Education in Hong Kong: Report by a Visiting Panel.* Hong Kong: Government Printer.
Lo, H.L. (1963). *Hong Kong and its External Communications before 1842: The History of Hong Kong prior to British Arrival.* Hong Kong: Institute of Chinese Culture.
Lofstedt, Jan-Ingvar (1984). Educational Planning and Administration in China. *Comparative Education* 20(1):57–71.
Lord, R., and T'sou, B. (1985). *The Language Bomb.* Hong Kong: Longman Books.
Lord, R., and Cheng, Helen N.L., eds. (1987). *Language Education in Hong Kong.* Hong Kong: The Chinese University Press.
Louie, Kam (1984). Salvaging Confucian Education [1949–1983]. *Comparative Education* 20 (1):27–38.
Lu Tongseng and Pei Haolin (1989). *Studies on the Economies of Taiwan and Hong Kong* [Taiwan Xiangang Jingji Yanjiu]. Zhenjian: Nongcun Duwu Chubanshe.
Lu Zufa et al., eds. (1985). *China's Urban Reform: The New Look of Shenzhen Special Economic Zone.* China's Urban Reform Series. Hong Kong: Economic Information and Agency and The Red Flag Publishing House.
Luk, Hung-Kay Bernard (1984). Lu Tzu-Chun and Ch'en Jung-Kun: Two Exemplary Figures in the Ssu-shu Education of Pre-War Urban Hong Kong. In *From Village to City: Studies in the Traditional Roots of Hong Kong Society,* ed. David Faure, James Hayes, and Alan Birch. Hong Kong: Centre of Asian Studies.
Luk, Hung-Kay Bernard (1989a). Education. In *The Other Hong Kong Report,* ed. T.L. Tsim and B.H.K. Luk. Hong Kong: The Chinese University Press.
Luk, Hung-Kay Bernard (1989b). Chinese Culture in the Hong Kong Curriculum. Paper presented at the annual conference of the Comparative and International Education Society, Harvard University, March 31.
Lukes, S. (1974). Power, A Radical View. *Studies in Sociology.* London: Macmillan.
Lulat, Y. (1988). Education and National Development: The Continuing Problem of Misdiagnosis and Irrelevant Prescriptions. *International Journal of Education Development* 8(4).
Luo Feng (1987). The Formation of Teachers' Professional Faith. *Educational Research,* September: 55–64.
Lyczak, R.; Fu, G.S.; and Ho, A. (1976). Attitudes of Hong Kong Bilinguals towards English and Chinese Speakers. *Journal of Cross-Cultural Psychology* 7:425–36.

Ma Lin (1986). "Commencement Speech at the 34th Session," The Chinese University of Hong Kong.
McGrew, A.G., and Wilson, M.M., eds. (1982). *Decision Making: Approaches and Analysis*. Manchester: Manchester University Press/Open University.
Mackerras, C. (1989). *Western Images of China*. Hong Kong: Oxford University Press.
Mak, Grace C. (1989a). People's Republic of China. In *International Handbook of Women's Education*, ed. G. Kelly. Westport, CT: Greenwood Press.
Mak, Grace C. (1989b). Development and Women's Access to Higher Education: A Comparative Study of the People's Republic of China and Hong Kong. Paper presented at The Chinese University of Hong Kong Conference on Gender Studies in Chinese Societies, Hong Kong.
Manley, J.F. (1983). Neo-pluralism: A Class Analysis of Pluralism I and Pluralism II. *The American Political Science Review* 77:368–83.
Mauger, Peter (1985a). Another Great Leap Forward? *The Times Educational Supplement*, 12 July, p. 11.
Mauger, Peter (1985b). China Breaks with Tradition. *The Times Educational Supplement*, 3 August, p. 8.
Maunder, W.F., et al. (1958). Survey of Student Life. *Journal of the Economics Society*, Hong Kong University: 11–68.
Mellor, Bernard (1980). *The University of Hong Kong: An Informal History*. Vol. 1. Hong Kong: Hong Kong University Press.
Mellor, Bernard (1988). *The University of East Asia: Origin and Outlook*. Hong Kong: UEA Press.
Menzel, J.M. (1963). *The Chinese Civil Service*. Boston: D.C. Heath.
Merelmann, R.M. (1966). Learning and Legitimacy. *American Political Science Review* 60(3):548.
Merton, R.K. (1957). *Social Theory and Social Structure*. Glencoe, IL: The Free Press.
Miners, Norman (1986). *The Governance and Politics of Hong Kong*. 4th ed. Hong Kong: Oxford University Press.
Miners, Norman (1990). Constitution and Administration. In *The Other Hong Kong Report: 1990*, ed. Richard Y.C. Wong and Joseph Y.C. Cheng. Hong Kong: The Chinese University of Hong Kong Press.
Mitchell, R.E. (1972). *Pupil, Parent and School: A Hong Kong Study*. Taipei: The Orient Culture Service.
Moon, B (1987). Who Controls the Curriculum: The Story of New Maths 1960–1980. In *International Perspectives in Curriculum History*, ed. I. Goodson. London: Croom Helm.
Morris, P. (1985). Teachers' Perceptions of the Barriers to the Implementation of a Pedagogic Innovation. *International Review of Education* 18(3).
Morris, P. (1988). The Effect on the School Curriculum of Hong Kong's Return to Chinese Sovereignty in 1997. *Journal of Curriculum Studies* 20(6):509–20.
Morris, P. (In press). Bureaucracy, Professionalization and School Centered Innovation Strategies. *International Review of Education*.
Murray, Thomas R., and Postlethwaite, T. Neville, eds. (1983). *Schooling in East Asia: Forces of Change*. Oxford: Pergamon.
Mushkat, Myron (1982). *The Making of the Hong Kong Administrative Class*. Hong Kong: Centre of Asian Studies, University of Hong Kong.
Mushkat, Myron (1989). *Hong Kong: The Challenge of Transformation*. Hong Kong: Centre of Asian Studies, University of Hong Kong.
Nurullah, Syed, and Naik, J.P. (1951). *A History of Education in India*. Bombay: Macmillan.
Ng Lun Ngai-ha (1984). *Interactions of East and West: Development of Public Education*

in Early Hong Kong. Hong Kong: The Chinese University Press.
Ng, Pedro (1975). *Access to Educational Opportunity: The Case of Kwun Tong.* Hong Kong: The Chinese University of Hong Kong Social Research Centre.
Offe, C. (1984) (J. Keane ed). *Contradictions of the Welfare State.* Cambridge: The MIT Press.
Offe, C. (1984) (J. Keane ed). *Disorganized Capitalism: Contemporary Transformation of Work and Politics.* Cambridge: Polity Press.
Oppenheim, F. (1968). The Concept of Equality. In *International Encyclopedia of the Social Sciences,* vol. 5, pp. 102–7, ed. David Sills.
Pelham, Margery (1956). *Luguard: The Years of Adventure 1858–1898.* London: Collins.
Perspectives on Education in Hong Kong [*Xianggang Jiaoyu Mianmian Guan*] (1988). Guangzhou: Guangdong Renmin Chubanshe.
Peters, B.G. (1977). Insider and Outsider: The Politics of Pressure Group Influence on Bureaucracy. *Administration and Society* 9(2):191–218.
Peters, B.G. (1984). *The Politics of Bureaucracy.* 2d ed. New York: Longman.
Phelps Brown, E.A. (1971). The Hong Kong Economy: Achievements and Prospects. In *Hong Kong: The Industrial Colony,* ed. Keith Hopkins. Hong Kong: Oxford University Press.
Pierson, H.D. (1989). Language Attitudes and Use in Hong Kong: A Case for Putonghua. Paper presented at the First Hong Kong Conference on Language and Society, Hong Kong, April.
Pierson, H.D., and Bond, M. (1981). The Impact of Interviewer Language on the Perceptions of Chinese Bilinguals. Occasional Paper No. 96. Social Research Centre, The Chinese University of Hong Kong.
Pierson, H.D.; Fu. G.S.; and Lee, S.Y. (1980). An Analysis of the Relationship between Language Attitudes and English Attainment of Secondary School Students in Hong Kong. *Language Learning* 30: 289–316.
Pierson, H.D.; Giles, H.; and Young L. (1987). Intergroup Vitality Perceptions during a Period of Political Uncertainty: The Case of Hong Kong. *Journal of Multilingual and Multicultural Development* 8: 451–60.
Podmore, D. (1971). The Population of Hong Kong. In *Hong Kong: The Industrial Colony,* ed. K. Hopkins. Hong Kong: Oxford University Press.
Post, David, and Pong Suet-ling (1989). Socio-economic Indicators and Higher Education Access in Hong Kong. Comparative and International Education Association Annual Meeting, Harvard University, March 31.
Postiglione, Gerard (1986). Higher Education and the Labor Market in Urban Hong Kong. In *Planning and Development in Open Coastal Cities,* ed. L.Y. Choi, K.W. Fong, and Y.W. Kwok. Hong Kong Center of Urban Studies and Urban Planning of the University of Hong Kong.
Postiglione, Gerard (1987). International Higher Education and the Labor Market in Hong Kong: Functions of Overseas and Local Higher Education. *International Education* 17(1):48–54.
Postiglione, Gerard (1988). The Structuring of Ethnicity in Hong Kong. *International Journal of Intercultural Relations* 12: 247–67.
Postiglione, Gerard (1991). Hong Kong Education within Transition. *Comparative Education Review* 35(5) November.
Postiglione, Gerard, and Shui Lai Hung (1986). Educational Expansion in Hong Kong: Contradicting Modes of Explanation. *Educational Research Journal* 1: 95–99.
Present State of Studies of Mainland China on Hong Kong, and Macau, The [Neidi Duiyu Gangao Yangiu Gaikuang, 1986]. *The Studies of Hong Kong and Macau [Gangao Yanjiu]* 1/2: 4–12.

Psacharopoulos, G. (1985). Returns to Education: A Further International Update and Implications. Paper presented at the Comparative and International Education Society Meeting, Stanford University, April.

Purves, W. (1989). Chairman's Statement to Shareholders at the Annual General Meeting on 9 May, Hongkong Bank.

Pye, Lucian W. (1983). The International Position of Hong Kong. *The China Quarterly* (95) September.

Quirk, R. (1886). Speculation on the Future Role of English in Hong Kong and the Implications for Educational Policy. *Future Directions in English Language Teacher Education*, ed. V. Bickley. Hong Kong: Institute of Language in Education.

Rafferty, K. (1990). *City on the Rocks: Hong Kong's Uncertain Future.* New York: Viking, 1990.

Rear, John (1971). One Brand of Politics. In *Hong Kong: The Industrial Economy*, ed. K. Hopkins. Hong Kong: Oxford University Press, p. 55.

Reform of China's Educational Structure: Decision of the CPC Central Committee [Zhonggong Zhongyang Guanyu Jiaoyu Tizhi Gaigede Jueding] (1985). *People's Daily*, May 29.

Reid, S.A. (1987). Validation: Setting the Scene. Paper presented at the conference of the Hong Kong Educational Research Association.

Reynolds, Bruce L. (1978). Two Models of Agricultural Development: A Context for Current Chinese Policy. *China Quarterly* 76 (December): 842–72.

Richardson, J.J., and Jordan, A.G. (1979). The Policy Process. In *Governing under Pressure*. London: Martin Robertson.

Roberts, D., ed. (1990). *Hong Kong 1990*, Hong Kong: Government Information Services.

Rosen, Stanley (1982). *Red Guard Factionalism and the Cultural Revolution in Guangzhou.* Boulder: Westview Press.

Salaff, Janet (1981). *Working Daughters of Hong Kong.* Cambridge: Cambridge University Press.

Salter, B., and Tapper, T. (1981). *Education, Politics and the State.* London: Grant McIntyre.

Sayer, G.R. (1975). *Hong Kong 1841–1862: Birth, Adolescence and Coming of Age* (with new introduction and additional notes by D.M. Emrys Evans). Hong Kong: Hong Kong University Press.

Sayer, G.R. (1975). *Hong Kong 1862–1919: Years of Discretion* (edited and with additional notes by D.M. Emrys Evans). Hong Kong: Hong Kong University Press.

Schon, D. (1973). *Beyond the Stable Sate.* London: Penguin.

Scott, I., and Burns, J.P. (1984). *The Hong Kong Civil Service: Personnel Policies and Practices.* Hong Kong: Oxford University Press, pp. 29–32.

Scott, Ian (1989). *Political Change and the Crisis of Legitimacy in Hong Kong.* Hong Kong: Oxford University Press.

Shawcross, W. (1990). *Kowtow!* Chatto Counterblast, no. 6. London: Chatto Counterblast.

Sinn, Y.Y.E. (1986). The Tung Wah Hospital, 1869–1896: A Study of a Medical, Social and Political Institution in Hong Kong. Ph.D. dissertation, University of Hong Kong.

Sino-British Joint Declaration on the Question of Hong Kong. Hong Kong: Xinhua News Agency, 1984.

Sit, F.S. (1981). The Population of Hong Kong. In *Hong Kong: The Industrial Colony*, ed. K. Hopkins. Hong Kong: Oxford University Press.

Sit, V., and Wong, S.L. (1988). *Hong Kong Manufacturing.* Tokyo: Institute of Developing Economics.

Sit, V.; Wong, S.L.; and Kiang, T.S. (1979). *Small Industry in a Laissez-faire Economy.* Hong Kong: Centre of Asian Studies.
Sixth Five-Year Plan of the People's Republic of China for Economics and Social Development (1981–1985), (1984). Beijing: Foreign Languages Press.
Skeldon, Ronald (1984). Hong Kong and Its Hinterland: A Case of International Rural-to-Urban Migration? Paper presented at the International Geographical Union Symposium No. 6, Commission on Population Geography, Migration, and Cities.
Smith, B. (1976). *Policy Making in British Government: An Analysis of Power and Rationality.* 2d ed. London: Martin Robertson.
So, D. (1988). Implementing Mother Tongue Education amidst Societal Transition from Diglossia to Triglossia in Hong Kong. *Language and Education* 3(1):29–44.
Sparks, D.W. (1978). The Teochiu of Hong Kong. Ph.D. dissertation, University of Texas at Austin.
Suttmeier, Richard P. (1989). Reform, Modernization, and the Changing Constitution of Science in China. *Asian Survey* 24(10) (October): 999–1015.
Sweeting, A.E. (1983). Hong Kong. In *Schooling in East Asia: Forces of Change,* ed. R. Murray Thomas and T. Neville Postlethwaite. Oxford: Pergamon Press, pp. 272–300.
Sweeting, A.E. (1989a). The Reconstruction of Education in Post-War Hong Kong, 1945–54: Variations in the Process of Policy Making. Ph.D. dissertation, University of Hong Kong.
Sweeting, A.E. (1989b). Snapshots from the Social History of Education in Hong Kong: An Alternative to Macro-Mania. *Education Research and Perspectives* 16(1): 3–12.
Sweeting, A.E. (1990). *Education in Hong Kong, pre-1841 to 1941: Fact and Opinion.* Hong Kong: Hong Kong University Press.
Szeto Wah (1987). Teaching Putonghua. *Asiaweek,* 6 September.
Tang, S.L.W. (1981). The Differential Educational Attainment of Children: An Empirical Study of Hong Kong. Ph.D. dissertation, University of Chicago.
Tang, Daniel C.C. (1982). An Evaluation of the Career Patterns and Attitudes of Upper Middle Civil Servants in Hong Kong. M. Soc. Sc. dissertation, University of Hong Kong.
Thirteenth Party Congress and China's Reform, The (1987). Beijing: Beijing Review.
Ting-Chau, Theodora (1980). Women Executives in Hong Kong. *Hong Kong Manager* 16(1):8–12.
Ting Wai (1988). What Will the Basic Law Guarantee?—A Study of the Draft Basic Law from a Political and Comparative Approach. In *The Draft Basic Law of Hong Kong: analysis and Documents,* ed. Hungdah Chiu. Baltimore: University of Maryland School of Law, 49–90.
Topley, M. (1969). The Role of Savings and Wealth among the Hong Kong Chinese. In *Hong Kong: A Society in Transition,* ed. I.C. Jarview. London: Routledge & Kegan Paul.
Tsang, S.Y.S. (1988). *Democracy Shelved: Great Britain, China, and Attempts at Constitutional Reform in Hong Kong, 1945–1952.* Hong Kong: Oxford University Press.
Tsang Wing-kwong (1985a). Equal Opportunity in University Education in Hong Kong. *Education Journal* [in Chinese] (CUHK) 13(1):10–27.
Tsang Wing-kwong (1985). Equality of Educational Opportunity in University, *Education Journal* (CUHK) 13(1):20–27.
Tsim, T.L. (1989). English Proficiency in Hong Kong. Manuscript.
Turner, Matthew (1988). *Made in Hong Kong: A History of Export Design in Hong Kong.* Hong Kong: Urban Council.
Tyler, W.B. (1988). The Organizational Structure of the School. In *Culture and Power in Educational Organizations,* ed. Adam Westoby. Milton Keynes, London: Open University Press, pp. 15–40.

UNESCO (1951). *The Use of Vernacular Languages in Education*. Paris: UNESCO.
University of Hong Kong Faculty of Law (1990). *Hong Kong's Bill of Rights: Problems and Prospects*. Hong Kong: University of Hong Kong Faculty of Law.
Vikner, David W. (1987). The Role of Christian Missions in the Establishment of Hong Kong's System of Education. Ed.D. dissertation, Teachers College, Columbia University.
Wai, S.W. (1986). Secondary Schools Favor Teaching through Chinese. *South China Morning Post*, November 12, p. 3.
Wan Chi-kie. Political Participation of Women in Hong Kong. B. Soc. Sc. thesis, University of East Asia (Macau).
Wan Ho-yee, Condy (1990). Issues of Efficiency and Equity in the District Subsidy Scheme from the Perspective of Parents. Master's thesis, University of Hong Kong.
Wang Gungwu (1988). Commencement speech, University of Hong Kong.
Wang Hsueh-wen (1988). Communist China's Educational Reforms: An Analysis. In *Changes and Continuities in Chinese Communism*, ed. Yu-ming Shaw. Vol. 2, *The Economy, Society, and Technology*. Boulder: Westview Press.
Waters, D.D. (1985). The Planning of Craft and Technician Education in Hong Kong, 1957–1982. Ph.D. dissertation, Loughborough University of Technology.
Watson, K. (1982). Colonialism and Educational Development. In *Education in the Third World*, ed. K. Watson. London: Croom Helm.
Watt, H.K. (1953). *Report of the Working Party on the Organization and Administration of National Vocational Training Programmes in Australia, the Philippines and Japan, Organized by the International Labour Organization Asian Field Office*. Hong Kong: Government Printer.
Weber, M. (1946). *From Max Weber: Essays in Sociology*. London: Routledge & Kegan Paul.
Weber, M. (1947). *The Theory of Social and Economic Organizations*. Trans. A.M. Henderson and T. Parsons. Glencoe: The Free Press.
Weber, Max (1951). *The Religion of China*. New York: The Free Press.
Weiler, H.N. (1985). Politics of Educational Reform. In *Innovation in the Public Sector*, ed. R.L. Merritt and A.J. Merritt. Beverly Hills: Sage, pp. 167–199.
Weiss, C., ed. (1977). *Using Social Research in Public Policy-making*. Lexington: D.C. Heath.
White Paper on Science and Technology No. 1: Directory of China's Policies on Science and Technology [*Kexue Jishu Baipishu Diyihao: Zhongguo Kexue Jishu Zhengce Zhinan*] (1986). Beijing: Xinhua Chubanshe.
Whitehead, C. (1981). Education in British Colonial Dependencies, 1919–39: A Re-Appraisal. *Comparative Education* 17(1):71–80.
Whitehead, C. (1989). Education in Far Away Places: Evidence from the Periphery of the Empire of the Problems of Developing Schooling in British Colonies. *Education Research and Perspectives* 16(1):51–69.
Williams, R. (1965). *The Long Revolution*. Harmondsworth: Penguin.
Wilson, Sir David (1989). Address by the Governor, Sir David Wilson, at the Opening of the 1989/90 Session of Legislative Council on October 11.
Wise, A.E. (1979). *Legislated Learning: The Bureaucratization of the American Classroom*. Berkeley: University of California Press.
Wolf, Margery (1985). *Revolution Postponed: Women in Contemporary China*. Stanford: Stanford University Press.
Wong, C.L. (1982). *A History of the Development of Chinese Education in Hong Kong* (in Chinese). Hong Kong: Po Nen Book Co.
Wong Kwan-yiu and Chu, David K.Y. (1985). Export Processing Zones and Special

Economic Zones as Locomotives of Export-led Economic Growth. In *Modernization in China: The Case of the Shenzhen Special Economic Zone*, ed. Kwan-yiu Wong and David K.Y. Chu. Oxford: Oxford University Press, pp. 1–24.

Wong Pui-kwong (1987). Chinese and Putonghua: A Combined Subject or Two Separate Subjects in a Society Where There Are Three Languages but Only Two Written Codes? [in Chinese]. Paper presented at the conference of the Institute of Language in Education, Hong Kong.

Wong, S. (1975). Development of Adult Education in Hong Kong since World War II. Ph.D. dissertation, Edinburgh University.

Wong, S.L. (1988). *Emmigrant Entrepreneurs: Shanghai Industrialists in Hong Kong*. Oxford University Press: Hong Kong.

World Bank (1975). *China: Issues and Prospects in Education*. Washington, D.C.: The World Bank.

Xianggang Jiaoyu Shouce (1988). Xianggang: Shangwu Shugan.

Xianggang Wenti Wenjian: Xuanji (1985). Beijing: Renmin Chubanshe.

Xiao Cuilin (1988). China's Open-Door Policy in Education: A Content Analysis of the Chinese Education Newspaper. *Compare* 18(2):163–72.

Xu Mingdi, Xu Jianquan, and Guo Sile (1986). An Experimental Reform in China's Primary and Secondary School Systems [Guonei Zhongxiaoxue Xuezhi Gaige Shiyan]. *Education Journal* (CUHK), December: 95–100.

Yee, Albert H. (1989). *A People Misruled: Hong Kong and the Chinese Stepping Stone Syndrome*. Hong Kong: API Press.

Yeung, K.Y. (1989). Manpower Training in New Technologies. Speech to Open the Hong Kong University/UNESCO Conference on the Popularization of Science and Technology, September 4.

Young L.; Giles, H.; and Pierson, H.D. (1986). Sociopolitical Change and Perceived Ethnolinguistic Vitality. *International Journal of Intercultural Relations* 10: 459–69.

Young, M.F.D., ed. (1971). *Knowledge and Control*. London: Collier Macmillan.

Youngson, A.J. (1982). *Hong Kong Economic Growth and Policy*. Hong Kong: Oxford University Press.

Youngson, A.J., ed. (1983). *China and Hong Kong: The Economic Nexus*. Hong Kong: Oxford University Press.

Yuen Yau (1984). *A Historical Study of the Educational System of Hong Kong* [in Chinese]. Hong Kong: Progressive Education Publishers.

Zhao Jian (1987). An Investigation into the Interest of the Students Who Are Sick of Schooling. *Educational Research* (July): 59–62.

Zhao Qiu (1988). *Yiguo liangzhi gailun*. Jilin University Press.

Zhao Xiaowang; Deng Yun; and Zhou Bingyin (1989). *Yige guojia liang zhong zhidu* (Liberation Army Press).

Zheng Deliang (1987). *A Preliminary Study of Hong Kong's Economic Problems* [Xianggang Jingji Wenti Chutan]. Guangzhou: Zhongshan University Press.

Zheng Deliang (1988). *Characteristics of Hong Kong's Development* [Xianggang Jingji Cheng Zhang Techeng]. Guangzhou: Zhongshan University Press.

Zhongshan University Economics Department. *Studies on Hong Kong's Economy* [Xianggang Jingji Kaocha] (1985). Guangdong: Guangdong Renmin Chubanshe.

Zhuang, J., and Thomas, R. M. (1987). Educational Radio and Television: Their Development in Advanced Industrial Societies. In *Educational Technology: Its Creation, Development and Cross-Cultural Transfer*, ed. R. Murray Thomas and Victor N. Kobayashi. Oxford: Pergamon.

Index

Abercrombie, Sir Patrick, 77*n.48*
Academic Aptitude Test, 153
Academy of Social Sciences of China (PRC), 243
ACEC. *See* Advisory Committee on Education in the Colonies
Administration. *See* Bureaucratization
Admissions, university, 12, 257
Adult education, 55, 77*n.44*, 207
Advisory Committee on Diversification of the Economy, 53
Advisory Committee on Education in the Colonies (ACEC), 62
Advisory Committee on Environmental Pollution, 78*n.56*
Advisory Inspectorate, 120, 122, 131
Africa, 62
Aid, financial
  Code of Aid, 13, 25
  fee remissions, 57
  for females, 169, 170–71
  scholarships, 57
  subsidies, 9, 11, 24–25, 113, 157, 158–61, 162–63, 276–77
Alice Memorial Hospital, 79*n.71*
Alumni Association of the Colleges of Education, 155
American Board of Foreign Missions, 84
Anglican Church, 84, 108

Anglo-Chinese College, 84
Antiquities and Monuments Office, 78*n.56*
Apprenticeships, 50, 76*n.42*
Asile de Sainte Enfance, 276
Australia, 90, 94*n.25*, 117, 174, 176, 179*n.43*, 223, 270

Baptist College, 12, 88, 216, 218
Basel Mission, 54
Basic Law, 5, 17, 34*n.11*, 246–47, 269–70
Beijing–Hong Kong Academic Exchange Center, 28, 267
Beijing University, 28, 244
Belilios, E.R., 76*n.44*
Belilios Reformatory, 76*n.44*
Bilingual Law Advisory Committee, 185
Blake, Sir Henry, 76*n.44*
Board of Chinese Vernacular Primary Education, 61
Board of Education, 13, 58, 108, 277
Bought Places Scheme, 25, 158
Brain drain, 63, 64, 65, 67, 120, 150, 164, 176–77, 184, 226–28, 281
Bridgman, Dr. E.C., 84
Brown, Reverend S.G., 60
Brown, S.R., 61
Bureaucratization, 39, 56–60, 79*n.68*, 101

305

Burney, Edmund, 58, 77n.45, 278
Burney Report, 43, 46, 278–79
Burt, S.J.G., 52
Burt Committee, 52, 54

Canada, 68–69, 90, 94n.25, 117, 174, 176, 179n.43, 223
Cantonese (language), 27, 61, 64, 183–200, 203–12
Catholic Board of Education, 156
Catholic Order of the Salesians of Don Bosco, 77n.49
Catholics. *See* Roman Catholic Church
CDC. *See* Curriculum Development Committees
Central School, 60, 76n.42, 85
Certificated Masters Dispute, 59
Certification, 55, 65, 68
Cha, Louis, 34n.11
Chamber of Commerce (U.S.), 9
Chamberlain, Joseph, 76n.44
Chao Zhouese, 27
Characters, Chinese. *See* Chinese characters
Chiang Kai-shek, 81n.86
Child labor, 7, 49
China. *See* People's Republic of China
Chinese (language), 10, 21–22, 61, 63–65, 269, 270. *See also* Cantonese; Putonghua
Chinese characters, 65, 186–87, 205–6
Chinese International School, 208
Chinese Language Movement, 63, 80n.79
Chinese Manufacturers' Association, 53
Chinese University of Hong Kong
admissions, 12
Chinese-medium, 88
creation of, 63, 80n.78, 178n.24
enrollment, 218
four-year program, 15, 16, 112, 269
teacher training, 259
Western influence, 88
women at, 170–71, 178–79n.25
working-class students, 164

Chou-Wang-Erh Kung College, 93n.4
Chu, Dominic, 204
Church of Christ in China, 108
Church of England. *See* Anglican Church
City Polytechnic of Hong Kong, 53, 216, 218
Civics, 45, 75n.24, 118, 120, 254
Civil service, 20–21, 22, 63, 175–76
Class, social. *See* Social class
Clementi College, 62, 63, 278
Code of Aid, 13, 25
Coeducation. *See* Females, education
Colonial Development and Welfare Acts, 62, 77n.47
Colonization, 14, 39–47, 84, 268, 276
Command Paper on the Organization of the Colonial Service, 62
Commission on Child Labour, 49
Committee to Review Technical and Higher Education, 105–6
Communications, 55, 191–94
Communist party, 118, 136. *See also* People's Republic of China
Compradores, 42, 73n.9
Compulsory education, 7, 49, 76n.40, 219
Computer studies, 54
Confucianism, 30
Conservancy Association, 78n.56
Crèches. *See* Nursery schools
Crozier, D.J.S., 67
Cultural tradition, 29–31
Curriculum. *See also* specific subjects
in Anglo-Chinese schools, 120
bureaucracy's influence on, 59
colonization's effect on, 8, 43–44, 84
control mechanisms, 120–22, 142, 144
democratization's effect on, 71
Great Britain's influence on, 120, 270
guidelines, 130–36
industrialization's effect on, 53–54
1997's impact on, 122–41, 142
and politics, 17–18, 118–19, 123

Curriculum *(continued)*
 reform, 18
 School-Based Curriculum Project Scheme (SBCPS), 137, 140–41, 142
 textbooks, 136–37, 211, 249, 269
Curriculum Development Committees (CDC), 120–22, 143
Curriculum Development Council, 59, 280

Day care. *See* Early childhood education
Decolonization, 15, 46, 268–70
Delinquents, 51
Democratization, 39, 69–71, 149–50
Deng Fuxie, 276
Deng Xiaoping, 235–37, 239, 266
Deng Ying-yuan, 276
Department of Technical Education and Industrial Training, 53
Depression, 51, 77n.45
Diocesan Native Female Training School, 276
Diploma inflation, 55, 60
Director of education, 12, 58
Direct Subsidy Scheme (DSS), 11, 24–25, 158–61, 162–63
Discrimination. *See* Racial discrimination
District Boards, 20, 70
District Office scheme, 70
DSS. *See* Direct Subsidy Scheme

Early childhood education, 54–55, 281
Ecology, 54
Economics and Public Affairs (EPA), 118, 123, 124–25, 129, 136
Economy, 23–25, 26, 257. *See also* Industrialization; specific industry, e.g., Textiles
Education Action Group, 155, 156, 157
Educational policy. *See* Policy, educational
Education and Manpower Branch (Government Secretariat), 53, 59

Education Commission, 13–14, 15, 25, 29, 59, 64, 87, 109, 113, 150, 189, 277–78, 281
Education Committee, 42, 57, 84, 277, 278
Education Department, 20, 43, 52, 59, 110, 120, 140, 150, 187–89, 207, 277, 278
Education Ordinance, 12, 45, 57, 168, 255
Education Tax, 76n.40
EEC. *See* European Economic Community
Eitel, Dr. E.J., 54, 61
Elections, 16–17, 71, 112
Electronics, 6
Elementary schools, 50, 76n.41, 278. *See also* Primary schools
Emigration, 9, 21, 63, 65, 66, 81n.87, 117, 223–25. *See also* Brain drain
England. *See* United Kingdom
English (language)
 vs. Cantonese and Putonghaua, 183–200
 international value, 91, 256
 in secondary schools, 42, 44–45, 54, 63, 255, 256, 269, 270
 teachers' knowledge of, 61, 64–65, 281
 at University of Hong Kong, 21, 22, 63, 88, 206
English Schools Foundation, 67
Environment, 54, 55, 78n.56
Environmental Protection Advisory Committee, 78n.56
Environmental Protection Department, 78n.56
EPA. *See* Economics and Public Affairs
Episcopal Church. *See* Anglican Church
Equipment, educational, 258–59
Ethnic groups, 27
European Economic Community (EEC), 49

Evening School for Higher Chinese Studies, 63, 80*n.78*
Examinations. *See also* Hong Kong Examination Authority
  Academic Aptitude Test, 153
  certificate of education, 11–12, 122
  Putonghua proficiency, 211
  Secondary School Entrance Examination (SSEE), 152–53, 158, 162
  standardized testing, 11
  syllabus, 123–30
  university admission, 12, 257
Executive Council, 107
Expatriate English Language Teacher Pilot Scheme, 281
Expatriates, 21, 64, 65, 85–86, 271. *See also* Immigration

Factory schools, 54
Federation of British Industries, 77*n.48*
Feeder and Nominated School System (FNSS), 152–54, 156
Fee remissions. *See* Aid, financial, fee remissions
Females
  education, 167–78, 217
  feminist movement, 54
  working mothers, 54
Filipinos, 66, 67
Financial aid. *See* Aid, financial
First Opium War, 14
Fisher, Norman, 76*n.41*, 279
FNSS. *See* Feeder and Nominated School System
Foreign study, 9–10, 56, 60, 90–96, 94*n.25*, 164, 173–74, 179*n.43*, 216, 220, 223
France, 90
French Sisters of Charity, 84
Friends of the Earth, 78*n.56*
Fujianese, 27

Gender, 11, 169, 173–77. *See also* Females

General Certificate of Education, 71
General Strike and Boycott, 61, 81*n.86*
Geography (subject), 126–27, 130, 137
Germany, 84, 90
Girls. *See* Females
Government and Public Affairs (GPA), 123, 125–26, 129–30
Government Central School, 44, 53, 75*n.23*, 277, 278
Government control. *See* Bureaucratization; Policy, educational
Government Information Services, 70
Government Normal School for Men, 62
Government Taipo Normal School, 62
Government Trade School. *See* Hong Kong Technical College
Government Vernacular Middle School. *See* Clementi College
Governor-in-council, 13
GPA. *See* Government and Public Affairs
Grantham Training College, 179*n.38*
Great Britain. *See* United Kingdom
Great Depression, 51, 77*n.45*
Green Paper
  of 1963, 109
  of 1977, 104, 109
  use in decision-making process, 107–8
Guangzhou Academy of Social Sciences (PRC), 243
Guomindang, 45, 118
Gutzlaff, Charles, 61

Hall, Bishop R.O., 59, 77*n.46*
Hamilton, Lee, 184
Hancock, Dr. Greg, 87, 110
Harbison-Myers composite index, 103
Harlow, F.H., 77*n.48*
Haw, Aw Boon, 77*n.49*
Hee, Young, 80*n.75*
Hennessy, Sir John Pope, 277
Heritage Society, 78*n.56*

History (subject), 68, 123, 127–29, 130, 137
HKCAA. *See* Hong Kong Council for Academic Accreditation
HKEA. *See* Hong Kong Examination Authority
HKTC. *See* Hong Kong Training Council
HKU. *See* University of Hong Kong
HKUST. *See* Hong Kong University of Science and Technology
Ho Kai, 60, 65, 79*n.71*
Hong Kong College of Medicine, 79*n.71*
Hong Kong Council for Academic Accreditation (HKCAA), 9, 86
Hong Kong Examination Authority (HKEA), 120–22, 129–30, 143
Hong Kong Legislative Council (Legco), 14, 15, 17, 70, 107, 112
Hong Kong Polytechnic, 52, 53, 173, 216, 218
Hong Kong Professional Teachers' Union, 14, 155, 156, 160, 209
Hong Kong Technical College, 52, 53. *See also* Hong Kong Polytechnic
Hong Kong Training Council (HKTC), 53, 103, 104
Hong Kong University. *See* University of Hong Kong
Hong Kong University of Science and Technology (HKUST), 53, 88–89, 216, 218, 219, 267
Ho Tung, Sir Robert, 52, 78*n.52*
Huang Shi, 276

Immigration, 26–27, 41, 46, 48, 66, 67, 68, 117, 169, 186, 218, 279
Income inequality, 23, 176
Indians, 43, 66
Industrialization, 6–7, 39, 47–56, 75*n.30*
Industrial Reformatory, 76*n.44*
Industrial Training Advisory Committee (ITAC), 103–4

Institute of International Education, 9
Institute of Language in Education, 187–88, 207, 210
Institute of Linguistics, 190
Internationalization, 270–71
International schooling, 271
Irving, E.A., 44, 49, 67
ITAC. *See* Industrial Training Advisory Committee
Italian Daughters of Charity, 84

Japanese, 43, 45–46, 48, 51, 62, 77*n.49*, 270, 279
Jiang Shi-yuan, 276
Jiang Zemin, 247, 266
Jian Manxiang, 238
JSEA. *See* Junior Secondary Education Assessment
Junior Secondary Education Assessment (JSEA), 11
Junior Technical School, 52, 77*n.45*

Kaifongs, 69
Kang Yu Wei, 81*n.86*
Keswick Report on Higher Education, 46, 63
Kiangsu Chekiang Primary School, 208
Kindergarten. *See* Early childhood education
Kirst, Professor Michael, 87, 110
Korea, 23, 66
Korean War, 48
Kotewall, Dr. Bobbie, 80*n.75*
Kowloon peninsula, 41
Kowloon Tang King Po School, 52

Labor
  functional core, 228–29
  manpower planning, 53, 56, 86–87, 103–6, 215–30
  shortage, 177, 224
  skilled, 10
  unemployment, 9
  women's participation, 174–77

Languages. *See* specific language, e.g., English; Putonghua
Lau Chu Pak, 53, 54
Lee Chu Ming, 34*n.11*
Legco. *See* Hong Kong Legislative Council
Legge, James, 61, 277
Legislative Council. *See* Hong Kong Legislative Council
Legitimacy. *See* Policy, educational, legitimacy
Lingnan College, 12, 216
Li Peng, 218, 247
Literature, 65
Li-ying College, 93*n.4*, 276
Llewellyn, Sir John, 87, 110, 189
Llewellyn Report, 59, 64, 87, 111, 150, 280–81
Lobschied, Reverend W., 84
Localization, 20–21, 39, 60–65, 85
London Missionary Society, 75*n.20*, 84
Lo Po Chun United World College, 271
Lugard, Sir Frederick, 85

MacDonnell, Sir Richard, 53
Management committee, 12–13
Mandarin. *See* Putonghua
Manpower planning. *See* Labor, manpower planning
Marquis of Ripon, 76*n.40*
Marsh-Sampson Report. *See* Green Paper, of 1963
Methodist Church, 108
Middle schools, 56
Missionaries, 84, 92
Mitchell, Robert, 103
Moral education, 131
Morrison Education Society School, 60, 84, 276

Nationalism, 61
National People's Congress, 17
Neighborhood associations. *See* Kaifongs

New Life Movement, 45, 118
New Territories, 41, 62, 69, 70, 93*n.4*, 278
New Zealand, 176
Ng Choy, 60, 65, 79*n.71*
Normal School, 74*n.18*, 278
Northcote Training College, 74*n.18*, 179*n.38*
Nursery schools, 54, 55, 281
Nursing, 12, 176, 216

OECD. *See* Organisation for Economic Cooperation & Development
Official Languages Ordinance, 185
One country, two systems, 4, 30, 65, 228, 242, 246, 247, 248, 249, 265–66
Open Learning Institute, 79*n.61*, 216
Organisation for Economic Cooperation & Development (OECD), 87, 110, 111, 280
Ottawa agreements, 48
Overseas studies. *See* Foreign study

Parents, school involvement, 19–20
Passports, 21, 225–26
Patriotic schools. *See* Secondary schools, patriotic
Peihua Foundation, 28
People's Republic of China (PRC)
  Cultural Revolution, 9, 35*n.29*, 99
  educational quality, 235–40
  educational system compared to Hong Kong's, 266, 285
  environmental protection in, 78*n.56*
  Hong Kong and Macau studies, 243–44
  interdependence with Hong Kong, 25–29, 265–68
  key-point school system, 238
  language medium in schools, 210–11
  May Fourth Movement, 54, 61, 278
  migration to Hong Kong, 26–27, 41, 46, 66, 68, 169, 186, 279
  open-door policy, 247

People's Republic of China (PRC) *(continued)*
  science and technology development, 238–39
  Special Economic Zones, 240–42
  State Education Commission, 28
  students in Hong Kong universities, 89–90, 267
  teachers from, 210, 218
  teaching about, 18, 136
  tertiary education, 238
  Tiananmen uprising, 142, 144, 184, 247
Phelps-Stokes Commission Report, 62
Plastics, 48
Policy, educational. *See also* Bureaucratization
  advisory bodies, 108–9
  decision making, 13–14, 107–8
  diagrammed, 275
  expertise, 100–101, 102–6, 112
  legitimacy, 13, 16, 32, 97–113
  participation, 101–2
  third-party consultation, 109–11, 112
Political system, 7, 14–20, 98–99
Politics. *See* Bureaucratization; Policy, educational
Pollution. *See* Environment
Polytechnical institutes, 12
Population, 26–27
Portuguese, 43
Pottinger, Sir Henry, 75*n.20*
PRC. *See* People's Republic of China
Precious Blood Jubilee School Dispute, 59, 71, 110, 280
Preschools. *See* Nursery schools
Primary One Admission Scheme, 11
Primary schools, 50, 119, 169–70, 208, 219, 279, 280
Principals, school, 13
Private education, 11, 13, 25, 67, 84, 152, 158–61, 219
Public Order Ordinance, 117
Putonghua (language), 22–23, 27, 64, 65, 183–200, 203–12, 249, 255, 267

Qinghua University, 28
Queen's College, 75*n.20*

Racial discrimination, 42–43, 62, 73–74*nn.12, 13, 14, 16, 17,* 75*n.20*
Rayson Huang Committee/Report, 59, 110, 111
Reform schools, 51, 76*n.44,* 77*n.49*
Reid, F.H., 77*n.48*
Reid, S.A., 87
Right of abode scheme, 225–26, 230, 269
Robinson, Sir William, 85
Roeloffs, Dr. Karl, 87, 110
Roman Catholic Church, 84, 108, 277
Rowell, T.R., 67
Rural Training College, 179*n.38*
Russia. *See* Soviet Union

St. Louis Reformatory, 77*n.49*
St. Paul's College, 60, 76*n.42,* 80*n.75,* 276
St. Saviour's College, 276
Salaries, teacher, 19, 62, 260
SAR. *See* Special Administrative Region
SBCPS. *See* School-Based Curriculum Project Scheme
SCHE. *See* Special Committee on Higher Education
Scholarships. *See* Aid, financial, scholarships
School-Based Curriculum Project Scheme (SBCPS), 137, 140–41, 142
Seaman's Strike, 61
Secondary Modern schools, 54
Secondary School Entrance Examination (SSEE), 152–53, 158, 162
Secondary School Places Allocation System (SSPA), 11, 153–54, 158–59, 162–63
Secondary schools
  Anglo-Chinese system, 21–22, 120, 168–69

Secondary schools *(continued)*
  Chinese-language, 22, 63, 207, 209
  elementary schools distinct from, 50, 76*n.41*
  expansion of, 219–20, 280
  girls in, 169–70
  patriotic, 9, 25, 35*n.29*
  places, allocation of, 11, 150, 151–64, 164*n.8*
  program, 119, 257
  subsidies to, 16
  transition to mass institutions, 150–52
Service industries, 48
Seven Year Plan, 46
Sex. *See* Females; Gender
Shanghai Academy of Social Sciences, 243
Shenzhen University (PRC), 241–42
Singapore, 23, 205
Sino-British Joint Declaration on the Future of Hong Kong, 4, 70
Sloss, Duncan, 62
Social class, 11, 23–24, 99, 171
Social studies, 131, 136, 148–49
South China Normal University, 243
Soviet Union, 91
Special Administrative Region (SAR), 5, 8, 204, 242–43, 254
Special Committee on Higher Education (SCHE), 103
Specialization, 57, 58
SSEE. *See* Secondary School Entrance Examination
SSPA. *See* Secondary School Places Allocation System
Standing Committee on Technical Education and Vocational Training, 52
Stewart, Frederick, 44, 58, 60, 61, 75*n.23*, 76*n.40*, 277
Student activism, 5, 34*n.13*, 71, 81*n.92*, 142
Students' Movement, 46, 63, 71, 81*n.92*
Subsidies. *See* Aid, financial, subsidies

Summers, James, 61
Sun Fong Chung Primary School, 208
Sung Hok-P'ang, 80*n.75*
Sun Yatsen, 34*n.18*, 81*n.86*
Supervisor, school, 13
Syllabus and Textbook Committee, 59. *See also* Curriculum Development Council

Taiwan, 23, 90, 185, 205, 210, 243
Teachers. *See also* Teacher training
  departures from profession, 65
  localization's effect on, 64–65
  non-Chinese, 44, 64, 218–19
  political involvement, 19
  salaries, 19, 62, 260
  shortage, 210–11
  women, 175
Teacher training, 12, 44, 60–61, 62, 69, 76*n.42*, 173, 179*n.38*, 187–88, 207, 216, 259–60
Teacher Training College, 74*n.18*
Technical Education and Vocational Training Investigating Committee, 52
Technical Institute, 52, 55, 74*n.18*, 76*n.42*
Technical institutes. *See* Vocational-technical education; specific institution
Technical School for Girls, 52, 78*n.52*
Tertiary education. *See* specific institution; specific type of institution, e.g., Colleges; Universities
Testing. *See* Examinations
Textbook Committee, 59. *See also* Curriculum Development Council; Syllabus and Textbook Committee
Textbooks. *See* Curriculum, textbooks
Textiles, 6, 7, 48
Thais, 66
T.K. Ann Commission/Report, 59, 110, 111
Topley, Kenneth, 105

Trade, 41–42, 47–48, 73n.9, 190, 205, 224
Transitization, 39, 65–69

Unemployment. *See* Labor, unemployment
UNESCO, 49
United Kingdom
  colonization of Hong Kong, 14, 41–47, 268, 276
  curriculum, influence on, 120, 270
  decolonization, 15, 46, 268–70
  Hong Kong students in, 90, 94n.25, 174, 179n.43, 220, 223
  "insurance" passports, 21, 226
United Nations, 48
United States
  equality of educational opportunity, 163
  Hong Kong students in, 9–10, 90, 94n.25, 179n.43, 220, 223
  income inequality in, 23
  investments in Hong Kong, 224, 270
Universities. *See also* specific institution
  academic exchange with China, 28–29
  admissions, 12, 257
  autonomy, 261–62
  expansion of, 12, 16, 120, 216–19, 220
  foreign students at, 89
  sixth form education, 15–16, 112–13, 120
Universities and Polytechnics Grants Committee (UPGC), 12, 13, 86, 87–88, 108–9, 110, 111, 261
University of Hong Kong (HKU)
  admissions, 12
  creation of, 85, 266
  English-medium, 21, 22, 63, 88, 206
  enrollment, 218
  student activism, 34n.13
  teacher training, 74n.18, 259, 267
  three-year program, 15, 112, 217, 255

University of Hong Kong (HKU) *(continued)*
  Western influence, 87, 88, 270
  women at, 169, 170–71, 179n.19, 178–79n.25
  working-class students, 164
UPGC. *See* Universities and Polytechnic Grants Committee
Urban Council, 16, 17, 71
U.S.S.R. *See* Soviet Union

Vernacularization, 39, 60–65
Victoria Technical School, 77n.45
Vietnamese, 66
Vocational-technical education
  early history, 76–78nn.44, 45, 46, 47, 48, 52
  expansion of, 12, 105–6, 216, 217, 220, 258
  industrialization's effect on, 50–54
Vocational Training Council (VTC), 13, 53, 59, 103, 106, 108, 258
Voting. *See* Elections
VTC. *See* Vocational Training Council

Wanchai Normal School, 76n.42
Wah, Szeto, 14, 34n.11, 59, 209
Weber, Max, 58
Wells, Reverend H.R., 49
West Germany. *See* Germany
West Point Industrial Reformatory, 51, 77n.49, 276
White Paper
  allocation of school places, 105, 151, 153
  on Colonial Welfare and Development, 77n.47
  on Educational Policy, 46, 279–80
  expansion of educational system, 150
  of 1940, 62
  use in decision-making process, 107–8
Williams, Peter, 86–87, 109, 111
Wilson, David, 218
Women. *See* Females
Woo, Dr. Catherine F.C., 80n.75

Woo, Chia-Wei, 89, 219
Working Group on Sixth Form
   Education, 18
World Bank, 28
World Wide Fund for Nature, 78*n*.56
Wright, Dr. George Bateson, 75*n*.20
Wu Ting Fang. *See* Ng Choy

Xinhua News Agency, 14–15, 178

Xun Yang, 204

Ying Wa College, 75*n*.20, 276
Young, Sir Mark, 70
Young Plan, 70
Yung Hung, 65

Zhongshan University (PRC), 243, 244

For Product Safety Concerns and Information please contact our EU representative GPSR@taylorandfrancis.com
Taylor & Francis Verlag GmbH, Kaufingerstraße 24, 80331 München, Germany